The Story of the Northern Pacific Railway's
Famous Domeliner

THE
VISTA-DOME
North Coast Limited

William R. Kuebler, Jr.

The eastbound *Vista-Dome North Coast Limited* follows the Yellowstone River at milepost 99, sixteen miles east of Livingston on November 24, 1955. The 13-car train includes four vista-domes. The photographer's father, H. E. McGee, is at the throttle of F 7A No. 6507C. With over 48 years of experience in engine service, Engineer McGee is highly qualified for the task of handling this train safely and efficiently on his trip from Livingston to Billings.
Warren R. McGee photo

PUBLISHED BY
Oso Publishing Company
P.O. Box 1349
Hamilton, MT 59840, USA
(800) 337-3547
www.osorail.com

Library of Congress Cataloging-in-Publication Data

Kuebler, William R., 1957-
    The Vista Dome North Coast Limited : The Story of the Northern Pacific Railway's
        Famous Domeliner / William R. Kuebler, Jr.
        p. cm.
    Includes bibliographical references and index.
    ISBN 1-931064-06-7
        1. Railroads–United States–Passenger Cars–History. 2. Northern Pacific Railway
        Company–History. I. Title.

TF455.K83 2003
385'.22'0973–dc21

                                                                                               2002044808

Printed and bound in United States of America

First Edition, First Printing

Copyright 2004 Oso Publishing Company, Incorporated.

All rights reserved. No part of this book may be reproduced or transmitted by any mechanical or electronic means, including photocopy, scanning, or digitizing, or any other means, without written permission from the publisher, except for purposes of critical review.

Production editor: Lynda Rygmyr
Copyeditor: Lynne Grimes
Editorial assistant: Jane Wyatt
Design and art: James D. Kramer design services, Everett, WA 98208

To the men and women of the Northern Pacific Railway,
especially those who made the *Vista-Dome North Coast Limited*—
in the words of Northern Pacific advertising—
truly "one of the world's *extra fine* trains."

Table of Contents

Acknowledgments ix
Foreword xi
Preface xiii

Part 1 — Northern Pacific's *Vista-Dome North Coast Limited*: An Overview

Chapter 1 What's In a Name? 3
Chapter 2 Northern Pacific's Vista-Dome Era: 1954–1970 7
Chapter 3 Scenic Route of the *Vista-Dome North Coast Limited* 15
Chapter 4 Equipment and Maintenance 23
Chapter 5 Schedule and Train Servicing 29

Part 2 — A 1959 Journey

Chapter 6 All Aboard! 39
Chapter 7 From Locomotive to Diner: A Tour 49
Chapter 8 First Class Luxury 101

Part 3 — *Vista-Dome North Coast Limited* Operation: An Inside Look

Chapter 9   Consist Evolution and Seasonal Changes 149
Chapter 10 Actual Consists 165
Chapter 11 Accidents 171
Chapter 12 The Crew of the *Vista-Dome North Coast Limited* 187

Part 4 — Highball into History

Chapter 13 Four Dome Train West 247
Chapter 14 The *Vista-Dome North Coast Limited* in Action: A Photo Gallery ... 265

Epilogue 293

Appendix Modeling the *Vista-Dome North Coast Limited* 297

Bibliography 319
    Sources 319

Index 325

About the Author

William R. Kuebler, Jr.

"Bill" Kuebler was born in Moorhead, MN, and grew up across the Red River in Fargo, ND, which was headquarters for Northern Pacific's (NP's) Fargo Division. From age seven through high school, he spent most of his free time around the NP depot and yards, as well as the roundhouse in nearby Dilworth, MN. Bill became acquainted with Fargo Division crews, many of whom indulged him with rides in locomotive cabs, cabooses, and all the NP passenger trains serving that area. His first trip on the *North Coast Limited* was at age nine, as a "guest" of the train crew who worked the train from Fargo to Mandan, ND. Within a few years, he became familiar with the other NP operating divisions and their crews as well. As a young lad, Bill once rode the engine cab of the *North Coast Limited* all the way from Fargo, ND, to Billings, MT, and return, a trip that involved six different engine crews each direction. This was probably a record for an "unauthorized" non-employee.

Mr. Kuebler has been an active member of the Northern Pacific Railway Historical Association (NPRHA) since its beginning in 1981. He served ten years on the NPRHA's Board of Directors and three terms as president. Bill has also authored several feature articles for the NPRHA quarterly journal, *The Mainstreeter*.

Mr. Kuebler graduated from the United States Air Force Academy in 1979, with a B.S. degree in Aeronautical Engineering. He spent the next several years in the Air Force as a T-38 instructor pilot (Vance AFB, OK) and as an F-4 pilot in Europe (NATO forces). Bill left the Air Force in 1987 and went to work for American Airlines as a pilot. He now flies Boeing 767s to various international destinations.

Bill currently resides in Apple Valley, MN, with his wife, Kim, and his two sons, Stephen and Kevin.

Acknowledgments

This account of the Northern Pacific's (NP's) *Vista-Dome North Coast Limited* would not have been possible without the help of several people.

Jim Fredrickson, David Hepper, Lorenz P. Schrenk, and Gary Wildung reviewed the text, pointed out various errors, and provided valuable suggestions. Lorenz Schrenk also prepared *North Coast Limited* car floor plan diagrams and provided information about dining car service. Pat Egan provided information regarding the Chicago, Burlington, and Quincy's (CB&Q's) operation of trains No. 25 and No. 26. Former Stewardess Nurse Lorain (Nygaard) Taylor provided original documents regarding her service on the *Vista-Dome North Coast Limited*. Phillip Beach provided timetable information. John Strauss and Warren McGee provided some of the "actual consist" information. Rick Leach of the Northern Pacific Railway Historical Association (NPRHA) provided all available painting diagrams for *Vista-Dome North Coast Limited* equipment.

Special thanks go to Norman Lorentzsen, who provided insights about executive officers' decisions regarding *Vista-Dome North Coast Limited* equipment and operation, and about the tragic Granite derailment. Special thanks also go to Don Angle, R. M. "Bud" Cain, Francis Scobee, and Glenn Hove for reviewing or discussing material concerning train handling, and air brake and steam heating equipment. Warren McGee offered unique insights that reflect his experience working as a passenger trainman between Billings and Butte. Jim Fredrickson's special interest in NP passenger service, his vast collection of photos and documents, and his experience as a telegrapher and train dispatcher made him an invaluable resource. The late Ron Nixon and Glenn Staeheli, gone but not forgotten, spent countless hours with me over the years answering question after question, filling in details, and telling it like it was on the NP as only they could.

Special thanks are due the photographers, men who had the wisdom and presence of mind to record scenes on film that would otherwise fade away in our memories. The other collectors, too, who have dutifully organized and generously made available their photographic collections to supplement my own, deserve my gratitude. Unfortunately, the proliferation of copies of photos and slides over the years has sometimes obscured the identities of photographers and collectors. Any incorrect photo credits that may appear in this volume are unintentional. Names of photographers, when known, and collectors appear under each photo, with the exception of one collector who wishes to remain anonymous.

One collector deserves special recognition. Gary Wildung is an invaluable resource of NP materials. Many photos from his collection appear in this book. His uncanny ability to "find" things and preserve them is matched only by his generosity in letting the rest of us enjoy them.

This account would have been woefully anemic were it not for the NP employees, initially on the Fargo Division and later on other divisions, who kindly allowed me dozens of opportunities to watch them ply their trades in locomotive cabs, vestibules, and cabooses, beginning in 1964. May this account in some way help preserve their outstanding record of service on the Northern Pacific Railway and bring it to the attention of future generations.

Oso Publishing Company's staff, under the direction of David and Lynda Rygmyr, has been outstanding throughout this challenging project. James D. Kramer deserves special recognition for the excellent design and artwork in this book.

Finally, I deeply appreciate the constant support and patience of my wife, Kim, and sons Stephen and Kevin. Without their understanding, this book could not have been completed.

Foreword

The author (William R. Kuebler, Jr.–Bill) grew up in Fargo, North Dakota. As a young lad, he became interested in the Northern Pacific Railway (NP), its trains, locomotives, and the train and engine crews that he observed. In spite of his love for railroad activities, he chose a career in aviation. Today, he is a senior pilot for American Airlines. Yet, his interest in the NP has continued unabated.

In this book, Bill has compiled a fascinating story about the *Vista-Dome North Coast Limited*, the NP's prime passenger train operating between Chicago and the west coast terminals, Seattle and Portland. His story covers most of the period between World War II and the beginning of Amtrak, focusing on NP's vista-dome era, 1954–70.

As in previous writings, Bill's research into the many details of the train's operation, color scheme, consist, and many other items, is meticulous. The book is a first-class manual for railroad modelers and historians alike. Many so-called minor items, easily overlooked, are part of the story. Bill spent many years of gathering data from many sources. This, combined with his extensive research and personal observations aboard the train, provides the reader a feeling of "being there."

Many photos in this volume depict the *Vista-Dome North Coast Limited* in the context of its magnificent—and, sometimes challenging—operating environment; others show the interesting details of the train's individual locomotive units and cars, including interior views. Many photos depict the beautiful scenery at various points along the train's route. Rolling hills and rocky buttes encompassing many colors mark the rare beauty of NP territory in eastern Montana, but the best scenery for the westward passenger aboard this train is yet to come, beginning with the foothills of the Rocky Mountain range, first seen shortly after leaving Billings, Montana. Various views taken from that point and west capture a scenic panorama that unfolds along the train's route. Perhaps the best of all this scenery is from Missoula west, where the Flathead River is a highlight, and then the Clark Fork River is ever present, up to its mouth at Lake Pend Oreille, near Sandpoint, Idaho. While some of the pictures have been taken by experienced amateurs, they equal the best professional quality.

One aspect of the *Vista-Dome North Coast Limited* that is easy to overlook is the vital part played by NP's operating personnel—the engine and train crews, and the dispatchers. These employees were hard working, dedicated people, many of whom worked behind the scenes, out of sight of the passenger, to make the *Vista-Dome North Coast Limited* an outstanding train. Bill gives due attention to these people in this book, and reading his account will give you the pleasure of experiencing this train from the unique perspective of NP employees directly involved in its daily operation. Indeed, it has given me the pleasure of reliving some of my days on the NP and brought to mind fond memories of working with or supervising the people whose names appear in this book. His account of the personnel who handled trains No. 25 and No. 26 reminds us all of the wonderful human element always present, ever vital, but not always appreciated, in railroad operations.

The three accidents that occurred with this train are described in this book as well—as they should be, for they are part of the story. Even so, Bill properly recognizes the outstanding safety record of NP's premier passenger train. In spite of its few dark moments, all of us who worked for the NP were proud of the *Vista-Dome North Coast Limited* and all the people who made it the top-notch train that it was.

For the rail modeler, the railfan, or an ordinary and occasional book reader, I recommend this book. Come along with Bill as he travels first class from Chicago to the Pacific Northwest on the *Vista-Dome North Coast Limited*. Enjoy!

Norman M. Lorentzsen
Vice President of Operations, Northern Pacific Railway

Norman M. Lorentzsen was promoted through the ranks of the NP, beginning his railroad career as a section laborer on the Fargo Division in 1935. He later became a brakeman and then a conductor on that division. His promotion to Assistant Trainmaster came in 1947, and to Trainmaster in 1949. He became Division Superintendent of the Rocky Mountain and Idaho Divisions in 1954 and 1957, respectively. He became NP's General Manager, Lines West, in 1964. In 1968, he became NP's Vice-President of Operations and held that post until the Burlington Northern (BN) merger in 1970. He then served as BN's Vice-President of Operations. In 1977, he became President of the BN, and in 1978 he became BN's Chief Executive Officer. He retired in 1981. He and his wife, Helen, currently reside in Arizona. During his service as an officer and executive on the NP and BN, he was known and respected by NP employees system-wide as a "railroad man's railroad man."

Preface

By the early 1950s, many United States railroads operated completely streamlined, lightweight high-speed passenger trains. Development of this equipment and service began in the mid 1930s, was interrupted during World War II because of the national war effort, and resumed in earnest soon after the war ended. The post-war period (roughly 1946–52) was a time of shiny new diesels, matching streamlined passenger cars, ever faster schedules, and unique and colorful paint schemes. Competition between railroads was stiff. Some western railroads were going beyond streamlining by equipping their passenger trains with dome cars. Known generically as a *vista-dome*, this type of car was designed to permit maximum viewing of passing scenery from an above-roof, glass enclosed dome section.

Not every railroad jumped on the streamlining bandwagon with such enthusiasm, however. As late as mid-1952, for example, it seemed unlikely to most railroad industry analysts that the Northern Pacific Railway (NP) would soon take its place among those United States railroads operating completely streamlined, high-speed passenger trains. The NP's top train, the *North Coast Limited*, was only partly streamlined, and it still operated on a slow, steam-era schedule, its new diesels notwithstanding. Even less probable to industry analysts was the notion of an NP streamliner one day carrying not only one, or even two, but *four* vista-domes. "A domeliner on the NP?" they wondered. Would it ever happen? Not likely, according to their common viewpoint. After all, the NP was so . . . so traditional, as traditional as the steel rail, semaphore, and wooden caboose. It was, some said, even too traditional for its own good. The elements of the road's image that supported this opinion were plentiful. What other railroad chose to represent itself with a symbol dating back nearly a *thousand* years? With a rugged route profile to prove it, the NP was the oldest of the northern "transcons," brought into existence by the signature of Abraham Lincoln. It was a road that looked long and hard at its abundant on-line coal supply before finally deciding to "dieselize" its entire locomotive roster. And, during the post-war period, it was a road few thought of when identifying the nation's most modern passenger trains. In short, the NP's premier passenger train lagged behind its competition. As late as 1952, many industry observers would have bet heavily against the NP ever offering the traveling public one of the greatest American passenger trains of all time. Fortunately for them, these observers did not place such bets, for they would have lost a great deal of money.

A great passenger train, indeed! In 1954, in one bold stroke, the NP's venerable *North Coast Limited* captured the spotlight again, just as it had done at the turn of the century when the beautiful train was inaugurated. This time, the train's name was prefixed with "*Vista-Dome*," turning the generic term into a title. Within a few years, after being updated with a fascinating lounge car, a luxurious new dining car, and the ever-popular "Slumbercoach," the *Vista-Dome North Coast Limited* made its indelible mark in the pages of railroad history and in the minds of millions of people. In the opinion of many, the train wore the most attractive and dignified paint scheme of all time, provided the best service to be found anywhere on the continent, and rolled through our nation's most fantastic scenery. It was an exciting time. And then, before we knew it, it was all over. In 1970, the Northern Pacific Railway was gone via merger with three other lines. The magnificent passenger train it had produced, the *Vista-Dome North Coast Limited*, would all too soon be a thing of the past as well.

Although NP's *Vista-Dome North Coast Limited* has received a fair amount of press over the years, railfans, historians, and modelers have had to hunt for information scattered about in books and periodicals, with most of these works focused on some other aspect of the NP. In the case of those precious few periodicals featuring this particular train, it was given but a cursory look, perhaps the only kind possible in a periodical—just enough to whet the appetite for most of us.

The Vista-Dome North Coast Limited

Thus, it is my intent to bring together, in this volume, a more detailed and comprehensive look at the NP's dome-bedecked streamliner. No claim is made that this volume exhausts the subject. Indeed, no such book would be possible. But, this material does represent a continuous effort that began more than 35 years ago, in the mid-1960s. At that time, I had the unique privilege of getting to know the *Vista-Dome North Coast Limited* operation rather intimately, thanks to NP enginemen and trainmen on the Fargo Division, and then on other NP operating divisions, who allowed me to accompany them while they performed duty aboard this and other NP trains. These employees gave generously of their time and knowledge, answered countless questions, and showed me the ropes. They explained rules, procedures, and techniques. On occasion, they even demonstrated some rather innovative, if non-standard, methods of railroading when faced with difficult and unusual circumstances. Most of all, they just went about their work with typical skill and professionalism, while I sat back and watched, listened, and learned. Dozens of such trips were made aboard the *Vista-Dome North Coast Limited*, many of them in the locomotive cab. It was a priceless education, one I shall cherish for the rest of my life.

Meanwhile, over the past 35 years or so, I've also spent countless hours researching, collecting photos and ephemera, and interviewing dozens of NP veterans across the Railway system, from former Vice President of Operations, Norman Lorentzsen, to a dining car waiter named Charlie Snodgrass—who nearly lost his life aboard the *North Coast Limited* on that fateful night in March 1962 when his dormitory car plunged over a steep embankment during a tragic derailment. While conducting this research, I also noticed railfans and modelers ponder, and sometimes struggle with, questions about this train. What was its consist? How did it evolve? Which cars had the "Vista-Dome North Coast Limited" slogan on their flanks, and which did not? What about that wide white stripe on the rear of the observation-lounge car? And, what about the operation of this train? Was it ever powered by four diesel units *east* of Livingston? Were the *North Coast's* diesel units assigned exclusively to this train? How did Raymond Loewy come up with the two-tone green scheme for the NP? What was dining car service like? What were those dome sleepers like? And, what about the crew—was service aboard this train a special assignment, something highly desired, the pinnacle of one's railroad career?

Many such questions have come up over the years. Bringing to this project the results of my research, and extensive personal experience with this train, I have attempted to answer thoroughly these questions and more. Even so, there is more about this fabulous train than any one author could say in a book.

This volume covers only the vista-dome era of the NP's *North Coast Limited*. Part I (five chapters) sets the stage with a general overview of the train's equipment and operation during the entire NP vista-dome era, with the year 1959 serving as a convenient reference point. That was when the train reached its peak in terms of equipment and service.

Part II (three chapters) starts us on a "you are there" journey aboard the *Vista-Dome North Coast Limited* in June 1959. In these chapters, written in the present tense, the reader will join me on a trip from Chicago to Seattle, and re-live (or find out for the first time) just what it was like to ride this superb train at the height of its existence. In two of these three chapters, I'll take you on a tour of the train during our stop at St. Paul. We will closely inspect the entire train there, inside and out, from locomotive to observation-lounge car, one piece of equipment at a time. We will also meet some of the crewmembers working aboard our train during our journey to Seattle.

Part III (four chapters) covers in detail the evolution and operation of the train during the vista-dome era. One chapter details consist evolution from 1954 to 1970 and describes seasonal changes in the consist, including a look at an interesting dome sleeper leasing arrangement. Another chapter covers the three serious accidents that occurred with the *Vista-Dome North Coast Limited*. Included is a discussion of one of the brake systems in use on this train, a possible factor in one of the accidents. Yet another chapter provides a "behind-the-scenes" look at the crew of the *Vista-Dome North Coast Limited*. We will consider locomotive engineers' passenger train handling techniques, particularly as they applied them to this train. We will also consider train performance, and the key role played by the various brake systems on the train. The system of crew districts and trip rotations that involved this train are an interesting part of the story, as well. Trainmen's duties and dispatching procedures involving trains No. 25 and No. 26 will also be described. Not least, we will take a close look at a unique and fascinating group of people who were identified with the *Vista-Dome North Coast Limited* more than any other employee group: the Stewardess-Nurses. In effect, this chapter puts the reader in the shoes of the employee—a rather interesting place to be!

Part IV (two chapters) resumes and concludes our 1959 trip on the *North Coast Limited*. In the first of these two chapters, I attempt to verbalize (admittedly a poor substitute for experiencing the real thing) many of the nuances peculiar to a journey aboard this train, those things railfans who rode it noticed but found difficult to describe to others. The return journey to Chicago is described only briefly, with emphasis on the differences from the westbound trip. The final chapter is a photo gallery of the *Vista-Dome North Coast Limited*. These superb scenes depict NP's famous domeliner in action during the 1954–66 period, the way the train is best remembered. It is fitting that, in the final chapter of this volume, we allow "one of the world's *extra fine* trains" (a phrase from NP advertising) to speak for itself through pictures. Thus, in Part IV this magnificent train highballs into history.

This, then, was Northern Pacific's *Vista-Dome North Coast Limited*!

Come along and enjoy the trip!

William R. Kuebler, Jr.
June 2003

The Yellowstone River and Elton bluffs form an impressive backdrop as the westbound *Vista-Dome North Coast Limited* sweeps around a curve 15 miles east of Livingston, Montana, in August 1956. This attractive 13-car train includes four vista-domes and is led by F-3A No. 6502A, assisted by F-3B No. 6507B and F-7A No. 6507A.
Warren R. McGee photo

Northern Pacific's
VISTA-DOME NORTH COAST LIMITED:
An Overview

Chapter 1

What's in a Name?

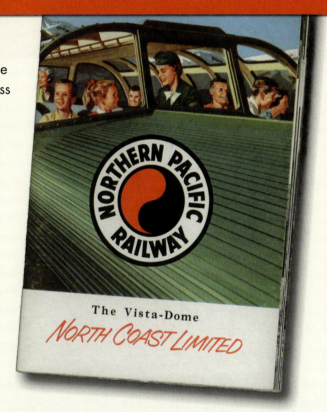

North Coast Limited. To those who rode her, those three words conjure memories of pleasant travel across prairies and alongside rivers, through forests and tunnels, over trestles and mountain passes, to places never before seen and people long-missed. For seven decades, those three words were synonymous with luxury and comfort on the Northern Pacific Railway (NP). Without a doubt, they brought much business to the road. They beckoned passengers and reminded shippers. They appeared in national advertisements, brochures, public timetables, and on drumheads, large wall calendars, neon signs, billboards, and even the sides of steel deck girder bridges seen by millions. They identified a train that carried everyone from our next door neighbors to movie stars, from common citizens to presidents and queens. It was a train that attracted railway employees of various crafts, and inspired generations of railfans to model, photograph, and sometimes just watch it. And, it was something to watch! The **North Coast Limited** was one of the most magnificent modes of transportation available to the traveling public, something extraordinary and unique in the overland transport experience of man. To the NP employee, from locomotive engineer to rear brakeman, the name meant pride, camaraderie, odd hours, the best available machinery for battling both mountain and weather, and, above all, a dependable paycheck. Under the NP corporate name, those mere three words did all that from April 29, 1900, until the Burlington Northern (BN) merger on March 3, 1970.

The Vista-Dome North Coast Limited

This photograph frequently appeared in NP public timetables and pamphlets. Train No. 26 descends a 1.8% grade with 12 cars at milepost 119, four miles west of Livingston, on December 6, 1954. Handling the train from Butte to Livingston this day is Engineer Charlie Graves. Hired as a fireman in 1901, he has been in engine service for 53 years, yet he will work another two before retiring with a near-perfect record. Dome sleeper 304 and sleeper 482, both owned by CB&Q, appear in the foreground.
Warren McGee photo

Sheep Mountain is an impressive backdrop as the eastbound *Vista-Dome North Coast Limited* splits a pair of semaphores at the east switch of Mission siding, six miles east of Livingston, on December 6, 1954. Warren McGee photographed this train west of Livingston about 30 minutes earlier (see photo above). Its 12-cars include unidentified water-baggage, mail-dormitory, and coach-buffet-lounge cars followed by dome coach 553, "Deluxe Day-Nite" coach 587, dome coach 558, dining car 455, 8-6-4 sleeper 372, dome sleeper 307, 8-6-3-1 sleeper 482, dome sleeper 304, and sleeper-observation-lounge 394. Chasing this train is now a lost battle for McGee. The position of the semaphore arm relative to the train's progress indicates a train speed of at least 75 miles per hour.
Warren McGee photo

Chapter 1: What's in a Name?

Billboards like this one in Tacoma, photographed on December 24, 1952, advertised the new, 45-hour Chicago-Seattle schedule that went into effect on November 16th of that year.
Jim Fredrickson photo

But, that's merely the short story of this famous train. The complete story involves many details, one of which has to do with the train's name itself.

NP's *North Coast Limited* had several official name changes, if advertising is any measure. These name changes were not mere plays on words; they reflected significant changes in the train itself. The "New" *North Coast Limited* and the "Air Conditioned Roller Bearing" *North Coast Limited* appeared in 1930s advertising. Beginning in early 1947, it was the "Streamlined" *North Coast Limited*. Then, in November 1952, NP told the traveling public that "You'll like the faster" *North Coast Limited*. Our focus here, however, is on what is arguably the most notable name modification, notable because it identified the most notable *version* of the train. This change occurred on a very memorable Monday in August 1954. With much fanfare and excitement, the westbound and eastbound streamliners departed Chicago and Seattle, respectively, with a brand new car in each train. This car was novel in design. It was attractive and functional. It was *very* expensive, yet its purpose was simple: to permit passengers to sit 14 feet above the rails in air-conditioned comfort, surrounded by tinted glass, and thus able to view 2,300 miles of fantastic scenery, including some 48 rivers and 28 mountain ranges, as well as lakes, prairies, and the big Montana sky, as never before. One NP advertisement accurately claimed that this car would "put the 'see' in scenery."

As for the fanfare, the NP had been advertising the new car type in on-line newspapers and national magazines. Prior to entering service, the car itself—three cars actually—had been displayed and opened to the public in major cities along the line. Car 550 was displayed in Missoula, Spokane, Yakima, and Tacoma. Car 551 was displayed in Bemidji, Fargo, Jamestown, Bismarck-Mandan, and Billings. Car 552 was displayed in St. Paul and Seattle. As intended, the fanfare generated much

As soon as the new dome coaches arrived in St. Paul from the Budd factory in Philadelphia, the NP set them up for service by installing P.A. system components, removing protective shipping covers from floors and seats, and thoroughly testing all electrical and mechanical devices. Then the cars were displayed in various on-line cities for several days. Dome Coach 550 is in pristine condition while on public display in Tacoma on July 30, 1954.
Jim Fredrickson photo

5

The Vista-Dome North Coast Limited

Judging from the visitors' apparel, it must be an exceptionally cool July morning as dome coach 551 is open to the public at Bismarck in 1954.
Photo C-697 courtesy of State Historical Society of North Dakota

excitement. The public turned out in droves to inspect these fascinating vista-dome cars, inside and out. Many visitors decided then and there to ride one soon, eagerly anticipating their first opportunity to do so.

On hand for the eastbound train's Seattle departure that Monday were Mr. F. G. Scott and other NP passenger department brass, as well as the Seattle Seafair Prime Minister, all of whom welcomed passengers on board. Riding the train to East Auburn, a reporter and camera crew from KING–TV Channel 5 (Seattle) recorded the event, as did NP dispatcher and noted railroad photographer Jim Fredrickson, movie camera in hand. After calling "All Aboard!" Tacoma Division Conductor William Brockelbank gave the highball precisely at the scheduled departure time, 1:30 P.M. A similar scene had transpired with the westbound train's departure exactly four hours earlier in Chicago. It was August 16, 1954, and a new era had just begun on *The Main Street of the Northwest*. A venerable name was modified once again, and for the last time, on the NP. From that day forward, the *Streamlined North Coast Limited* would be known as The *Vista-Dome North Coast Limited*. And, with that name change, the famous train reached the pinnacle of its existence.

For the *Vista-Dome North Coast Limited*, the NP spared no efforts in advertising. Media included national publications, print and radio ads in on-line communities, and the newest form of mass communication at the time—television. This TV ad appeared on Tacoma stations in August 1954.
Jim Fredrickson photo

6

Chapter 2
Northern Pacific's Vista-Dome Era: 1954–1970

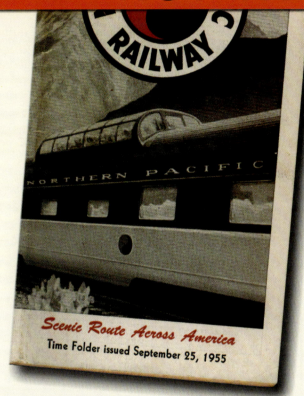

In retrospect, the Northern Pacific Railway's (NP's) vista-dome era was a remarkably short one, a mere 15½ years in duration. (See the chronological overview of the entire *Streamlined North Coast Limited* era, 1946–70.) Fifteen years is not a long life span for a public transportation entity, especially for railroad equipment designed for several decades of service. When compared with other forms of transportation, it seems an even shorter life span. As of this writing, several major airlines have been operating Boeing 727 jet transports continuously for 39 years, and 737s for 34 years. Even though its 15 years was rather short, NP's *Vista-Dome North Coast Limited* made an indelible mark upon those of us who experienced it, whether as passenger, observer, or employee. The train's reach even exceeded its setting. Photographs from that era have captured the interest of those too young to have experienced it firsthand, and more than one modeler born *after* that period has committed substantial funds toward depicting the train accurately on his layout.

7

The Vista-Dome North Coast Limited

Even within that short span of time, the *Vista-Dome North Coast Limited* changed somewhat. Schedules were adjusted and improved, and the full summer season consist grew slightly to accommodate new equipment. Apart from this slight overall growth, the consist also fluctuated in length from season to season, and altered its line-up as car positions in the train were periodically changed. The crew expanded, too, with the introduction of Stewardess-Nurses in 1955. Generally, the period 1954–59 was one of continual improvement in equipment, service, and schedule. The period 1959–66 amounted to a plateau; the height achieved in late 1959 was maintained for a little over seven

The *North Coast Limited*

Evolution and Competition During the Streamlined Era

January 1946: NP orders 78 new lightweight passenger cars from Pullman-Standard at a cost of $9 million, along with six new 4,500 horsepower, three-unit, passenger diesel sets (6500–6505) from Electro-Motive Division (EMD) for the *North Coast Limited*. A seventh diesel set (6506) is ordered later in the year. Diesels are painted in a scheme of two-tone green with imitation gold striping. New lightweight cars are painted to match.

November 1946–February 1947: New lightweight 56-seat "Day" and "Day-Nite" coaches delivered for *North Coast Limited* service. A test run of the first group of these new cars behind EMD F-3 demonstrator No. 754 in November 1946 is made to develop a fast, 45-hour schedule for the *North Coast Limited*. Implementation of the fast schedule is deferred until November 1952.

1947–52: Even though the *North Coast Limited* is advertised as "Streamlined," new lightweight cars are gradually added during 1947–48; some older, heavyweight cars operate in the train until November 1952.

January 1947: New coach-buffet-lounge cars (NP 494–498, Chicago, Burlington, and Quincy (CB&Q) 499) received for use by coach passengers on the *North Coast Limited*.

March–April 1947: Six water-baggage cars (NP 400–404, CB&Q 405) delivered for *North Coast Limited* service.

April–June 1947: Six mail-dormitory cars (NP 425–429, CB&Q 430) delivered.

September 1947: Six diner-lunch counter cars (NP 450–455) delivered.

June–July 1948: Sleeper-observation-lounge cars ("Club" series; later numbered NP 390–394; CB&Q 483) delivered.

July–August 1948: All-room Pullman sleepers (named for towns along the line; later numbered NP 350–363; Spokane, Portland, and Seattle (SP&S) 366; CB&Q 480–482) delivered.

March 1949: *California Zephyr* begins vista-dome service on the CB&Q, Denver and Rio Grande Western (D&RGW), and Western Pacific (WP) railroads. This move sets a new standard of service and equipment for passenger trains on western railroads.

January 1951: Robert S. Macfarlane, executive vice-president of the NP and a supporter of improved passenger service, becomes NP president.

June 1951: The Great Northern Railway's (GN's) fully streamlined *Empire Builder* is completely re-equipped with new streamlined cars.

November 1952: Raymond Loewy & Associates hired by NP to advise on design of new and existing passenger equipment.

November 16, 1952: *North Coast Limited* renumbered 25 and 26, and put on fast, 45-hour schedule; *Mainstreeter* inaugurated as secondary train, given nos. 1 and 2, and operated on old *North Coast Limited* schedule, except via Helena instead of Butte.

January 1, 1953: Milwaukee Road's *Olympian Hiawatha* equipped with full-length dome lounge car, the first dome service in the Northwest.

March 1953: First NP car painted in new Loewy two-tone green scheme, Day-Nite coach 589, followed shortly by Day-Nite coach 588. First diesel set, 6506A, B, C, painted in Loewy scheme. "Main Street of the Northwest" slogan on 6506 cab units first painted in dark green, changed to white very shortly thereafter.

September 1953: First cars with Loewy-designed interiors (new diners 456 and 457, and rebuilt diner 453) enter service.

September–December 1953: Diner-Lunch Counter cars rebuilt to full diners (NP 450–455) for *North Coast Limited* service; No. 455 sold to CB&Q in early 1954, but remains in NP service, paint scheme, and lettering.

March 1954: Modernized sleeper-observation-lounge cars (NP 390–394; CB&Q 483) begin *North Coast Limited* service.

Chapter 2: Northern Pacific's Vista-Dome Era: 1954–1970

years. Then, the *Vista-Dome North Coast Limited* began a gradual change in the other direction, particularly its equipment. Patronage had declined, though not nearly as much as on other roads, and in the spring of 1967, the luxurious Pullman sleeper-observation-lounge cars were removed from service. In spite of this new trend, the *North Coast's* service, schedule, and remaining equipment kept it well ahead of most other named trains during the rather depressing final years of the 1960s. Indeed, many well-known trains had pitifully declined in appearance and service, and others had even disappeared from the railroad scene entirely.

The *North Coast Limited* (continued)

August 16–September 1954: Dome coaches (NP 550–556; CB&Q 557–558; SP&S 559) enter service on the *Vista-Dome North Coast Limited*.

August 1954: NP begins to advertise the *North Coast Limited* as a "Four dome train."

September–October 1954: Dome sleepers (NP 307–313; CB&Q 304–305; SP&S 306) enter service on *Vista-Dome North Coast Limited*.

October 1954: Six lightweight sleepers (NP 367–372) and two Deluxe Day-Nite coaches (NP 586–587) enter service on *Vista-Dome North Coast Limited*.

1955: NP 1955 wall calendar features the "*Vista-Dome North Coast Limited*."

March 1955: NP receives 1954 Passenger Award from the Federation for Railway Progress.

May 29, 1955: GN's *Empire Builder* begins dome-coach service.

June 1955: NP inaugurates "Stewardess-Nurse" service on *Vista-Dome North Coast Limited*.

June–September 1955: "Traveller's Rest" lounge cars (NP 494–498, CB&Q 499; rebuilt from coach-buffet-lounge cars) enter *Vista-Dome North Coast Limited* service on the 150th anniversary of the Lewis & Clark expedition.

October 1955: GN's *Empire Builder* begins full-dome service.

November 1956: New toy American Flyer train from A. C. Gilbert features the *Vista-Dome North Coast Limited*.

March 1957: NP orders six new diners, one dome coach and one dome sleeper from the Budd Company.

April 1957: *Vista-Dome North Coast Limited* schedule between Chicago and west coast reduced by 45 minutes. Line changes and more efficient signaling systems make this schedule reduction feasible.

December 1957: New dome coach (NP 549) and dome sleeper (NP 314) enter service. These extra cars in the *North Coast Limited* fleet facilitate protection of vista-dome service during scheduled maintenance of vista-dome cars.

January 1958: New Budd diners (NP 459–463, CB&Q 458) enter *Vista-Dome North Coast Limited* service, displacing older Pullman-Standard diners (rebuilt in 1953) to *The Mainstreeter*.

November 30, 1959: New Budd "Slumbercoach" cars enter *Vista-Dome North Coast Limited* service and carry 30,000 passengers in first year of operation.

February 14, 1960: *Empire Builder* sleeper-observation-lounge car is withdrawn from service.

December 6, 1960: Milwaukee Road applies with the ICC to discontinue the *Olympian Hiawatha*, citing insurmountable operational losses.

July 1961: NP passenger revenue reaches 15-year high.

January, March, June 1962: The *Vista-Dome North Coast Limited* has three derailments; suffers only passenger fatality ever.

April 1965: Westbound *Vista-Dome North Coast Limited* schedule reduced by 20 minutes. Line changes and more efficient signaling systems make this reduction feasible.

October 1966: Louis W. Menk becomes NP president upon leaving the presidency of the CB&Q.

March–April 1967: Six dome sleepers rebuilt to "Lounge-in-the-Sky" configuration for service on the *Vista-Dome North Coast Limited*; sleeper-observation-lounge cars removed from service.

July 1967: NP announces that its famous fruit cakes will no longer be sold to the public, ending a decades-old tradition of mail-order sales during the winter holidays.

March 3, 1970: Burlington Northern (BN) merger.

Compiled by William R. Kuebler, Jr. and Lorenz Schrenk, June 1993; revised by William R. Kuebler, Jr., June 2000.

The Vista-Dome North Coast Limited

Although the *Vista-Dome North Coast Limited* car line-up changed somewhat during the vista-dome era, and from season to season, from 1955 on, the train almost always included the following equipment (not necessarily in the order shown):

- Diesel Units: EMD F-3/5/7/9s (3 or 4 units)
- Water-Baggage Car
- Mail-Dormitory Car
- Budd Dome Coaches (2)
- Day-Nite (leg rest) Coaches (1–3)
- Lewis & Clark Traveller's Rest Lounge Car
- Dining Car
- Pullman-Standard Sleeping Cars (1 or 2)
- Budd Dome Sleeping Cars (1 or 2)
- Pullman Sleeper-Observation-Lounge Car (discontinued in 1967)

A detailed account of car line-up and changes in consist will appear later in this book.

1959: A Reference Point

With so many changes in the train's make-up during the vista-dome era, a representative focal point is useful for a detailed look at the *North Coast Limited* operation. The year 1959 serves this purpose well for several reasons. Most details of the train's operation during 1959 would generally apply to the entire period, 1958–66, except for a few slight variations in car line-up. This period includes several of the highest revenue-producing years, it is the period most railfans like to remember, and it is the period that most *North Coast Limited* modelers prefer to depict. In short, it is the period of the train's most glorious existence. While considering the 1959 edition of the *Vista-Dome North Coast Limited* at length in the next several chapters, brief comments about the domeliner's evolution before and after that period will be included wherever fitting. A more detailed account of changes in its consist over the years, however, appears in Chapter Nine.

Budd dining cars joined the *Vista-Dome North Coast Limited* fleet in January 1958, displacing Pullman-Standard dining cars to *The Mainstreeter*, NP's secondary transcontinental passenger train. Slumbercoaches were added to the *North Coast* in November 1959. At that time, NP's top train was fully equipped. After 1959, the only "new" cars to join the fleet were five 48-seat leg-rest coaches that had been removed from Holiday Lounge service on *The Mainstreeter* and rebuilt into coach configuration. These Holiday Lounge cars were built in 1956 and entered service on *The Mainstreeter* that year. Upon being rebuilt into coaches in 1962, they were placed in *North Coast Limited* service. Other than that addition to the fleet, the *North Coast's* appearance and operation were essentially unchanged and maintained at a peak level from 1959 until spring 1967.

As for the Slumbercoach, that car is a matter of some controversy. Generally, historians recognize its excellent record: it was very popular with passengers and a true moneymaker for the NP. In contrast, modelers tend to dislike the car because it was unpainted stainless steel, the only car in the train not given Loewy colors. It stood out either like a sore thumb or a functional novelty, depending on one's perspective. The year 1959 gives modelers the option of including or excluding the car.

Chapter 2: Northern Pacific's Vista-Dome Era: 1954–1970

All things considered, the *Vista-Dome North Coast Limited* was one of the best, if not *the* best, passenger trains in the country. The crack Limited topped the choice train lists of many industry critics who never earned a dime from the NP. Members of the Interstate Commerce Commission (ICC) recognized the excellence of its operation, as well. It commanded respect throughout the railroad industry. That is all well and good, but the *Vista-Dome North Coast Limited* was more than just a showpiece on rails. It was a free-market enterprise intended to *make money* for the NP. Thus, the most important measures of the train's success were the traveling public's opinion and especially the Railway's bottom line.

To be sure, the public gave the *Vista-Dome North Coast Limited* rave reviews. "Fan mail" received from passengers at NP headquarters in St. Paul between 1955 and 1963, for example, included such remarks as these:

"A great train. Gives the average man a feeling of traveling like a millionaire...I found the equipment the most comfortable in which I have ever ridden..."

"You have a train to be proud of..."

"Flew west, railroaded east. Will never fly again. Did not know a train trip could be so much fun..."

"I'm an experience air traveler. But after my trip aboard your North Coast Limited, I've decided to become an experienced rail traveler. I had no idea that a train trip could be so pleasant..."

"There is nothing to compare with this train...it is outstanding!"

Even as late as 1968, the train was bringing some travelers back to the rails from the hectic pace and discomfort of air travel. Ironically, actor Dean Martin elected to study his script for the movie *Airport* in a bedroom aboard the *North Coast Limited* on a trip from Seattle to Minneapolis, where the movie was filmed in 1969–70. (He made more than one rail journey in the course of the filming, too.) He stated that the relaxing trip enabled him to prepare for his leading role. Even nationally syndicated newspaper columnists opined in print about the train's merits. One wrote in 1958, "I wouldn't want my airline friends to hear me say it, but that train trip was just wonderful . . . and what a panorama it is!" In 1961, another wrote a column aimed at his "friends back east" who made fun of rail travel (and perhaps for good reason, given their setting), telling them and readers, "Come out west and ride *this* one some time!"

As for the bottom line, that is a matter of record, a record with very little red ink. During the summer travel season in the late 1950s, the train grossed close to three-quarters of a million dollars a month for the NP ($709,586 in August 1958, for example), which figures out to an average of just over $6 per train-mile. Even during the winter season, the train grossed almost $4 per train-mile. Year round average was about $5 per mile. With an average out-of-pocket cost in 1958 of $3.76 per train-mile, $1.25 per train-mile reached the bottom line as net profit, a very respectable figure. Annual passenger revenue on the NP *increased* during each of the four consecutive years of 1959–62, with the *North Coast Limited* accounting for the bulk of this income. While other railroads' premier passenger trains were bleeding red ink during those years, the *North Coast Limited* was still making a profit. By 1968, however, it was barely breaking even. Even though the traveling public was opting

The Vista-Dome North Coast Limited

When this photo was taken on August 19, 1954, dome coach 550 was on its first revenue trip from Chicago to Seattle and was the only dome car in this train. Train No. 25 approaches Highview Tunnel, its east portal just out of view to the left, with diesel units 6500C, B, A and 11 cars. Highview Tunnel is about one mile west of the top of this pass at Homestake, on the Butte line. This train includes cars 400, 428, coach-buffet-lounge 494, "Day-Nite" coach 588 (hidden by the rock cut), dome coach 550, "Day-Nite" coach 591, and diner 451. Vista-dome cars were designed with scenery like this in mind, so the *North Coast Limited* will soon carry four domes per train.
Ron Nixon photo; Bill Kuebler collection

for the automobile and airplane in ever-increasing numbers, the *North Coast Limited* had chalked up a profitable record for the NP during almost the entire vista-dome era.

Whatever else can be said, the *Vista-Dome North Coast Limited* certainly served as a standard against which other trains were compared, particularly those of western railroads, including the Milwaukee Road's *Olympian Hiawatha* and Great Northern's (GN's) *Empire Builder*. Officials of these railroads were acutely aware of this fact. Even GN president John Budd was once overheard saying to a fellow officer that with the *North Coast Limited* around, the GN advertising department might have chosen a more accurate adjective than "incomparable" when promoting their premier train. Milwaukee Road executives felt the pressure of competition from the NP's top passenger train to an even greater degree.

Let's put this in proper perspective, however. In 1952 the NP was still considered by many, especially the GN (and even some embarrassed NP employees), to be a distant second in terms of passenger service. This was arguably a well-deserved reputation. In 1947, when the GN and other western roads were speeding up the schedules of their top trains, the NP kept its top train, the *North Coast Limited*, on a slower, steam-era schedule, diesels notwithstanding, so as to be able to serve a greater number of small on-line communities. Moreover, the NP did not streamline the entire *North Coast Limited* in 1947, but gradually did so over the next few years. Meanwhile, in 1951, the already streamlined *Empire Builder* was completely re-equipped with new streamlined cars. Then, on January 1, 1953, the Milwaukee Road initiated dome service in the Northwest. The *Olympian Hiawatha* was equipped with a full-length dome lounge car that had a café on its lower level.

Chapter 2: Northern Pacific's Vista-Dome Era: 1954–1970

The same train pauses at Butte on a misty, overcast day, August 19, 1954. Vista-dome service began just three days earlier.
Ron Nixon photo; Bill Kuebler collection

From 1947 until late 1952, in the eyes of passengers, employees, and railfans the NP's *North Coast Limited* lagged behind the competition. Then things changed.

In his book, *Great Northern Pictorial, Volume 3*, former GN Traveling Passenger Representative, John Strauss, states that the GN may have become careless and even elitist in its response to the increasing popularity of dome cars on other western roads. He quotes several members of GN's board of directors and other Railway officials as publicly saying, "We do not need domes to be the leader in the Northwest!" For whatever reason, the GN chose not to purchase dome equipment for delivery in 1954. But, the NP did. Practically overnight, the *North Coast Limited* grabbed the spotlight, and by October 1954, each train carried *four* domes while the *Olympian Hiawatha* carried only one and the *Empire Builder* carried none. Dome-wise, the NP had achieved a substantial advantage over its competitors. The GN finally did acquire domes for its *Empire Builder* in 1955, equipping each train with three dome coaches and one full-length dome lounge. The GN was late in the game, but its top train entered that game in style. Even so, from 1954 on, the *North Coast Limited* had earned its place in the streamlined, vista-dome era and would be a train with which NP's competitors would have to reckon.

Chapter 3
Scenic Route of the Vista-Dome North Coast Limited

The *Vista-Dome North Coast Limited* operated daily between Chicago and Seattle as train No. 25 westbound and No. 26 eastbound. Some historians have said that the Northern Pacific (NP) chose those train numbers because the New York Central's famous *Twentieth Century Limited* trains (one of the connections to the east of Chicago) operated with the same numbers, but according to Richard Mossman, former Passenger Traffic Department Vice-President in Seattle, this is not true. Rather, the NP and the Chicago, Burlington, and Quincy (CB&Q) simply found a number pair they could share without conflicting with other train numbers. Three railroads were involved in the *Vista-Dome North Coast Limited* operation. The CB&Q handled the entire train between Chicago and St. Paul, an arrangement that dated back to 1918. (From December 17, 1911 until 1918, the Chicago and North Western (C&NW) handled the train over its line via the North Shore suburbs, Milwaukee, and Wyeville, Wisconsin, and before that, the *North Coast Limited* was a St. Paul-west coast operation.) In the mid- and late-1960s, the CB&Q regularly operated the *North Coast Limited* and *Empire Builder* combined as one long train between Chicago and St. Paul. The NP handled the *North Coast Limited* over its own line between Minneapolis and Seattle, via Butte, and exercised trackage rights over the $10\frac{1}{2}$-mile Great Northern (GN) line between St. Paul and Minneapolis. Cars to and from Portland were routed over the Spokane, Portland, and Seattle (SP&S). At Pasco, westbound Portland cars were switched out of NP train No. 25 and into SP&S train No. 1, and eastbound Portland cars were switched out of SP&S No. 2 and into NP No. 26. A similar arrangement with these SP&S trains existed in Spokane for GN's *Empire Builder* cars assigned to Portland service. Known as "The Streamliner," SP&S trains No. 1 and No. 2 operated between Spokane and Portland on SP&S rails, following the north bank of the Columbia River between Pasco and Portland.

The Vista-Dome North Coast Limited

Viewed from the rear cab unit, train No. 25 stretches back over Skones trestle as the domeliner descends a 2.2% grade into Butte on June 28, 1955. This is one of the most spectacular trestles on the NP main line, and it is situated on a 12-degree curve. Whenever westbound dome riders reached this bridge, they often gasped in awe at the magnificent view of Butte and the Silver Bow valley stretched out to the west, nearly 1,000 feet below this trestle.
Ron Nixon photo; Bill Kuebler collection

Photographed from a footbridge extending over Missoula yard, Train No. 25 departs with 12-cars on June 13, 1955, with diesel units 6507C, B, A leading the way. It is about 6:20 p.m., and passengers on this train will be able to see some of the best scenery on the Northern Pacific Railway during the next three hours.
Ron Nixon photo; Bill Kuebler collection

Chapter 3: Scenic Route of the Vista-Dome North Coast Limited

Many NP freight cars doubled as rolling billboards advertising the road's "Scenic Route" and premier passenger train. *Above*: New mechanical refrigerator N.P.M.X. No. 500 at the Pacific Car and Foundry Company plant in Renton, Washington, in September 1957. *Below*: "DF" (for "Damage Free") boxcar 1143 appears at Missoula in May 1955.

Top: Photo courtesy of Tacoma Public Library & Jim Fredrickson

Bottom: Ron Nixon photo; Bill Kuebler collection

"Scenic Route of the Vista-Dome North Coast Limited." Thus proclaimed the NP on rolling billboards known more commonly as boxcars. If anything, this advertising slogan was an understatement. The late David P. Morgan, editor of *Trains*, summed it up best when he penned the following lines:

> Some railroads . . . never matched in person the image they cast in photo or timetable or history book. A publicized canyon was gone in the blink of an eye, a vaunted engine fell shy of its builder photo, a union station proved to be less than august. But not the Northern Pacific. NP exceeded its press. Nothing I'd read had prepared me for the breathtaking descent of [the westbound North Coast Limited] into Butte. Or the climb of No. 26 out of Auburn to Stampede Pass.
>
> "The All-American Railroad"
> *Trains*, Vol. 46, No. 2, December 1985

Without a doubt, the *North Coast Limited* rolled through some of the most beautiful and spectacular scenery in the United States, and lots of it. This is where the NP had a substantial advantage over its chief rival, the GN. Although *Empire Builder* passengers enjoyed beautiful views of Glacier National Park and the western Montana Rockies, viewing time was rather limited. Only a few daylight hours on the *Builder*—in the summer, that is, and even fewer in the winter—were spent in mountainous territory. Most of the territory from Havre east was hardly the kind that would move a passenger to a dome seat; if anything, it did the opposite.

In contrast, the NP had interesting scenery to offer during almost all daylight hours, even on long summer days. That scenery varied, too; it was not monotonous. All these could be seen from the train: Minnesota's lake country; the North Dakota badlands (early morning westbound, evening

The Vista-Dome North Coast Limited

eastbound, the best times for viewing this territory); the bluff-lined Yellowstone River (for 344 miles); Bozeman Pass; Homestake Pass; Evaro hill; the Jocko and Flathead River valleys; the Clark Fork River valley, perhaps the most beautiful segment of all (second evening, westbound); and the beautiful Cascade Mountains and the Green River valley. Even non-railfans have told this author about vivid memories of magnificent views seen through NP dome windows decades earlier. A first viewing of the Montana Rockies from a vista-dome west of Billings, for example, was utterly breathtaking and very exciting, especially for those of us who grew up in prairie states. The view often reduced conversation in the dome to mere whispers of awe. It gave the passenger a chance to reflect on the important questions of life, while the barracuda telephone and other daily demands were a world away. For some, the view even seemed to add years to one's life span and somehow made time stand still. As the road's executives wisely understood, the vista-dome was a passenger car made just for the kind of scenery that was in such abundance on the NP.

But, we're getting a little ahead of ourselves. No discussion of the 1959 *North Coast Limited* is proper without a brief look at some of the corporate decisions that brought it about. Back in 1951, some of these issues were not so clear to railroad executives. Difficult questions confronted NP's new

Long summer days permit westbound *North Coast Limited* passengers maximum daylight viewing along the scenic Clark Fork River. Sleeper-observation-lounge 390 brings up the rear of this 13-car train, photographed near Turah, Montana, in June 1957. In two hours this train will enter Idaho Division territory at Paradise and continue its early evening run alongside the Clark Fork. Passengers and employees deemed the territory west of Paradise to be the most scenic on the entire NP, and it was especially magnificent during sunset.
Ron Nixon photo; Bill Kuebler collection

Chapter 3: Scenic Route of the Vista-Dome North Coast Limited

president, Robert S. Macfarlane. Namely, how does a railroad under new management come from behind in the passenger business as quickly as possible? Yes, we can implement a new, faster *North Coast Limited* schedule, thought Macfarlane, and yes, we can order new equipment for the train, but is that enough? Maybe something more—or some*one*—was needed, a real expert in those nuances of image, someone who could really give the NP's premier passenger train—even the road's entire passenger department—a badly needed boost in the public's eye. Perhaps a new paint scheme and interior decor for all NP passenger equipment were in order.

President Macfarlane found just such a man. This man was an outsider, but he was well known, and the results of his labors for the NP would turn out to exceed all the hopes and dreams of NP management. He gave the NP's passenger department, including the *North Coast Limited*, an entirely new look. His name was Raymond Loewy.

For the NP assignment, Loewy did not simply engage in guesswork. When he and his associates were retained by the NP in 1952, he was on NP property almost daily for a period of several weeks, searching for clues, ever so perceptively creating a whole new image for the road's passenger department. The results of his work were stunning!

We may never know with certainty just how Loewy decided upon the colors that would dress NP's passenger trains. Thus far, only one account has emerged. It is said that after some time of observing NP's passenger operation and making mental notes, Mr. Loewy himself was standing

Raymond Loewy

Who was the man behind Northern Pacific's (NP's) new passenger train image? Born in 1893, Raymond Loewy had a life-long love of trains, for starters. He was also fascinated by machines, especially locomotives, later automobiles, and just about anything else having to do with industry and progress. As a young lad in his native France, he frequented roundhouses and rail yards, observing the designs of various locomotives and cars. He had an eye for detail. With a few design adjustments here and there, either on paper or simply in his mind, he would try to turn an otherwise plain or ugly object into something attractive, something that might appeal to the general public.

After moving to America as a young man, he offered his design skills to a number of people and companies, but most seemed to have no time for him. Finally, in about 1930, Loewy landed a job in a department store as a window display designer. His ideas immediately clashed with the traditional thinking of management. Whereas they wanted the window to show almost everything the store had to offer, Loewy preferred something much less cluttered, a display that presented a "picture," a setting that enticed the viewer to enter the store and see what else was inside. For this untraditional thinking, Loewy was fired!

But, he never gave up. In fact, his personal motto as well as the title of his autobiography was "Never leave well enough alone." So, he pursued his dreams and ideas. Loewy was also a clever man. That, combined with his eye for detail, gave him an advantage when he needed it. For example, shortly after coming to America, when jobs were rather scarce, he approached a tobacco company with an offer they couldn't refuse: He would present a logo "design package" to them. If they accepted it, they would pay him $50,000; if they rejected it, they owed him nothing. A few days later he returned to the company's offices and presented his "package." The logo itself was the same as before—except that he had put it on *both* sides of the cigarette pack. That way, regardless of how someone tossed the pack on a table, the logo would be on top and plainly seen, in effect doubling advertising exposure. The company accepted the result, Loewy was paid $50,000 and from that day forward, the "Lucky Strike" logo has appeared on both sides of the cigarette pack!

Respect for Loewy and his work began to grow. Eventually, he did considerable design work on everything from cookie cutters to refrigerators, office furniture, automobiles (especially the Studebaker) and even ocean liners. He also did comprehensive design work on Pennsylvania Railroad passenger trains and most notably on that road's famous GG-1 type electric locomotive. By the 1950s, his work in industrial design was highly respected, well known and liked by many among the discerning. In 1962, President Kennedy asked Raymond Loewy to design a new exterior paint scheme for the Presidential aircraft, at that time a new Boeing 707. Adapted to a Boeing 747, that scheme is still in use on the Presidential aircraft today. Loewy continued his work over the years and earned his place as the most influential industrial designer in American history. He died in July 1986, at his home in Monte Carlo. He was 92.

The Vista-Dome North Coast Limited

trackside near milepost 28 on the Rocky Mountain Division's 2nd Subdivision, between Logan and Butte. That's near the spot where NP's Ron Nixon coincidentally stood some six years later to photograph the eastbound *Vista-Dome North Coast Limited*—a famous photo that adorned dining car menu covers for several years. As Loewy stood there, observing the limestone mountains across the Jefferson River at high noon, something about the scene held his attention, namely the warm shade of green he saw in the distant trees under the noon sun. Perhaps it could be complemented by some other hue. Just maybe . . .but what? What other hue in NP territory would go with it? Everywhere he looked, Loewy found green. Perhaps a second shade of green would work, but what shade? Then, another thought occurred to him.

According to this account, there was a full moon and a clear sky that night. And there, in the middle of the night, stood Mr. Loewy again, looking across the river at those same green trees on the hillside. This time, under a full moon, the trees had a soft, cool, deeply pleasing dark shade. There it was! He had found his complementary shade of green—from the same trees! It was simply a matter of day and night, or in this case, moonlight. (Although the human eye does not see colors in very low light, it is interesting to note that a phenomenon known as the "Purkinge effect" could have played a role. In reduced light the eye's sensitivity to color shifts so that greens stand out. That is why grass tends to look better in the late evening.) To Mr. Loewy, a white accent against these two shades of green seemed natural, an accent possibly inspired the previous day by high cirrus clouds overhead. However Loewy decided upon the colors, they have been lauded by railfans and passengers, alike. It is worth noting that the use of a two-tone green color scheme on the NP predates the

This is the area where Raymond Loewy is said to have observed two shades of green from the same trees in the limestone hills across the river, under different lighting conditions. Train No. 26 approaches milepost 28 in the upper Jefferson River canyon, three and a half miles east of Cardwell, Montana. In the foreground, "Day-Nite" coach 594 and dome coach 557 make up part of the 14-car consist, led by three F-units on a bright June day in 1959. This classic photo by Ron Nixon adorned NP dining car menu covers throughout the 1960s.
Ron Nixon photo; Bill Kuebler collection

Chapter 3: Scenic Route of the Vista-Dome North Coast Limited

designer. The NP's passenger equipment scheme previous to his consisted of two tones of green accented by imitation gold striping.

It is also difficult to know the full reach of his design work for the NP. On the Pennsylvania, his passenger train design work covered all the details, right down to the road's matchbook covers. Consider NP dining car china, for example. In about 1947, a rather drab two-tone charcoal gray pattern was given colors, becoming a two-tone green version with the NP insignia, known as the "Park Line" pattern. After about 1953, this pattern was replaced with a new one, the "Monad" pattern. It was a slight modification of the 1947 pattern and probably the work of Loewy.

In any case, Loewy was busy searching for not only the right exterior paint scheme, but the right interior decor for NP's passenger cars as well. He decided upon a formula of western themes, rich but not loud or ostentatious, combined with various soft colors lightly accented, modern furnishings, and plenty of lighting. To top it all off, he went so far as to advocate a new and unique lounge car for the *North Coast Limited*, one with a Lewis and Clark theme literally painted all over its interior walls. Before it was over, he did just what he had been asked to do. He offered NP man-

Wintertime scenery on the NP was also spectacular. Train No. 26 meets a snowplow clearing the westward main track near Borup Loop, west of Stampede, on January 11, 1964. Ron Nixon took this picture from the rear vestibule of a dome sleeper. The Budd dining car ahead is car 458. The car in front of the diner is Traveller's Rest 496, and ahead of that is leg rest coach 584, one of five cars converted from Holiday Lounge cars 487–491 in 1962.
Ron Nixon photo; Gary Wildung collection

The Vista-Dome North Coast Limited

agement a whole new package for its passenger department. Wisely, President Macfarlane accepted Loewy's results.

And the rest, as they say, is history. Beginning in 1953, the NP painted all of its passenger cars, even those assigned to trains other than the *North Coast Limited*, in a new "Loewy green" exterior paint scheme. Passenger diesel locomotives (F-units) were painted to match. So, when the *North Coast Limited* was fully equipped with dome cars the following year, it presented a stunning appearance. It was a handsome train, inside and out; but, its most striking feature was its exterior paint scheme. While other roads may have had flashier schemes, the two tones of green separated by a thin white stripe resonated deep within the psyche of the viewer, just as industrial designer, Raymond Loewy, had intended. Something seemingly magic about this paint scheme has withstood the test of time, for even today, its positive effect upon viewers is the same as when it debuted in 1953. It is one of the first reasons given by many NP fans when asked why they favor the road. Even non-railfans have been permanently impacted by the scheme. Famous jazzman and bandleader Duke Ellington once said in an interview, "Back in '56 we did a gig in Minneapolis, and then one out in Seattle. By the way, we went by train as usual, but this one was different. I remember it so well. It was the most beautiful train, a fascinating mixture of greens . . . I've always wanted to go back and ride that one . . ."

The westbound *Vista-Dome North Coast Limited* pauses at Billings, Montana, on a sunny day in September 1954. Two dome coaches appear in the train, but dome sleepers have not yet arrived on NP property. Most of the cars in the rear half of this train have not yet been painted in the new two-tone Loewy green paint scheme.
Bill Kuebler collection

Chapter 4
Equipment & Maintenance

Cars assigned to *North Coast Limited* service operated in a pool. The same three railroads involved in the train's operation: the Northern Pacific (NP), the Chicago, Burlington, and Quincy (CB&Q), and the Spokane, Portland, and Seattle (SP&S), owned cars in this pool. Five complete *North Coast Limited* trains, known in the industry as "train sets," were required to fill the daily schedule between Chicago and Seattle-Portland. Extra cars amounting nearly to a sixth train set were maintained as protection equipment in St. Paul and Seattle. Railroads used the phrases "protection equipment" and "protection cars" to refer to those cars in a fleet that were on stand-by status. Protection cars were available to fill in for cars taken out of service for any reason. Generally, cars rotated between in-service, out-of-service (usually for routine maintenance), and stand-by status. Of all 88 cars assigned to *North Coast Limited* service in 1959 (that figure excludes Slumbercoaches), the CB&Q owned the equivalent of one complete train set, whereas the SP&S owned one dome coach, one dome sleeper, and one 350-series standard sleeping car. (Until 1954, the SP&S also owned one Day-Nite coach.) These CB&Q and SP&S cars were painted and lettered to match the NP cars, except for small ownership letters appearing on each side of these cars in the upper corners. The NP cars did not have ownership letters.

The Vista-Dome North Coast Limited

This ownership arrangement included maintenance; the CB&Q and SP&S were responsible for maintaining the *North Coast Limited* cars they owned. If the NP actually did any work on their cars, the NP would bill the owner accordingly. The ownership arrangement also included equitable distribution of revenue generated by the cars, according to some rather complicated formulas. By this method, the CB&Q and SP&S were compensated for their part in the *North Coast Limited* operation. This rather unusual system worked well, especially because it permitted great flexibility in how the train could be made up.

This pool system meant that the NP rotated the cars owned by CB&Q and SP&S in and out of service along with the NP cars. A car's position in a train and its routing (Seattle *vs.* Portland) had no relation to which railroad owned the car. For example, on any given trip, SP&S dome sleeper 306 could operate in either the train's Seattle line or its Portland line.

In actual practice, the nearly six trains' worth of cars were individually rotated in- and out-of-service on a regular operating cycle that provided for major maintenance every two years at NP's Como Shops in St. Paul or, in the case of the Pullmans (see the sidebar), at the Pullman Company's Calumet, Illinois, Shops. Some "running repairs" were made at Seattle and at St. Paul Union Depot as necessary. Routine maintenance was also done as needed at Burlington's 14th Street Yard in Chicago, including replacement of 30 pairs of wheels per week (about every four months for each car) and almost twice that many in the winter on account of "shellout" on those cars equipped with clasp brakes. "Shellout" occurred when rapid wheel cooling took place after braking in low temperatures, causing steel fragments to flake off the wheel tread. This did not occur on cars equipped with disc brakes. Budd cars came equipped with disc brakes; Pullman-Standard cars came with clasp brakes. In 1956–62, NP replaced all clasp brakes on Pullman-Standard lightweight cars with disc brakes.

Northern Pacific maintained its passenger car fleet (except Pullmans) at Como Shops in St. Paul, Minnesota. In this north-northeastward view, shop buildings appear in the center of the photo, just to the south of the NP main line. The Great Northern's line is about a half-mile further south, at the bottom of the photo. This aerial view of the Como shop complex was made in 1957.
NP photo; Gary Wildung collection

Chapter 4: Equipment & Maintenance

The Pullmans: Railroad Sleeping Cars

The name "Pullman" can be a source of confusion, because it appears in the name of more than one company. "Pullman-Standard" and the "Pullman Company" were not one and the same during the *Vista-Dome North Coast Limited* era. Pullman-Standard was a railroad car builder (since 1927); the Pullman Company (often referred to as "Pullman") operated sleeping cars as a concessionaire. That is, Pullman maintained, staffed and equipped sleeping cars in revenue service on the railroads. During the 1950s and 1960s, this arrangement was spelled out in contracts between the individual railroads and the Pullman Company. Essentially, the sleeping cars were built by any of the major car builders (Pullman-Standard, Budd, American Car and Foundry, etc.), they were owned by the railroads, and they were maintained, staffed, and operated by the Pullman Company. But, this arrangement was not always so. A very brief account of the events that led to it may be of interest.

The sleeping car ownership and operation arrangement that existed in the 1950s really had its beginnings several decades earlier. Since long before World War I, the Pullman Company (known as the "Pullman Palace Car Company" in the 1800s) developed, built, and operated sleeping cars. The Pullman Company maintained a virtual monopoly on sleeping car construction and operation by acquiring what few other companies had attempted to engage in the sleeping car business. By the early 1900s, "sleeping car" and "Pullman" had become essentially synonymous terms in American culture, such was the monopoly. In 1927, the Pullman Company became Pullman Incorporated with two subsidiaries, the Pullman Company as the operating side and Pullman-Standard Car Manufacturing Company (Pullman-Standard), the car-building component. By the mid-1930s, a fleet of 8,500 sleeping cars operated under the Pullman name in North America, and some 30,000 employees were on the Pullman Company's payroll.

By the late-1930s, the construction side of the business (Pullman-Standard) had expanded to include several types of passenger cars (sleepers, coaches, diners, lounge cars, etc.), freight cars, trams, buses, track maintenance machines, and even boats. Six Pullman-Standard works handled the construction side at places ranging from Bessemer, Alabama, to the original Pullman shops at Chicago, Illinois. The Chicago shops built most of the railroads' passenger cars, including all the NP Pullman cars (or Pullman-Standard cars, after 1927). Then, in 1940, inspired by a construction competitor, the United States government brought a successful lawsuit against Pullman Incorporated under the Sherman Anti-Trust Act, claiming an unlawful monopoly had been created. The United States government gave Pullman Incorporated the choice either to build railroad cars or to operate sleeping cars, but it could not do both. Pullman Incorporated selected the construction side. Car building thus continued under the Pullman-Standard name, and Pullman-Standard continued as a subsidiary of Pullman Incorporated.

Equipment Trust plate on sleeper-observation-lounge car 390. This plate is located on the right side of the car, just behind the vestibule and above the rear of the end skirt.
Bill Kuebler photo

The United States government, however, allowed Pullman Incorporated to defer this separation of business until after World War II, so as not to disrupt the nation's war effort in any way. Thus, in 1947, the Pullman Company—the company that had operated railroad sleeping cars—was bought out by a consortium of 59 American railroads. Carroll Rede Harding from the Southern Pacific (SP), who had played a leading role in the purchasing negotiations, was elected its president and the Pullman Company continued to operate as previously, but as a concessionaire, for another 22 years. Shortly before the Burlington Northern (BN) merger in 1970, the railroads assumed the responsibility for catering and all other on-board services in the sleeping cars. In 1979, Pullman Incorporated, the original company, now an even more diversified enterprise with 14 plants in the United States and Canada, announced that no more passenger cars would be built by its Pullman-Standard subsidiary. Since the railway passenger car side of the business at the Chicago shops was no longer financially viable, the shops closed. The years 1980-81 marked the end of the Pullman car in the United States after some 112 years' service.

Thus it was that during the *Vista-Dome North Coast Limited* era, a contract between NP (or CB&Q or SP&S) and Pullman, a concessionaire company owned by several dozen railroads, called for Pullman to staff and operate the sleeping cars of the owning road, regardless of the car's builder, and thereby ensure quality service to all sleeping car passengers. Each railroad paid an annual fee for Pullman service. The small "PULLMAN" lettering on the sides of NP sleeping cars indicated this contractual arrangement.

The Vista-Dome North Coast Limited

There were two major maintenance programs at Como for lightweight passenger equipment: a four-year overhaul and a less extensive program at the two-year mid-point between overhauls. Similar programs existed at Pullman's Calumet shops for all *North Coast Limited* sleeping cars. The shorter, mid-point program included replacement or repair of brake equipment, heating and air conditioning equipment, replacement of truck springs, new belts and drives for generators, new batteries, refurbishing of some interior equipment (seats, shelves, doors, etc.), and other repairs to trucks and wheels as necessary.

The four-year overhaul program included all the items from the mid-point program, plus the complete stripping of the car's interior and exterior, removal and re-sealing of all windows, disassembly or replacement of many major parts, and repainting. In the words of Como veteran, Don Kjellberg, "We completely stripped the cars and practically rebuilt them." An overhaul typically kept a car in the shop for two to three weeks. Prior to repainting, each car was completely stripped and sanded *by hand*. Repainting was accomplished with a large spray-painting rig rolling along rails placed outside those upon which the car sat. This rig applied only one color at a time, and one full day was required for the application of each color. The Loewy scheme had four colors, each getting multiple coats, and these colors were applied as follows: first, a one to two foot wide area just below the windows was painted white the full length of the car; then the actual white stripe was masked off and the dark green was applied to the top half of the car; then the light green was applied to the bottom half and, finally, the black to the underside. After these colors were applied the lettering was applied, usually requiring an extra day. Thus, five days were required just to repaint one car!

The *North Coast Limited's* Budd-built cars were made of stainless steel, substantially reducing rust problems. But, this material also presented some unusual challenges to shop forces because it was very difficult to work with and especially to weld. Even the task of merely drilling a hole through stainless steel was very difficult compared with the steel used in Pullman-Standard cars. Heat during the welding process would usually cause the surrounding stainless steel to buckle or warp. To solve this problem, Como shop forces devised a crude but effective technique of using large burlap bags soaked in water to confine heat transfer from the welding process to the smallest possible area. After some trial and error, the men at Como were able to work quite skillfully with these stainless steel cars. (It is interesting to note that most of the "trial and error" was conducted not on the dome cars, but on one of the Budd Rail Diesel Cars, which was of similar construction. It proved to be a very good "practice" vehicle.)

Como shops maintained all the NP's passenger cars, except the Pullmans, with a force of about 275 men working on a five-day week, single shift basis. These employees worked especially hard on those occasions when repairing passenger cars that had been badly damaged in an accident. Generally, Como shop personnel were known to be a very productive and close-knit group of employees.

A *North Coast Limited* train set arriving Chicago would layover about 22 hours before beginning its westbound trip, but a set arriving Seattle had a mere six hours before heading back east. These layover times resulted from NP's decisions regarding scheduling at each terminus. Departure and arrival times at Chicago and Seattle were chosen so as to facilitate connections with certain trains running between Chicago and points east (e.g., New York Central's *Twentieth Century Limited* and Pennsylvania Railroad's *Broadway Limited*), and NP and GN trains running between Seattle and Portland—trains generally referred to as "west coast pool trains." At both Chicago and Seattle, the *Vista-Dome North Coast Limited* was fully cleaned inside and out, serviced, and then restocked with water, propane, food, sleeping car linens, and numerous other supplies. Young women, working in pairs, required 1 hour 45 minutes per Pullman to vacuum, dust, scrub, and wipe, while porters made up some 86 beds (126 beds with a Slumbercoach in the train). At Seattle, if the westbound arrived more than an hour and a half late, servicing time would be very tight and No. 26's on-time departure, jeopardized. In a bit of a paradox, NP's conservative decision to keep

Chapter 4: Equipment & Maintenance

the *North Coast Limited* on the slower schedule during the period 1947–52 resulted in considerably higher operating costs during those years. *Six* train sets, rather than five, were required to cover the slower schedule (plus extra cars for protection), increasing equipment, maintenance, and crew costs accordingly.

In 1959, each *North Coast Limited* consisted of 11 to 14 cars, depending on the season. The 1959 summer season consist was 14 cars. The Slumbercoach, which began operating in late November 1959, increased the train's length to 12 to 15 cars. During the fall, winter, and spring seasons, the train ran a reduced consist, except from about December 10 until mid January, when it ran a full 14-car "mid-winter" season consist to accommodate holiday season traffic. In the mid-winter season of 1959-60, however, the train ran a 13-car consist because three of the fleet's 11 dome sleepers were leased-out for Miami service. No doubt this leasing arrangement was a business decision. Perhaps it was intended to help pay for expensive dome sleepers that would be difficult to fill with revenue passengers on the NP during periods of low, off-season demand, but the specific reason for it is unclear in NP records. Dome sleeper leasing occurred again in later winter seasons, beginning in late 1963. (The lease arrangement itself will be described in detail in Chapter 9.)

With few exceptions, NP management did not permit the train to grow beyond 14 cars (15 with a Slumbercoach), because company executives thought that the train's dining facilities were insufficient to handle more passengers than a 14- or 15-car train could carry. President Macfarlane, in fact, had decreed early in his tenure that the *North Coast Limited* would be kept to a maximum of 11 cars, perhaps a rather conservative limit. When the fast schedule went into effect in November

Only four days after entering revenue service, dome coach 550 gets a bath at Seattle on August 20, 1954. During their six-hour layover here, these cars will be thoroughly cleaned, inside and out, and restocked for the eastbound journey to Chicago, scheduled to begin later this day at 1:30 p.m.
Ron Nixon photo; Lorenz P. Schrenk collection

1952, Macfarlane's 11-car rule was imposed, but with the addition of domes two years later, the train was allowed to expand slightly. After all, there were plenty of revenue passengers to haul and dollars to earn. The demand for space aboard trains 25 and 26 in the mid-1950s (and during several years in the following decade, for that matter) was enough to fill 14 or more cars during the heavy travel seasons, and even as many as 12 cars during the periods of lowest demand.

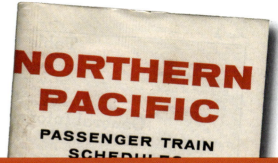

Chapter 5
Schedule & Train Servicing

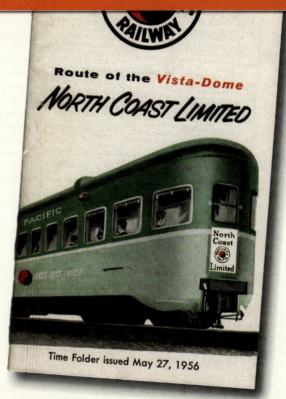

Time Folder issued May 27, 1956

The Northern Pacific (NP) went to great lengths to schedule the *Vista-Dome North Coast Limited* competitively, and in this department it was at a disadvantage to the Great Northern (GN) and Milwaukee Road. Between St. Paul and Seattle, via Butte, in 1959 lay 1,892 miles of track, all NP except for 10 1/2 miles of GN track between St. Paul and Minneapolis. The 427 Chicago, Burlington, and Quincy (CB&Q) miles between St. Paul and Chicago brought the total to 2,319. That was 109 miles more than the *Empire Builder* covered between Chicago and Seattle, and 130 more than covered by the *Olympian Hiawatha*. Besides that, the *North Coast* faced a much tougher profile, with three formidable mountain passes rather than two, some 52 miles of grades exceeding 1.8%, and enough degrees of curvature to keep car shop forces rather busy with wheel replacement programs as previously noted. In spite of these disadvantages, the 1959 *North Coast Limited* took less than two hours longer than the *Empire Builder* and less than an hour longer than the *Olympian Hiawatha*. Westbound, the *North Coast* took only five minutes more than the *Hiawatha*!

From the moment the wheels began turning at Chicago until the train stopped at Seattle, average speed for the *North Coast Limited* in 1959 was 51 miles per hour, including all intermediate stops. Eastbound, the average was 50 miles per hour. These are remarkable figures, given the physical properties of the route. One way the NP compensated for its tough profile was by keeping its station dwell times to a bare minimum. Average scheduled dwell time at intermediate stops (Fargo, Jamestown, Billings, etc.) was a mere four minutes, another remarkable figure and considerably less than what most

The Vista-Dome North Coast Limited

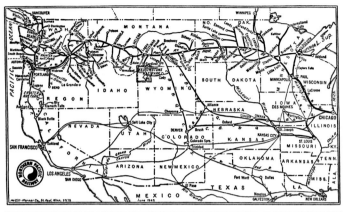

Stewardess-Nurse Service...
Exciting Traveller's Rest
Buffet-Lounge Car...

Extras on the VISTA-DOME

NORTHERN PACIFIC RAILWAY

NORTH COAST LIMITED

CONDENSED PASSENGER SCHEDULES
Issued June 14, 1959

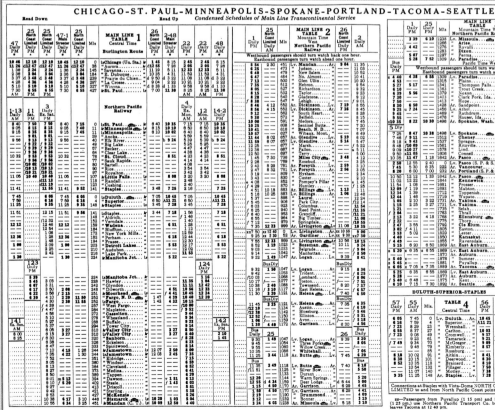

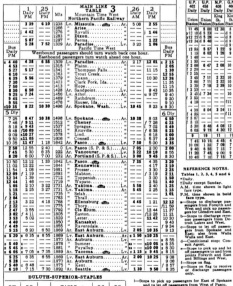

Chapter 5: Schedule & Train Servicing

When this photograph was taken in June 1955, the dome window-washing procedure was still performed at Missoula, so the Livingston depot platform is sans two-story wash rigs as No. 25 arrives with 13 cars. As soon as this train stops, the three diesel units, 6507C, B, A, will be exchanged for another set of three, fully fueled and ready to begin a 16-day operating cycle on NP's main line passenger trains.
Ron Nixon photo; Gary Wildung collection

Highball! Anticipating his boss's next move, the rear brakeman carefully watches the conductor from the edge of the depot platform at Livingston. Departure time is seconds away, so all vestibules save two are closed and the train is ready to go. As soon as the conductor raises his arm to give the highball, the rear brakeman will return the signal and waste no time crossing the eastward main track. He will then follow the porter (in white jacket) aboard sleeper-observation-lounge car 391. The next two cars forward are dome sleeper 313 and 8-6-3-1 sleeper 354. June 1955.
Ron Nixon photo; Bill Kuebler collection

The Vista-Dome North Coast Limited

Servicing the Vista-Dome North Coast Limited (as of June 1959)

Chicago	22-hour layover for equipment and dining car crew: 46-hour (two-day) layover for Stewardess-Nurse
	Some scheduled maintenance performed at Chicago, Burlington, and Quincy's (CB&Q's) 14th St. Yard
	Unscheduled maintenance performed on cars as required
	Train fully serviced, cleaned, and re-stocked for westbound trip
	CB&Q engine and train crews operate train between here and St. Paul
St. Paul	
Westbound:	CB&Q locomotive units exchanged for Northern Pacific (NP) units
	Inbound CB&Q engine and train crews relieved by outbound NP engine and train crews
	Train inspection by carmen
	Electrician on call
	Cars scheduled for regular shopping at Como, if any, switched out (usually these were deadheaded in from Chicago)
Eastbound:	NP locomotive units exchanged for CB&Q units
	Traveler's Rest and dining cars exchanged with freshly re-stocked cars from the commissary; new dining car crew begins St. Paul-Chicago-Seattle-St.Paul trip
	Train inspection
	Electrician on call
	Inbound NP engine and train crews relieved by outbound CB&Q engine and train crews
	Cars that just completed scheduled shopping at Como, if any, switched in (usually deadheaded to Chicago to enter revenue service next day)
Staples	Carmen meet train
	Electrician on-call (will accompany train, if necessary)
	Engine crew change
Dilworth	Engine crew change (this stop was usually less than one minute in duration; there was no passenger service here)
Fargo	Carmen meet train
	Train crew change (conductor and brakemen)
	Water-baggage car's water tanks refilled
Jamestown	Carmen meet train
	Engine crew change
Mandan	Carmen perform mandatory 500-mile Interstate Commerce Commission (ICC) train inspection and brake test
	Cars watered
	Locomotive units refueled (winter and as required during other seasons)
	Water added to water-baggage car as necessary (winter)
	Engine and train crews change
Dickinson	Engine crew change
Glendive	Carmen meet train
	Electrician meets train (will accompany train, if necessary)
	Locomotive units refueled
	Engine and train crews change
Forsyth	Engine crew change
Billings	Carmen perform mandatory 500-mile ICC train inspection and brake test
	Electrician meets train; not a traveling electrician
	Engine and train crews change
Livingston	Locomotive units exchanged (outgoing units fully-fueled)[1]
	Carmen meet train
	Dome windows washed
	Dining car re-supplied if required
	Engine crew change
	Cars watered as needed

Chapter 5: Schedule & Train Servicing

Servicing the *Vista-Dome North Coast Limited* (continued)

Butte	Carmen meet train
	Electrician meets train
	Engine and train crews change
Missoula	Carmen perform mandatory 500-mile ICC train inspection and brake test
	Electrician meets train (will accompany train, if necessary)
	Locomotive units refueled
	Cars watered
	Water added to water-baggage car as required (winter)
	Engine crew change
	Train crew change, westbound trips only[2]
Paradise	Engine and train crews change
Spokane	Carmen perform mandatory 500-mile ICC train inspection and brake test
	Electrician on call
	Engine and train crews change
Pasco	Portland cars switched out (westbound) or in (eastbound)
	Carmen perform 500-mile ICC train inspection and brake test
	Electrician on call
	Locomotive units refueled
	Engine crew change
Yakima	Carmen meet train
	Locomotive fireman change[3]
Ellensburg	Train crew change
	Locomotive engineer change[3]
Seattle	Train fully-serviced, cleaned, and re-stocked (about four hours required)
	Unscheduled maintenance performed as required
	Some *North Coast Limited* cars kept on standby to replace inbound cars as needed
	Carmen perform 500-mile ICC inspection and brake test
	Stewardess-Nurse begins six-day trip here (four days off upon return)

1 Exchanging locomotive units required breaking and re-coupling of steam lines, air brake line, signal line, and special connections for the electro-pneumatic brake system in use only on the *North Coast Limited*.

2 Rocky Mountain Division passenger train crews had a "step off" agreement, whereby they would begin a trip westbound, Missoula to Paradise, layover at Paradise, then work east all the way to Butte, layover there, then work back west to Missoula where they would "step off" at their home terminal. They then had two days off before their next trip.

3 In accordance with union agreements after 1952, passenger engineers changed at Ellensburg, but passenger firemen changed at Yakima.

    As noted above, carmen met the train at most division points. They inspected the train's exterior, including hose and cable connections, trucks, wheels, and under-body equipment. With the assistance of local carmen at each division point, the engine crew performed a standing test of the train's brakes. To accomplish this, the engineer made a 20-pound brake-pipe reduction immediately after stopping, allowing carmen to check train line integrity by observing this brake application on all cars. In addition to this, a "running test" of the train's brake system was required when departing a terminal or anyplace where there was a change in engine crew, train crew, locomotive units, or any combination of these.

    Finally, NP Special Rules and Instructions governing employees in passenger train service stated the following: "Frequent running inspection shall be made from the vestibules in various parts of the train" (Rule 37g).

other western roads allowed their named trains. Seldom recognized for their contribution, the NP's water-baggage cars did as much as anything else to make these figures possible. (The term "water-baggage" may seem strange at first sight. A "water-baggage" car was a baggage car with large water tanks installed at one end of the car. The water was pumped to steam generators on the diesel units; the steam generators produced steam for train heating and for hot water systems. I will describe this operation in more detail later in this book.) Large water tanks in this car made time-consuming *en route* water servicing for the locomotive's steam generators unnecessary, with very few exceptions.

33

The Vista-Dome North Coast Limited

Some names on the timetable were scenes of daily (or nightly) wonders as the train was serviced in only minutes, with minimal interruption to the passenger boarding process. Most passengers, in fact, hardly noticed all the activity going on around the train during these brief stops. Even before the train's wheels stopped turning at these places, men would converge upon it from every direction, with blue flag, fuel and water hoses, and other tools of the trade in hand. The "blue flag" was a blue metal flag hung on one of the diesel units or on the front end of the first car in a passenger train. Its display indicated that carmen were under or about the train and that the train must not be moved or coupled to, and that the engine crew must not apply or release the train's brakes. At Livingston, locomotive units were exchanged while several men on two-story rigs washed all the dome windows. Timetable allowance for this: a mere 10 minutes. A complete list of *en route* servicing demonstrates just how labor-intensive the operation of the *Vista-Dome North Coast Limited* was, even in 1959.

Livingston, I presume? Dome coach 552 gets a window wash during No. 25's stop at Livingston on a sunny day in August 1959. Livingston shop forces built two-story wash rigs especially for this purpose. Normally, two rigs were used, one on either side of the train. When this duty was performed at Missoula prior to summer 1955, carmen placed large wooden ladders alongside the train, a method that required the carmen to walk atop the cars in order to reach all the dome windows. Thus, these rigs enhanced safety and efficiency.
Ron Nixon photo; Lorenz P. Schrenk collection

Chapter 5: Schedule & Train Servicing

From the compilation of terminal and *en route* servicing shown in the table, one can see that many people were involved in the safe and successful operation of this train. A trip from St. Paul to Seattle involved 16 engine crews and 11 train crews (10 train crews, eastbound), and an army of carmen, electricians, and other shop personnel. The *North Coast Limited* and other passenger trains surely kept many people employed on the NP!

With such a demanding schedule and operation, how did the *Vista-Dome North Coast Limited* actually perform? In a word, excellently. Its "off-season" on-time performance was a stunning 98%, in spite of some very tough weather conditions. Larger passenger loads and increased station work adversely affected the train's summer and mid-winter season on-time performance, as did track maintenance (summers) and very harsh weather (winters). Even so, on-time performance during those seasons was about 93%. In this category overall, the *North Coast Limited* was one of the top performing trains in the industry.

Two carmen are busy cutting the air, signal, and steam lines between locomotive and water-baggage car on No. 25 at Livingston in September 1967. This set of diesel units will be cut off and replaced by another set in less than ten minutes. This maneuver requires the coordinated work of several men. The respective incoming and outgoing road engine crews are handling the two sets of locomotive units during this exchange.
Bill Kuebler collection

The Vista-Dome North Coast Limited

On-time performance was defined by the NP as the percentage of arrivals at Seattle and St. Paul that occurred on-schedule. (When a train was late, the degree of tardiness was irrelevant to this computation.) While that definition may seem obvious, it is interesting to consider the following items of comparison with today's airlines:

- Today's airlines and the Federal Aviation Administration define "on-time" as the arrival of a flight at its scheduled destination not more than *15 minutes after* its scheduled arrival time. The NP defined "on-time" as arrival at Seattle or St. Paul *not later than* scheduled arrival time. If the train stopped even one minute behind schedule at either of these places, it was considered late and executives in St. Paul knew about it the same day—and, called division superintendents for explanations.

- In 1989, American Airlines was in first place among major United States air carriers for "on-time" performance (see definition in item 1 above), hailing itself in ads as "the on-time machine." Its on-time performance that year: 92%. The second-place airline was not even close to that figure. In recent years, figures in the mid 80's have been typical for most major airlines, including those with the best records.

- As the airlines do today, the NP "padded" the *North Coast's* schedule, but only over certain districts, whereas the airlines do this with all flights. That is, the westbound *North Coast Limited* was given a rather loose schedule from Yakima to Seattle, and the eastbound one a similar schedule from Staples to St. Paul. This made it easier to make up time lost across the system, so that on-time arrivals and connections would be more likely in those important terminals. As a result of this "padding," on-schedule running speeds from Staples to St. Paul, mostly double track territory designed for 75 miles per hour, were typically around 55 miles per hour.

Train No. 26, the eastbound *Vista-Dome North Coast Limited*, is switched at St. Paul Union Depot in August 1969. Dome sleeper 306, foreground, is owned by SP&S and is operating from Seattle to Chicago on this trip. Just ahead of it are diner 463 and Traveller's Rest Lounge car 494. The diner and lounge cars are about to be replaced with freshly stocked cars staffed by a new dining car crew.
Jim Fredrickson photo

Part 2
A 1959 JOURNEY

Chapter 6
All Aboard!

"Hello, I'm Sue, Your Stewardess-Nurse"

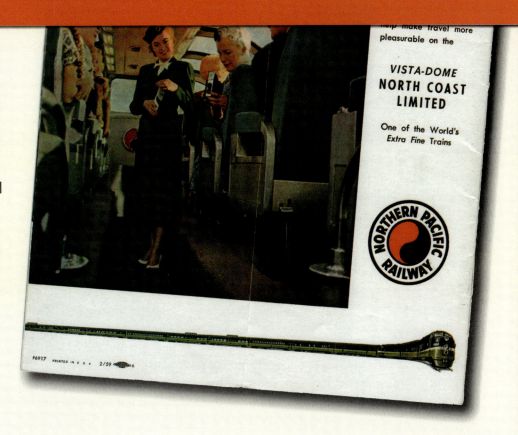

Decisions, Decisions!
Now, let's turn the clock back to 1959. We are planning a trip from Chicago to Seattle and return, and we face several choices. Automobile, train, or plane? (Let's forget the bus. After all, bus companies have just figured out how to squeeze a toilet into the back of one of these noisy vehicles.) If by train or plane, first class or coach? What route shall we take?

The westbound *Vista-Dome North Coast Limited* highballs along the CB&Q double track sandwiched between high palisades and the Mississippi River. The river is just out of view to the left. Photographed in late April 1955, this 12-car train is powered by a CB&Q E-8 and a pair of Denver Zephyr power units known as "Shovelnoses." There is no lounge in the coach section of this train, because the coach-buffet-lounge car has been removed from service for conversion to the Traveller's Rest configuration.
A. C. Kalmbach photo; Bill Kuebler collection

39

The Vista-Dome North Coast Limited

Let's see what the typical automobile has to offer us in June 1959. A great amount of freedom, to be sure, plus a convenient means of local transportation at Seattle, but . . . no air-conditioning; hot, cramped quarters; limited space for bags; about 80% of our journey on narrow, two-lane roads (although this is slowly changing, thanks to new freeways); plus constant interruptions for decent meals and, unless one's constitution is rather peculiar, the usual physical needs. At a safe pace without sightseeing, the round trip will take eight days and seven nights, assuming some long days at the wheel. Cost: $80 for fuel. Add to that: $65 for food (assuming three square meals a day at decent restaurants), $75 for lodging (seven nights in modest but dependable motels), and $20 for routine automobile maintenance resulting directly from the trip (assuming that it's an excellent car that began the trip with fairly new tires and fresh motor oil). Total: $235. This, incidentally, is to say nothing about the drunk drivers headed your way at who knows where or when.

The airplane? Well, speed far exceeds that of other modes of travel, but the deafening pistons (there are very few jets in service) will still need some seven hours to get us to the coast and six going back to Chicago, what with several intermediate stops each direction. Space is rather limited, even in first class, and weight is also a significant, limiting factor—only a couple of small bags, please. Food? Well . . . perhaps that can wait. Surely the phrase "airline food" is an oxymoron, and besides, it is served, more or less, in your lap. For a restroom, there's that "phone booth" somewhere down the aisle, but get in line while the seat belt sign is off. Cost: $175 for a tiny coach seat; almost twice that amount for first class. You're safer than in an automobile, but statistics favor the train over the airplane by a considerable margin. Besides, the mid-air collision over the Grand Canyon back in May 1956, only three years ago, is still fresh in your mind. There were no survivors, and the weather was clear!

As for the train, one shining offering that presents itself every afternoon on track 22 at Chicago Union Station is the *Vista-Dome North Coast Limited*. At 45 hours 20 minutes (westbound) and 46 hours 15 minutes (eastbound), it is considerably faster than the automobile—by four days and three nights, in fact—since, while you sleep comfortably through the night on this train, it will achieve 70 miles per hour routinely and average anywhere from 49 to 57 miles per hour, depending on the territory. (Westbound, the Fargo and Idaho divisions are covered on the first and second nights, respectively.)

As for accommodations, well . . . If funds are limited, a mere $95 round trip fare will get you a coach seat, but let's put this in perspective. Your personal sitting space in a "Day-Nite" coach would be about the same as that in a first-class airline seat, plus you get a full leg-rest and almost twice the angle of recline. Your coach seat window on a train is at least ten times the size of the little window adjacent an airline seat, but that's okay; there is usually little to see from an airplane anyway. Meals on the train are extra, but they may be enjoyed at a modest cost in a nifty lunch counter car that doubles as a lounge with a unique Lewis & Clark theme, a history book on wheels.

If funds are not a limiting factor, you may go first class. But if you do, be prepared for pampering!

After your stroll down the platform to your sleeping car, a porter will greet you, take your carry-on bag and show you to your room. Your *bedroom*, that is, where you will have a large, plush sofa by day, and a $6^1/2 \times 3$-foot bed by night, next to your personal picture window. This porter will be at your beck-and-call around the clock by the mere push of a button. Unless you want them delivered to your room, meals are served in what amounts to a first class restaurant of the highest quality, in an atmosphere of white linen, white uniforms, etched glass panels, fine china, and picture windows with some rather incredible western real estate passing by in a continuous real-time panorama—to say nothing of the "famously good" cuisine. You will have the option of visiting the plush observation-lounge, a place of comfortable seats, tables for card games, picture windows at the sides and rear, and the pleasures of conviviality among some of the world's most interesting people.

Chapter 6: All Aboard!

As for your safety, you will have to make several dozen round trips on a train such as this to put yourself at the same risk incurred during a single journey by air. Several thousand trips by rail will put you at the same risk as that incurred during only one by automobile. On the *North Coast Limited* in particular, your odds of fatal injury are immeasurably small, for since its inaugural run in April 1900, there have been no passenger fatalities aboard this train.

Cost for first class, with a double bedroom (the largest space available for single occupancy) is surprisingly reasonable and confounds expectations. The fare is $126.80; plus bedroom space ($91.80); plus meals (about $30). Total: $248.60 (excluding tips).

Why, this decision is easy!

Shall we take the train?

> **WESTBOUND - 1st Day - Commentary No. I**
> Good afternoon...and welcome aboard* the Vista-Dome NORTH COAST LIMITED.
>
> This is your Stewardess-Nurse, Miss Hamilton.
>   The train crew and I are here to help make your trip enjoyable.* Please let us know* if we may be of assistance to you.
>   Our train has many facilities* that can add to your travel pleasure. Vista-Dome seats* are available for both coach* and Pullman passengers. These are for your enjoyment* at no extra cost...and* they are not reserved. Please be careful* when using the stairway in the dome cars...and remember* there is a step down* from your dome seat to the aisle.
>   The dining car* is located in the center of the train. Meal times* except breakfast* will be announced over the public address system.
>   Just ahead of the diner* is the Traveller's Rest buffet-lounge car. Here you can order a la carte meals* light snacks* or beverages from 7:00 A.M. until 10:00 P.M.. In this car* you will also find magazines* stationery* post cards and a mail box...and you can purchase postage stamps* from the attendant.
>   For Pullman passengers* the observation-lounge car at the rear of the train* provides magazines and writing material. Beverage service is available* from 7:00 A.M. until midnight.
>   All of these and other facilities on the train* are described in our "Train Service Guide" booklet. If you would like a copy* I'll be glad to give you one.
>   We invite you to make use* of the services and facilities on the train. Make yourselves comfortable* and we hope you have a pleasant trip.
>   Thank you!
>
> *Denotes breath pauses, while giving the commentaries. If a breath pause is not necessary for you, please pause for a moment. A period, of course, always denotes a breath pause.

> **Note**
> During the journey described below and in the following chapters, names of personnel will be actual names of Northern Pacific (NP) employees who worked aboard the *Vista-Dome North Coast Limited* during the summer of 1959.

Going in Style

Our decision made, we are traveling together aboard the *Vista-Dome North Coast Limited*, departing Chicago's Union Station on a warm sunny day in June 1959. First class space has been sold out for weeks, and coach reservations (yes, they're required on this train) have already filled that section of the train to about 95% of its capacity, so our decision last February to reserve double bedrooms "C" and "D" in car 256 aboard this rolling Hilton was probably a wise one.

The crew has backed the train into position and the rear of the observation car is about five feet from the bumper. Suddenly, a voice on a loudspeaker announces boarding time for first class passengers. It is 11:30 A.M. Even though we have 40 minutes until departure time, let's head for our car right away instead of first walking along the train. It would be tempting to enjoy the Loewy colors on all 14 cars, washed this morning to spotless condition, but getting settled in now will give us a chance to become acquainted with our Pullman porter (R. H. "Robbie" Robinson, 31 years on NP trains) and our rooms, their facilities and controls. Besides, the activities in St. Paul this evening will make a walk along the platform there even more interesting than one here.

As we step through the gate and toward the train platform, we encounter the first two crewmembers we see from our train: the Pullman conductor, who checks our tickets, and—a young woman. She is our Stewardess-Nurse, whose nameplate reads "Miss Hamilton –R.N." She is, in fact, Miss Rita Hamilton, whose sister, Mary, was also a Stewardess-Nurse until a few months ago, when she resigned to get married. (Stewardess-Nurses are required to be single.) This pretty, smiling young woman (she can't be more than 23 years old) greets us and welcomes us aboard. A short chat with her reveals her to be more than warm and friendly; she appears to be a rather perceptive person, able to carry on an intelligent conversation about many subjects while discreetly noticing things that are going on around her. She seems quite mature for her age. Time to board our car, the forward dome sleeper. It is just up ahead, three cars ahead of the observation-lounge car.

What more fitting way is there to identify a crack passenger train than this lighted tail sign? Sleeper-observation-lounge car 392 on train 25 awaits boarding time at Chicago Union Station in 1964. A red Mars warning light for use in CB&Q territory has been temporarily attached above the coupler. Carmen will remove the light at St. Paul.
NP Photo; Bill Kuebler collection

Chapter 6: All Aboard!

As we walk down the narrow aisle to our bedrooms, the only sound we hear is soft music coming from the train's sound system—an orchestra playing Gershwin's "Rhapsody in Blue." At the end of the tune, the dining car steward announces that luncheon will be served in the dining car as soon as the train departs Chicago. Having had a late breakfast, we opt for sandwiches in the observation-lounge car, if necessary, to sustain us until an early dinner.

A few minutes after first class passengers board the train, an announcement is made for coach passengers to board. The platform is a busy place as they stroll past our dome sleeper to the coaches ahead. Between Chicago and Pasco there are exactly 250 coach seats available for sale aboard this train, and rooms for 82 first class passengers. Space is always set aside in various cars for the following crew members: the conductor, head brakeman, coach attendants, the Pullman conductor, the Stewardess-Nurse, and the sleeping car porters. Each sleeping car has a porter assigned to it, but each coach attendant generally covers two coaches. Sleeping space for the dining car crew is far up ahead, in the mail-dormitory car. Even though coach attendants are not assigned space in the dormitory car, they are all members of the dining car crew and work under the direct supervision of the steward.

About five minutes before departure time, the dining car steward repeats his announcement regarding luncheon. Background music continues to play throughout the train, but it will be turned off (except in the lounge cars) during the afternoon hours between lunch and the first dinner seating.

At precisely 12:08 P.M., the Burlington conductor calls, "All Aboard!" Less than two minutes later, he repeats the call. Then, at precisely 12:10 P.M., this edition of the westbound *North Coast Limited* begins rolling, imperceptibly at first. On-time. Another train awaits its departure on the next track. Our start is so smooth, it appears that the adjacent train has started moving instead and is about to back into the station!

The trip on the "Q" (a common nickname for the Chicago, Burlington, and Quincy (CB&Q)) is fast and a little rough in places, but the 85–90 mile-per-hour ride is comfortable enough. The sweeping curve at Naperville is along a triple track main line governed by searchlight signals. There are several stops along the way to St. Paul, each very brief. This is the route, according to NP and Burlington advertisements, "where nature smiles for 300 miles," the approximate distance remaining to St. Paul once the train pulls alongside the Mississippi River near Savanna, Illinois. Our train will closely follow the river for the remainder of the CB&Q segment. As dining car steward Frank Houska (38 years with NP) takes dinner reservations from first class passengers, our choice is for the first seating, which will commence in just a few hours. That will allow plenty of time to dine before arrival in St. Paul at 6:55 p.m.

Shortly before 5 P.M., the traditional dining car chimes (a hand-held set with the four notes of the C-major chord) are sounded over the train's PA system, followed by an announcement calling passengers with reservations to the first seating. Entering the dining car from the Pullmans, we are immediately greeted by Steward Houska, who hands us a menu and escorts us to our choice of seats. When traveling alone, it is not unusual for a patron to be seated with other dinner guests so as to maximize use of the space available. After we take our place and examine the menu, Houska takes our orders verbally. Yes, *verbally*! The NP is the only railroad with this practice; others traditionally leave you to write your own order for the waiter. But here, the steward takes our order and delivers the original to the kitchen while our waiter (who serves only two tables, permitting lots of attention to our needs) studies the copy left on our table and does his best to memorize it verbatim.

The Vista-Dome North Coast Limited

Our selections from the dinner menu comprise typical NP cuisine:

chicken noodle soup
a relish tray with celery, green olives, and pickled mushrooms
prime rib
a "big baked potato"
peas and carrots
dinner rolls and butter
pear and cottage cheese salad
coffee and milk

The rear cover of a 1968 dining car menu featured this NP coach attendant. *Bill Kuebler collection*

Chapter 6: All Aboard!

The ice water pitcher in the center of our table comes in handy, as well. Topping off this delicious meal is a generous slice of freshly baked apple pie a la mode. Total cost: $4.00 plus tips.

Although the dining room is nearly full during our seating, the atmosphere is quiet and relaxed, with taped music in the background. Patrons' dress varies from casual to formal. There are a few children, as well. One of them, a quiet but observant boy named "David," who appears to be about 10, studies the finger bowl before him. The expression on his face reveals that this is probably the first time he has seen one. *"What is it for?,"* he seems to wonder, *"Does one drink this?"* Better not, not yet anyway. When his dessert arrives, his expression changes to one of anticipation.

> **WESTBOUND - 1st Day - Commentary No. 2**
> As train leaves Savanna (about 2:40 P.M.)
>
> Good afternoon! This is your Stewardess-Nurse, Miss Hamilton
>   We have just left Savanna* Illinois. In a few minutes*, we'll see the Savanna Military Ordnance Depot (dep'o)...the buildings are located on both sides of the track. Then* for nearly 300 miles* we will be riding along one of the most beautiful stretches* of the Mississippi River. The scenery is interesting* and it's a pleasant ride* at any time of the year.
>   The Upper Mississippi River* has a rich historical background. This was the route of the early explorers* such as Fathers Hennepin and Joliet. Then came the fur traders* soldiers and settlers. Some of the towns we will ride through today* were early French forts or military posts.
>   Before you reach your destination* we would like you to tell us how you like our train...we welcome your suggestions. Please ask me for a comment card* designed for this purpose. Just fill it in* and return it to me...or drop it in a mail box—no postage required.
>   Thank you for your attention.
>
> *Denotes breath pauses, while giving the commentaries. If a breath pause is not necessary for you, please pause for a moment. A period, of course, always denotes a breath pause.*

After our delicious meal in the dining car and some relaxation in the observation-lounge at the rear of the train, we notice our approach to St. Paul. It is 6:30 P.M. and time to find a dome seat, a good place to watch the train maneuver itself into St. Paul Union Depot (known by railroaders, frequent rail travelers, and St. Paul citizens simply as "SPUD"). The procedure for train No. 25 is to approach from the southeast on the CB&Q westward main, pass by SPUD on the northeast side of the depot complex, head up Westminster Hill on the Great Northern (GN) westward main far enough to clear the cross-overs, then, after receiving a signal from the switchtender, to back slowly through the cross-over and puzzle switches, around the sharp curve and into the station. This is a busy place and an interesting operation. According to St. Paul Union Depot and Minnesota Transfer Special Instructions, there is no superiority of trains here. Everything is done by hand signal from switchtenders on the ground, who control all train movements. It is a labor-intensive operation, but well-coordinated and efficient. At precisely 6:50 P.M. (five minutes early), No. 25 completes its maneuvers and stops on SPUD track 17. Time to get out and watch the action as Q units are swapped for NP ones. During this swap, each set of diesel units is handled by the respective road's engine crew as part of their normal duty on a trip to or from St. Paul. Departure of train No. 25 is scheduled for 7:15 P.M., so this is also a good opportunity to "inspect" the train. We will have to move right along, though, as we have only about 25 minutes to accomplish this. When we hear the first "All Aboard!" from the NP conductor, we had best be either on the train or very near an open vestibule, for he normally makes the first call two minutes before departure and the second one when departure is imminent.

Walking alongside our train, we admire its beauty. Our 14 cars look resplendent in the Loewy green paint scheme. In spite of the dust kicked up by the 85-90 mile-per-hour sprint from Chicago, our train is still nearly spotless. As we pass the vestibule of the "Day-Nite Coach" between the two dome coaches, we overhear the Burlington conductor exchanging information with the NP conductor about to take command of our train. The NP man is Ray Lundberg (41 years with the NP). He seems to have a personality that reminds us of a favorite uncle or grandfather. His uniform is pressed and spotless, and his shoes, shined to a luster. The Burlington man's conversation is interspersed with

The Vista-Dome North Coast Limited

"Famously good food" was how NP advertising described meals served in its dining cars. Waiter Eugene Shepherd presents a meal fit for a king aboard one of NP's new Budd diners in 1958.
NP photo; Bill Kuebler collection

numbers that sound like code, probably having to do with seat assignments for various coach passengers. The Pullman conductor, Ivan Roskaft, has already informed both men regarding Pullman occupancy, including a roomette that has just become available due to a "no show." If this roomette is not filled either here or in Minneapolis, it will be "released" to down-line locations for sale.

As we walk past the head end cars, there is a flurry of activity at both the water-baggage car and the mail-dormitory car, especially the latter. Two postal clerks, one of them assigned to the mail-dormitory car and the other to the nearby post office, toss mail sacks back and forth between rail car and cart. Several boxes of live baby chicks wait to be loaded onto the baggage car. Baby chicks? Now, what could possibly be their destination?

As we walk further ahead, we can see four NP F-units just around the curve, poised to back into position. Two Burlington E-8s have just rolled away from the train. Handling our train to Staples tonight are Engineer Art Kath and Fireman Archie Reid. Kath has 50 years with the NP and is number two man on the engineer's seniority roster for this district. Reid has been with the NP for 12 years and is a qualified engineer. They went on duty about forty minutes ago over at Mississippi Street roundhouse, where their quartet of fully fueled, freshly washed diesel units awaited them. Three units are standard power for this train, but with 14 cars, four are sometimes used when an extra unit is available. The mountainous territory west of Livingston usually has priority for a fourth unit, but on occasion four units are used on the flatter terrain east of Livingston as well. No doubt the engine crew is pleased with having an extra diesel unit today, because their pay for this trip will consequently be greater (an engine crews' pay is proportional to the total weight on driving wheels of all the units in a diesel locomotive).

Chapter 6: All Aboard!

As the NP F-units slowly approach the water-baggage car, Kath brings them to a stop before moving them into position and coupling them to the train. This is in compliance with an NP company rule that requires a locomotive to be stopped within 15 feet of a passenger train before being coupled to it. The rule is meant to reduce the likelihood of misjudgment and a hard coupling, lest passengers be jostled.

It is surprising how much action we've already seen in less than five minutes. Even so, we must move along now, so as to see the rest of the train before departure. As we tour the train, inside and out and from front to rear, we'll stop at every piece of equipment and discuss its appearance and operation, and maybe digress a little as we consider some related items of interest.

WESTBOUND - 1st Day - Commentary No. 3
10 minutes before arrival St. Paul (about 6:35 p.m.)

Hello: This is your Stewardess-Nurse, Miss Hamilton.
 The correct Central Standard Time is now _____ p.m.. In a few minutes we will arrive in St. Paul. The capitol of Minnesota* St. Paul is an important manufacturing* wholesale and retail center...and a major distribution point for the Northwest. This city is also a leading educational center* with several accredited colleges and universities.
 After stopping in St. Paul* we will cross the Mississippi River to Minneapolis* the city of lakes. There are 22 lakes and lakelets* within the city limits. The basic industry during the city's early history* was flour milling. Today* Minneapolis has also become* a diversified industrial city* with more than 1,300 manufacturing plants. This is the home of the University of Minnesota* and the famed Minneapolis Symphony Orchestra.
 Thank you!

*Denotes breath pauses, while giving the commentaries. If a breath pause is not necessary for you, please pause for a moment. A period, of course, always denotes a breath pause.

Chapter 7
From Locomotive to Diner: A Tour

A 14-car North Coast Limited powered by three or four diesel units represents a substantial investment of Northern Pacific (NP) dollars. A view of the entire train is something to behold, too. Today, including four diesels, our train is 1,396 feet long and 10 feet wide, weighs 1,426 tons (excluding the weight of occupants, mail, and baggage), and rests on 144 flanged steel wheels. Ready to run, it's worth about 3½ million dollars. (That figure represents 1959 dollars; in 1999 dollars the figure would be about $20 million.)

Engineer Howard McGee and Fireman Jerry Peterson are assigned to handle train No. 25 from Billings to Livingston on March 24, 1956. The engineer's son, Warren McGee, made this photo at Park City, 23 miles west of Billings. The three-unit F-3 diesel, lead by No. 6500A, has a booster unit in place of a trailing cab unit. The NP began mixing F-units from various sets at about this time period.
Warren R. McGee photo

49

The Vista-Dome North Coast Limited

The *Vista-Dome North Coast Limited*

How Much Did It Cost and How Much Did It Weigh?

The costs shown are acquisition costs at the time of purchase for each piece of equipment. These figures include the purchase price plus costs for initial inspection and installation of train radio and public address (PA) equipment. The car weights shown are average weights. Weights varied slightly within each group of cars of the same type. A full, 14-car summer season consist of 1959, powered by a three-unit diesel, is shown.

Equipment	Year Delivered	Cost	Weight (lbs.)
3-unit Diesel (assuming F-3/7 combo)	1947–1949	$589,707	733,500
Water-Baggage	1947	59,240	119,000
Mail-Dormitory	1947	80,299	118,000
Dome Coach[1]	1954	243,738	147,000
Day-Nite Coach	1946/47	192,199	118,000
Dome Coach[1]	1954	243,738	147,000
Day Coach	1946/47	190,249	117,000
Day-Nite Coach	1946/47	192,199	118,000
Traveller's Rest[2]	1947	133,750	137,000
Diner (Budd)	1957/58	252,996	140,000
Sleeper (8-6-4)	1954	226,173	134,000
Dome Sleeper (4-4-4)[1]	1954	283,783	155,000
Sleeper (8-6-3-1)	1948	228,180	139,000
Dome Sleeper (4-4-4)[1]	1954	283,783	155,000
Obs-Lounge-Sleeper[3]	1948	130,294	126,000
Totals		**$3,330,328**	**2,603,500 lbs (1,301.75 tons)**

1. Vista-Dome Coach 549 cost $335,275. Dome sleeper 314 cost $368,190. Both cars were delivered in December 1957. Each car weighed approximately the same as one of the other cars in its respective group.
2. Cost shown is the purchase price of one coach-buffet-lounge car in 1947. Converting these cars to the Traveller's Rest configuration in 1955 cost $95,055 per car, a figure that included $3,500 per car for Chicago artist, Edgar Miller. This conversion also added about 15,000 pounds weight to each car. Original average weight was 122,000 pounds.
3. The 1953 re-styling involved only the lounge section of these cars. The cost of this re-styling was about $42,000 per car. Each car's weight remained about the same.

Locomotive by Electro-Motive Division

Our tour starts with the locomotive. Today our train is powered by four Electro-Motive Division (EMD) F-units: 6507A, 6504C, 6508B, 6701A. These engine numbers identify an F-7A, an F-5A (strictly an NP designation; technically it is a late-model F-3A), an F-3B, and an F-9A. The first, second, and fourth units are "A-units" (cab units); the third unit is a "B-unit" (booster unit). Three diesel units can maintain the demanding schedule with a 14-car train. The addition of a fourth unit allows for better acceleration from stops, however, which can make a difference when trying to make up any lost time. On a level or ascending grade, the extra unit also means that a lower throttle setting—about one or two notches lower—is required to maintain speed. (There are eight running notches on an F-unit throttle.) For example, when climbing the 2.2% grade of Butte Mountain with a 14-car train, the seventh notch is usually required to maintain 30 miles per hour with three diesel units, whereas with four units, the fifth notch usually suffices.

Chapter 7: From Locomotive to Diner: A Tour

Northern Pacific F-unit Models and Numbering Schemes

In the years that have passed since early F-units were common on United States railroads, and since the NP's existence, certain terms and numbering schemes may no longer be familiar, even to rail enthusiasts. A brief summary of these matters may be helpful here. Moreover, a look at the history of NP's F-unit numbering practices might be of special interest, even to long-time NP fans who are familiar with those practices, but who may not know the full story behind them.

Model Designations

Various models of first-generation F-units, such as F-3, F-7, and F-9, came as single units or in multiple-unit sets. A locomotive engineer could simultaneously control all the units in a set from one control cab by use of multiple-unit (M.U.) control cables connecting the units. Each unit had several M.U. cables at one end (or both ends) for this purpose. Furthermore, if multiple-unit sets were equipped with standard couplers between the units, as opposed to semi-permanent drawbars like the ones connecting steam engines to their tenders, they could be easily split up and reassembled in various combinations if the operating road so chose, although most roads did not to do this for the first several years of F-unit operation.

In terms of basic design, there were two versions of each F-unit model, a unit with a control cab and a unit without a control cab. Units with cabs were designated as "A-units," and this designation appeared as a letter suffix to the model type, such as F-7A or F-9A. Units without cabs, the "booster units," were designated as "B-units," such as F-7B or F-9B. This model letter suffix was independent of the operating road's numbering scheme; model suffixes and engine number suffixes were two different things, though on the NP they were related. Booster units were essentially identical to cab units, except for the lack of a cab and, in some cases, the addition of a large water tank inside the unit at the end where the cab would be if the unit had one. A passenger B-unit had a large water tank that contained water for the steam generator. A freight B-unit did not have a water tank or a steam generator; instead, it had concrete ballast installed in place of the tank, for weight and balance purposes.

When the NP first acquired F-units in the mid- and late-1940s, the road ordered them in multiple unit sets and initially intended them for use as complete sets, not to be split up or mixed with other sets. The NP ordered its passenger F-units in three-unit sets, and its freight F-units in four-unit sets. Although NP's passenger sets were originally A-B-B (cab-booster-booster) sets, they were changed to A-B-A sets (cab-booster-cab), with the two cab units facing opposite directions so as to avoid having to turn the set at the end of a run. This change in passenger diesel locomotive sets occurred in 1948 and 1949. The NP did this as a one-time change; and, when this change occurred, the intention was to continue operating these passenger F-units as complete and permanent sets.

Numbering Schemes

When the railroads first acquired F-units, several railroad managements were concerned that labor unions might claim that each unit in a multiple-unit diesel locomotive warranted an engine crew, even though only one crew was actually needed to operate a diesel locomotive, regardless of the number of units. Steam engines were still common in those days, and if more than one steam engine powered a train, one crew was needed for each engine. Thus, concern about potential union claims regarding manning of multiple-unit diesel locomotives was not unreasonable.

To help prevent such claims, several railroads, including the NP, numbered each multiple-unit set of F-units with a single engine number—the entire set had but one engine number. This worked for a while, but only until railroads decided to break up sets and intermingle them. The flexibility of intermingling was very useful when assigning power to various trains. When railroads first began seriously considering the idea of breaking up and intermingling sets in the early 1950s, however, it did not take long for someone to realize the problem that would ensue as long as each set had been assigned but one engine number. More than one train, each with the same engine number, could end up operating on the railroad at the same time. In fact, two trains could conceivably meet each other, each with the same engine number in the lead! Operating rules were such that prevention of such a situation was an absolute must. Train orders usually identified trains by use of the lead engine number, and serious accidents could occur because of confusion among crews.

Therefore, the NP and other roads assigned engine number letter suffixes to its F-units to distinguish them, first to freight A-units, beginning in about 1954, then to passenger A-units, and eventually to all B-units as well. NP's numbering scheme involved using letter suffixes that related to the original set, so, for example, the three-unit passenger set 6507 became units individually numbered 6507A, 6507B, and 6507C. So from the time that engine number letter suffixes first appeared on passenger cab units in early 1955, a passenger F-unit number suffix of "A" or "C" indicated an "A-unit" (cab unit). The number suffix "B" indicated a B-unit (booster unit). This scheme resulted from the fact that these units had been assembled earlier as A-B-A sets.

In similar manner, the NP ordered its freight F-units as four-unit A-B-B-A sets. When engine number letter suffixes were adopted, NP's number scheme assigned letter suffixes of A, B, C, and D, respectively, to the four units of a set. Thus, freight cab units were numbered with "A" and "D" suffixes, and booster units with "B" and "C" suffixes.

The NP began breaking up its F-unit sets on rare occasions in about 1954, and gradually moved toward doing this on a regular basis during the period 1957–60. The NP routinely split its F-unit sets and mixed them from 1960 on. The NP's F-unit numbering scheme evolved in a way that allowed the NP to accomplish two goals: it prevented frivolous union claims, and it allowed flexibility in splitting up and mixing F-units in any combination the road desired.

The Vista-Dome North Coast Limited

Even though our train has four units today, an A-B-A three-unit combo is still the most common mix on NP transcontinental passenger trains. An A-A-B-A combo is the most common lash-up whenever there are four units, but only because there are about three times as many cab units as booster units on the roster. In 1947, it was the other way around. Passenger diesels were originally ordered as 3-unit, A-B-B sets, but in 1948 and 1949 these sets were changed to A-B-A sets as new individual units and new three-unit sets were purchased. An A-A-B-A combo is not the only four unit one seen, however, as just about any combination may occur, including A-B-B-A, depending on availability. Our four-unit locomotive provides 6,250 horsepower and about 237,000 pounds of tractive effort, more than enough to handle the task of rolling our train into Livingston, 999 miles west, on time. There these units will be replaced by another set of four; it will probably be another A-A-B-A set.

The NP maintains a fleet of 52 EMD F-units in a transcontinental passenger locomotive pool that, in 1959, looks like this:

Engine Type	Engine Numbers	Horsepower/unit	No. of Units
F-3A	6500A-6506A	1500	7
F-3B	6500B-6509B	1500	10
F-5A	6503C-6506C	1500	4
F-7A	6501C, 6502C, 6507A, C-6513A, C	1500	16
F-7B	6510B-6513B, 6550B	1500	5
F-9A	6500C (rebuilt from F-7A in 1955 after an accident); 6700A,C-6701A,C 6702A-6704A	1750	8
F-9B	6700B-6701B	1750	2
		Total Units in Pool:	52

F-3s 6506A and 6505A, coupled elephant-fashion, comprise half of the four-unit locomotive on train No. 25 near Silver Bow, about seven miles west of Butte, on July 21, 1960. Just a few miles ahead this 15-car train will reach the upper waters of the Clark Fork River. Except for 64 miles between DeSmet and Paradise, this train will closely follow the Clark Fork all the way to where the scenic river flows into Lake Pend Oreille at Hope, Idaho, now some 286 miles ahead of this train.
Bill Kuebler collection

Chapter 7: From Locomotive to Diner: A Tour

Train No. 26 prepares to leave King Street Station in Seattle on a hazy afternoon in April 1958. The lead diesel unit is a late model F-3A, built in 1948, but the NP has designated it an F-5A. Essentially, it is an F-3 mechanically, but with electrical components more like an F-7's, an even later model that first arrived on NP property in 1949. An A-B-A combination is the most common arrangement of F-units on trains 25 and 26.
William A. Raia collection

All diesel units in the transcontinental passenger locomotive pool are equipped with steam generators (boilers which make steam for heating all the cars in the train), dynamic brakes, and 59:18 gear ratios that permit a maximum speed of 85 miles per hour. This is EMD's limit, shown on a placard in each cab and protected by a speed governor. If this speed limit is closely approached, a warning sounds in the cab, giving the engineer a few seconds to apply the brakes himself, or else experience an automatic penalty brake application and idling of all engines. Several lower speed limits, however, are imposed on NP crews. The Interstate Commerce Commission (ICC) imposes a limit of 79 miles per hour on passenger trains in territory equipped with block signals but no cab signaling. (Chicago, Burlington, and Quincy (CB&Q) engines are equipped with cab signaling and higher gear ratios, so speeds of 90 miles per hour are common in that territory.) The NP's maximum speed for main line passenger trains is 75 miles per hour, officially stated in all operating divisions' Special Instructions. Finally, there are many curves on the NP that have lower speed limits posted trackside, and other sections of track with speed limits imposed by Special Instructions. In all cases, the lowest applicable speed limit governs the operation.

In actual practice, where conditions permit, if not the rules, NP enginemen operate at speeds up to about 80 miles per hour when making up time. Most men in passenger service are quite comfortable at that speed. A few even exceed it. As long as they exercise good judgment, carefully consider existing conditions, and maintain a safe operation, enginemen who operate in 75 mile per hour territory at speeds up to about 80 miles per hour are not challenged by supervisors.

Meanwhile, from the platform at SPUD, we contemplate the four-unit diesel locomotive that has just coupled to our train, and the passenger locomotive fleet to which these units belong. Of the

The Vista-Dome North Coast Limited

52 units assigned to the transcontinental passenger locomotive pool, 45 are actually in regular scheduled service at any one time. The rest are either undergoing periodic maintenance, or are available for assignment as extra units when needed. The transcontinental passenger diesel fleet is assigned to the Rocky Mountain Division and maintained at Livingston. The train assignment system for these locomotive units is complex, but ingenious and efficient. It covers all main line passenger trains except those operating between the Twin Cities and Duluth. (Those trains are powered by passenger locomotives assigned to the St. Paul Division, consisting of two FP-7As, three GP-7s, and three GP-9s that will be supplemented by two more GP-9s in 1962.) Each diesel unit in the transcontinental pool averages over 600 miles per day on a 16-day cycle that amounts to a marathon, such is the resulting high utilization rate. At the end of each cycle, a diesel unit either begins another 16-day cycle after a 24-hour rest, or is removed from service for scheduled maintenance. Although this 16-day cycle has varied over the years, the accompanying table shows how it looks in June 1959.

NP Passenger Diesel Assignment Between St. Paul-Seattle-Portland

June 1959

Terminal	Time	Day	Train	Units[1]
Lv. Livingston	12:33 p.m.	1	25	3
Ar. Seattle	7:30 a.m.	2	25	3
Lv. Seattle	12:30 p.m.	2	408	3
Ar. Portland	4:30 p.m.	2	408	3
Lv. Portland	5:30 p.m.	2	407	3
Ar. Seattle	9:30 p.m.	2	407	3
Lv. Seattle	8:25 a.m.	3	6	2
Ar. Spokane	6:50 p.m.	3	6	2
Lv. Spokane	7:25 a.m.	4	5	2
Ar. Seattle	6:10 p.m.	4	5	2
Lv. Seattle	9:35 p.m.	4	2	3[2]
Ar. Livingston	10:48 p.m.	5	2	3
Lv. Livingston	7:25 a.m.	6	1	3
Ar. Seattle	7:15 a.m.	7	1	3
Lv. Seattle	1:30 p.m.	7	26	3
Ar. Livingston	10:56 a.m.	8	26	3
Lv. Livingston	11:06 p.m.	8	2	3
Ar. St. Paul	10:15 p.m.	9	2	3
Lv. St. Paul	8:40 a.m.	10	1	3
Ar. Livingston	7:00 a.m.	11	1	3
Lv. Livingston	11:06 a.m.	11	26	3
Ar. St. Paul	6:40 a.m.	12	26	3
Lv. St. Paul	9:30 p.m.	12	3	2
Ar. Mandan	9:55 a.m.	13	3	2
Lv. Mandan	4:40 p.m.	13	4	2
Ar. St. Paul	7:25 a.m.	14	4	2
Lv. St. Paul	7:15 p.m.	14	25	3
Ar. Livingston	12:23 p.m.	15	25	3
Lv. Livingston	12:33 p.m.	16/1	25	3

Total Units in Service: 45   **Average Mileage:** 613 miles/day

1 Four diesel units are sometimes used on trains 1, 2, 25, and 26, depending on loads and availability of units. In these cases, the extra unit is an otherwise unassigned cab or booster unit from the pool and is added to the three units normally assigned.

2 Third unit to be used on No. 2 is the unit off No. 407 not used on No. 6.

Chapter 7: From Locomotive to Diner: A Tour

As Engineer Kath couples his four F-units to the water-baggage car, we notice all the connections: train line air for the brakes; signal line (so the conductor can signal the engineer from any vestibule); steam line (for train heat); connections for the electro-pneumatic brake system; and finally, the large hose for carrying water from the water-baggage car to the locomotive units for use in steam generators. Booster units came equipped with a steam generator at the rear and a large water tank at the forward end of the unit. Cab units came with only a steam generator at the rear of the unit, so the NP added sidewall water tanks to all passenger cab units shortly after their delivery. These sidewall tanks make for some rather tight quarters when a crew member walks through the engine room. All this water capacity is the railroad's answer to the challenge of operating in winter temperatures as low as 40-below, since at those temperatures steam for heating is consumed rapidly throughout the train.

These four diesel units will burn, on average, a little more than five gallons of no. 2 diesel fuel per mile, including what the steam generators consume. (A steam generator consumes considerably more fuel in the winter than it does in the summer, but only three diesel units are normally used during that season.) For each gallon of fuel consumed by the steam generators, about $11^1/_2$ gallons of water are needed to keep up the heat on a 13-car train in mid-winter.

A look at Engineer Kath is reassuring. Surely a man in engine service would not likely reach his age (69 years) or years of service (50) unless he knew what he was doing. In this business, there is little room for incompetence, carelessness, or neglect. Kath appears quite relaxed but all business; he knows his job well. Although it is common for an engineer to permit his fireman to run the locomotive for part of a trip, Kath is at the controls this evening. Fireman Reid will probably handle No.

Even during the diesel era, the NP exchanges power on every through passenger train at Livingston. F-7A 6512C and two other F-units, fully fueled and ready to begin another 16-day cycle of passenger train service, have just been coupled to train No. 25 on a blustery January day in 1965. The incoming power, led by No. 6511A, heads for the diesel maintenance facility. Did some of the snow on the front of No. 6511A originate in Minnesota?
Gil Hulin photo; Warren Wing collection

The Vista-Dome North Coast Limited

26 from Staples to St. Paul tomorrow morning. This practice allows a younger man to develop his train handling skills while the "old man" takes a break. Responsibility cannot be delegated, however, so whenever he's on the left side of the cab, Kath will keep a close eye on his fireman's performance and offer appropriate guidance.

A Word About "Car Lines"

The phrase "car number" can be confusing. To a carman or railfan, it refers to the equipment number or car number as shown on a roster and painted on the side of the car, but to a passenger, an

Train No. 25 is serviced at Missoula on June 15, 1955. Dome coach 556 occupies car line C-250 (above), and dome sleeper 313 is in line 258 (below). CB&Q ownership letters identify the sleeper-observation-lounge car in line 259 as car 483. It is very unusual that there are two 8-6-4 sleeping cars (series 367–372) in this train rather than one 8-6-4 and one 8-6-3-1 sleeping car.
Ron Nixon photos; Bill Kuebler collection

Chapter 7: From Locomotive to Diner: A Tour

agent, or a Pullman conductor, the phrase is loosely used to refer to the "car line." Generally, a "car line" denotes the position in the train of a "revenue car," a car in which space can be sold to passengers. On the *North Coast Limited*, the first two digits of a car line denote the train number and the third digit (beginning at zero) is the position in the train relative to other revenue cars. Coaches have line numbers preceded by the letter "C." Thus, car line "C-250" is the first coach in train No. 25, and "C-260" is the corresponding coach in train No. 26. Pullman sleeping car lines do not have a letter prefix. Non-revenue cars—the water-baggage, mail-dormitory car, Traveller's Rest, and diner—are in the train but are not assigned car line numbers. When the Slumbercoach joins the train's lineup, it will occupy lines "SC-25" and "SC-26" on trains No. 25 and No. 26, respectively. The Slumbercoach will retain these car line numbers even when, in later years, its position in the train changes.

On a passenger's ticket, the car line number appears in the space marked "Car. No." Also, the car line number for each revenue car is installed in a small, lighted fixture and mounted in a window or on the outside of the car, near the vestibule, for easy viewing from the station platform. A similar fixture is mounted near the top of each end door window, so that a passenger, entering that car from an adjacent car, can more easily identify the car. The digits in these fixtures can easily be changed as needed. This number is what the passenger looks for when walking along the platform or through the train to his assigned car. Today, we are assigned Bedrooms C and D in Car 256, which is the forward dome sleeper. It operates from Chicago to Seattle.

North Coast Limited Car Lines–Summer 1959

Car Lines[1]		Car Type	Between
WB 25	EB 26		
		Water-Baggage	Chicago-Seattle
		Mail-Dormitory	Chicago-Seattle
Note: after November 1959, the Slumbercoach operated Chicago-Seattle here, ahead of the coaches, in line "SC-25" or "SC-26".			
C-250	C-260	Dome Coach	Chicago-Seattle
C-251	C-261	Day-Nite Coach	Chicago-Seattle
C-252	C-262	Dome Coach	Chicago-Portland
C-253/700	C-263/800	Day Coach[2]	Chicago-Portland
C-254	C-264	Day-Nite Coach	Chicago-Seattle
		Traveller's Rest Buffet Lounge	Chicago-Seattle[3]
		Diner	Chicago-Seattle[3]
255	265	Standard Sleeper, 8-6-4[4]	Chicago-Seattle
256	266	Dome Sleeper, 4-4-4	Chicago-Seattle
257	267	Standard Sleeper, 8-6-3-1[4]	Chicago-Portland
258	268	Dome Sleeper, 4-4-4	Chicago-Portland
259	269	Observation-Lounge Sleeper, 4-1	Chicago-Seattle

1. These lines represent a full, 14-car consist in 1959. See Chapter 9 for details about consist evolution and seasonal changes.
2. When a full 14-car consist was operated, in some cases Day coaches from the series 500–517 operated in lines C-253/263 and NP travel brochures and timetables' equipment listings showed this. When there were only four coach lines, a Day-Nite Coach usually operated in line C-253/263.
3. Traveller's Rest Buffet Lounge cars and dining cars were changed out at St. Paul on eastbound runs. After being switched out of train No. 26 at St. Paul, they were inspected and maintained as needed; then they were cleaned and restocked. With a new dining car crew, they were switched into train No. 26 the next day. Dining car crews worked a 5-day, St. Paul-Chicago-Seattle-St. Paul circuit.
4. The 8-6-4 standard sleepers were numbered 367–372 (Pullman-Standard, 1954). The 8-6-3-1 standard sleepers were numbered 350-363, Spokane, Portland, and Seattle (SP&S) 366, CB&Q 480–482 (Pullman-Standard, 1948).

In addition to the use of car lines, sleeping cars are number-coded according to the available accommodations in each type of car. Generally, only passenger agents and Pullman conductors use these codes. For example, standard sleeping cars noted as "8-6-3-1" have eight duplex roomettes, six

The Vista-Dome North Coast Limited

roomettes, three double bedrooms, and one compartment, whereas dome sleepers, noted as "4-4-4," have four roomettes, four duplex single rooms, and four double bedrooms. This coding is somewhat inconsistent and mysterious to those not used to working with it, but Pullman conductors and passenger agents work with it routinely and understand the numbers.

Let's "inspect" the rest of the train!

> **Note**
>
> In the following headings, car line numbers (where applicable) appear first, followed by the type of car. The type of car is followed by the corresponding car number series. Any one car of the series could appear in that position in the train. Car numbers are NP cars unless shown otherwise. Following the car number series is the name of the cars' builder and the approximate date of delivery to the NP. In most cases, cars were delivered in groups of two or three, with the groups spaced a few days apart. The last line in the heading shows the routing of the car in *North Coast Limited* service, whether between Chicago and Seattle or between Chicago and Portland. Actual equipment numbers of several *North Coast Limited* trains on specific dates appear in Part 3, to provide some real life examples.

Water-Baggage
400–404, CB&Q 405; Pullman-Standard, March 1947.
Chicago-Seattle

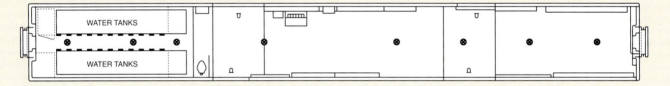

This view shows the left side of water-baggage car 404. Its A-end, the end with the water tanks, is coupled to the A-end of mail-dormitory car 429. This is not the normal arrangement in a train. Both cars are in St. Paul's coach yard, awaiting their next assignment in April 1970. The size and number of truck springs on a passenger car vary according to load and weight distribution. Under a full load, the A-end of these water-baggage cars is considerably heavier than the B-end. Though the A-end is still supported by a four-wheel truck, that truck has heavy-duty springs.
Bill Kuebler collection

Chapter 7: From Locomotive to Diner: A Tour

In this interior view of water-baggage car 401, two 1,300-gallon overflow tanks appear just ahead of the forward sliding doors. The main 1,500-gallon tanks are further ahead. The baggage man's station is at the right. This builder's photo was taken on March 20, 1947, not long before this car was delivered to the NP. The interiors of these cars remained essentially the same throughout their NP careers.
Pullman-Standard photo; Bill Kuebler collection

Unlike NP's 200-series baggage cars, this car is not a "shorty." It is 85-feet long, as are all the other cars in our train. The section forward of the forward side doors is occupied by two large tanks that hold 1,500 gallons of water. There are also "overflow" tanks that hold another 1,300 gallons. A floor-level crossover pipe keeps the water load balanced between these tanks. An electric motor in the forward left corner of this car pumps water from these tanks into the large water tank in the B-unit. A float switch inside the B-unit's tank controls this pump. Each tank in the water-baggage car is equipped with a steam coil to keep the water from freezing in cold weather. The large connecting hose between the water-baggage car and the rear diesel unit is also equipped with an attached steam line for heat, to prevent water from freezing in the connecting hose during cold weather. Malfunctions of this system are not uncommon, especially in super-cold weather, because the steam coil does not protect the metal couplings—only the rubber hose is protected. Firemen (or even Road Foremen), thus, often end up balancing themselves between rear unit and water-baggage car, trying to thaw a frozen hose coupling while the train is moving at 70 or 80 miles per hour. To accom-

View of the baggage area in car 401, looking aft from the forward set of sliding doors. The baggage man's station at the left includes a drop table, letter case, and water cooler. Note the two U-shaped stretcher mounting racks at the upper right. "Fish racks" (floor slats) can be seen in the distance beyond the rear set of sliding doors. March 20, 1947, builder's photo.
Pullman-Standard photo; Bill Kuebler collection

plish this, they use a temporary steam line connected to the rear steam generator, or a fusee. (A fusee is essentially a 10-minute red flare; railroad crews normally use them as emergency signals by throwing or placing them in the track as warnings to a train that there is danger ahead.)

The section aft of the rear baggage doors contains "fish racks" (floor slats) for draining melt water. Other items of interest include a storage area for emergency equipment, an electric locker, and a drop table, letter case, water cooler, cup dispenser, and toilet for the baggage man. A stretcher is mounted up high on one of the walls. The baggage doors are of two sizes, seven foot and five foot, one opposite the other and alternating sides, fore and aft. The rear baggage doors are closer to the rear of the car than the front ones are to the front end because of the large water tanks. This car is not reversible. The "A" end must always go forward if water is to be available to the diesel units. There is an end door at each end of this car, but neither one has a window. A peek inside this car reveals quite a diversity of passenger baggage, including trunks, suitcases, boxes, and even a couple of bicycles.

Mail-Dormitory
425–429; CB&Q 479 (renumbered from CB&Q 430 in 1954)
Pullman-Standard, April–June 1947
Chicago-Seattle

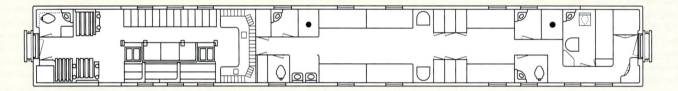

Mail-dormitory 426, dome coach 550, and "Day-Nite" coach 597 are three of the thirteen cars in train No. 26 at Livingston on June 28, 1955. Station work is nearly complete. Conductor Quinn, standing near the open vestibule, will soon give a "highball" signal to the engineer for an on-time departure at 10:51 a.m.
Ron Nixon photo; Bill Kuebler collection

Chapter 7: From Locomotive to Diner: A Tour

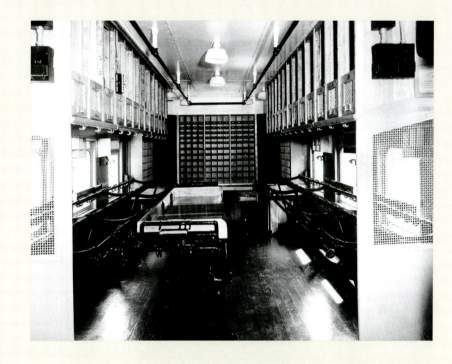

This June 1947 builder's photo shows the R.P.O. section of mail-dormitory car 430 before its delivery. This view is looking aft from the area near the sliding pocket doors. A crawl-through type door below the pigeonhole rack at the back wall of this section allows passage to the dormitory section.
Pullman-Standard photo; Bill Kuebler collection

As we continue inspecting our train, we note that this car is a combination mail car and dormitory for the dining car crew. A 30-foot mail section, or Railway Post Office (R.P.O.), occupies the forward end of the car. A crew of two postal workers sorts mail *en route*. On trains No. 25 and No. 26, postal clerks are assigned to R.P.O. divisions as follows: St. Paul to Jamestown (345 miles); Jamestown to Miles City (393 miles); Miles city to Butte (383 miles); Butte to Spokane (378 miles); and Spokane to Seattle (396 miles). A postal clerk's job is very demanding, and annual mail sorting proficiency tests are quite difficult. These tests are designed to ensure consistently high standards. (See the Northern Pacific Railway Historical Association's (NPRHA) quarterly, The Mainstreeter (vol. 16 no. 1, Winter 1997), for detailed coverage of NP's R.P.O. operation.)

The R.P.O. section includes a specially designed security end door at the forward end of the car, a closet on

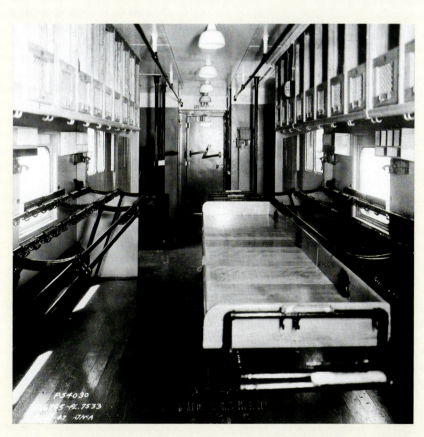

View looking forward in the R.P.O. section of car 430. Note the security end door. This mail-dormitory car was owned by CB&Q but lettered for Northern Pacific; it was renumbered 479 in 1954. June 1947 builder's photo.
Pullman-Standard photo; Bill Kuebler collection

The Vista-Dome North Coast Limited

View looking aft in car 430 (later 479). The waiter's dormitory section appears in the foreground of this June 1947 builder's photo. Just beyond the lockers is the cook's dormitory section, which consists of two sets of double bunks. In the distance the aisle bends around the steward's private room. This car is equipped with two showers.
Pullman-Standard photo; Bill Kuebler collection

the car's left side, an enclosed lavatory on the right side, removable stanchions, and two bag catchers. There is a 3-ft. 2-in. sliding pocket door on each side of the car over the forward truck. The R.P.O. also includes mailbag racks with wire mesh dividers to minimize sway, a pigeon hole mail sorting rack (forming a blind wall at the rear of the R.P.O. section), and a crawl-through door below the sorting rack, leading to the dormitory section.

The steward's private room is located at the rear of the dormitory section and contains two berths situated cross-wise, as seen in this June 1947 builder's photo of car 430 (later 479). The upper berth is normally not used, but it is available for use by steward trainees, men who have acquired enough seniority in dining car service for promotion. One wonders who might own that caboose-style chair today.
Pullman-Standard photo; Bill Kuebler collection

Chapter 7: From Locomotive to Diner: A Tour

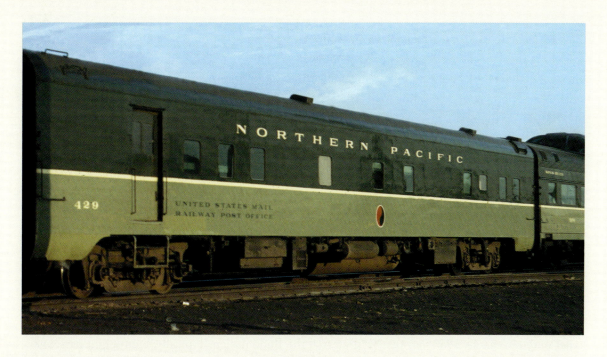

Mail-dormitory car 429 is still in service on May 26, 1972, but the R.P.O. section of the car is no longer in operation. The car number at the forward end is not positioned over the truck center. This is due to the location of the sliding door. After only one number was applied to each side of passenger cars beginning in 1958, the other five cars in this series (except car 427 during the late 1960s) had the number at the B-end, rather than at the A-end as seen here. Note the dark green lettering aft of the sliding door.
Bill Kuebler collection

    The dormitory section of this car looks rather plain. Its capacity is 14 men, one more than a full dining car crew of 13. A full crew consists of the dining car steward, three cooks, six waiters, plus the cook, the waiter, and the "waiter-in-charge" assigned to the Traveller's Rest car. Walking through this section from the crawl-through door (from the mail section) toward the rear, we see a washroom and enclosed toilet on our right and a dressing room and shower on our left. Then, we see the waiter's section, consisting of four sets of double-deck bunks, two sets on each side. Next, is a pair of caboose chairs, followed by several sets of lockers on each side. Then, we come to the cook's section, consisting of one set of double-deck bunks on each side. Next, there is a washroom and toilet on our right, and another dressing room and shower on our left. This is the only car in the train with shower facilities. Finally, the aisle winds around to our right to accommodate the steward's space, a private room, equipped with two berths positioned crosswise, a caboose chair, and a lavatory and toilet. At the rear of the car are a large linen closet and an electrical cabinet.

C-250
Vista-Dome Coach
550–556; CB&Q 557, 558; SP&S 559; Budd, July 1954
549; Budd, December 1957
Chicago-Seattle

63

The Vista-Dome North Coast Limited

Now we come to the first vista-dome in our train. One of the first things we notice upon entering this car is that several of the seats on the main level are empty, even though every seat has a hat check. The hat checks indicate full occupancy in this car, not unusual for C-250. Most of these passengers are "long hauls" traveling to Seattle. A few are traveling to Spokane or points between there and Seattle. At the moment, most passengers assigned space in this car are elsewhere on the train. Some are up in the dome; others are eating dinner in the Traveller's Rest car or in the diner.

Without a doubt, this car is one of the most novel in design and attractive in appearance. The dome itself is the most obvious external feature. Its curved glass windows are specially shaped and tinted a dark bluish-green to reduce glare and daylight illumination levels. They are all double-pane windows, designed to prevent condensation and frost, and each is set in a thick rubber seal for noise reduction and insulation. Replacement of one of the side or overhead dome windows (24 windows per dome) costs the NP about $600. A new forward or rear end window costs over $800! (Remember, these are 1959 dollars. In 1999 dollars, these figures would be about $3,400 and $5,100, respectively.)

Building a dome section into a lightweight passenger car presented some interesting engineering challenges, and Budd met those challenges well. While other builders had produced various types of dome cars by 1953–54, the NP preferred the Budd design. Typically, lightweight passenger cars have a critical load-bearing center sill running the full length of the car along the bottom, between truck centers. The sheer weight of an 85-foot car supported at two truck center pins causes large bending forces at the center of this sill, so the sill is designed for minimal deflection under load. It is pre-stressed and cambered, so as to be level when under static load. Thus, it forms the car's "backbone." The main level of a vista-dome, however, had to be lowered under the dome to allow passengers easy passage through the car. To accommodate this requirement, the center sill was specially formed as an integral unit with the necessary depression under the dome section. Lesser forces normally distributed throughout the roof of lightweight cars also had to be accommodated, in spite of the presence of the dome section. Budd accomplished this without the use of unsightly load bearing members, so the car retains a streamlined appearance inside and out.

The mechanical equipment on these cars is the most modern available in the 1950s. Electrical generators are of the "Spicer Drive" type, which employs a gear and universal shaft drive, avoiding use of cumbersome belts. Steam-based heating is unizone, and fairly easy to regulate. Most notable to passengers is the comfort maintained by the superb air-conditioning system, even in the dome section. Each dome car has two complete Trane air-conditioning units, more than enough to handle the main level as well as the dome section, where radiant sunlight on a hot summer day must be offset by plenty of cooling power. Conditioned air for the dome section is routed through ingeniously hidden ducts behind bulkheads and flows between glass panels of the dome's center end-windows. The inside center window at each end of the dome can be opened for access to the duct. From there, air flows along the narrow, above-the-aisle ceiling and then into the dome section through several overhead vents, the proper exit point for cold air circulation. Under certain conditions diesel exhaust (its source is only about 200 feet ahead of car C-250) can find its way into this car's ventilation system. It is seldom a serious problem, however.

As we walk through the train we notice certain features common to modern passenger cars. Cars built in 1954 and later, for example, including these vista-domes, have pneumatically powered end doors. Gently depressing the latching bar on the outside, or pulling the latching handle on the inside, opens the door with a hiss of pneumatic power. After being held open a few seconds by a timer, the door slowly closes and latches. A crewmember can adjust or, in the event of malfunction, disconnect this pneumatic feature.

Chapter 7: From Locomotive to Diner: A Tour

Builder's photos of dome coach 553 were taken in July 1954, just before it left Philadelphia for St. Paul. Budd designed NP's dome coaches to operate with the vestibule to the rear. They are some of the most modern and well-constructed cars in the industry.
Budd photos; Bill Kuebler collection

The Vista-Dome North Coast Limited

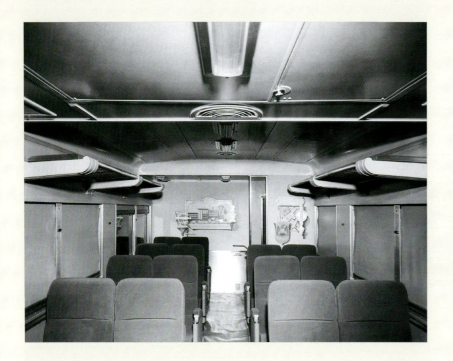

Looking aft in the forward coach section of newly built dome coach 553, July 1954. Temporary protective covering is taped to the floor for shipment of this car to the NP. *Budd photo; Bill Kuebler collection*

A dome seat in this particular car, the third behind the locomotive, offers some advantages, particularly to the railfan. At night, it means seeing occasional sparks from the locomotive exhaust fly up and back in the slipstream; the sparks are quickly extinguished by the cool air. In searchlight or color light signal territory, the locomotive exhaust causes an interesting, shimmering effect as the green block signal light changes to red. This shimmering effect is less pronounced with semaphores, because their lights are higher above the exhaust, due to taller signal masts. Riding in this dome also means being able to hear the whistle and throttle changes very clearly. Locomotive sounds are not loud or obnoxious, but are quite audible and remind the observant dome rider that the engineer is a busy man. Otherwise, this car is quiet inside at any speed. On both levels of the car, the clicks, clacks, and rattles of high-speed travel, so pronounced on heavyweight equipment, are subdued to a soft, muffled sound. Even at speeds as high as 80 miles per hour, the ride is smooth.

Main level steps leading to the passageway under the dome of car 553. This is at the rear of the forward coach section. Note the emergency equipment storage area and ice water tap. July 1954 builder's photo. *Budd photo; Bill Kuebler collection*

66

Chapter 7: From Locomotive to Diner: A Tour

The aft end of the passageway under the dome. Stairwell railings in all NP dome cars are stainless steel rather than plastic. Each step has a small light on each side of the stairwell. Soft theater-style lighting illuminates steps and dome aisle without causing glare or reflection off the dome windows at night. July 1954 photo.
Budd photo; Bill Kuebler collection

The rocking and swaying motion caused by track irregularities is minimized, thanks to a new, "outside swing hanger" truck design. Essentially, this truck design allows the weight of the car to be supported by a wider truck "platform," because the hangers are positioned outside the drop-type equalizing bars of the truck rather than inside them. Thus, rocking motion, especially, is minimized. All NP passenger cars built in 1954 and later are equipped with this new truck design. Older lightweight cars have inside-hanger trucks. The ride they provide is only slightly less smooth, but far better than any ride in a heavyweight.

The main level of this car contains 46 fully reclining seats with leg rests, 18 in the forward section and 28 in the rear section. The leg rests fold back under the

The dome section features 24 seats and 360-degree vision. Even aisle seats have windows overhead. The red and black NP monad on the forward bulkhead is a radio speaker. Signs on seat backs advise passengers to watch their step when leaving their seats, because the center aisle is a step lower than the floor under the seats. The NP will install antimacassar seat covers on dome seats a few years hence. This builder's photo of car 553 was taken at Philadelphia in July 1954.
Budd photo; Bill Kuebler collection

67

The Vista-Dome North Coast Limited

View looking aft in the dome section of car 553. The inside pane of the center end window at each end of the dome opens inward for access to the air conditioning ducts. July 1954 photo.
Budd photo; Bill Kuebler collection

seats for stowage. Every coach seat in this car, and on the train, has an antimacassar cover on the seat back. The NP added these to all coach seats, including those in "flat top" (a car without a dome) coaches, shortly after each car was delivered. Each cover displays the NP monad with the words "NORTHERN PACIFIC." Two seats at the right forward end of the rear coach section face rearward, creating a "family section." Seats in this car are numbered from the vestibule end forward. Neither the dome seats nor the ones on the main level are reversible, so this car is always operated with the vestibule to the rear. The area under the dome contains the men's and women's lavatories and dressing rooms (each quite large), and an aisle for passage around them along the left side of the car. There are two steps down as the main aisle bends around under the dome. A water cooler mounted flush into the wall is located at each pair of steps.

Seven carpeted and lighted steps lead to the rear of the dome section in a slightly curving, narrow stairwell. Handrails on NP domes are stainless steel. (The handrails in Great Northern (GN) dome cars are plastic.) The dome section contains 24 non-reserved, non-revenue seats open to passengers on a first-come-first-served basis. Dome seats also have antimacassar covers on the

Looking aft from the forward end of the rear coach section in Dome Coach 553. Part of the temporary floor covering has been removed, revealing the wide stripe pattern on the hard rubber tile floor. July 1954 photo.
Budd photo; Bill Kuebler collection

Chapter 7: From Locomotive to Diner: A Tour

Looking forward from the aft end of the rear coach section. The forward pair of seats on the right side face aft, creating a four-seat "family section." July 1954 photo.
Budd photo; Bill Kuebler collection

seat backs, but these were not added until a few years after dome cars entered service. With 360-degree vision, every seat is a window seat. Although there is no bad place to sit here, the ideal spot is probably in one of the forward seats, a great place to observe the railroad operation as well as the approaching scenery. Dome seats do not recline, as space is limited, but each has a footrest.

Interior decor is also the work of Raymond Loewy Associates. On the main level, the ceiling is painted an off white color, and the walls, a light beige. End walls are aqua with white stripes, and seats are cocoa colored. The floor is made of dark rubber tile, with wide off-white stripes running cross-wise. The bulkheads display murals and plaques with a railroad theme. These displays are identical in Dome Coaches 550–558; cars 549 and 559 have slightly different displays, as noted below. One interesting feature is the red and black NP monad on the forward bulkhead in the dome

Coach Attendant Clyde Williams and Passenger Representative Earl Smith serve as tour guides in new dome coach 550 during its public display at Tacoma, July 30, 1954. The NP's first locomotive, "Minnetonka," is depicted on the rear bulkhead of the forward coach section. Cars 550–558 have identical displays, but cars 549 (built in 1957) and 559 depict an American Standard locomotive instead of the "Minnetonka."
Jim Fredrickson photo

section; this serves as the cover for a radio speaker. Dome seats are turquoise, and the entire dome floor is carpeted. Small signs remind passengers to step down when leaving their dome seats, as the aisle is one-step lower than the rest of the floor in this section. Distance from aisle to ceiling in the dome is a little over six feet. At night, soft "theater style" lights illuminate just the aisle and steps, enough for safe passage but not enough to ruin night vision through dome windows. Bright fluorescent lights along either side of the dome center ceiling are usually left off at night.

As we walk through this car on the main level, we note one other thoughtful feature. Most windows are double-length, each one serving two pairs of seats. Rather than having one long shade, NP opted for two individual shades in each double-length window, made possible by use of a narrow metal track that splits the window vertically. This allows individual shade positioning on a double-length window. We also observe that the overhead luggage racks are of the metal tube design rather than solid shelves. The disadvantage of this design is that small objects could easily fall through the rack. On the other hand, this design makes the car seem more open, allows for better distribution of light, and reduces the likelihood of passengers leaving things behind.

Car 549, built in 1957, is nearly identical to the original 10 dome coaches. The only internal difference is a slightly different wall mural and engine display on the rear bulkhead of the forward coach section. Cars 550–558 display the "Minnetonka," the name given to NP's first locomotive, a

Day-Nite coach 594 normally operates in trains 25 and 26 with the vestibule forward, but when this photo was taken at Seattle, the car's seats were turned to face the other way after service on another train. Although they were assigned exclusively to the *North Coast Limited* when delivered in 1947, Day-Nite coaches in series 588–599 have since served on several other NP passenger trains as well.
Rick Leach photo, 1969

Chapter 7: From Locomotive to Diner: A Tour

small steam engine used during the construction of the railroad. Cars 549 and 559 show an American Standard 4-4-0 locomotive, instead; this was the most common type in regular service on all railroads during the mid- and late-1800s. Car 549 has only one external difference: the car's bearings. They are Timken roller bearings, whereas the original 10 cars have Hyatt roller bearings. The difference between the two makes is minor, but it was enough to cause President Macfarlane to have his business car, Yellowstone River, re-equipped with Timken bearings while the other two lightweight business cars retained their original Hyatts. He believed that the Timkens provided an even quieter ride.

The overall design of the vista-dome creates a modern and rather timeless appearance. Indeed, some three or four decades after 1959, a freshly painted Budd dome will hardly look out of place in a passenger train. Appearances are not deceiving, either. These cars are definitely not "under-engineered," as are some home-built dome cars on other roads. They are solid and exceptionally well built, fully capable of many decades of service. Little wonder they are so expensive!

One last glance into the dome section of this car reveals that all 24 seats are occupied. The buzz of conversation is fairly loud up there. After all, there is little to see out the windows at the moment; SPUD activity hardly keeps the attention of anyone except a serious railfan. But, you can safely bet the price of your first class ticket that the group's idle chat about Mantle and Maris and Ike and America's first seven astronauts will have been reduced to insignificance by about noon tomorrow. That's when No. 25 will blast out of the curve near Big Timber, its four F-units in the eighth notch, and aim for a narrow gap between the snow-capped Gallatin and Bridger ranges looming ahead. That gap is Bozeman Pass.

C-251
Day-Nite Coach
588-597; CB&Q 598, 599; Pullman-Standard; 1946–47
586, 587; Pullman-Standard; 1954

On the *North Coast Limited*, coaches are normally oriented with the vestibule forward, even though these cars are reversible. Seats can be reversed by depressing a locking lever with the foot and turning a pair of seats on a center pivot to face them in the opposite direction. This feature is intended to make the cars reversible, not to create facing-seat arrangements. In fact, company rules state that crewmembers are to discourage passengers from creating facing seat arrangements, because doing so restricts recline of seats that would, thus, be back-to-back. Also, leg rests on cars 588–599 fold down out of the back of the seat ahead or, in the case of the forward row, from the bulkhead.

> **Note**
> The car in the following car line could be either a Day-Nite Coach or a "Deluxe" Day-Nite Coach.

The Vista-Dome North Coast Limited

Day-Nite coach 589 was the first passenger car to be painted in the new Loewy scheme. Car numbers were originally dark green to match the top half of the car, as seen here, but were changed to white very shortly after this photo was taken in March 1953. Cars 589 and 588 were probably the only ones ever given dark green numbers; the change to white was adopted before other cars were painted in this scheme.
Jim Fredrickson photo

Day-Nite coach 598 is owned by CB&Q but painted and lettered for Northern Pacific. Note the small ownership letters in the upper corners. Coach 599 is also owned by CB&Q. Day-Nite coach 597, identical to the other cars in the series 588–599, was originally painted and lettered for SP&S and numbered 300, but it was sold to the NP in 1954, given number 597, and painted in the Raymond Loewy two-tone green scheme.
Bill Kuebler collection

Chapter 7: From Locomotive to Diner: A Tour

The aisle on all *North Coast Limited* Day-Nite Coaches runs straight through the center of the car. In a few years, newer leg rest coaches will join the fleet (cars 581–585, rebuilt from the Holiday Lounges in 1962); these will have a substantially different floor plan and window arrangement.

Day-Nite Coaches in series 588-599 are noticeably different from Deluxe Day-Nite Coaches 586 and 587, so these series will be discussed separately. Even so, either type of car can appear in this coach line.

Day-Nite Coach Series 588–599

These cars contain 56 fully reclining, "Sleepy Hollow" Heywood-Wakefield seats with a fold-down leg rest for each passenger's use. As we enter this car from the vestibule (forward) end, we note the women's and men's dressing rooms and lavatories on our left and right, respectively. Each dressing room has enough space to accommodate three people comfortably, but it is less space than we found in the dressing rooms under the dome in the car ahead. Built flush into the aisle side of the men's room wall is an ice water tap and cup dispenser. Every revenue car on this train has ice water on tap. Just beyond these rooms we find three large, equally spaced, linoleum covered luggage shelves on the left and a large supply locker on the right for the coach attendant. The supply locker contains pillows, playing cards, portable tables, drinking cups, paper supplies for the lavatories, and cleaning supplies for use by the coach attendant en route. Generally, each coach attendant is responsible for two coaches during the trip.

The coach section has one three-foot long window per pair of seats, allowing for ample viewing and individual shade positioning. Each pair of seats has a wall plate for fastening tables. The coach section extends all the way to the opposite end of the car; there is no smoking section in Day-Nite coaches.

Seats in cars 588–599 are numbered from the vestibule end (see accompanying diagram). The first seats on either side, seats 1–4, are assigned to the train crew. In 1954, the NP installed a conductor's section in place of seats 3 and 4 in cars 589, 594, 597, and 599. This section consists of a single sofa-type seat and a large non-portable table. (The conductor's section in these cars will be removed and seats 3 and 4 reinstalled in 1963.) Therefore, these four specially equipped cars are usually assigned specifically to line C-251/261. When other cars in this series operate in line C-251/261, the conductor is assigned seats 3 and 4. The brakeman is always assigned seats 1 and 2 in this car. Attachment plates on the forward bulkhead accommodate portable tables for the conductor (if there is no conductor's section) and brakeman. The coach attendant is assigned seats 5 and 6; he attends this car and the one ahead. Thus, only 50 seats are available for revenue sale in C-251. Several of them, however, are reserved for the conductor's discretionary use, so as to provide protection space in the event of duplicate sales. Duplicate sales are unusual, so these seats are also available for passengers needing to board without reservations. Although this is a reserved-seat-only train, these protection seats serve as the conductor's "ace-in-the-hole." Should a distraught passenger need to board without a reservation—such as someone traveling to a funeral on short notice—the conductor

73

can sell these seats at his discretion. In this car, these are seats 7–12. Other coaches on this train also have protection seats, as will be noted during our inspection.

Mechanically, these cars are well built. Each one has a Waukesha type air conditioning system capable of maintaining comfort even on the hottest days. Generators are belt driven. Like other lightweight cars, cars in this series have steam-radiation heating systems; some are a unizone type, the others are a zone type. These two systems have only minor differences. Car 590 also has a steam radiation heating system, but it is a unique Minneapolis-Honeywell system that has turned out to be a moderately successful experiment.

Interior decor in this car is simple, yet pleasant. The floor is a plain rubber tile, and the seats are a cocoa brown color. Lighting is ample and includes bright fluorescent lights over the center aisle and individual reading lights above each seat. The reading lights project a narrow beam so as to minimize inconvenience for nearby passengers trying to sleep. Overhead luggage racks run the full length of the coach section. Although cars 588–599 are equipped with the older, inside hanger type trucks, the ride is quite smooth and very quiet. Even at high speeds, the loudest noise in this car during daylight hours is the buzz of conversation among the passengers.

Like the car ahead, this car is nearly full. Most of its passengers are going to Billings or points west of there. Only four of the "conductor's seats" for discretionary sale in this car are yet unsold. Several other seats are currently unoccupied, though. Are these passengers enjoying a meal in the Traveller's Rest car?

"Deluxe" Day-Nite Coaches 586, 587

These two cars, known as "Deluxe Day-Nite" coaches or simply as "Deluxe" coaches, were delivered to the NP from Pullman-Standard in October 1954 as part of an order which included six sleeping cars numbered 367–372. These two coaches were purchased as substitution equipment for dome coaches. Since the NP originally had only 10 dome coaches, whenever one of them was in the shop, it meant that one train set would be missing a dome coach. The NP thought that substituting a more modern Day-Nite Coach would help make up for the loss of the dome. In 1957, the NP invested some additional capital in another dome coach from Budd, car 549. When that car was delivered in December 1957, scheduled maintenance for dome coaches was protected by an 11th dome coach, so the substitution role for cars 586 and 587 was no longer necessary. These two cars were then simply put into the pool of Day-Nite Coaches operating on the *North Coast Limited*, increasing that fleet from 12 to 14 cars. Cars 586 and 587 are usually assigned specifically to line C-251/261.

The dressing rooms and lavatories in this car are located at the end opposite the vestibule; on the older Day-Nite coaches they are at the vestibule end. Inside, these lavatories are more modern than those in the older Day-Nite coaches, but they are about the same size. The interior decor of this car is noticeably brighter than that of the older ones. The rubber tile floor has wide stripes, alternating light and dark colors, running crosswise. This is intended to "break up" the monotony of the long, narrow tube effect of a railroad coach interior, causing the passenger to feel that the coach

Chapter 7: From Locomotive to Diner: A Tour

Deluxe Day-Nite coach 587 poses for the company photographer at the Pullman-Standard factory in Chicago, just prior to delivery to the NP in October 1954. Rather than car line number boxes affixed to the inside of a window on each side of the car, these coaches have a more modern fixture at the end of the car, next to the vestibule. The NP paid about $199,000 for this car, about $7,000 more than it paid for each Day-Nite coach (series 588–599) in 1947. Although seats are reversible, the NP normally operates this type of car vestibule forward.
Pullman-Standard photos; Bill Kuebler collection

75

The Vista-Dome North Coast Limited

Wide floor striping in Deluxe Day-Nite coach 587 creates the impression that this car is wider than it is, reducing the "tube effect." This view is looking toward the vestibule end of the car. October 1954 builder's photo.
Pullman-Standard photo; Bill Kuebler collection

section is wider than it is. This car contains the same number of seats as the older cars, and they are likewise numbered from the vestibule end. The leg rests, however, fold back under the seat for stowage, like those in the dome coaches. This car is reversible, but it is normally operated with the vestibule forward, just like the other Day-Nite coaches. The purpose of this orientation is to be able to service two adjacent coaches more efficiently at station stops, the dome ahead and the coach behind the dome. That way, both vestibules can be opened, if needed, with only one crewmember attending the boarding of two cars. Generally, the head brakeman attends one pair of vestibules, the conductor the other pair. Coach attendants (sometimes called coach porters) handle passengers' luggage. When line C-254 operates, boarding of this coach is handled by its attendant, since company rules prohibit requiring boarding passengers to walk through another car to get to theirs.

Cars 586 and 587 have more modern mechanical equipment than the 1946–47 cars. This equipment includes a Trane air-conditioner, unizone heating, and a Spicer Drive generator. These cars also have outside swing hanger trucks.

Coach 587, looking toward the restroom end of the car. The ceiling is painted an off white color, and the walls, a light beige. End walls are aqua with white stripes, and seats are cocoa colored. The NP will add antimacassar covers to seat backs before this car enters service a few days hence.
Pullman-Standard photo, October 1954; Bill Kuebler collection

Chapter 7: From Locomotive to Diner: A Tour

"Deluxe" Day-Nite coach 586, built in 1954, is easily distinguished from the cars in series 588–599 by the location of the restrooms at the end opposite the vestibule. The end skirt under the restrooms was originally much shorter, but Como shop personnel applied a longer one to this car during repair work following its involvement in the derailment of train No. 25 at Granite, Idaho, in March 1962.
Duane Durr photo; Bill Kuebler collection

Deluxe Day-Nite coach 587, Seattle, September 1971. Built in 1954, this car has more modern external features than the Day-Nite coaches in series 588–599. Note the more streamlined roof vents.
Bill Kuebler collection

The Vista-Dome North Coast Limited

This is the type of Pullman-Standard truck used on Deluxe coaches 586 and 587, and on 8-6-4 sleepers 367–372. It is an outside swing hanger design, equipped with disc brakes (two discs on each axle). The "swing hanger" is the short, flat horizontal member positioned just outside the longer horizontal equalizers. The weight supported by this truck is distributed by the hangers to the truck frame and then to the four wheels. The equalizers compensate for normal track irregularities by continually "equalizing" the weight on the four wheels. Trucks built by Budd for *North Coast Limited* equipment are nearly identical, except that the center pin is on the truck. On Pullman-Standard cars, the center pin is on the car.
Pullman-Standard photo; Bill Kuebler collection

C-252
Vista-Dome Coach
550–556; CB&Q 557, 558; SP&S 559; Budd, July 1954
549; Budd, December 1957
Chicago-Portland

Information regarding line C-250 would apply to this car, except its routing. This car will go to Portland, so almost all of its passengers are destined for that city.

Being a little further back in the train means that a passenger in the dome can see more of the train ahead. And, the further back in the train, the fainter the sounds of the diesels. The presence of the flat top Day-Nite coach ahead is in compliance with an unwritten but long-standing rule on the NP to try to keep dome cars separated by at least one flat top car as much as possible. That way, the dome ahead does not interfere with the forward view from the one behind. Surely a minor

Chapter 7: From Locomotive to Diner: A Tour

Dome coach 549 rolls across the grade crossing just west of the Ellensburg depot on September 5, 1971. Built in 1957, this car was equipped with Timken roller bearings, whereas the original ten dome coaches, built three years earlier, were equipped with Hyatt roller bearings.
Bill Kuebler collection

point, but it shows the desire of NP management to look out for its passengers and consider the details. (After 1961, both dome sleepers will operate to Seattle, so west of Pasco, depending on the season and consist, they will sometimes have to operate one right behind the other.)

The major figure behind such considerations in 1959 is the 65-year-old energetic head of NP's passenger traffic department, G. Walter Rodine, who has held the post since 1949. This man, as much as any other, looks for every possible way to maximize the pleasures and convenience experienced by NP passengers. He strongly advocates use of the best possible equipment in the most sensible fashion, especially on the *North Coast Limited*. President Macfarlane respects him greatly. (One senior NP official has told this author, "In top level meetings, if Mr. Rodine wanted something done, or done a certain way, it would happen. His influence was very great.") The idea for separating dome cars from each other on the NP is Rodine's, and from 1955 until after his retirement (in August 1963) the rule will stick.

Continuing our walk-through, we note that the front row of seats in the forward coach section of this car, the row with seats 43–46, is still unoccupied. These are the conductor's "discretionary" seats, available as protection space for duplicate sales, passengers without reservations, etc., especially for those traveling to points Pasco-Portland.

As we walk through car C-252, we contemplate the well-orchestrated maneuvers that these unaware passengers will sleep through just 32 hours, 15 minutes from now. That is when the Portland cars will be switched out of this train in the middle of the night at Pasco. Behind the scenes, the *North Coast Limited* is a round-the-clock adventure!

The Vista-Dome North Coast Limited

Things are not quite what they seem. This familiar NP publicity photo seems to show a Stewardess-Nurse and dome passengers enjoying the scenery and each other's company aboard the *Vista-Dome North Coast Limited*. The Stewardess-Nurse and passengers are advertising models, however, and this car is at the CB&Q coach yard near Chicago Union Station, between runs in May 1955. Northern Pacific's Chicago advertising agency, Batten, Barton, Durstine & Osborn, Inc., shot several publicity photos in this car a few hours before it was due to leave Chicago in train No. 25. This view is not entirely misleading. Indeed, passengers did enjoy Stewardess-Nurse service aboard NP's finest passenger train and took many photos from its domes. Wouldn't it be interesting to see some of those amateur snapshots taken throughout NP's vista-dome era?
NP Publicity Photo; Bill Kuebler collection

Another photo taken during the same advertising photo session in Chicago, May 1955. The absence of a nameplate on the Stewardess-Nurse's left uniform pocket indicates that she is a model and not a real Stewardess-Nurse.
NP photo; Bill Kuebler collection

80

Chapter 7: **From Locomotive to Diner: A Tour**

A coach attendant has positioned window shades evenly with each other while dome coach *556* lays over at Chicago on March 22, 1969. NP's dome coaches have individual window shades for each row, made possible by a vertical track in the middle of each double-length window.
William A. Raia collection

Pasco Operations

Operations at Pasco will require the crew to advise passengers to be in their assigned cars during switching moves there. Westbound, the schedule calls for this switching to occur between 1:18 and 1:33 A.M., hardly a time when passengers are likely to be away from their assigned space. Nevertheless, at various times during the day and evening prior to arrival at Pasco, announcements will be made over the train's PA system, lest somebody ends up on the wrong train. Additionally, the Idaho Division conductor and brakeman will walk through the cars just prior to arrival at Pasco, making sure that everyone is where they are supposed to be, and then close all eight end gates in the four places where uncoupling will occur. Specifically, these end gates will be the rear one on car C-251 and the forward one on car C-252. Similarly, the pairs between cars C-253 and C-254, and between cars 256 and 257, and cars 258 and 259, will be closed.

In spite of the potential for mistakes regarding passengers' assigned space, the crew usually knows who belongs where. (As conductor Warren McGee has said, "We passenger conductors had a sixth sense about who was on our train, where their assigned space was, and where they were going. It was just something we always knew. A really good conductor could even discreetly punch tickets in the dining car for those who went there right after boarding—and he could do it without the other passengers even noticing. On the Rocky Mountain Division, no passenger conductor was better at these kinds of things than Jimmy Quinn. I always admired him for the way he handled things. He was my mentor.")

Switching at Pasco is another example of efficiency, perhaps the best. When the *North Coast Limited* approaches Pasco, the switcher, usually a Baldwin DRS 4-4-15 (either 500 or 501), will be ready and waiting. Several switchmen and carmen will be on the ground, ready to begin the procedure at their assigned spots. As soon as the train stops and the few arriving passengers begin to step off, carmen will be busy disconnecting lines and pulling coupler pins. A minute or two later, one of these men will give a signal and the switcher will pull the first cut of cars back while the road units are being serviced up ahead. Four switching moves will be required, two for coaches and two for sleeping cars. Usually, the two Portland sleeping cars are set out first, and then the two Portland coaches. For the eastbound *North Coast*, the coaches are coupled in first, and then the sleeping cars. In just a few minutes the *North Coast Limited* will be back together, and a few departing passengers will board as the carmen reconnect all the lines. The last item will be the standing air brake test. In only 15 minutes, the train will be ready to go.

The Vista-Dome North Coast Limited

C-253/700[1]
Day Coach
500-517; Pullman-Standard; 1946–47[2]
Chicago-Portland

Windows in day coaches (series 500–517) are spaced slightly closer together than those in "Day-Nite" coaches (series 588–599). Day coaches also have two additional windows on each side of the car, on the end opposite the vestibule. The extra windows are for the smoking room and the aisle around it. Coaches 500 (above) and 515 (below) are on stand-by status at Seattle in 1971 and 1969, respectively.
Both photos: Rick Leach

1. Records conflict regarding this line number. Some show it as C-700/800, others as C-253/263, and still others give both numbers. The C-700/800 designation was in use for only a few years in the late 1950s and early 1960s.
2. As of 1959, only six-day coaches were "train lined" for North Coast Limited service. This meant that they were equipped for the train's PA system and electro-pneumatic brake operation. These cars were as follows: 502, 505, 506, 511, 513, and 516.

Chapter 7: From Locomotive to Diner: A Tour

Day coach 517 still wears NP paint and lettering in June 1974 at Dilworth, MN. The generator and its drive belt are visible under the car, near the truck. Brake cylinders for disc brakes are mounted inside the truck, out of view.
Duane Durr photo, Bill Kuebler collection

Looking toward the smoking lounge of day coach 502 at the Pullman-Standard factory. Each pair of seats in the main coach section of this car is reversible. When this car is operated vestibule forward, the usual orientation for line C-253, these seats would be facing the other way. October 7, 1946, builder's photo.
Pullman-Standard photo; Bill Kuebler collection

83

The Vista-Dome North Coast Limited

Smoking lounge of newly built day coach 502, October 7, 1946. Note the small fixture in the window for displaying the car line number. *Pullman-Standard photo; Bill Kuebler collection*

Most NP passenger timetables and brochures dated Summer 1959 show a day coach in this line, but in actual practice, any of the Day-Nite coaches can appear in this line, instead, and occasionally do. The reason for using a day coach is a simple matter of availability. As of June 1959 the NP has 14 Day-Nite coaches in the *North Coast Limited* pool, cars 586–599. With a full 14-car summer season consist, however, 15 Day-Nite coaches would be required to fill out all five train sets with three coaches each. That means that one of the five train sets (or more than one, if a Day-Nite coach is in the shops) has to have a day coach in one of its five coach lines, or else the line would have to be dropped. The NP often puts a day coach in this line in more than one train set, so as to free up some Day-Nite coaches for service on *The Mainstreeter*.

Perhaps the NP could have ordered an extra Day-Nite coach or two at some point, as it did the extra dome coach, but by the time the requirement was realized (remember, the consist of this train evolved considerably from 1946 to 1955), only one or two new cars would have been needed. Ordering one or two cars of a particular type means greatly increased unit costs, a major consideration. Indeed, the cost of dome coach 549 in 1957 was a whopping 38 percent more than one of its 10 mates acquired only three years earlier. So, if a choice has to be made, management reasons that such limited capital is better spent on domes than on coaches.

Chapter 7: From Locomotive to Diner: A Tour

Day Coach Series 500–517

As we continue our inspection of the train at St. Paul, we observe a day coach in line C-253. Several differences are immediately apparent. These seats have only footrests and no leg rests, and they are spaced a little closer together than seats in the Day-Nite coaches. Windows are therefore a little shorter in length and closer together than those in the Day-Nite coaches. This car is also operated vestibule forward, and restrooms are located at the vestibule end. This car and its seats are reversible. At first glance from the forward toward the opposite end, the aisle appears to go straight through the car, but this is an illusion. At the rear (non-vestibule) end is a small smoking lounge with only a front entrance. The aisle bends around this room, but it's easy to miss the turn since the back wall of the smoking lounge contains a large pane of clear glass through which is seen the car's end door. The scene can easily lull one into a dead-end. More than once, a hurrying passenger has come rushing into the smoking lounge only to come up against its back wall, an embarrassing moment.

Other features of this car are the same as those on the 1946–47 Day-Nite coaches, such as the air conditioning and heating systems, electrical system, and inside hanger trucks. All *North Coast Limited* coaches are 85-foot cars; there are no "shorties."

Whether a day coach or a Day-Nite coach operates in this line, seats 1–4, the first row behind the vestibule and restrooms, are reserved for the conductor's discretionary sale as protection space. Seats 29 and 30 are reserved for the coach attendant working this car and the dome coach ahead. Long-haul traffic to Portland is rarely enough to fill a second coach line, so some passengers in this car are "short hauls," whereas almost all the passengers in the dome coach ahead are "long hauls" traveling to Portland.

C-254
Day-Nite Coach
588-597; CB&Q 598, 599; Pullman-Standard; 1946–47
Chicago-Seattle

Most of the commentary for line C-251 applies to this one, except for the conductor's section, seat assignments, and destinations of the passengers. No space in this car is assigned to the train crew (they are assigned seats in C-251), but seats 29 and 30 are assigned to the coach attendant. Also, seats 1–4 are available to the conductor for discretionary sale as protection space, usually for passengers traveling short distances. Sometimes, depending on expected loads, additional seats (5–8) are set aside for discretionary sale. Rare is the occasion of turning someone away who is willing to pay the fare. While the NP doesn't have a "shorts" coach—one exclusively reserved for short-haul passengers—those traveling shorter distances during the summer or winter-holiday seasons are generally assigned to this car or the one ahead.

The Vista-Dome North Coast Limited

Day-Nite coach 588 waits for its next assignment in Seattle, in 1969. Day-Nite coaches in series 588–599 do not have smoking rooms.
Rick Leach photo

Even though cars 586 and 587 are operated in a pool with other Day-Nite coaches, they do not appear in line C-254/264, simply because this line is operated only during certain times of the year, and even then somewhat sporadically. Cars 586 and 587 are assigned specifically to line C-251/261.

As we walk through C-254, we notice that there are more unfilled seats in this car than in any of the other coaches. In effect, this is the "extra" car, used only during the busiest times. Even so, the load factor on this train (percentage of sellable seats sold), especially during the summer, is typically very high.

Lewis & Clark Traveller's Rest Lounge
494–498; CB&Q 499; Pullman-Standard; 1947
Rebuilt at NP Como Shops, 1955
Chicago-Seattle

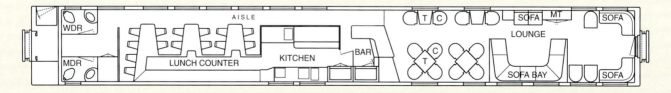

Chapter 7: From Locomotive to Diner: A Tour

Traveller's Rest car 494 poses for a company photographer before being released from NP's Como shops in June 1955. Both of these views show the car's left side. The NP will add VISTA-DOME NORTH COAST LIMITED slogans to the sides of this car in early 1956.
NP Photos; Bill Kuebler collection

87

The Vista-Dome North Coast Limited

The right side of Traveller's Rest car 494, Como shops, June 1955.
NP Photo; Bill Kuebler collection

Nineteen fifty-five, the year these cars entered service, marked the 150th anniversary of the famous Lewis and Clark expedition. Since the NP operates over a route that closely follows much of the famous explorers' trail, Raymond Loewy's concept for these cars seemed very fitting to NP executives. President Macfarlane is well aware of historical matters pertaining to the NP, so he accepted Raymond Loewy's recommendation for a Lewis and Clark theme. Perhaps the word "theme" is an understatement, for these cars literally are a Lewis and Clark history lesson on wheels. We will find it difficult to walk through this car quickly; there is much to see. Ever popular and truly unique, it is the most talked-about car in the train. The decision to rebuild the coach-buffet-lounge cars that had been built for the *North Coast Limited* in 1947 into the Traveller's Rest configuration has proved to be a very wise one. The older lounges were not popular;

Chicago artist Edgar Miller puts the finishing touches on the wall mural in car 494. Artist Miller had to devise a special mixture of oil-based paint and ground plastic in order for the paint to adhere to the walls. Finishing nails are hidden beneath the plastic "cross stitches" in the wall seams.
NP photo; Bill Kuebler collection

Chapter 7: From Locomotive to Diner: A Tour

in fact, they were a flop. Their design was plain; they were just another lounge. But, not so are these cars! The handiwork of NP's Como shops is nowhere better seen than here.

Rebuilding these cars from the coach-buffet-lounge into the Traveller's Rest configuration was a challenging task, but Como shop personnel did a good job. The first NP car (car 497) was removed from service for remodeling in spring 1955. (CB&Q car 499 was actually the first car to be converted.) It is interesting that Como shop forces did the entire job *without use of blueprints* for wiring, a rather unusual feat. Electricians faced some interesting challenges when installing the hanging light fixture above the buffet counters and the mural lights in the lounge. Shop personnel developed some procedures and techniques as the job progressed, so by the time they worked on the last car (car 496), things were running smoothly. Windows had to be completely removed and filled in, and new ones installed. New plumbing was installed for water, drainage, and the propane fuel needed for the gas grill in the kitchen, while Como shop carpenters were busy making lounge tables, chairs, and sofas. Last, but not least, was mural artist Edgar Miller's work (but, more on this later.) All in all, it was a big job.

At last, by the end of May 1955, the first car from Como, car 497, was ready to enter service. When it was rolled out of the shops, however, a minor problem was discovered in the placement of some under-body equipment. One Como shop veteran has said that the car was actually leaning slightly to the left. After a short time back in the shop, it was rolled out again, truly level and ready this time. It entered service at the end of May or early June, and by the end of the summer, all the other cars were also in service. The last to enter service was car 496. It is equipped with a Trane air-conditioning system, whereas the other five cars are equipped with a Waukesha system, typical for cars of 1947 vintage. Let's take a closer look at this fascinating lounge car . . .

Even the vestibule of this car is unusual. Located at the forward end, it is really only half a vestibule. There is a standard Dutch door with retractable steps on the car's right side, but not on its left side. Instead, a large, four-shelf storage area for equipment, including a small closet insert for cleaning materials, occupies that space. As we step through the forward end door we notice women's and men's lavatories on our left and right, respectively. These do not include dressing rooms. Just aft of the men's lavatory is a large, four-shelf locker. Here, we go left and around a wall; an aisle along the side of the car allows passage through the lunch counter section.

Lunch Counter Section

What an attractive setting! Instead of the monotonous, long-

Lunch counter section of car 494. This seating arrangement is very unusual in the railroad industry. On other roads, the lunch counter is typically one long, L-shaped counter, curved at one end. The arrangement seen here forms a cozier setting and is very popular with passengers. Note the spaces for small handbag stowage underneath the tables.
NP photo; Bill Kuebler collection

The Vista-Dome North Coast Limited

counter, elbow-bumping arrangement common on other roads, this lunch counter section features three neat lunch counters where passengers can sit facing each other, fore and aft, as in a dining car. The forward counter has six seats, the middle and aft counters have four seats each. Passengers can enjoy each other's company as well as their meals. The middle and aft lunch counters have small cutouts, permitting the waiter easy access to all four places at a counter while serving. All three counters have inset compartments beneath them for purses and packages. Sparkling white Formica counter tops accent the more rustic motif of the large hanging light fixture in this section. The stools are leather cushioned and comfortable. Select and *a la carte* meals and snacks are served all day here from 7 A.M. until about 10 P.M. It is a busy place throughout the day, because about two-thirds of the coach passengers will eat meals here. Some, mainly the short hauls, will not eat on the train; others will eat in the dining car, space permitting, as first class passengers always get priority for dining car seats.

A kitchen and buffet are located at the car's mid-point, neatly hidden behind walls. The kitchen area has a door at each end; one is used to access the lunch counters, the other, the bar in the lounge section to the rear. The crew of this car consists of a cook, a waiter, and the "waiter-in-charge."

Lounge Section

The lounge is comfortable and roomy, with seats for 30 passengers. An attractive color scheme gives this section a feeling of luxury and restfulness. Colors of warm sienna and ochre, highlighted by aqua, blend with natural cherry planking. The carpet is actually a colorful Indian rug, custom woven. Copies of Lewis and Clark correspondence are displayed, lending authenticity to the theme.

Mounted in brass letters on the side of the service bar is this phrase from the entry of September 9, 1805, in the Journals of Lewis and Clark—"We called it Traveller's Rest." "Traveller's Rest" is the name they gave to their campsite along the Bitterroot River, at Lolo Creek,

Looking aft in the lounge of Lewis and Clark Traveller's Rest 494. This car is fresh out of Como shops in June 1955 and will soon enter *North Coast Limited* service. A peek under those tables would reveal carved initials and names of NP Como Shop carpenters.
NP photo; Bill Kuebler collection

Chapter 7: From Locomotive to Diner: A Tour

This forward view of the lounge in Lewis and Clark Traveller's Rest 494 presents an attractive setting. Mounted in brass letters on the side of the service bar are the words, "'We called it Traveller's Rest' ...Journals of Lewis and Clark, September 9, 1805." A company photographer took this June 1955 photo just after the car rolled out of Como Shops.
NP photo; Bill Kuebler collection

south of present-day Missoula. (Lewis and Clark spelled "Traveller's" with two l's, and so does the NP.) Four tables and chair sets complement the sofa bays, the latter upholstered in aqua, antique white, and burnt sienna. Music is provided by radio and by the train's high fidelity sound system. Beverage service, magazines, tables for cards, and a wonderful western atmosphere make this lounge an ideal place for relaxation, reading, and conversation.

This view of the right side of Traveller's Rest 498 shows a vestibule door and a row of windows along the aisle of the lunch counter section. There is no vestibule door on the opposite side. Windows in the lounge section are irregularly spaced much further apart to allow room for the large interior wall murals depicting a map and scenes from Lewis and Clark's journey. This photo of train No. 26 was taken during its brief stop at Ellensburg in September 1970.
Bill Kuebler collection

The Vista-Dome North Coast Limited

Traveller's Rest car 495, which arrived SPUD this day at about 6:40 a.m. on train 26, is spotted at NP's St. Paul commissary for its usual 24-hour layover between trips in 1968. Carmen inspected this car soon after it was spotted here, and the next day's outgoing dining car crew will soon begin thoroughly cleaning the car's interior and restocking it. Tomorrow at about 6:45 a.m., a yard crew will switch this car into train 26 for another five-day St. Paul-Chicago-Seattle-St. Paul trip.
John Kennedy photo

The most striking features of all, however, are the colorful, curving wall-to-ceiling murals, designed and executed by famed Chicago artist, Edgar Miller. These murals are done on a light beige, buckskin-like plastic material, cross-stitched at the seams, an appropriate background for the graphic portrayal of scenes and episodes taken from the *Journals of Lewis and Clark*. (The "cross stitches" actually hide the nails used for construction of the buckskin-like wall, an ingenious detail.) The central feature is a large map in the lounge section, which shows the route followed by the explorers to the Pacific Northwest and back. Pictured are Fort Mandan, first winter's camp, and Fort Clatsop, where the party spent its second winter. Other points of interest depicted include Three Forks and the Traveller's Rest camp. Scenes from a buffalo hunt appear below the map, and throughout the car there are paintings of Indians and wild animals encountered by the explorers.

Artist Edgar Miller used a special type of paint for the murals since ordinary oil paint would not work on the plastic background. He made his paint by hand-grinding colored plastic cubes of the same material as the background into a fine powder, which he then put into a solvent. The result was a paint that was both durable and able to stick to the walls. Since these murals are all hand painted, each car is unique. That is, the exact positions and rendering of the various scenes are not the same in each car, but only approximately the same. In the event of accidental damage to one of these cars, mural repair and touch-up would present a challenge. (Cars 499 and 496 had to be repaired after being damaged in derailments at Granite and Evaro, respectively, in 1962.)

Chapter 7: From Locomotive to Diner: A Tour

One point of interest gets very little attention. Como shop personnel were justifiably proud of their work on these cars. As we walk through this car, we contemplate the rumor that various carpenters at Como carved their names or initials under the tables in these cars, a little known signature on their handiwork. While nobody's looking, we chance a peek under a couple of lounge tables in search of these carvings. Sure enough, they are there.

Just before we head back to the diner, we observe the Stewardess-Nurse, Miss Rita Hamilton, chatting with a cute little four-year-old boy about the relative virtues of a new cartoon character named Yogi Bear. "Jellystone Park, Miss 'Sue' . . . that's the one we're going to!" he proclaims with

In early June 1955, before this Traveller's Rest car (no. 498) entered service, these models posed for the NP's Chicago advertising agency photographer during a photo shoot in St. Paul. The "Waiter-in-Charge," however, is not a model. He is an NP waiter performing this additional duty on his day-off. The meals seen in this photo appeared on the 1955 Traveller's Rest menu; they were actually cooked in this car for this advertising session. In reality, this was a busy place aboard the *North Coast Limited* as most coach passengers who ate aboard the train ate here.
NP Publicity photo, Bill Kuebler collection

The Vista-Dome North Coast Limited

all seriousness. Indeed, he and his family will step off this train at Livingston tomorrow, bound for summer vacation in nearby Yellowstone Park. Miss Hamilton is a Registered Nurse, as are all nine of the other NP Stewardess-Nurses. She is a 1957 graduate of Holy Cross Central School of Nursing and St. Mary's college at Notre Dame, Indiana. Prior to joining the NP a year ago, she served as nurse at the Illinois Braille and Sight Saving School in Jacksonville, Illinois, her hometown. Her new job with the NP moved her to Seattle, where all her trips begin and end with six days on, and four days off rotation. Back at Seattle, her supervisor is Miss Elaine Rath, but on board the train, she answers directly to the conductor.

Stewardess-Nurses wear an attractive uniform consisting of a white blouse, dark green jacket and skirt, and a matching cap sporting an NP logo and the words "NORTHERN PACIFIC." The uniform is not cheap, at $150, and the topcoat and raincoat cost an additional $115. The NP initially pays one-half the entire cost of the uniform and coats, and maintains their cleaning. The NP pays the full cost of the uniform if the Stewardess-Nurse stays on staff at least a year. There are very few other expenses for Miss Hamilton. The company also pays for her two-night Chicago layover at the Palmer House and provides all meals on board the train. She is not expected to tip the dining car waiters. The Palmer House allows the Stewardess-Nurses free entrance to shows in the hotel's famous "Empire Room," space permitting. Even though a day working aboard this train is usually very long and tiring, Miss Hamilton considers this to be a very good—and interesting—line of work.

Miss Hamilton is young, attractive, and does her job well. At times, especially when the conductor is somewhere else on the train, passengers see her as *the* person with answers and solutions. After 12 months on the job, she now has most of her 16-page commentary for PA announcements about points of interest along the route memorized, and should a passenger ask her how opposing trains manage to "pass each other" under single track operation, she has the correct answer from her secret "Q&A guide" memorized as well. One moment, she is likely to be helping a young mother prepare formula for her infant, time permitting; the next moment she is exchanging pleasantries with dome passengers and answering questions about the train and its route. ("Miss, how much fuel do our locomotives burn on a trip?" "What is the cost of this train?" "When were domes added?" "What is the relation of the Burlington to the Northern Pacific?" Miss Hamilton has the correct answers to all these questions and more.) After a long day of service on this train, a short night's rest in Roomette 2, car 255, will be well deserved. She definitely earns her monthly salary of $360, not a bad income in 1959.

Dining Car
459–463; CB&Q 458; Budd; 1958
Chicago-Seattle

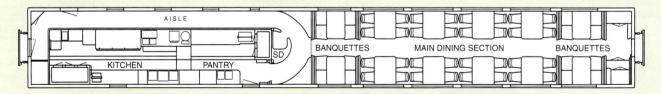

When the NP ordered an extra dome coach and dome sleeper from Budd in 1957, the Railway also ordered six new dining cars, one of which was for CB&Q ownership. (These were the last full diners built for an American railroad prior to Amtrak, and they represented the best money could buy in 1957.)

As we enter the forward end of the car, the pneumatic end door is automatically held open just long enough for our passage, and then gently closes behind us. This is a mealtime—the second seating for dinner is nearing completion—so, the sounds and aromas of this unique and fascinating facil-

Chapter 7: From Locomotive to Diner: A Tour

In this December 1957 builder's photo of the left side of Budd diner 463, the journal covers are painted silver. Although they would appear that way on rare occasions during the next 12 years, this was not standard NP practice.
Budd photo; Bill Kuebler collection

ity multiply the input to our senses. The well-lighted passageway immediately bends to our left and around the enclosed kitchen, from which the faint sounds and not so faint smells waft out through the pantry to permeate the car's atmosphere. In spite of excellent air-conditioning, the passage around the kitchen is a little warmer than the rest of the train, but not uncomfortably so. Unlike dining cars on some other roads, there is no lineup of people waiting to be seated here; dinner on the *North Coast Limited* is always by reservation.

At the steward's desk in the middle of the car, we stop to take in the scene—a waiter carrying a tray of dessert over here, Steward Frank Houska receiving compliments from a dinner guest over there. Of the 48 seats, 44 are occupied; of these, coach passengers occupy only four. Several patrons

Steward Frank Houska invites us to a table in this gleaming, well appointed Budd dining car, where etched glass panels divide the banquette sections from the main dining room. This 1958 publicity photo was taken the day before this car made its first in-service trip.
NP publicity photo, 1958

The Vista-Dome North Coast Limited

This view of the right side of Budd diner 458 shows that the forward end skirt is missing. Otherwise, the car is still in its *North Coast Limited* livery at Seattle on January 8, 1972.
Bill Kuebler collection

are establishing new friendships at their tables, and everyone seems to be thoroughly enjoying the cuisine. The seated and relaxed passengers contrast with the swift and sure motion of the waiters. Later, when the *North Coast* will again be moving, this scene will be even more impressive and enhanced by the cinema of scenery passing slowly in the distance and flashing by quickly in the foreground, an unexcelled experience for any traveler. Each table is located adjacent to a generous double-length picture window furnished with Venetian blinds and drapes.

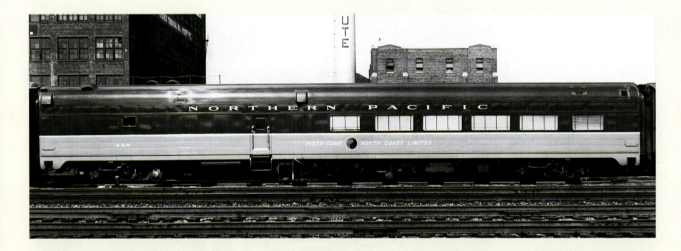

The left side of Budd diner 459 shines in the late morning sunlight on July 13, 1968. In a few minutes this equipment will be backed into position at Chicago Union Station for boarding of train No. 25. The dining car crew lowered all the Venetian blinds the previous day after this car's arrival on train No. 26, to help keep the dining room cool in the event electrical power was temporarily cut during the train's 22-hour layover.
William A. Raia collection

Chapter 7: From Locomotive to Diner: A Tour

There usually is very little passenger traffic through this car because NP positions it between coaches and Pullmans; it is a natural dividing point between coach and first class. Coach passengers heading toward the rear of the train are discreetly, and sometimes not so discreetly, stopped here by the dining car crew. "Only first class passengers to the rear of this car, folks." But, we are first class passengers, and the crew recognizes us. Before we chance a conspicuous walk through the dining area in the rear half of this car, a study of the interesting railroad murals behind the steward's desk is worthwhile. Stepping into the dining room, we notice a sudden transition from linoleum flooring to carpet. The latter muffles sound, especially when the train is in motion. Six tables on either side of the aisle are covered in white linen and support an interesting array of china, glassware, and appetizing food. Our decision to eat earlier was a wise one, for the food seen here would otherwise look all the more tempting.

A detailed description of a typical table setting and the dinner menu is in order. On any given table we see crisp, white Irish linen with the NP Monad woven into the center. The dining car crew places fresh linen on each table after every seating. The china is white with rim stripes in two shades of green set off by orange pin stripes. Except for coffee cups, each piece displays NP's red and black Monad. Each setting includes finger bowls. The silver serving pieces and flatware, which are in attractive, art-deco patterns, are kept at a high shine by regular polishing. The full dinner menu is extensive. Typically, there are as many as four kinds of soup, several types of seafood, nine entrees, four or five kinds of vegetables and five or six dessert choices, plus a variety of relishes, breads, and beverages *a la carte*, in addition to other choices on a *table d'hôte* menu and a budget 'Plate Dinner." There is also a separate menu for children. So concerned is the NP with food quality that the railroad has its own bakeries and butcheries in St. Paul and Seattle and runs its own dairy and poultry farm.

Baking potatoes are a specialty item on NP diners. These Idaho russet potatoes, actually harvested from Washington's Yakima Valley, are baked on board the train. The "Great Big Baked Potato" began on the NP as a way to support Washington farmers. In those days, minimum weight of a potato was two pounds! The idea for this specialty originated in 1909 with Dining Car Superintendent Hazen J. Titus, who found a way to market the giant potatoes by selling them on NP dining cars. They became so popular that the road eventually was buying several hundred tons per year. The NP became known as "The Road of the Great Big Baked Potato." The price for one baked potato in June 1959: 30-cents.

Official NP Recipe for Baking & Serving Potatoes (1959)

Minimum Weight: 20 ounces.

After being washed, the big potatoes are pierced with an ice pick at both ends and placed in a moderate oven. During fall and winter months it requires approximately 2 hours to bake them. The potatoes should be turned several times during the process of baking. In spring and summer they will bake in about an hour and a half. At that time of year, it is well to place a pan of water in the oven with the potatoes to compensate for some of the natural moisture which has evaporated during the storage period. When the potatoes are done, they are taken from the oven and rolled gently to loosen the meaty part from the skin. Cut from end to end, spread open, and serve with a large piece of butter in the center.

A study of the pantry and kitchen area reveals plenty of activity. Space is at a premium there, and every item—food stock, utensils, dishes, pots and pans—has its place. Keeping track of supplies and equipment is a major task. Average food supply loaded on a diner includes 55 loaves of bread, 19 dozen sweet and dinner rolls, 23 dozen hamburger buns, 66 pies, 50 orders of chicken, 80 orders of turkey, 100 of seafood, as well as 480 cuts of meat and 13 gallons of ice cream. Then there's raisin bread, rye bread, baby foods, apples, melons, potatoes, shortening, salad oils, fresh vegetables, fish and

The Vista-Dome North Coast Limited

Train No. 25 pauses at Forsyth, Montana, in November 1968, while passengers in dining car 459 enjoy breakfast, a meal given as much care and attention by NP dining car crews as any other. For example, chefs prided themselves at being able to make perfectly round (and tasty) pancakes in spite of the kitchen's tight quarters and the train's motion at high speeds.
Bill Kuebler collection

many other items. And, besides all that, this car is equipped with over 650 pieces of silver flatware and hollowware, over 200 glasses of various types, and more than 650 pieces of china. Woe unto a green "mule" who misplaces something! The nickname "mule," usually waiter no. 6 who is also the junior waiter, is an old one that refers to his having to serve the wishes of the "pantryman," or waiter no. 1.

The seniority system among cooks and waiters is less apparent during a meal service than it would be during the hours between and after meals, when these men perform several assigned duties. Each man is traditionally assigned tasks according to his seniority and consequent position. The pantryman, also the first waiter, is usually the senior waiter. As his nickname implies, he and his "mule," assisted by waiter no. 3, are responsible for the pantry, keeping it clean and making sure everything is where it belongs. The pantryman, assisted by the third cook, is also responsible for mopping and scrubbing the protective wooden floor slats (designed to prevent slipping in the event of spills) in the pantry and kitchen and, after raising the slats, the metal floor. Waiter no. 2, known as the "linen man," is assisted by waiter no. 5 in changing tablecloths and bagging all soiled linen after each seating. Waiter no. 2 is also responsible for keeping the carpet in the dining room clean. Waiter no. 4 is responsible for sweeping and mopping the linoleum-covered passageway around the kitchen. He is also responsible for serving meals to train personnel, who usually eat between passenger seatings. The Stewardess-Nurse usually takes her dinner meals during the last seating. Although she sits with dining car patrons during that time, the NP requires her to remain "on the job" and attend to any passengers needing assistance.

A division of labor also exists for the three cooks. During meals the chef, or first cook, oversees all orders, making sure that the second and third cooks meet the wishes of each patron as they prepare the various portions of the entrees. He also prepares food himself, specializing in coffee brewing, potato scrubbing and baking (some 100 pounds worth per dinner), preparation of various meat entrees such as prime rib and steaks, and baking of pies and other pastries. The preparation of some of these items, such as the baked potatoes and pies, begins several hours before dinnertime.

Chapter 7: From Locomotive to Diner: A Tour

The chef on our train is Bill Nelson, who has 38 years of service in NP's dining car department. He is highly experienced and enjoys his work. And, it shows. Between meals the cooks are assigned specific clean-up duties, including washing dishes and utensils (nicknamed "pearl diving"), cleaning the stove and oven to spotless condition, and returning everything to its proper place.

Overseeing all of these activities is the dining car steward, whose success in finding a place for everything on a dining car has to be either a major mystery or a minor miracle. Resourcefulness is an absolute requirement, and Frank Houska refined the tricks of his trade early in his long and successful career. Above all, meeting every wish of the dining car patron is his primary concern, and no detail escapes his notice. Should a waiter get careless and violate a rule of the dining car department, however minor the infraction, Houska takes him aside and discreetly reprimands him. And, there are many rules, too. Some show up almost daily as bulletins and curt messages at the commissary in St. Paul. These come from Superintendent, Bill Paar, a man who also attends to the smallest details. ("Under no circumstances should a waiter bring a full jar of mustard . . . to the table . . . bring a small mustard pot about half full" is an example of one of Paar's bulletins.)

Steward Houska looks sharp. He wears dark blue trousers and matching coat with a white vest and black tie. His black shoes are shiny enough to serve as mirrors. His upper left coat sleeve sports a monad, with the letters "N" and "P" prominent in the red and black halves, respectively. His smile and kind demeanor do not reveal his experience level, but his lower left sleeve does, for it has embroidered upon it a three-quarter inch gold star (for 25-years' service) plus two 1½ inch gold bars (five-years' service each). He has been in the dining car service for nearly four decades and will soon qualify for a third gold bar. Houska also serves as an instructor in the dining car department.

An interesting agreement exists between dining car stewards of the NP and CB&Q. Since stewards on the *North Coast Limited* work in CB&Q territory between St. Paul and Chicago, it seems fair to unions representing stewards of both roads to allow a CB&Q steward to work *North Coast Limited* trips, each of which would involve compensatory NP mileage. Equitable balance is based on monthly mileage accumulated over each road by the stewards. Houska happens to be an NP employee, but his uniform is not proof of this. About one of every 10 *North Coast* stewards wears an NP uniform, but is actually a CB&Q man "working off mileage." Whatever employing road, though, all stewards maintain the same high standards in accordance with NP dining car department directives.

The dining car crew works very hard to make this more of a production than a

Between meal seatings the dining car crew is very busy preparing for the next seating. Their work has to be accomplished in minimal time and, when complete, the dining room looks like this to a first class passenger upon entry from the sleeping car section of the train. Everything in this dining room is spotless and in its place, an inviting setting, indeed!
NP photo; Bill Kuebler collection

99

mere dining experience. They have little time for rest and relaxation, and their days are very long. As we turn our attention from the pantry and kitchen back to the dining room, the contrast in atmosphere is startling. The latter place is far more elegant and relaxed. Judging from the beads of perspiration on the cooks' foreheads, the dining room is also a considerably cooler place.

In the rear banquette section, a party of eight dines at the two tables there. Rather than individual chairs, banquette tables are furnished with sofas even more comfortable than the individual padded chairs in the main dining area. The two banquette sections at either end of the dining room are set off by glass partitions, beautifully etched with alternating monads and an interesting leaf design; these panels help create a cozier and more private setting than exists at one of the eight main tables. The windows in each banquette section are slightly shorter than those in the main dining area. The latter ones are $67\frac{1}{2}$ inches long, to be precise, whereas the banquet section windows are $54\frac{1}{2}$ inches long.

Soft background music draws our attention to the train's PA system, which pipes recorded music during meal times to all but the first two cars in the train. Taped music, radio, and paging equipment for this train is located in a locker at the forward end of the dining car. Master control switches permit taped music, radio, or paging to be directed either to the forward or rear half of the train, or simultaneously to both halves. Paging microphones are located at three places: the conductor's desk in C-251, the Stewardess-Nurse's station mounted flush into the wall of the dining car kitchen on the aisle side, and the dining car steward's desk. Independently operating entertainment radios are available for use in the Traveller's Rest car and in the observation lounge car. The latter two cars usually play either recorded music or locally broadcast radio programs during all hours of the day. Each car in this train has individual volume control for loudspeakers. Before stepping out of the dining car, we pause to reflect once again on the delicious meal enjoyed here only two hours ago.

It is time to move on. This car's pneumatic end door at the rear of the dining room, however, is unique on this train, and it is unique in two respects. First, unlike the swinging, forward end door on this car, the rear end door slides open. Instead of a pull handle, this door has a flat rectangular push button about three by five inches in size mounted flush on the door. An identical push button is on the other side of the door. A push of either button causes the door to slide neatly into a pocket for a few seconds before it slides back closed.

The other way in which the rear door on the dining car is unique is in what it represents, for it is a very real boundary. Coach passengers are not permitted to pass beyond the dining car, for behind its rear door are the sleeping cars—the section of the train reserved for first class passengers. It is an area of plush carpet, heavy curtains, private rooms, and a luxurious lounge.

Not least, there are two glass penthouses back there as well.

Chapter 8

First Class Luxury

The Northern Pacific (NP) has gone to great lengths to make the first class section of the *Vista-Dome North Coast Limited* as luxurious as possible. Unlike other famous, named trains, there are no open sections in the sleeping cars on this train. Except the first class lounge (in the rear car) and the two dome sections, these cars are "all-room" Pullmans, a world of complete privacy, where it is *quiet*. First class accommodations range from as small as a duplex roomette to as large as a compartment, with several options in between. Anywhere from one to four people can travel together in a private room with the right choice of accommodation. As we tour the last five cars in our train, we will get a better idea of what is back there. We will even get a chance to peek into most of the rooms.

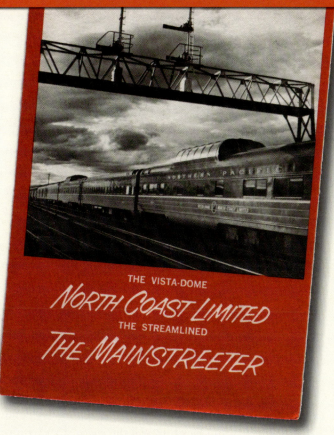

101

The Vista-Dome North Coast Limited

255
Sleeper (8-6-4)
367–372; Pullman-Standard; 1954
Chicago–Seattle

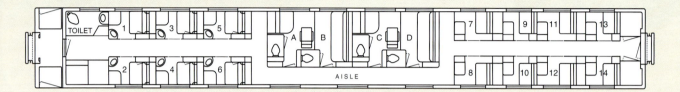

Stepping into car 255, we notice its vestibule at the forward end. All standard (flat top) sleeping cars on the *North Coast* are designed to be operated this way. Although some sleeping car seats face rearward, most face forward and none can be pivoted or otherwise reversed. The designation "8-6-4" signifies eight duplex roomettes, six roomettes, and four double bedrooms. These cars have more modern features than the 1948 350-series cars, as we shall see.

Just inside the forward pneumatic end door, we find a single restroom (no dressing room) on our left, an electric locker, and controls next to a trio of luggage shelves on our right. Carpeted flooring begins just as we step ahead into the roomette section. Sleeping cars are noticeably quiet, regardless of train speed or time of day. The carpet is fairly thick and, aided by roomette curtains, muffles sounds. There is no porter's section in this car; he is assigned to duplex roomette 14 (a "lower" roomette) at the back of the car. A roomette is slightly larger than a duplex roomette, but both are designed for single occupancy. Roomettes 1, 3, and 5 are on the right side of the car (our left when walking toward the rear of the train). Roomettes 2, 4, and 6 are on the left side of the car.

Roomette 1 in this car is assigned to the Pullman conductor. He is a Pullman employee, whose job is to manage the sale and occupancy of first class space aboard this train, striving for the highest possible load factor. An empty room is wasted space and revenue, part of a fixed supply that cannot be reduced to match demand by leaving the room behind for another trip. The Pullman conductor collects fare (the term "fare" can refer either to the price of a ticket or to the ticket itself) and room tickets (which show the assigned room and associated space charge) from first class passengers; he later provides these and occupancy information to the train conductor. This is not always as simple as it sounds. Sometimes there are "no-shows" or other last minute changes to reservations. Generally, if a room suddenly becomes available, the Pullman conductor communicates that fact to down-line ticket agents who may then sell the space. This requires a fair amount of coordination, but the system has been refined and works well.

Roomette 2 in this car is assigned to the Stewardess-Nurse, who is required to be on duty from 7:30 A.M. until 10:00 P.M., local time. She is allotted a one hour break in mid-morning and another hour in the afternoon of the second day out, each direction. Generally, the train conductor and Pullman conductor screen passengers' requests for her services when she is off duty, and, during those hours, she is called upon only in cases of emergency.

One of the other roomettes appears to be unoccupied at the moment. (It is sold to a passenger who will board at Minneapolis.) A peek inside reveals a small, carpeted room with a plush seat large enough for one to spread out a little, a full-size "Murphy-type" bed stowed vertically in the wall behind the seat, a sink and mirror, and a toilet covered by an oversize, rectangular padded lid doubling as a footstool. With a turn of the locking lever (usually by the porter), the bed rotates down into horizontal position, causing the seat back to fold neatly against the matching-shaped seat bottom. Controls for this room are several,

Chapter 8: First Class Luxury

These builder's photos of car 370, taken on October 26, 1954, show that 8-6-4 sleepers had no porter's section. Although these cars appear to be similar to the 8-6-3-1 sleepers, there are differences in mechanical equipment, the B-end skirts, roof vents, and window size and position, including the window on the vestibule door. These cars operate with the vestibule forward.
Pullman-Standard photos; Bill Kuebler collection

103

The Vista-Dome North Coast Limited

Center aisle, looking toward the forward entry area of 8-6-4 sleeper 370. This section of the car contains six roomettes. Curtains have not yet been installed over the roomette doors. October 26, 1954, builder's photo. *Pullman-Standard photo; Bill Kuebler collection*

all within arm's reach: individual light controls for overhead and reading lights; a control for the rubber-bladed fan (blades are harmless to the touch even when the fan is on); heating and air-conditioning controls; a speaker control; and a porter call button. Ice water is on tap in every Pullman room. A small wardrobe is tucked in between the seat and aisle-side wall. A sliding door can be closed and latched from the inside for privacy and sound insulation. Ceiling-to-floor curtains outside the door can be zipped closed, permitting the occupant some privacy when standing in the aisle to raise and lower the bed. Finally, there is a large picture window with a shade designed to make the room truly dark inside during broad daylight, if so desired. For a single occupant, there is enough room and plenty of comfort and privacy.

Double bedrooms A, B, C, and D (lettered from the forward end aft), are located in the middle of the car; the aisle bypassing them extends along the car's left side. Bedrooms A and C are arranged with the beds lengthwise and daytime seats facing rearward. Bedrooms B and D have crosswise beds with a daytime sofa facing forward. The rearward facing seats in rooms A and C are a little smaller than a full sofa, so an extra sitting chair is included in these rooms. The sofas in bedrooms B and D are each large enough for three adults, even though the room is designed for two. Each bedroom has a separate, enclosed lavatory. This is one of the more modern features of this car as compared with the 1948 cars, which do not have enclosed lavatories in their double bedrooms. Equipped with an upper and lower berth—uppers in B and D rotate down and those in A and C drop straight down into the nighttime position—each double bedroom can accommodate two adults or one adult and two children. Adjacent rooms (A-B and C-D) can be arranged as a suite by folding back the

Chapter 8: First Class Luxury

These two photos show Roomette 4 in car 370. The sink is fixed in the position shown. A small shelf on the front wall is just large enough for a small carry-on bag. Large luggage pieces may be stowed on one of the luggage shelves located just inside the car's forward entry door. October 26, 1954.
Pullman-Standard photos; Bill Kuebler collection

wall dividing them. Each room has a large picture window and the same controls found in the roomette, with more options for lighting.

The aisle returns to the center of the car as we enter the rear third, where the duplex roomettes are located. These carpeted rooms are arranged in an alternating "upper" and "lower" fashion, giving this car its distinctive window arrangement. This design allows for an extra pair of rooms by permitting slide-away stowage of a lower room's berth under the floor of the upper duplex roomette ahead, an ingenious method that maximizes use of available space. Upper rooms' Murphy-type beds are rotated down in the usual fashion. Space in duplex roomettes is conserved by use of fold-away washbasins above the toilet, whereas the

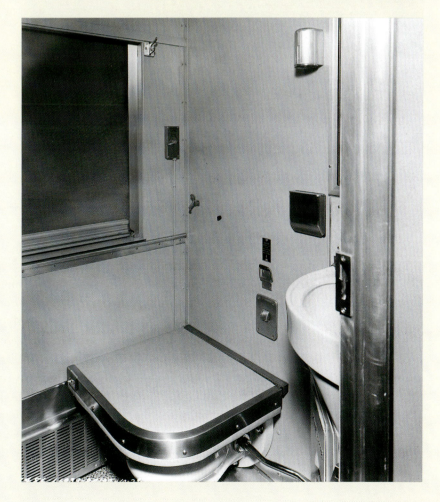

105

The Vista-Dome North Coast Limited

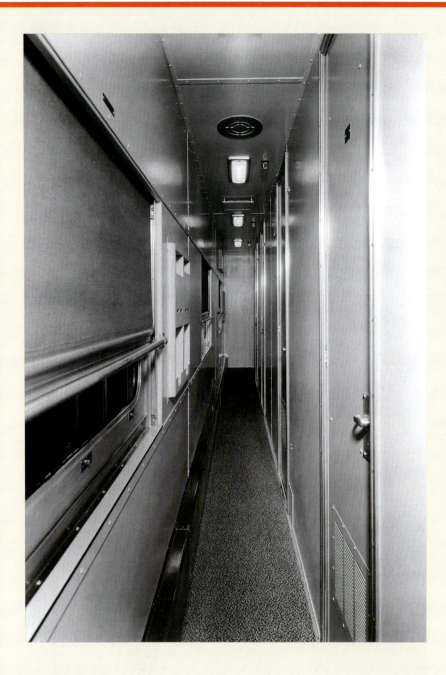

Looking forward along the side aisle around the double bedrooms in car 370. The aisle window in the foreground is hinged for emergency egress. Just ahead of it is a rack for timetables, the hotel "Red Book," and telegram blanks. The aisle returns to center for the eight duplex roomettes in the rear third of the car, and for the six roomettes in the forward third. Double bedrooms do not have curtains outside their doors. October 26, 1954.
Pullman-Standard photo; Bill Kuebler collection

washbasins in this car's roomettes are fixed. A duplex rommette is a little less expensive than a roomette, since it is slightly smaller. Controls are the same as those in roomettes, as are the long curtains hanging outside each sliding door. Each upper duplex roomette is equipped with a semi-recessed step in the aisle.

Each room in this car (and all the other sleeping cars) has a compartment just large enough for one or two pairs of shoes. It is accessible from inside the room and from the aisle outside. Leave your shoes and a tip inside this compartment before retiring to bed, and your nicely polished shoes will be waiting for you when you awake in the morning. This is a tradition maintained by porters, one of whom is available around the clock by the push of your call button.

Sleeping car porters are Pullman employees and are supervised by the Pullman conductor. They work very long hours, the longest of any employees on the train. Each is allotted a mere four hours off per night. Porters in adjacent cars must alternate their time off, so that the on duty one can cover both cars during the time the other one is off duty. During two-car duty, a porter will set his call button controls so that any call button in either car will ring at his station. When there are five sleeping cars in the train, the porter in 259 (the sleeper-observation-lounge) usually covers cars 257, 258, and 259 as the porters in cars 257 and 258 take the same rest period; that way, all five porters can be off duty during night hours. Most porters are very friendly, and all of them are professional and justifiably proud of their work.

Chapter 8: First Class Luxury

Double bedrooms B and D in car 370 are arranged crosswise and face forward. The small sign above the window reads "HINGED SASH," so this is Bedroom D. The hinged egress window has a stainless steel frame around it, unpainted on both sides. Protective webbing for the upper berth is not yet installed in the night set-up, but the porter would be sure to do so whenever "turning down" the berth for nighttime use. October 26, 1954.
Pullman-Standard photos; Bill Kuebler collection

Cars 367–372 are very well built and provide a smooth, quiet ride. Every revenue space in this car is occupied or reserved at this point, not unusual during summer travel. In fact, this car was probably sold out weeks in advance. Passengers' destinations vary in this car, most of them traveling to Spokane or points west, and two or three traveling overnight to points Missoula and east. On this train, the bedrooms usually sell out first, then the roomettes, then the duplex roomettes. There are no sections in this car or anywhere else on this train. The NP learned a lesson from other railroads by observing that open sec-

107

The Vista-Dome North Coast Limited

Double Bedrooms A and C in car 370 are arranged lengthwise and face rearward. This view depicts Bedroom C set up for daytime use. The washroom annex is compact, but it affords privacy. Its stainless steel sink rotates up and into the back wall for drainage and stowage. Double bedrooms in 8-6-4 sleepers are almost identical to those in dome sleepers. The layout is the same, but the light fixtures and a few other details are slightly different. October 26, 1954.
Pullman-Standard photo; Bill Kuebler collection

tions were almost always the last spaces to sell, because they were the least plush and were hardly private.

Mechanically, these cars are very similar to Deluxe Day-Nite coaches 586 and 587. Air-conditioning is by Trane, the generator has a Spicer drive, but each room has individual heating.

Double Bedroom C in car 370 is set up for single occupancy nighttime use. For double occupancy, the upper berth can be lowered straight down from the ceiling. October 26, 1954.
Pullman-Standard photo; Bill Kuebler collection

Chapter 8: First Class Luxury

One of the upper duplex roomettes in car 370 is set up for night time use, showing how the seat back folds down neatly against the bottom seat cushion. October 26, 1954. *Pullman-Standard photo; Bill Kuebler collection*

When 8-6-4 sleeper 372 was built in 1954, it was equipped with the most modern features available, including a Trane air conditioning system and a Spicer drive generator. Several differences in external details may be seen when comparing this car to the 1948 sleeping cars in the 350 series. Note the more streamlined appearance of the roof vents, the shorter B-end skirt, and the unpainted frame around the egress window. Minneapolis, July 1971. *William A. Raia collection*

109

The Vista-Dome North Coast Limited

256
Dome Sleeper (4-4-4)
307–313; CB&Q 304, 305; SP&S 306; Budd; 1954
314; Budd; 1957

Chicago–Seattle

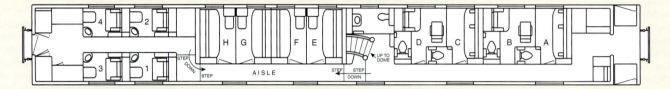

This is our assigned car. Dome sleepers on the *North Coast Limited* are unique, the only cars built to this floor plan. They are also the most expensive and heaviest cars in the train, at some $284,000 and $77\frac{1}{2}$ tons each, respectively. (Car 314 was purchased in 1957 for $368,000. In 1999 dollars, these two figures would be about $1.59 million and $2.06 million, respectively.) The "4-4-4" floor plan means four roomettes, four duplex single rooms, and four double bedrooms.

An NP dome sleeper is cause for a little digression. The road faced some interesting decisions before purchasing these cars.

Many observers have wondered why the NP did not purchase full dome cars for its first class passengers as did chief rivals Great Northern (GN) and Milwaukee Road. A popular misconception is that the NP could not (or would not) afford the cost of full domes. This is untrue. The NP paid a total of $4.4 million for all its dome cars, and the GN paid about $4.6 million for its dome car fleet, including five full domes. These figures exclude cars owned by Chicago, Burlington, and Quincy (CB&Q) or Spokane, Portland, and Seattle (SP&S). This difference in expenditure is insignificant, and NP company annual reports reflect that capital was available for purchase of full domes, if that were the choice. Some have suggested that a full dome presents a greater risk in the event of overturning in an accident. While that may be true, no evidence has yet surfaced to show that this was a factor in the decision.

The reason for NP's decision is much simpler and more logical—and, seems obvious to those who have ridden in both types of dome cars. According to former NP Vice President of Operations, Norman Lorentzsen, the decision boiled down to which type of car was deemed to be the best for the purpose, and on this point, NP officials simply believed that a "short dome" was the better choice. Their rationale makes sense. The purpose of a vista-dome, by definition, is to afford passengers maximum viewing of the passing scenery, and we have already noted the abundance of scenery on the NP. According to available evidence, the NP decided that a full-length dome actually defeats the purpose implied by an elevated dome section. Structural integrity and other factors require a full dome's roof to be much wider than that of a conventional, "short" dome. This cuts down substantially on the available angle of upward view, while the sheer length of the full dome cuts down substantially on the forward vision afforded most of its occupants. In a full dome, passengers in some 14 rows of seats on the left side and almost as many on the right have their forward vision obstructed by a long roof or the back of someone's head. (The forward most seats on the right side are some distance back from the front window, to accommodate a stairwell.)

What about passengers' preferences? Ironically, the GN experiences the phenomenon of first class passengers frequently seeking space in the dome *coaches* ahead when the scenery gets interesting. By now, in 1959, GN passenger department personnel have learned that, in terms of viewing

Chapter 8: First Class Luxury

Dome sleeper 310 poses for the Budd Company photographer in Philadelphia, October 1954. It is painted and lettered for NP service, except VISTA-DOME NORTH COAST LIMITED slogans will be added by Pullman shop forces in Calumet, Illinois, in early 1956. Budd designed dome sleepers to be operated with the vestibule to the rear.
Budd photos; Bill Kuebler collection

111

Just inside the forward entry door on dome sleeper 310 are these luggage shelves and the clean linen locker, on the car's right side. Normally, roomette and duplex single room occupants keep their luggage here or on similar shelves at the rear of the car, whereas double bedroom occupants stow their luggage inside their rooms, atop the washroom annex. October 1954.
Budd photo; Bill Kuebler collection

scenery, their "short domes" are more popular than the full dome, a result that validates NP's choice not to buy the latter type. As for lounge space, the full domes are hard to beat. But, that makes the point: they are more appropriate for lounging than for viewing scenery. The NP, on the other hand, prefers to ensconce its first class lounge space where it has traditionally been for decades, at the end of the train in a plush observation-lounge car. Finally, in retrospect, the full domes have turned out to be under-engineered, rather unusual for Budd equipment of this era. (They will suffer air-conditioning problems during most of their GN careers.)

In all respects, NP's dome sleepers are probably *the* nicest cars in its flagship train. There is something to be said about rising from bed, getting dressed, and finding stairs to a true *vista*-dome a few feet down the aisle. Not only that, the design of this car affords some of the best single-occupancy space on the train. Shall we take a look?

As noted earlier, dome sleepers are designed to be operated vestibule to the rear. Immediately inside the front pneumatic end door we find linen lockers on either side. Next are three stacked luggage shelves on our left, and a cup and ice water dispenser across the aisle, with more luggage shelves above the dispenser. Next is the roomette section, containing four roomettes. These roomettes are very similar to those we saw in the previous car, except that roomettes 3 and 1 are on our right, 4 and 2 on our left, as we walk back. Since the vestibule is at the rear, rooms are numbered from that end forward.

Just aft of roomettes 1 and 2, the carpeted aisle bends to our right as we walk back and simultaneously drops two steps to allow passage under the dome, along the car's left side. This under-the-dome section is where the four duplex single rooms are located. This type of room is found only in the dome sleepers and is arguably the best space available for the dollar. Space charge is slightly higher than that for a roomette, but the extra space is substantial. The toilet, with a large padded cover, is like those found in roomettes, and a sink above rotates up into a recess, just below an ice water dispenser. The window is slightly smaller than a roomette's, however. Instead of a wide, single

Chapter 8: First Class Luxury

seat, each of these rooms has a full-length sofa positioned crosswise, alternately facing fore and aft from one room to the next. One can really stretch out here! The bed rotates down from the wall behind the sofa to a crosswise orientation, causing the sofa back to fold down like a roomette seat. Some experienced passengers prefer crosswise orientation for sleeping, believing that it has less of a tendency to roll one out of bed on curves. This author, however, has found the difference in orientation to be minor. What is more noticeable about these duplex single rooms is that they are located where the ride is best—down low, under the dome and just below the car's center-of-gravity, and approximately in the middle of the car. Motion caused by curves and track irregularities is minimal here, and the clickety-clack of jointed rail almost unheard. These rooms probably accommodate the best possible night's sleep on a fast streamliner, and more than one traveler with funds enough for a double bedroom has opted for one of these rooms instead. Duplex single rooms are lettered as bedrooms E, F, G, and H, from the rear forward. Adjacent duplex single rooms (E-F and G-H) can be opened into a suite arrangement, perfect for two travelers.

Just aft of the duplex single rooms, the aisle steps up twice, back to the main level. At chest height on our left between these two steps is a large, curved speaker for public address messages and music. Next to the speaker is the narrow stairwell to the dome section. It has seven carpeted and lighted steps and is slightly curved, identical to the stairwell in a dome coach. Stair railings in this car are also stainless steel.

The dome section is identical to that in a dome coach, except that the 24 seats are a slightly different color in the sleepers. These are a medium blue, instead of turquoise. It is not uncommon to find several empty dome seats here, even during the daytime, because the ratio of supply and demand for dome seats in the first class section of this train is far better than in the coach section. A maximum of only 82 first class passengers compete for dome space;

Across the aisle from the forward luggage shelves is an extra luggage shelf situated atop an ice water and cup dispenser. Just forward of these is the soiled linen locker. At the top of the forward entry door is the equipment number indicating car 310. Just below are number boxes for the car line number. This car's entry doors have pneumatic door opening devices. October 1954.
Budd photo; Bill Kuebler collection

The Vista-Dome North Coast Limited

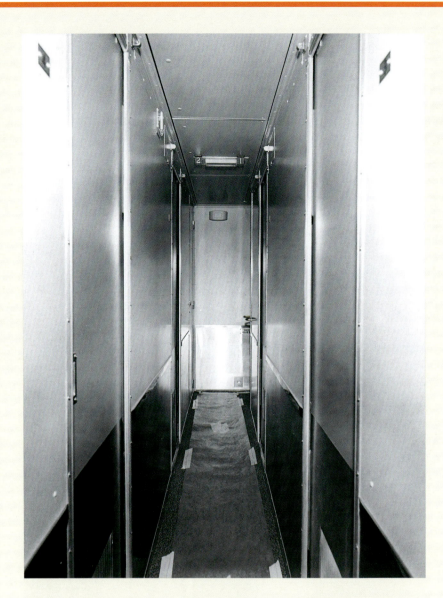

Four roomettes are at the forward end of Dome Sleeper 310, as seen in this view looking aft. Curtains have been removed for this photo. In the distance the center aisle bends to the right and drops two steps to provide a passageway under the dome and along the side of the car. October 1954.
Budd photo; Bill Kuebler collection

there are about three times that many people in the coaches. Between the dining car, the observation-lounge car, and well-appointed private rooms, first class passengers have more than one desirable place to ride on this train.

As we reach the bottom of the stairs to head back, we notice the main level restroom on our left (car's right side). A peek inside reveals a room that looks unused, just as shiny as it was the day this car rolled out of the Budd factory. Is this place a well-kept secret, or a testimony to the standards of cleanliness for this train?

Four double bedrooms, all located on the main level behind the dome section occupy the last section of this car. They are lettered as bedrooms A, B, C, and D from the rear forward. They are nearly identical in arrangement and appearance as the ones we saw in car 255. All four have enclosed washroom facilities. The aisle around the duplex single rooms continues along the car's left side to bypass all four double bedrooms. The window for bedroom C, my assigned space, is a hinged egress window, as is the one in the aisle opposite this room. Let's step inside bedroom C and take a closer look.

The door opens inward, as usual. Immediately on our right is a just-right size wardrobe, enough space for two or three suits. Behind the door is the entrance to the enclosed washroom. It is compact, but everything we need is right there: covered toilet with sink above that rotates down into position (the sink drains water just by rotating up for stowage); ice water dispenser; mirror; plenty of good lighting; a razor blade receptacle; and ventilation controls. The floor inside the washroom is hard rubber. There is plenty of linen on hand. If one were so inclined, a sponge bath here is feasible. Back inside the room, we find a sofa long enough for three adults, even though this room is designed for two. The sofa has three armrests; they can be stowed to a neat, flush position, into the

Chapter 8: First Class Luxury

The wardrobe of Roomette 2 in Dome Sleeper 310 is small but adequate for one person's use. The porter call button on the control panel is within arm's reach of the passenger, day or night. All roomettes face forward. October 1954.
Budd photo; Bill Kuebler collection

back of the sofa, making it easy to stretch out. The lower berth is stowed in the wall behind this sofa. The berth rotates down to a horizontal position, causing the sofa back to fold down to the seat, much like the seats in roomettes. The upper berth rotates down for nighttime use, and when the birth is lowered, nylon webbing may be clipped into place to keep the sleeping passenger from accidentally rolling out of bed—it's about five and a half feet to the floor. The steps on the upper berth's ladder are carpeted. A large picture window and the usual controls complete the room. As with the double bedrooms seen earlier, the walls between bedrooms A and B, and between C and D, can be opened to create a suite arrangement. At the moment, the wall between our rooms is folded back.

Roomette seats have armrests that can be folded up flush with the seat back. This is Roomette 2 in car 310. October 1954.
Budd photo; Bill Kuebler collection

The Vista-Dome North Coast Limited

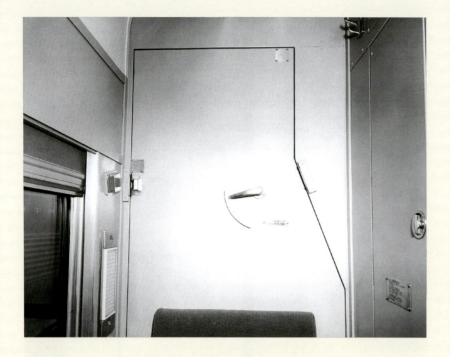

Murphy bed stowed for daytime use in Roomette 2, dome sleeper 310. October 1954.
Budd photo; Bill Kuebler collection

Your room, bedroom D, faces bedroom C. It, too, has a separate enclosed washroom, this one oriented sideways rather than fore-aft. Otherwise, the annex is identical to mine. This room's seat is about half a sofa, or a little less, so an extra sitting chair is present. The lower berth—a Murphy-type bed—rotates down to a lengthwise horizontal position alongside the large picture window. The upper berth is stowed in the ceiling and drops straight down (it is countersprung) for nighttime use. Since our rooms each have only one occupant, the upper berths will remain stowed at night. Single occupancy is permitted in a double bedroom with the purchase of a single first class fare plus the space charge.

The large mirror above the lavatory and toilet make a roomette seem larger than it is. Note the ice water tap above the sink. Roomette 2, car 310. October 1954.
Budd photo; Bill Kuebler collection

116

Chapter 8: First Class Luxury

Looking aft along the side aisle under the dome in car 310. Duplex Single Rooms E–H are in the left foreground. Double Bedrooms A–D are further down the aisle, just beyond where the aisle returns to main level. The seat visible at the far end of the corridor is for the porter. October 1954.
Budd photo; Bill Kuebler collection

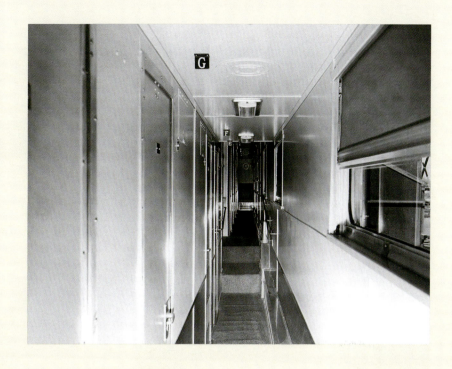

At the end of the aisle is a porter's seat and annunciator controls. Porter "Robbie" Robinson is occupied at the moment, "turning down" another passenger's berth in bedroom A for nighttime use. As we pass by the room, he greets us with a nod. Shall we ask him to turn down our beds next and close the partition between the rooms?

Duplex Single Rooms E and F in dome sleeper 310 are opened "en-suite" to form one larger room by folding back the dividing wall, a perfect arrangement for two travelers. The best possible night's sleep on the *Vista-Dome North Coast Limited* is probably had in one of these rooms. They are located low under the dome and near the center of the car, providing the best ride. Each room has a large daytime sofa with arms that can be stowed flush, so a person can really stretch out here. The fan in each room has rubber safety blades. The sink under each ice water tap has been rotated up into the stowed position. October 1954.
Budd photo; Bill Kuebler collection

117

The Vista-Dome North Coast Limited

The stairwell in a dome sleeper is identical to the one in a dome coach. Note the radio and P.A. speaker just to the left of the stairwell. A public restroom is located on the main level, just out of view to the right of the stairwell. What can compare with waking up at sunrise feeling refreshed, getting dressed, and climbing these stairs to take in the beauty of North Dakota's badlands or Washington's Green River Valley (westbound), or the Clark Fork River valley east of Missoula (eastbound)? This is truly first class travel!
Budd photo; Bill Kuebler collection

Chapter 8: First Class Luxury

The Budd Company photographer took this picture looking forward in the dome section while dome sleeper 310 was still inside the shop complex. The author's first dome ride was in this car from Fargo to Mandan in May 1966, a splendid "midnight ride" on the *North Coast Limited*. (See NPRHA's quarterly, *The Mainstreeter*, Summer 1998 and Spring 1999 for a full account of that trip.) Any dome seat in one of the *North Coast Limited's* dome sleepers is the best seat in the house. October 1954.
Budd photo; Bill Kuebler collection

Sure, why not? We do, he nods, and the job is as good as done. The next time we step into our rooms, say, about 10 P.M., we will find them partitioned and ready for nighttime use, reading lights left on for us.

That will present some delightfully difficult decisions, however. Does one crawl into bed with a good book? Or, does one head for the dome to take in a little more night time railroading along the double track of St. Paul Division's 2nd Subdivision, highlighted by the moon's reflection off Lake Detroit? Or, does one head back to join the group of 10 or so people in the obs-lounge having a wonderful time telling stories and drinking and snacking? After all, one of them could be (and once was, in 1956) Elvis Presley himself. Or maybe Bing Crosby or Tennessee Ernie Ford. Or how about Johnny Carson, Dean Martin or Jerry Lewis, or Duke Ellington, or even Walt Disney? Not least, there's NBC's Chet Huntley (who was born in the NP depot at Cardwell, Montana) and Weyerhaeuser's namesake founder and president. Yes, all these names have appeared at least once

The Vista-Dome North Coast Limited

on a Pullman conductor's *North Coast Limited* passenger manifest, and some of them will appear several times again. That *would* be interesting company, now, wouldn't it? So, what's it going to be, bedroom, dome, or lounge? Ah, the difficulties facing the first class passenger on this train! I, for one, will opt for the lounge for a short while, and then the dome, perhaps in time to take in the lake country, Hawley cut, and Stockwood fill. At that time of night, the dome will be peaceful and quiet, and the "movie" up there unbeatable—and in "3-D."

Meanwhile, let's finish our tour. At the porter's seat in our dome sleeper the aisle re-aligns to the center of the car. There are some more luggage shelves on our left, a small broom closet on our right, and a large electric locker and controls opposite the closet. Next we step through the end door into the vestibule.

Mechanically, these cars are identical to the dome coaches. Car 314, the dome sleeper built in 1957, is equipped with Timken roller bearings; the original 10 dome sleepers are equipped with Hyatt bearings. Otherwise, car 314 is identical to the other 10 dome sleepers. Unlike GN's full domes, these dome sleepers rarely experience air conditioning problems. Like the dome coaches, they are very well engineered.

Dome section of car 310, looking aft. This car has just been rolled out of the shop and is ready for delivery to the NP. Note the emergency equipment locker on the main level bulkhead, visible just beyond the stairwell. The small rack just to the right of the locker will soon be stocked with NP public timetables and various brochures. October 1954.
Budd photo; Bill Kuebler collection

Chapter 8: First Class Luxury

The seat in Double Bedroom D in dome sleeper 310 faces rearward, and the bed is arranged lengthwise. In this view the room is set up for daytime use. For nighttime use the upper berth can be lowered straight down out of the ceiling, but only after the lower berth has been rotated out of the back wall and down into the nighttime position. The door at the left is to the washroom annex. The extra sitting chair in this room is not visible in this view. October 1954. *Budd photo; Bill Kuebler collection*

Double Bedroom D is now set up for nighttime use—sans linen, however. How many passengers will occupy this room during car 310's NP career, and how many of their names would we recognize? October 1954. *Budd photo; Bill Kuebler collection*

121

The Vista-Dome North Coast Limited

Double Bedroom C in car 310 is arranged cross-wise, set up for day occupancy (above) and night occupancy (below). The entrance to the washroom annex is out of view, just to the photographer's right. October 1954.
Budd photo; Bill Kuebler collection

Chapter 8: First Class Luxury

The porter's seat in car 310 is located at the aft end of the side aisle. The annunciator panel and chime can be seen in the upper right corner of this October 1954 photo. When a passenger rings for the porter, the chime sounds and the annunciator panel indicates which room is calling. This system can be connected in series with that of adjacent cars so one porter can cover two cars during nighttime rest periods when the other porter is off duty. During his four-hour rest period each night, the porter in a dome sleeper usually finds space in an unoccupied room, either in his car or in one of the other sleepers, or he uses the porter's section in one of the older sleeping cars.
Budd photo; Bill Kuebler collection

The Vista-Dome North Coast Limited

During most of 1961, dome sleepers operated in car lines 255/265 and 257/267, not their usual positions. Photographed in November 1961 from the dome in car line 255, train No. 26 is safely in the siding at Greycliff to meet its westbound counterpart. Train No. 26 is lead by F-9A no. 6700A. Depending on the year, this was usually the scheduled meeting point for trains 25 and 26 on the Yellowstone Division. The car ahead of 255 is a Pullman-Standard diner in the 450–457 series, substituting for a Budd diner undergoing periodic maintenance at Como Shops.
A. C. Kalmbach photo; Bill Kuebler collection

Moments later, No. 25 rounds the curve at milepost 72 on a northwesterly heading and appears to assault the Crazy Mountains, looming ahead. It is an illusion, however, for less than eight miles ahead, near Big Timber, No. 25 will change to a southwesterly heading and continue following the Yellowstone River. From there it will approach an even more formidable barrier, formed by the Gallatin and Bridger ranges and crossed via Bozeman Pass. The westbound approach to the Montana Rockies is very dramatic when seen through the front window of a dome.
A. C. Kalmbach photo; Bill Kuebler collection

Chapter 8: First Class Luxury

On an overcast day in November 1961, No. 25 approaches the east portal of Bozeman Tunnel, built in 1945 to replace the older, original tunnel. The original tunnel's portal, boarded up, can be seen to the left. The summit of Bozeman Pass is just outside the west portal of the new tunnel, so these three diesel units are still working upgrade at a high throttle setting, evidenced by the cloud of exhaust above them. This photograph was made from the dome sleeper in line 255, an unusual car line arrangement that dated back to the early weeks of 1961 and would end about two weeks after this photo was taken.
A. C. Kalmbach photo; Bill Kuebler collection

257
Sleeper (8-6-3-1)
350-363; SP&S 366; CB&Q 480-482
Pullman-Standard; 1948
Chicago–Portland

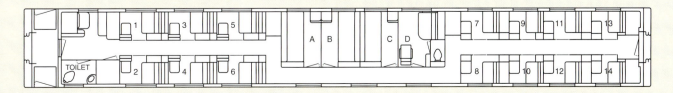

The Vista-Dome North Coast Limited

The designation "8-6-3-1" indicates eight duplex roomettes, six roomettes, three double bedrooms, and one compartment. These cars were originally named after cities along the NP line. (See accompanying table.)

This car is designed to operate vestibule forward. Apart from its floor plan, its basic construction is very similar to that of coaches in series 588–599, including its mechanical equipment. Immediately after entering the forward end of this car, we see a linen storage cabinet, ice water dispenser, porter's section, and an electrical cabinet on our left. On our right there is a restroom and, just aft of it, a luggage locker. The porter's section is open with a rear-facing seat. At night, a bed is created by rotating down halves which, when horizontal, rest upon the cabinets fore and aft of the section. A curtain can then be drawn for some privacy. Roomettes are numbered the same as those in the 8-6-4 sleepers. Their features are very similar, except that the washbasin is not fixed; it is stowed by tipping it up and into a recessed space. This was done not to conserve space, but because the toilet is located directly under the sink in these cars, rather than alongside the opposite wall. An equipment locker accessible from the aisle is tucked in behind Roomette 5.

The most notable differences in accommodations between this car and the newer, 8-6-4 sleepers is the porter's section (the newer cars do not have one) and the double bedrooms. Like the newer cars' double bedrooms, this car's are located in the center third, but there are only three instead of four. All three are equipped with a crosswise sofa by day and crosswise upper and lower berths by night, rather than alternating fore-aft and crosswise orientations. Each double bedroom has no washroom annex. Rather, the toilet in each room is tipped up and into a metal cabinet for stowage. A sink is fixed above the metal cabinet. These double bedrooms are a little less modern than those in the newer cars, but they were certainly state-of-the-art in 1948. Double bedrooms are lettered from the front aft, A, B, and C.

Rather than a fourth double bedroom, there is one compartment lettered D. The term "compartment" is deceiving, perhaps leading one to believe that it is smaller than a double bedroom. A compartment affords slightly *more* space and commands a slightly higher charge than a double bedroom. It has a forward-facing half-sofa by day (with extra sitting chair) and lengthwise upper and lower berths by night. It also has an enclosed washroom similar to those found in the newer cars' double bedrooms. It is definitely the largest and nicest room in this car. Double bedrooms A and B can be opened *"en suite"* as in other cars; double bedroom C and compartment D can also be opened into a large suite, ideal for a family of four or five.

8-6-3-1 Sleeping Car Names and Numbers

Pullman-Standard sleeping cars of the 8-6-3-1 plan were given numbers when repainted into the "Loewy scheme" beginning in 1953. In the pre-Loewy scheme these cars had names but no numbers; they did not simultaneously carry both name and number. Numbering in 1953 was as follows:

Loewy Scheme No.	Pre-Loewy Scheme Name
350	Detroit Lakes
351	Billings
352	Fargo
353	Walla Walla
354	Missoula
355	Bismarck
356	Aberdeen
357	Brainerd
358	Butte
359	Valley City
360	Pasco
361	Helena
362	Jamestown
363	Dickinson
SP&S 366	Portland
CB&Q 480	Chicago
CB&Q 481	Savanna
CB&Q 482	Dubuque

Chapter 8: First Class Luxury

Pullman-Standard 8-6-3-1 sleeping car 361, formerly "Helena," carries the markers of Train No. 2, the eastbound *Mainstreeter*, at Mandan in November 1961. In a few months this car will rotate back into *North Coast Limited* service.
Slide courtesy Northern Pacific Railway Historical Association

Named "Portland" from 1948 until it was repainted into the Loewy scheme and given number 366 in 1953, this 8-6-3-1 sleeper was owned by SP&S (until the BN merger), as denoted by the ownership letters in the upper corners. It is on stand-by status at Seattle in April 1971. For some strange reason, NORTHERN PACIFIC does not appear on the letterboard. It was probably removed sometime after the BN merger in March 1970.
Rick Leach photo

The Vista-Dome North Coast Limited

An open end door invites us into the forward end of an 8-6-3-1 sleeper. When this car was given Loewy colors in 1953, number 352 replaced the name "Fargo," but otherwise the interior of the car remained the same. The porter's section appears on the left. Just beyond are six roomettes. This builder's photo was taken in July 1948.
Pullman-Standard photo; Bill Kuebler collection

Chapter 8: First Class Luxury

This July 1948 view shows the cup dispenser, ice water tap, and porter's section of 8-6-3-1 sleeper "Fargo," numbered 352 in 1953. For nighttime use, the porter opens the door above the seat and positions a bed on top of the cabinets. He then can hang a privacy curtain on the rod just below the ceiling. *Pullman-Standard photo; Bill Kuebler collection*

The rear third of the car contains duplex roomettes 7 through 14, numbered front to rear as in the 8-6-4 cars. These are also arranged in the alternating upper and lower fashion, giving this car its staggered window pattern. With only minor differences in controls and interior decor, these duplexes are the same as those in the newer cars, curtains and all. At the back of the car are the soiled and clean linen lockers, on our left and right, respectively as we walk back.

These cars are not equipped with egress windows. In an accident, egress through any window can still be accomplished, however, by use of emergency equipment mounted in a small cabinet on an aisle wall.

This car is destined for Portland, as are most of its passengers. In future years (after 1960), however, the 8-6-4 sleepers will swap line numbers and positions in the train with the 8-6-3-1 sleepers. Whichever type of car is between the domes will operate in line 257 to Portland.

The Vista-Dome North Coast Limited

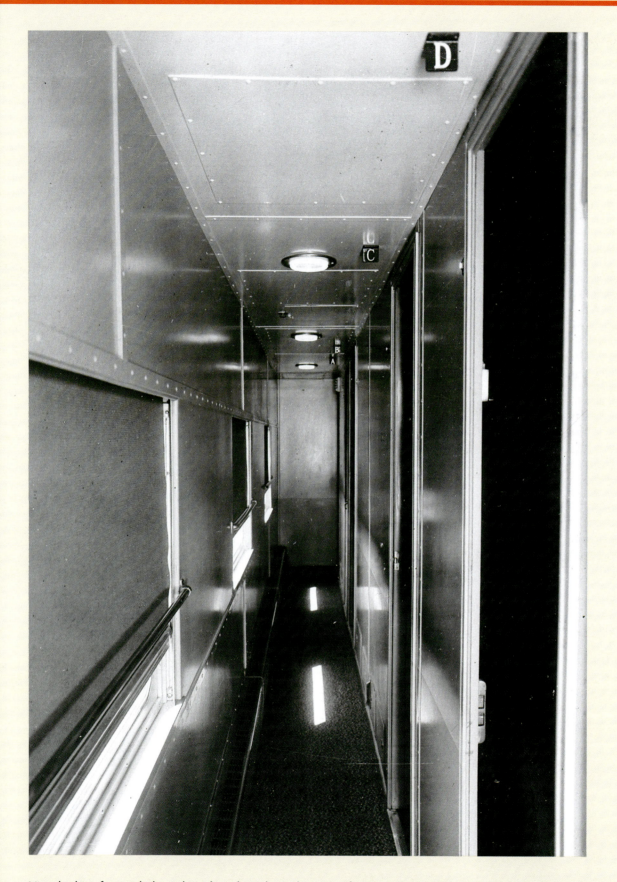

View looking forward along the side aisle in the mid-section of 8-6-3-1 sleeper "Fargo." Double Bedrooms A, B, and C and Compartment D are identified by letters affixed to the ceiling above the aisle. July 1948 builder's photo.
Pullman-Standard photo; Bill Kuebler collection

Chapter 8: First Class Luxury

The dividing wall between Bedroom C and Compartment D in sleeper "Fargo" (352) has been folded back, creating a suite arrangement. This view is looking forward from Compartment D into Bedroom C. July 1948.
Pullman-Standard photo; Bill Kuebler collection

View looking rearward from Bedroom C into Compartment D. A compartment is slightly larger than a bedroom. In an 8-6-3-1 sleeper, Compartment D is the only room with a separate enclosed washroom. Its door is at the right. July 1948.
Pullman-Standard photo; Bill Kuebler collection

131

The Vista-Dome North Coast Limited

These two views show Lower Duplex Roomette 13 in 8-6-3-1 sleeper "Fargo" (352). The bed is stowed directly under the upper duplex roomette ahead, in a space hidden by a small curtain. For nighttime use, the bed is rolled straight back and locked into position. It must be rolled forward to gain access to the toilet. Upper duplexes have a Murphy bed that rotates down from the wall behind the seat. July 1948. *Pullman-Standard photos; Bill Kuebler collection*

Chapter 8: First Class Luxury

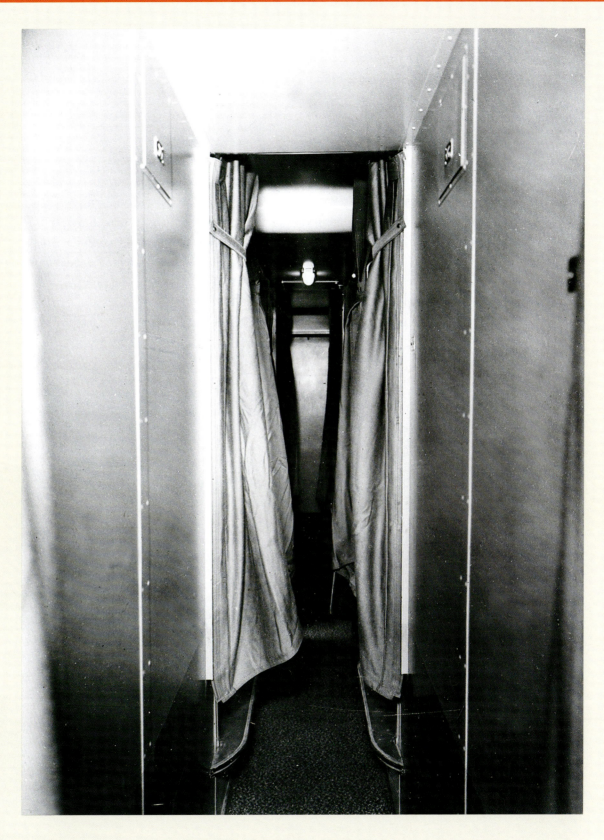

July 1948 view looking forward in the duplex roomette section of 8-6-3-1 sleeper "Fargo." Upper duplex roomettes 11 and 12 appear on either side of the aisle in the foreground. Note the small doors near the ceiling on either side of the aisle. They are access doors for shoe compartments that have similar access doors on the inside of the rooms; the porter shines shoes left in these compartments at night.
Pullman-Standard photo; Bill Kuebler collection

The Vista-Dome North Coast Limited

258
Dome Sleeper (4-4-4)
307-313; CB&Q 304, 305; SP&S 306; Budd; 1954
314; Budd; 1957
Chicago–Portland

The entire description given for the first dome sleeper (car line 256) applies to this car, except this one operates to Portland and it is next to the last car in the train. Being at this location, this is arguably the best dome in the train to ride. First, it is the furthest from the locomotive and, thus, the quietest dome. Second, it is within easy reach of the plush observation lounge car behind. A perch in this cool glass penthouse affords a fascinating view of 12 cars' worth of *North Coast Limited* ahead, winding its way along "the scenic route." The sight of the long train snaking around curve after curve is spellbinding, and no two curves seem exactly alike. By carefully watching the car tops and angles between them, one can detect vertical curves, places on a well-engineered railroad where the track gradually changes grade to ascend or descend hills. The careful observer can also detect a compound curve, one with varying degrees of curvature to the left or right. In single-track territory,

Dome sleeper 313 is unoccupied as it waits for its next assignment at Seattle in February 1970. The four windows for the duplex single rooms under the dome and the lower placement of the VISTA-DOME NORTH COAST LIMITED slogan give the right side of this car its distinctive appearance. The silver journal box covers, however, are not in accordance with standard NP painting practices, even though some of the Budd cars appeared this way at various times over the years.
Rick Leach photo

Chapter 8: First Class Luxury

When numbers are installed, the small, lighted number box just to the left of the vestibule indicates the car line, enabling passengers walking along the platform to find their assigned car. Note the small disc brake indicator plunger above the truck. When the car's brakes are applied, the plunger extends out about one inch, allowing brakemen to check train line integrity from the vestibule during running brake tests. Every car with disc brakes has a plunger on each side of the car. October 1954 builder's photo.
Budd photo; Bill Kuebler collection

a rather enjoyable neck exercise results from a strange obligation to watch every receding eastward semaphore behind the train, to see whether it clears after our passage or remains red for whatever reason.

By day or night, this is the best place on this train to repose in wonderful solitude and watch the quiet action. Even changes in weather, adverse for the motorist, can be welcome to us here. There is little to compare with the fascinating dances performed by lightning bolts across the Minnesota or North Dakota night sky, each flash, were it harnessed, enough electricity to power a city for who knows how long, yet rendered of no potential harm to us. What is better grounded than a steel train on steel rails extending, practically speaking, forever in either direction along the earth's surface?

In about two years time (in fall 1961), the NP will designate this rear dome as a Chicago–Seattle car line, leaving only one standard sleeping car to operate to Portland. Traffic patterns for Portland are barely sufficient to justify operating two sleeping cars to and from that city. Furthermore, loads in the Portland lines are decreasing somewhat, while Seattle loads are increasing slightly. The choice to operate one standard sleeping car rather than one dome sleeper to Portland following this

The Vista-Dome North Coast Limited

change is probably a simple matter of space. A standard sleeping car, depending on which type is used (8-6-3-1 vs. 8-6-4), can accommodate 21 or 22 adult passengers, whereas a dome sleeper has spaces for only 16. Matching available space to expected demand is both an art and a science, the latter involving statistical analysis done by hand.

We have just enough time to check out the sleeper-observation-lounge before departure time . .

259 Sleeper-Observation-Buffet Lounge (4-1)
390-394; CB&Q 483; Pullman-Standard; 1948

Chicago—Seattle

As fitting a car as this one was for the rear end of the *North Coast Limited* in 1948, it is even more so for the *Vista-Dome North Coast Limited* of 1959. While the two dome sleepers are designed for best viewing of the passing scenery, they are not designed as lounge cars (at least not in 1959). True, a Lounge-in-the-Sky modification will occur to six of the 11 dome sleepers in spring 1967, when the observation-lounge car will be discontinued, but even the new dome-lounges will not serve the purpose of providing lounge space as well as does the car we are about to inspect. This car was modern and plush in 1948; it is even more so now, thanks to the handiwork of Raymond Loewy. Let's step in from the vestibule and take a look.

The "4-1" designation indicates four double bedrooms and one compartment. Just inside the forward end of this car, we see an arrangement like the 8-6-3-1 sleeper two cars ahead, but this similarity ends about six feet past the forward end door. Immediately inside on our right is a restroom, and on our left, a porter's section. In this car the ice water tap just forward of the porter's section on our left has a "commissary storage locker" above it, no doubt containing items for use in the buffet further back. Instead of extending straight through a roomette section (no roomettes in this car), the aisle bends right, abeam the porter's section. A linen locker and table and chair storage cabinet are against the bulkhead directly ahead of us as we walk back. From there the aisle runs along the car's left side (our right) to bypass the four double bedrooms, the compartment, and the buffet.

Lounge-In-The-Sky

During March and April 1967, six dome sleeping cars were reconfigured to "Lounge-in-the-Sky" cars as follows:

Original No.	Lounge-in-the-Sky No.
307	375
308	376
311	377
312	378
314	379
CB&Q 304	CB&Q 380

Duplex single rooms E and F were removed from these cars and replaced with a buffet for preparing snacks and drinks to be served in the dome. The two windows for the buffet remained in place, but they were given prism type glass. Dome seats were replaced with six tables. Each table had four facing seats and a small rheostat-controlled table lamp with a gold-colored shade. Total seating capacity in the dome remained at 24. From 1967 until 1970, Lounge-in-the-Sky domes were normally operated just behind the Slumbercoach, which was immediately behind the diner. If there was a second dome sleeper in the train—one of the unmodified cars—it would usually operate one or two cars behind the Lounge-in-the-Sky.

The other five dome sleeping cars remained in their original configuration and continued in *North Coast Limited* service until after 1970.

Chapter 8: First Class Luxury

Double bedrooms A and B are identical to those in the 350-series sleeper. They face each other and can be opened into a suite arrangement. Double bedroom C faces forward, but it is a loner; its forward wall cannot be folded back to create a suite. Double bedroom D faces rearward and can be opened *en suite* with compartment E, identical to its counterpart in the 350-series sleeper, except that this one has about six more inches of length than the other car's compartment. Therefore, compartment E in this car is technically the largest room on this train.

The buffet is just aft of the mid-point in this car. A two-way swinging door separates the aisle around the bedrooms ahead from the buffet and lounge behind. A buffet-lounge attendant is on duty from 7 A.M. until about 11 P.M., although the porter assigned to this car sometimes fills in for him during breaks. The attendant is a Pullman employee, as are the sleeping car porters, and not a member of the dining car crew. The buffet-lounge attendant serves drinks and snacks, including sandwiches, fruit, and ice cream.

Only the lounge section was remodeled in 1953. The forward half of this car remained unchanged. The lounge seats 27, one more than it did before its Loewy re-styling in 1953. Admittedly the pre-1953 arrangement was rather plain, with rather boring, straight rows of seats facing inward from alongside the walls along with two facing-seat tables. The new lounge, however, is a dramatic improvement. Stepping into the lounge from the buffet area, we note a square Formica-top table with four facing seats on our left, a small writing desk and chair on our right. Next are five lounge chairs facing inward from the sides, two on our left, three on our right. Aft of these are a two-chair table and a

Bedroom C in sleeper-observation-lounge "Montana Club" (numbered 394 in 1953) is unique; its forward wall is permanent and cannot be folded back to create a suite arrangement. Bedrooms alternately face forward and rearward, permitting suite arrangements, but this car has five rooms (four bedrooms and one compartment) and Bedroom C is the odd loner. Otherwise, its facilities are the same as those in the other three bedrooms. The small metal cabinet door opens to allow a toilet to rotate down into position. The sink above the toilet has a stainless steel cover in place. This builder's photo was taken in July 1948.
Pullman-Standard photo; Bill Kuebler collection

The Vista-Dome North Coast Limited

Compartment E in sleeper-observation-lounge "Montana Club" includes a half-sofa and an extra sitting chair. A Murphy bed behind the sofa rotates down for nighttime use, and the upper berth can then be lowered from the ceiling. The door just to the right of the sofa is for the washroom annex, and the door on the far right is for the wardrobe. The term "compartment" is misleading, for this room is slightly larger than a double bedroom and commands a slightly higher space charge. Only the lounge section of this car was modernized in 1953; the forward half of the car—the buffet, bedrooms, compartment, and porter's section—remained unchanged. July 1948 builder's photo. *Pullman-Standard photo; Bill Kuebler collection*

forward facing three-seat sofa. An attractive etched glass partition extends up behind the sofa; the partition has a magazine rack on the back of its supporting structure. Behind the partition is a four-chair table, opposite a smaller one with two chairs. Finally, the rear section contains more lounge chairs along the curved, "teardrop" end of the car. The rear two chairs can be moved to face any direction, permitting viewing out the rear windows.

This is a cozy setting, the scene of countless card games, storytelling, informal meetings, and general conviviality, and a place where the cares of this world—even civilization—will seem to recede further and further behind as we head west. Watching the receding scenery and railroad fascinates more than a few passengers and will provide the careful observer with an education on NP main line traffic capacity and patterns. An average trip from Minneapolis to Seattle on this train, for example, will involve meeting more than 40 trains, including seven passenger trains, and passing about a dozen freight trains. (In railroad terms, opposing trains *meet*; same-direction trains *pass* one another. And, incidentally, to pass or meet each other, trains on the NP use a *siding*, not a "passing track." Woe unto the operating employee who uses the wrong term before a rules examiner!) Between observing traffic and the engineering of this line, a historical landmark in its own right, there is much to see and contemplate from these comfortable seats.

Chapter 8: First Class Luxury

The buffet in sleeper-observation-lounge "Montana Club" (394) was constructed almost entirely of stainless steel. The Pullman lounge attendant prepares snacks and drinks here for first class passengers using the lounge section. The counter-top cover just to the left of the sink is for an ice cream well. July 1948 builder's photo.
Pullman-Standard photo; Bill Kuebler collection

The Vista-Dome North Coast Limited

Interior of "Montana Club" lounge before being restyled by Raymond Loewy and Associates. This builder's photo was made on July 30, 1948.
Pullman-Standard photo; collection of Bill Kuebler

A common misconception exists that the last car of a passenger train is always a very uncomfortable ride, a place where one is subject to a "crack of the whip" on curves. While there is some truth to this when poor train handling occurs, the ride here is actually quite smooth most of the time, especially when the train is on time. When a locomotive engineer is doing his best to make up time, however, things can get a little dicey here for the Pullman attendant carrying a tray of drinks and snacks. It is interesting to note the heavily weighted bases of the various beverage and smoking stands throughout this lounge. Even when passengers are humbled by a curve taken at 75 miles per hour, the stands do not move.

This is the car where the rear brakeman, also called a flagman, usually rides. At almost any time of the day or night (when he is not making an observation of the train from the car's vestibule), he can be seen sitting at one of the lounge tables or perhaps in an unoccupied bedroom. In any case, his duties require him to be in or near this car at all times, ready to flag and protect the rear of the train as necessary. There are exceptions, however. Tonight, for example, somewhere between Windsor and Dawson, North Dakota, say about 1:45 A.M., the Fargo Division train crew will meet in the otherwise empty Lewis and Clark Traveller's Rest car for their traditional coffee break and "bull session," while the rest of North Dakota sleeps.

The rear brakeman also has switch-throwing duties whenever this train takes a siding in non-Centralized Traffic Control (CTC) territory. One very important duty is participation in a "running air brake test." This test is required after departure from a terminal, and after any change in engine crew or train crew, or both. A running brake test is also required prior to passing the summit of a mountain grade. The rear brakeman that has just come on duty here at St. Paul will participate in a running brake test a few minutes from now, as our train departs from St. Paul Union Depot (SPUD). After accelerating to about 30 miles per hour, Engineer Kath will apply the brakes just long enough for the rear brakeman to observe the disc brake indicator plunger on the rear car (or the brake cylinder on the one observation car still awaiting its disc brake conversion). As soon as the rear

Chapter 8: **First Class Luxury**

Looking aft in the observation-lounge of car 392 in 1955. In this setting first class passengers enjoy comfort, relaxation, and conviviality during a journey between Chicago and Seattle. Tables, chairs, and sofa form an interesting and modern arrangement which differs from the rather boring straight rows of sitting chairs along the side walls, typical of other observation cars—and these cars before their Raymond Loewy re-styling. The glass panel behind the sofa has etched gold leaf patterns.
Jim Fredrickson photo

Observation-lounge of car 392, formerly "Tacoma Club," looking forward. These 1955 photos were taken prior to the boarding of train No. 26 at Seattle.
Jim Fredrickson photo

The Vista-Dome North Coast Limited

brakeman observes this brake application, train line integrity is assured and he will wave a highball to the engineer. If handled properly, this test will result in minimal deceleration of the train—an important factor on Westminster Hill. As usual, the key to the operation is good crew coordination.

An emergency air brake valve is located in each car's vestibule. Next to the rear door on the observation car is another air valve, this one with about seven or eight notches, permitting varying amounts of brakepipe reduction (brake application). It is designed for normal air or electro-pneumatic brake operation. The rear brakeman uses this valve to precisely stop the train whenever it backs into SPUD or Chicago Union Station.

A backing maneuver can be tricky and requires a good deal of thinking, planning, and understanding of train length by the engineer, as well as coordination between him and the rear brakeman. Air brake rules governing backing maneuvers are strict and include a requirement for both a standing test and a running test of the rear valve. The running test must be accomplished within 200 feet of first rearward movement, or else the engineer is required to stop the train himself before backing further. Generally, after successful completion of both tests, the engineer establishes a slow and steady rearward approach, and then closes the throttle to let the train slowly drift back toward the bumper. Then, it's up to the rear brakeman to control the rate of deceleration with his air brake valve, hopefully spotting the train about five to ten feet from the bumper, without a jolt. Some SPUD tracks are through tracks, but the *North Coast* usually uses one of the stub tracks. Most CB&Q flagmen (on train No. 25) and NP St. Paul division flagmen (on train No. 26) take pride in

Formerly "Montana Club," sleeper-observation-lounge car 394 probably retained its original tail sign—with the words NORTHERN PACIFIC—for its entire NP career. The tail signs on cars 390–393 and 483 received updated NORTHERN PACIFIC RAILWAY logos; the NP gradually made this change during the period 1958–1965. This photograph was taken on July 30, 1961, at East Auburn.
Bill Kuebler collection

Chapter 8: First Class Luxury

Sleeper-Observation-Lounge Names and Numbers

Sleeper-observation-lounge cars were given names in the "Club" series, rather than numbers, when painted in the 1948–53 scheme. When the NP painted these cars in the Loewy scheme in 1953, the road dropped their names and gave the cars numbers as shown:

Loewy Scheme No.	Pre-Loewy Scheme Name
390	Rainier Club
391	Arlington Club
392	Tacoma Club
393	Spokane Club
394	Montana Club
CB&Q 483	Minneapolis Club

perfectly spotting a train at SPUD, but all of them have had to learn by trial and error over the years. Even so, mishaps have been rare.

Mechanically, these cars are similar to the 1948 sleeping cars in the 350 series. The rear door is not opened during a trip and is not designed for passengers' use. There is no rear diaphragm on this car; it is completely streamlined. A company rule prohibits coupling other passenger cars to the rear of this one, even business cars. Those are usually handled on the *Mainstreeter*, but should an executive need his car included in this train, it would normally be coupled in somewhere up ahead, usually ahead of the mail-dormitory car so as to isolate the business car from unwanted intruders.

Builder's photo of "Montana Club" taken July 30, 1948. This car was given number 394 in the Loewy scheme. Shadowing tends to obscure its center skirt, which was removed in 1952.
Pullman-Standard photo; collection of Bill Kuebler

143

The Vista-Dome North Coast Limited

Brakeman John Cunneen stands at the rear of sleeper-observation-lounge car 394 while train No. 26 boards passengers at Livingston on June 8, 1955. He is assigned as rear brakeman on this train from Butte to Billings. His conductor on this trip is 41-year NP veteran Jimmy Quinn, who is assisted by head brakeman Bob Dubois. Some trainmen, including Brakeman Cunneen, choose to remain brakemen for their entire careers and enjoy their seniority in that position, rather than accepting promotion to conductor and having to compete for jobs against other conductors, men with more seniority. The NP hired Brakeman Cunneen on June 1, 1914. He has been a rear brakeman (flagman) in passenger service for many years and is known for top-notch performance of his duties. He will retire in just six months.
Jim Fredrickson photo

Our tour of the train is complete, and just in time: the departure from SPUD is mere moments away. We had best stand near the observation-lounge car's vestibule and be ready to board. As we look toward the head end of the 14-car train, we see that the platform is now devoid of people and activity, except for a few friends and family members waiving goodbye to passengers aboard the train. This is quite a contrast to the busy platform scene we saw only a few minutes ago. Conductor Lundberg calls "All Aboard!," which actually sounds more like "Boooard!" Most conductors, in fact, have somehow compressed this call to a single syllable. Little matter, for his first call means that departure is now about a minute or two away. Anticipation is high.

Chapter 8: **First Class Luxury**

This is how 8-6-3-1 sleeper 358 appeared when it was named "Butte." The number replaced the name in 1953, when this car was painted in the "Loewy" scheme. The outside diaphragms on this car were removed in about 1951. This builder's photo was taken on August 24, 1948.
Pullman-Standard photo; collection of Bill Kuebler

> **Note**
>
> We have just toured the *Vista-Dome North Coast Limited* as it appeared in 1959. At this point some readers may be curious about ways in which this train changed during NP's vista-dome era, and about its operation "behind the scenes" during those years. The following chapters provide a detailed account of consist evolution and an inside look at the operation of the *Vista-Dome North Coast Limited* during the entire period 1954–70. Our 1959 journey west resumes in Part IV. Those who wish to continue the journey without interruption may skip ahead to Chapter 13.

VISTA-DOME NORTH COAST LIMITED OPERATION:
An Inside Look

Part 3

Chapter 9
Consist Evolution & Seasonal Changes

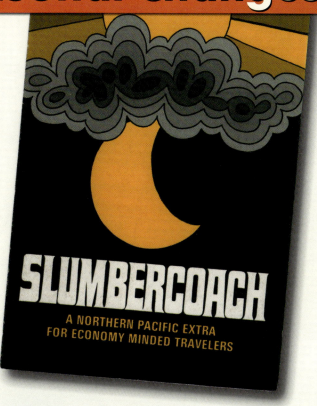

In 1954, when domes first appeared on the *North Coast Limited*, the Northern Pacific (NP) usually operated the two dome coaches together, behind the coach-buffet-lounge car and a Day-Nite Coach, and just ahead of the diner. The practice of separating all domes with at least one flat top car began in late 1954, soon after the addition of dome sleepers.

In 1953–54, the coach-buffet-lounge car operated behind the mail-dormitory car, but by spring 1955, the NP had relocated it to just ahead of the diner. The coach-buffet-lounge cars were removed from service for conversion to Traveller's Rest cars in spring and summer 1955, as previously noted. When the Traveller's Rest car entered service, the NP placed it just ahead of the diner, and there it remained until December 1961.

Train No. 25 sweeps around a curve on the CB&Q near Savanna, Illinois, in July 1961. Speeds up to 90 miles per hour are common in this territory. The last two cars in the train are 8-6-3-1 sleeper 482 and sleeper-observation-lounge car 390. Car 482 is operating in Portland line 258. The NP exchanged the position of dome sleepers and standard sleepers in the *Vista-Dome North Coast Limited* car lineup during most of 1961.
Bill Kuebler collection

149

The Vista-Dome North Coast Limited

From then until about May 1962, the Traveller's Rest operated in the midst of the coach section, usually behind the first dome coach and ahead of a Day-Nite Coach, or just ahead of the second dome coach. The reason for this odd placement is unclear. It is odd, indeed, for it meant a couple of extra switching moves when the Traveller's Rest and dining cars were changed out of train No. 26 at St. Paul. One possible explanation for this placement of the Traveller's Rest car is that the NP experimented with the train's dining facilities in anticipation of greatly increased demand during

Train No. 25 snakes its way alongside the Jefferson River, just west of milepost 28, in November 1954. Until December 1954 dome coaches operated one right behind the other, usually just ahead of the diner. A standard sleeping car, on the other hand, always separated dome sleepers from each other as soon as there were two dome sleepers in each train (beginning in October 1954). This photograph was made from dome coach 552. The following cars include dome coach 553, diner 457, 8-6-4 sleeper 368, dome sleeper 311, 8-6-3-1 sleeper 352, another dome sleeper, and a sleeper-observation-lounge car.
Ron Nixon photo; Bill Kuebler collection

Chapter 9: Consist Evolution & Seasonal Changes

summer 1962. (Extra dinner seatings were typical that summer.) Perhaps management wished to make the diner a little more accessible to coach passengers. After so experimenting, the NP may have simply decided to go back to the tried and true consist for this train, probably to reduce the number of required switching moves with train No. 26 at St. Paul. As it was, the practice of placing the Traveller's Rest car amidst the coach section was short lived, and the car was back in its normal place just ahead of the diner by the summer of 1962. Between 1962 and 1967, changes in its placement were rare and exceptional. On a few occasions in 1968 and 1969, the Traveller's Rest was once again amidst the coaches, two or three cars ahead of the diner. In most cases during the late 1960s, however, it operated just ahead of the diner.

Another interesting change in the standard *North Coast Limited* consist occurred in 1961, this one in about March. During the spring, summer, and fall seasons, the NP exchanged the standard sleeping car lines with the dome sleeping car lines. That is, dome sleepers operated in Seattle and Portland lines 255/265 and 257/267, respectively. The 8-6-4 sleeper operated in Portland line 256/266 (between domes), and the 8-6-3-1 sleeper operated in Seattle line 258/268, just ahead of the observation-lounge car. This marked a change in assignment for the 8-6-3-1 sleepers. At this point (spring 1961), they began operating in Seattle service instead of Portland service.

Train No. 26 approaches Stampede Tunnel No. 4 in May 1962, with F-units 6508C, 6509B, and 6506A handling eleven cars. A Budd Slumbercoach is in its usual position behind the mail-dormitory car, but the Traveller's Rest lounge car is cut in behind the first dome rather than in front of the diner. This was a temporary practice during the winter and spring of 1962. From this vantage point, three levels of track can be seen on the west side of Tunnel No. 4, the lower two levels forming Borup Loop, just out of view to the left. What outstanding composition by the photographer in capturing NP action on Stampede Pass! **Jim Fredrickson photo**

151

The Vista-Dome North Coast Limited

The dome sleepers were back in their previous positions by the end of 1961, but they both served Seattle from then on. Portland dome sleeper service ended at that time, although Portland dome coach service continued.

When the NP moved the dome sleepers back to their previous positions in late 1961, it moved the standard sleeping cars as well, but not to their 1950s positions. Rather, the 8-6-3-1 sleeper went to Seattle line 255/265, and the 8-6-4 sleeper operated in Portland line 257/267, the opposite of their 1950s positions when both cars operated. From the end of 1961 until spring 1967, the standard sleeping cars remained in those positions except when the 8-6-3-1 sleeper in Seattle line 255/265 was dropped during the off-season. The 8-6-4 sleeper operated in Portland service year round from spring 1961 through the remainder of the 1960s, but it moved to the end of the train when the sleeper-observation-lounge car service was discontinued in 1967.

The most notable event in the evolution of the *North Coast Limited* during the 1960s was the discontinuance of the sleeper-observation-lounge car in spring 1967. From then on, the *North Coast Limited* was something much less attractive than before, at least in appearance if not also in accommodation. Not only did passengers notice the loss of the observation car, so did rear brakemen, who now had to find space in an unoccupied roomette, bedroom, or even in a dome seat (where they really weren't supposed to be, if it wasn't the last car in the train). Six dome sleepers were converted to "Lounge-in-the-Sky" configuration, so as to provide first class passengers with lounge space. Passenger opinion, however, was that the Lounge-in-the-Sky was an inadequate substitute for the observation-lounge car. In fact, during 1967–70, the *North Coast Limited* developed a reputation among

After pivoting around to face the other direction (see photo on previous page), the photographer captures the same train on film just after it exits Tunnel No. 4. Eastbound *North Coast Limited* passengers enjoy viewing the lush green Cascades in mid-afternoon, but westbound, one would have to rise at or before dawn to see this territory from a dome seat.
Jim Fredrickson photo

Chapter 9: Consist Evolution & Seasonal Changes

Train No. 26 slips into Stampede Tunnel No. 4 on a cool day in April 1963. Just over one mile ahead this train will enter Stampede Tunnel No. 3, a nearly two-mile bore situated at the summit of this pass. Dome sleepers 305 and 307 are followed by sleeper-observation-lounge car 391, formerly "Arlington Club." Two dome sleepers in each train have been operating in Seattle lines year round since late 1961 and will continue doing so until late 1963, when one dome sleeper will be dropped during winter seasons.
Jim Fredrickson photo

experienced travelers as lacking adequate first class lounge facilities, although demand for first class space had declined to the point where an 8-6-3-1 sleeping car rarely appeared in the *North Coast Limited* during its last three years of NP service.

It is also worth noting that when the observation-lounge cars were discontinued, NP executives' business cars began making rather frequent appearances on the rear of the *North Coast Limited*. This was cause for many sarcastic, under-their-breath remarks from NP trainmen who had to offer explanations to inquiring passengers. Several trainmen reasoned that a wise executive either would have put his business car ahead in the train as before (ahead of the mail-dormitory car), or would have put it on another train, if only to avoid the appearance of displacing a first class lounge car merely for personal convenience. Accusations to that effect continued among active and retired

The Vista-Dome North Coast Limited

Clearance between the dome of car 555, foreground, and the platform awning appears to be rather close in this 1968 view of No. 26's morning stop at St. Paul Union Depot. The NP was less consistent with train makeup in the late-1960s as compared with earlier years. The car behind dome coach 555 is a Budd diner, indicating that the Lewis and Clark Traveller's Rest is not in its usual place between the coaches and diner. Trains 25 and 26 usually used one of the stub tracks at SPUD, rather than a through track as seen here.
Bill Kuebler collection

Business car *Yakima River* is on the rear of train No. 25 at Billings, September 25, 1967. Soon after the NP discontinued sleeper-observation-lounge car service the previous spring, NP executives' business cars began appearing quite frequently on the rear of trains 25 and 26, instead of trains 1 and 2.
Matt Herson photo

Chapter 9: Consist Evolution & Seasonal Changes

Although passengers enjoyed the "Lounge-in-the-Sky" on the *Vista-Dome North Coast Limited,* some said that it was an inadequate replacement for the luxurious sleeper-observation-lounge cars that were discontinued in the spring of 1967. Dome sleeper 379 appears on train No. 26 at St. Paul in 1968. This car was built by Budd in 1957 and carried number 314 until its conversion to "Lounge-in-the-Sky" configuration. The NP purchased it in order to provide protection equipment for dome sleeper service on trains 25 and 26.
John Kennedy photo

NP employees for at least the next three decades, long after the *North Coast Limited* had disappeared from the scene.

Slumbercoaches

When the Slumbercoach was added to the *North Coast Limited* in November 1959, the NP placed it between the mail dormitory car and the first dome coach. There it stayed until summer 1965, when it began "migrating" toward the rear of the train. The Slumbercoach appeared just ahead of the Traveller's Rest car for a very brief time in 1965, then *between* the Traveller's Rest and diner. In the summer of 1966 it often appeared between the Traveller's Rest and diner. This was not consistent, however; there were times during both periods when it appeared behind the mail-dormitory car as usual. Finally, in spring 1967, when the observation cars were removed from service, the Slumbercoach found its final spot on the NP's *North Coast Limited*—just behind the dining car. By that time, it was treated more as a sleeper than as a coach, since it was in the first class section of the train.

A couple of reasons account for this inconsistent migration. The railroad industry originally deemed a Slumbercoach to be more a coach than a sleeper; hence, the name Slumber*coach* and its location in the coach section of the train. The philosophy in 1959 was to sell private room space on a *coach* ticket, rather than on a first class ticket, for a nominal additional charge. This idea was very popular with passengers. Many who could not afford first class space found a Slumbercoach room to be within easy reach. In 1960, a mere $19.10 room charge on a $59.10 coach fare would get a coach passenger a single room in a Slumbercoach, one-way between Chicago and Seattle. (The least expensive first class accommodation available on trains No. 25 and No. 26, a duplex roomette, cost $26.60 plus $82.75 for first class fare.) Also, Slumbercoaches were not wired for music and the public

155

The Vista-Dome North Coast Limited

"Loch Leven" Slumbercoach 326 has just arrived on NP property at St. Paul in November 1959, ready to enter *North Coast Limited* service. NP Slumbercoaches had no center skirt; they had only a short skirt under the vestibule. CB&Q Slumbercoaches in the "Silver" series had full car-length skirts. Slumbercoaches operated vestibule to the rear.
NP Photo; Bill Kuebler collection

address (PA) system during their first five or six years of operation, so they had to be in front of the coaches during those years in order to maintain PA system continuity through all the cars behind the Slumbercoach.

Slumbercoach single rooms were compact but private. Seats and beds were narrower than those in roomettes, allowing toilet and sink to be located beside the seat rather than across from it. The occupant had convenient access to all facilities even when the bed was down. 1959 photo.
Bill Kuebler collection

Chapter 9: Consist Evolution & Seasonal Changes

Beds in Slumbercoach double rooms were as narrow as those in single rooms. Even though compact, these beds were more comfortable than a reclining seat and leg rest in a Day-Nite coach. 1959 photo.
Bill Kuebler collection

Slumbercoaches were sometimes nicknamed "cheaper sleepers." To make ends meet for the operating railroads and Pullman, these had to be high capacity cars as compared with standard sleeping cars. Slumbercoaches, thus, had 24 single rooms and eight double rooms, for a total capacity of 40. (One single room was reserved for the Slumbercoach porter, leaving space for up to 39 revenue passengers.) The layout of the car was simple when compared with that of standard sleepers. The Slumbercoach had a single center aisle running the full length of the car, with 12 alternating "upper" and "lower" single rooms and four double rooms on each side of the aisle. Budd designed these cars to be operated with the vestibule to the rear. The rooms were very small but entirely private. The beds were a couple of inches shorter and several inches narrower than those in standard sleeping cars; beds in all rooms were oriented lengthwise. Each room had a sink, toilet, mirror, and a few switches for lights and temperature control. A "Slumbercrib" was specially designed for use by mothers traveling with small children. Slumbercoach rooms were modest, but far better for privacy than any coach seat. The cars lettered for NP were given names of Scottish lakes, to suggest thrift.

From 1959 until 1964, eight leased Slumbercoaches—four lettered for NP in the *Loch* series and four lettered for Chicago, Burlington, and Quincy (CB&Q) in the *Silver* series—operated in an NP-CB&Q pool arrangement between Chicago and Seattle (on the *North Coast Limited*); and between Chicago and Denver, and Chicago and Colorado Springs (on CB&Q trains). The NP and CB&Q cars were easily distinguished by the full car-length skirt on the CB&Q cars, whereas the NP cars had only an end skirt under the vestibule. The *North Coast Limited* was the only NP train equipped with a Slumbercoach during this period. This arrangement lasted until the NP purchased its four leased cars in 1964, and then purchased second hand another six. At the same time, the

157

The Vista-Dome North Coast Limited

CB&Q purchased the four cars it had been leasing, plus two more cars; these two, also skirtless, were lettered to match the 10 NP cars, but they had CB&Q ownership letters in the upper rear corners. This new arrangement in 1964 brought NP's fleet to 12 cars, counting the two CB&Q-owned cars. That was enough to put a Slumbercoach in both of NP's transcontinental named trains, so beginning in 1964, the *Mainstreeter* also carried a Slumbercoach.

Slumbercoaches on the *North Coast Limited*

- 1959–1964 Pool Arrangement
    Leased to NP
    　325 "Loch Sloy"
    　326 "Loch Leven"
    　327 "Loch Lomond"
    　328 "Loch Ness"
    Leased to CB&Q
    　"Silver Repose"
    　"Silver Rest"
    　"Silver Siesta"
    　"Silver Slumber"

- NP Fleet 1964–1970
    　325 "Loch Sloy"
    　326 "Loch Leven"
    　327 "Loch Lomond"
    　328 "Loch Ness"
    　329 "Loch Tarbet" (ex-T&P "Southland")
    　330 "Loch Katrine" (ex-B&O "Restland")
    　331 "Loch Long" (ex-B&O "Sleepland")
    　332 "Loch Lochy" (ex-B&O "Thriftland")
    　333 "Loch Tay" (ex-NYC 10800)
    　334 "Loch Rannoch" (ex-NYC 10801)
    　CB&Q 335 "Loch Arkaig" (ex-NYC 10802)
    　CB&Q 336 "Loch Awe" (ex-NYC 10803)

Seasonal Changes

Generally, the heaviest travel seasons were between June 1 and September 15, and between December 10 and about January 10. These dates varied somewhat from year to year. During these heavy travel periods, the *North Coast Limited* ran a full consist until dome sleeper leasing occurred in winter 1959–60. During off-seasons, the NP dropped one or more car lines. Initially this occurred only in the coach section; car line C-254/264 was the first to be dropped as passenger loads decreased, followed by line C-253/263. Prior to 1957–58, all five sleeping car lines operated year round, but when demand for first class space declined somewhat in late 1957, the NP dropped one sleeping car line during the off-season. When this first happened, the 8-6-3-1 sleeper was dropped, the 8-6-4 sleeper operated in its place (between dome sleepers) in line 257/267, and line 255/265 was not operated. Later in the winter season of 1957–58, the 8-6-3-1 sleeper returned to its usual location in line 257/267, the 8-6-4 sleeper moved back to line 255/265, and the NP dropped dome sleeper line 258/268, instead, during the

Chapter 9: Consist Evolution & Seasonal Changes

"Loch Sloy" was one of the four original Slumbercoaches leased by the NP from 1959 to 1964. The NP purchased all four in 1964. Car 325 lays over at Chicago on September 13, 1969.
William A. Raia collection

"Lounge-in-the-Sky" dome sleeper 380 (ex-304) lays over at Chicago on July 13, 1968. As indicated by lettering in the upper corners, CB&Q retained ownership of this car after it was converted to "Lounge-in-the-Sky" configuration in April 1967. The train has been turned but not yet washed; by the time it departs the following day, it will likely be spotless.
William A. Raia collection

The Vista-Dome North Coast Limited

The car number, 378, and the prism glass in the rear two lower windows (formerly duplex single rooms E and F and now a buffet section) identify this car as a "Lounge-in-the-Sky" dome sleeper. This photograph was taken at Ellensburg in September 1971. The adverse effects of Amtrak operation are evident in the scratched and fading exterior paint. Car 378 was formerly No. 312.
Bill Kuebler collection

remainder of the off-season. From then on, whenever a dome sleeper line was dropped during an off-season (a dome sleeper line was not always dropped, as we shall see), it was line 258/268.

There were special occasions when the NP needed to operate extra cars on the *North Coast Limited*, especially during the record-setting summer of 1962 and the Seattle World's Fair, and during summer 1966, when the airlines experienced a prolonged strike. Generally, if the NP needed an extra sleeping car in the train, it placed one of the 350-series cars between the rear dome car and the sleeper-observation-lounge car. This was sometimes done to accommodate special tour groups traveling to and from Seattle. Sleeping car 364 or 365 (10 roomettes, six double bedrooms) occasionally appeared in the train as an extra car during the 1960s, but until the late 1960s this was less common than the appearance of an extra 350-series car.

Passenger cars from foreign roads appeared in *North Coast Limited* service on some occasions in the latter half of the 1960s, particularly during 1966–70. In 1962, when heavy Seattle World's Fair traffic was a factor, the NP still had enough 8-6-3-1 sleepers to provide extra equipment as needed. But by 1966, when a prolonged airline strike created increased demand for rail travel, five of these sleepers had been converted the previous year to dormitory service and renumbered 440–444. Thus, the NP needed a car from a foreign road on occasion to meet demand. These included cars from the Pennsylvania, New York Central, Santa Fe, New Haven, and Union Pacific Railroads. Finally, a few Illinois Central sleeping cars appeared on the *North Coast Limited* in the mid-1960s—and in Loewy colors, too—but this was part of a special arrangement having to do with NP's dome sleepers.

Chapter 9: **Consist Evolution & Seasonal Changes**

Dome Sleepers

During the 1959–60 winter season, some dormant NP dome sleepers began operating on other railroads, in Chicago-Miami service. These cars operated on the *City of Miami* and the *South Wind* under a lease agreement with the Illinois Central (IC) and Pennsylvania Railroads. While leased to the IC, dome sleepers were painted in IC colors (chocolate brown and orange), but retained their NP numbers. They were repainted into NP colors upon return to the home road. When used on the Pennsylvania Railroad, dome sleepers remained in NP colors. In spring 1960, these cars returned to full-time *North Coast Limited* service.

During the next three years, the NP normally operated two dome sleepers in each *North Coast Limited*, even during the off-season. Then, from late 1963 until spring 1969, the NP again removed one dome sleeper from each train during the winter season. In 1963–64, dome sleepers were used in New Orleans service on the IC's *Panama Limited*, instead of the *City of Miami*. Beginning in 1964–65, the wintertime Miami service arrangement resumed on the *City of Miami* and *South Wind*, as was done in 1959. By 1965, this arrangement was more of an exchange than a simple lease. During these exchanges in the latter half of the 1960s, IC gave several of its sleepers Loewy colors and unique lettering, and loaned them to the NP during the summer seasons in exchange for use of

This is how the dome section looked in six of the eleven dome sleepers following their 1967 reconfiguration to "Lounge-in-the-Sky" cars. The other five dome sleepers remained in their original configuration during their last years of NP service.
NP publicity photo, April 1967

the NP dome sleepers during the winter seasons. When in Loewy colors, these IC sleeping cars' names (all started with a "B") appeared in place of the monad on the side of each car, below the windows, and PULLMAN appeared on the letterboard. These cars even appeared in *North Coast Limited* service on a few occasions during the 1966 airline strike. The names of these cars were as follows; "Baton Rouge," "Belleville," "Benton," "Bloomington," "Bradley," and "Brookhaven."

Dome sleepers repainted to chocolate brown and orange IC colors during the various winter seasons were as follows:

1959: NP 307, 308, 310
1963: NP 308, 310
1964: CB&Q 304, NP 308, 309, 310
1965: NP 310, 312, 313
1966: CB&Q 304, NP 311
1967: CB&Q 305, NP 313

Chronology of *Vista-Dome North Coast Limited* Consist Changes, 1954-1970

This summary merely presents NP's standard practices. As always, there were exceptions, especially during the 1960s. Regardless of car routing (Seattle *vs.* Portland), line numbers always reflect relative position in the train. If lines were not operated, the surrounding lines simply closed the "gap." For example, line 255, when operated, was always the first sleeping car behind the diner, and 256 was the next sleeping car, etc. But if, for example, line 255 was not operated, then line 256 was the first sleeping car behind the diner. Also, this summary does not show head-end cars. The water-baggage and mail-dormitory cars always operated at the head-end of the train and in that order. Standard NP practice throughout the 1954–70 period was to operate the diner between the coaches and the Pullmans, with the Pullmans in the rear portion of the train.

Abundant photographic evidence, and other evidence, proves that timetable equipment listings and brochures do not always accurately reflect even standard practices. In those cases where public timetable equipment listings are in conflict with sufficiently ample photographic coverage, or other compelling evidence, I have given priority to the photos and supporting evidence.

- **Early 1954:** Coach-Buffet-Lounge operates just behind mail-dormitory car. Diner operates between coaches and sleeping cars.

- **August 1954:** As soon as two dome coaches join each train set, they operate together, just ahead of diner, until late 1954.

- **Late 1954:** Dome coaches separated by a Day-Nite Coach. First dome coach operates behind the coach-buffet-lounge car, which, in turn, is still behind the mail-dormitory car. The 8-6-4 sleeper operates in Seattle line 255/265, 8-6-3-1 sleeper in Portland line 257/267. Dome sleepers operate in lines 256/266 and 258/268. Coach lines C-254/C-264 and C-253/C-263, behind the second dome coach, are dropped, in that order, during off-seasons, from late 1954 on. All five sleeping car lines operate year round until late 1957.

- **Early Spring 1955:** Coach-Buffet-Lounge moves to just ahead of diner.

- **April–August 1955:** Coach-Buffet-Lounge cars removed from service for conversion, one at a time, to Traveller's Rest configuration. Traveller's Rest car placed in front of diner as each one enters service. On most occasions, substitute coach lounge service is provided by "Holiday Lounge" car 492 or 493. On a few occasions, there is no substitute coach lounge service during this period.

Chapter 9: Consist Evolution & Seasonal Changes

- **Fall 1957:** First off seasonal reduction of sleeping car lines. Seattle line 255/265 dropped and 8-6-4 sleeper moved to line 257/267 during off-season, bumping 8-6-3-1 sleeper to dormant status.

- **Winter 1957–58:** Line 255/265 resumes. The 8-6-4 sleeper moves back to line 255/265, 8-6-3-1 sleeper returns to line 257/267, and dome sleeper line 258/268 dropped during off-season. Line 258/268 dropped during off-season of 1958-59 also.

- **Late November 1959:** Slumbercoach placed behind mail-dormitory car.

- **Winter 1959–60:** Three dome sleepers not used in line 258/268 are leased for Miami service; return in the spring of 1960.

- **Fall 1960–Spring 1963:** During off-seasons, two dome sleepers usually operate, and the 8-6-3-1 sleeper is dropped. Line assignments vary, however. (See the following entries.)

- **Spring–Fall 1961:** Dome sleepers shift to lines 255/265 (Seattle) and 257/267 (Portland until October, then Seattle); 8-6-4 sleeper operates in Portland line 256/266. During the summer '61 season, 8-6-3-1 sleeper operates in Seattle line 258/268.

- **October 1961:** Both dome sleepers operate in Seattle service. This practice continues throughout remainder of 1960s whenever there are two dome sleepers in each train.

- **Winter 1961–62:** Dome sleepers move back to usual locations and lines 256/266 and 258/268 (both in Seattle service), but 8-6-4 sleeper operates in Portland line 257/267. When operated, 8-6-3-1 sleeper operates in Seattle line 255/265. This lineup continues through the following winter season also.

- **Winter–Spring 1962:** Traveller's Rest operates in midst of coach section, usually behind first dome coach or just ahead of second dome coach. Returns to usual location just ahead of diner by summer 1962.

- **1963–70:** Second dome sleeper dropped during off-season.

- **Summer 1965:** On various occaisions, Slumbercoach operates behind mail-dormitory car, or just ahead of the Traveller's Rest, or between Traveller's Rest and diner.

- **Summer 1966:** Slumbercoach frequently operates between Traveller's Rest and diner.

- **April–May 1967:** Dome coaches operate together, usually behind a 581–585 series leg rest coach. Dome coaches usually not separated by another car during off-season, but are separated by Day-Nite Coach during 1967–1969 summer and mid-winter seasons. Slumbercoach moves to just behind diner. Sleeper-observation-lounge car discontinued, Lounge-in-the-Sky enters Seattle service, and 8-6-4 Portland sleeper moves to end of train. When operated, second dome sleeper is positioned behind Lounge-in-the-Sky and ahead of 8-6-4 sleeper and operates in Seattle service. On some occasions the two dome sleepers exchange positions. This "standard" line-up continues until the Burlington Northern (BN) merger, though with more frequent deviations than occurred with standard lineups in previous years.

Chapter 10
Actual Consists

Northern Pacific (NP) assigned certain groups of cars to specific car lines on trains No. 25 and No. 26 at any one time. Management changed these assignments periodically (generally, every few weeks), because of equipment rotation into and out of service for scheduled maintenance. Some cars were taken out of *North Coast Limited* service and exchanged with same-type cars assigned to other trains, and vice versa. (Recall that the Loewy paint scheme was common to all NP passenger trains and equipment.) Cars serving in the *North Coast Limited* and other trains included Day Coaches in series 500–517, Day-Nite Coaches in series 588–599, and 8-6-3-1 sleeping cars. The other types of cars assigned to trains No. 25 and No. 26 were normally assigned exclusively to those trains. In addition to these equipment rotations, there were seasonal changes in the *North Coast Limited* consists. For all these reasons, the specific consists of the five *North Coast Limited* train sets were not permanent. They frequently changed.

    The following table lists specific car assignments to the various lines on trains No. 25 and No. 26 as of July 10, 1958. It serves merely as an example. These lists and notes are taken, verbatim, from a directive issued by the General Superintendent of Transportation and sent to all personnel concerned. The General Superintendent of Transportation sent such directives out periodically, generally every few weeks, as assignments changed due to the reasons stated above. The order of the individual car numbers under each car line is not significant. In other words, just because, say, cars 400, 425, 550, etc., happen to be listed first under their respective car line assignments does not mean that those cars all appeared in the same train set. These assignments are strictly car line assignments; they are not train set assignments.

    Extra cars at either Seattle or St. Paul protected most car lines. The Traveller's Rest car and dining car were not protected, however, because of extensive trip preparations with them while they lay over between trips. These preparations took place each day at the St. Paul commissary. Carmen could perform maintenance on these cars

165

The Vista-Dome North Coast Limited

The rest of the story... NP fans will probably recognize this photo but may not know the full story behind it. On a pleasant spring day in March 1962, after chasing Milwaukee Road trains in an NP company car and ending up at Three Forks, Ron Nixon raced to Homestake and then walked a mile west to Tunnel No. 5 at Highview. He lugged his Speed Graphic and other photographic equipment to a perch above the tunnel's east portal, just in time to photograph No. 25's approach. In spite of slipping on some loose granite and nearly falling to his death, he created a photo image that adorned NP's 1963 desk calendars! The calendar photo, reproduced here, was appropriately entitled, "On Top of the World." Number 25 is led by 6510C, 6507B, and 6505A, and includes water-baggage 401, mail-dormitory 429, and a Slumbercoach (in the rock cut). The Traveller's Rest lounge car is just ahead of the second dome coach, out of its usual position in front of the diner.
Ron Nixon photo; Lorenz P. Schrenk collection

Chapter 10: Actual Consists

This is a much easier way to get to the same spot! Train No. 25 negotiates a 12-degree curve on approach to Highview Tunnel, one mile west of Homestake, on June 28, 1955. This view was made from the rear cab unit. The first nine cars in this train are cars 402, 427, 551, 589, 554, 596, 493, 454, and 350. Car 350 is substituting for a car in series 367–372. The car behind the first dome sleeper is also a 350-series car. Parlor-bar-lounge car 493, a "Holiday Lounge," is substituting for a coach-buffet-lounge that has been sent to Como shops for conversion to the Traveller's Rest configuration.
Ron Nixon photo; Lorenz P. Schrenk collection

during their 24-hour layover at the commissary, but whenever one of these cars was taken out-of-service for major maintenance, the NP operated other equipment in its place. Holiday Lounge cars in series 487–493 and Pullman-Standard dining cars in series 450–457 from trains No. 1 and No. 2, or trains No. 407 and No. 408, substituted for Traveller's Rest cars and Budd dining cars, respectively.

The Vista-Dome North Coast Limited

Cars Assigned to North Coast Limited #25 & #26

General Superintendent of Transportation
St. Paul, Minnesota
July 10, 1958

Water-Baggage
Chicago-Seattle
400
401
402
403
405
404 on hand, Como

Mail-Dormitory
Chicago-Seattle
426
427
428
429
479
425 at Seattle for protection

Dome Coach C-250/260
Chicago-Seattle
552
554
555
557
559
553 at Seattle for protection

Day-Night Coach C-251/261*
Chicago-Seattle
586
587
589
597
599
594 at Seattle for protection
*These six Day-Night Coaches are equipped with conductor's desk and should stay in #25-26 in this position.

Dome Coach C-252/262
Chicago-Portland
549
550
551
556
558

Day Coach C-700/800**
Chicago-Portland
502
505
511
513
516
506 at St. Paul for protection
**These six Day Coaches are all train lined and should be kept in lines C-700 and C-800 at all times.

Day-Nite Coach C-254/264
Chicago-Seattle
592
593
594
595
598

Traveller's Rest
Chicago-Seattle
494
495
496
497
498
499

Diner
Chicago-Seattle
458
459
460
461
462
463

8-6-4 Sleeper 255/265
Chicago-Seattle
367
368
369
370
371
372 at Seattle for protection

Dome Sleeper 256/266
Chicago-Seattle
304
306
309
311
314
312 at Seattle for protection

8-6-3-1 Sleeper 257/267
Chicago-Portland
354
357
358
359
362
additional cars on hand, St. Paul

Dome Sleeper 258/268
Chicago-Portland
305
307
308
310
313

Observation-Lounge 259/269
Chicago-Seattle
390
391
392
393
483
394 at Seattle for protection

Chapter 10: Actual Consists

Following are several actual consists of the *Vista-Dome North Coast Limited*. Most are from 1962, one is from 1959, and two are from 1966. These serve as a few real life examples. The train shown departing Seattle was without Portland cars west of Pasco.

Train No. 25 departing St. Paul on June 8, 1962:

403 Water-Baggage
425 Mail-Dormitory
326 "Loch Leven" Slumbercoach
556 Dome Coach
594 Day-Nite Coach
CB&Q 558 Dome Coach
516 Day Coach
590 Day-Nite Coach
498 Traveller's Rest
463 Dining Car
352 8-6-3-1 Sleeper
309 Dome Sleeper
367 8-6-4 Sleeper
310 Dome Sleeper
365 Sleeper (extra car; 10-6; Pullman-Standard; 1950)
392 Sleeper-Observation-Lounge

Sleeper no. 365, the extra car, was in this train because of the heavy demand for space aboard the *North Coast Limited* during the Seattle World's Fair. This car was normally used in NP-SP pool service on the west coast.

Train No. 26 departing Seattle on June 8, 1962:

404 Water-Baggage
427 Mail-Dormitory
"Silver Repose" CB&Q Slumbercoach
553 Dome Coach
587 Deluxe Day-Nite Coach
SP&S 559 Dome Coach (added to train at Pasco)
505 Day Coach (added to train at Pasco)
588 Day-Nite Coach
497 Traveller's Rest
CB&Q 458 Dining Car
SP&S 366 8-6-3-1 Sleeper
CB&Q 305 Dome Sleeper
372 8-6-4 Sleeper (added to train at Pasco)
314 Dome Sleeper
355 8-6-3-1 Sleeper (extra car)
391 Sleeper-Observation-Lounge

Train No. 25 departing St. Paul on June 9, 1962:

400 Water-Baggage
426 Mail-Dormitory
"Silver Slumber" CB&Q Slumbercoach
549 Dome Coach
597 Day-Nite Coach
555 Dome Coach
506 Day Coach
596 Day-Nite Coach
494 Traveller's Rest
459 Dining Car
CB&Q 481 8-6-3-1 Sleeper
308 Dome Sleeper
370 8-6-4 Sleeper
313 Dome Sleeper
CB&Q 483 Sleeper-Observation-Lounge

Train No. 25 departing St. Paul on July 10, 1962:

403 Water-Baggage
425 Mail-Dormitory
328 "Loch Ness" Slumbercoach
551 Dome Coach
589 Day-Nite Coach
554 Dome Coach
511 Day Coach
591 Day-Nite Coach
495 Traveller's Rest
460 Dining Car
355 8-6-3-1 Sleeper
311 Dome Coach
369 8-6-4 Sleeper
312 Dome Sleeper
361 8-6-3-1 Sleeper (extra car)
392 Sleeper-Observation-Lounge

169

The Vista-Dome North Coast Limited

Train No. 25 departing St. Paul on July 7, 1959:

(Date may be slightly in error; it is partially illegible on the document.)
403 Water-Baggage
428 Mail-Dormitory
CB&Q 557 Dome Coach
587 Deluxe Day-Nite Coach
556 Dome Coach
CB&Q 599 Day-Nite Coach
595 Day-Nite Coach
494 Traveller's Rest
459 Dining Car
371 8-6-4 Sleeper
SP&S 306 Dome Sleeper
357 8-6-3-1 Sleeper
314 Dome Sleeper
390 Sleeper-Observation-Lounge
Note the positions of the 8-6-3-1 and 8-6-4 sleepers in the 1962 consists as compared with the one from 1959.

Train No. 25 departing Fargo on June 3, 1966:

6508C F-7A
6700A F-9A
6701B F-9B
6512A F-7A
401 Water-Baggage
CB&Q 479 Mail-Dormitory
CB&Q 557 Dome Coach
586 "Deluxe" Day-Nite Coach
555 Dome Coach
596 Day-Nite Coach
595 Day-Nite Coach
498 Traveller's Rest
329 "Loch Tarbet" Slumbercoach
460 Dining Car
CB&Q 481 8-6-3-1 Sleeper
SP&S 306 Dome Sleeper
371 8-6-4 Sleeper
311 Dome Sleeper
390 Sleeper-Observation-Lounge
The crew on this train included Engineer Roy Peterson and Conductor Kenny Dahl.

Train No. 26 arriving Fargo on June 5, 1966:

6506A F-3A
6513C F-7A
6510B F-7B
6701A F-9A
404 Water-Baggage
427 Mail-Dormitory
553 Dome Coach
583 Day-Nite Coach (rebuilt from Holiday Lounge 489 in 1962)
549 Dome Coach
593 Day-Nite Coach
590 Day-Nite Coach
494 Traveller's Rest
332 "Loch Lochy" Slumbercoach
461 Diner
358 8-6-3-1 Sleeper
307 Dome Sleeper
369 8-6-4 Sleeper
310 Dome Sleeper
391 Sleeper-Observation-Lounge
The crew arriving on this train included Engineer Fred J. "Fritz" Lewis and Conductor Kenny Dahl.

Chapter 11

Accidents

The *North Coast Limited* had a superb safety record during its seven decades of Northern Pacific (NP) operation. Millions of passenger-miles were accumulated, year after year, with very few accidents, a remarkable achievement, especially considering that the train operated daily in some of the most challenging conditions ever faced by a railroad. The NP's tough operating environment included some of the harshest winter weather found anywhere within the 48 contiguous states. Snow and ice played havoc with men and equipment, and temperatures across much of the system sometimes dipped as low as 35 degrees below zero. In these conditions steam line connections would freeze up, and during prolonged station stops more than one carman gave his all in trying, sometimes in vain, to thaw the frozen lines with live steam drawn from special trackside equipment. In some cases, signal lines snapped from the weight of ice on them. The fail-safe design of automatic block signals usually brought a failing signal to its most restrictive, and safest, indication. Even so, such operating conditions constantly tested the mettle of NP men everywhere. In spite of it all, their work ethic and "can do" attitudes carried them through the day—or night.

For the most part, the NP was at least as safety-conscious as any other large railroad, and probably more so. Supervisors regularly held safety meetings at various places on the operating divisions. Crewmembers openly discussed, and sometimes debated, rules and their proper application in complicated situations. The NP gave a coveted annual safety award to the operating division with the best safety record for a given calendar year. Competition for this award was stiff. One man on the Rocky Mountain Division even went so far as to draw daily cartoons for his fellow employees, cartoons that humorously raised awareness of safety issues. Perhaps his effort had a positive effect, because, at a time when some NP men said that the annual safety award would "never go to a division west of Livingston" (because of the more difficult operating conditions in mountain territory), the

171

The Vista-Dome North Coast Limited

At 32 degrees below zero, it is a bitterly cold day in Butte as Engineer P. R. "Pat" McGee walks away from his locomotive in January 1966. He has just brought train No. 26 in from Missoula. McGee (no relation to Warren McGee) began his career in engine service in 1918. Severe winter weather such as this challenged NP crews year after year, and it is a remarkable achievement that very few mishaps occurred with the *Vista-Dome North Coast Limited*.
Bill Kuebler collection

Rocky Mountain Division won this award for 1956 and 1957, two consecutive years! This was unprecedented for a western division.

Operating employees took mandatory, periodic rules examinations. Supervisors rode with enginemen and trainmen to see that these employees developed and maintained good practices. Road foremen tested each road engineer under their supervision with a surprise block signal test about once every other month. Typically, the road foreman would place a shunt in

Cover of the May 1957 issue of The Tell Tale, NP's safety magazine for Employees, shows presentation of the 1956 safety award to Rocky Mountain Division. Immediately to the left of the plaque in the upper photo is Vice President C H. Burgess, to the right of the plaque is Rocky Mountain Division Superintendent Norman M. Lorentzsen. This was the first time the coveted annual safety award went to a western division.
Bill Kuebler collection

Chapter 11: Accidents

the track at some location where an engineer would least expect it. Then, the road foreman would hide nearby and watch to see if the engineer stopped his train at the red block in accordance with the rules. Trains No. 25 and No. 26 were *not* exempt from these tests. Even the crack *Vista-Dome North Coast Limited* was fair game; such was the NP's concern for safety. On one occasion, a road foreman tested train No. 25 *twice* in the middle of the night within a distance of about 10 miles! He actually chased the train from one spot to the other, to observe the results of each test. In this instance, he suspected that the engineer expected the first test, but not the second one. Incidentally, the engineer passed both tests, but he was very upset about being tested twice on the same run, and let the road foreman know it when they met at the end of his trip.

In spite of all these efforts, an operation as large and complex as a major transcontinental railroad is bound to suffer an accident from time to time. The NP was no exception, and neither was its

Carmen on the Northern Pacific faced some very tough winter conditions when servicing the train during station stops. Imaging trying to troubleshoot a problem under a car that looks like this! This is Traveller's Rest car 499 on train 26 during a pause at Livingston. It is January 3, 1969, and a very cold day.
S. W. Leach photo; Rick Leach collection

The Vista-Dome North Coast Limited

famed *Vista-Dome North Coast Limited*. Over the years, few mishaps occurred with this train, and most of them were minor. On one occasion, for example, while moving at 70 miles per hour about three miles east of Glendive, the Traveller's Rest lounge car on train No. 25 separated from the car ahead, due to mechanical failure. Fortunately, no one was walking between the two cars at the moment of the mishap, which occurred about 6 A.M., so there were no casualties. When the train parted, both halves made an uneventful, emergency stop and came to rest several feet apart. The automatic air brake system functioned properly and effected the quick stop.

By January 1962, the *Vista-Dome North Coast Limited* had racked up a nearly perfect safety record. The efforts of the road's safety department, and especially of NP operating employees across the system, seemed to be paying off. No major accidents had occurred with the train. But, then . . . the NP's luck ran out when it experienced three major derailments within about six months. We will look at each of these three accidents in detail in this chapter.

This string of accidents began in late January 1962, when there was a serious derailment of train No. 26 west of Glendive. There were no fatalities, but there were some serious injuries. As if that weren't bad enough, in less than six months there were two more major derailments with the *Vista-Dome North Coast Limited*, and both of these were fatal. The only good news was that the number of fatalities was surprisingly low, considering the catastrophic nature of the derailments. The toll from the two fatal accidents stood at only three people, and two of these were enginemen. There was only one passenger fatality during the entire history of *North Coast Limited* operation. That fatality occurred at Evaro, Montana, in June 1962. Coincidentally, all three major derailments occurred that year, one of the busiest travel years during NP's modern streamlined passenger train era.

Regarding two of these three major accidents, official documents list some locomotive units and cars as "destroyed." This was a technical term used by the Interstate Commerce Commission (ICC) in its accident reports. Some of the equipment listed as "destroyed" was actually rebuilt and placed back into service, however, as will be noted below.

Train No. 26 Derails West of Glendive

Train No. 26, traveling at 43 miles per hour, struck a large rock and derailed 12 miles west of Glendive at 5:05 P.M. on Monday, January 29, 1962. The rock fell from a nearby bluff and lodged against one of the rails shortly before the train reached the spot. As the train rounded a curve and the engineer saw the rock, it was too late to stop. The train struck the rock, and the three diesel units and first six cars derailed. The consist of this train was as follows:

- 6701C F-9A
- 6501B F-3B
- 6512A F-7A
- CB&Q 405 Water-Baggage
- 429 Mail-Dormitory
- 327 "Loch Lomond" Slumbercoach
- CB&Q 557 Dome Coach
- 498 Traveller's Rest
- 554 Dome Coach
- 589 Day-Nite Coach
- CB&Q 458 Dining Car
- CB&Q 305 Dome Sleeper
- 371 8-6-4 Sleeper
- 310 Dome Sleeper
- 393 Sleeper-Observation-Lounge

This consist shows the unusual placement of the Traveller's Rest car behind the first dome coach, a practice lasting only a few months during the winter of 1961–62 and occurring on rare occasions in later years. During the derailment, the mail-dormitory car "popped" out of the train from

Chapter 11: Accidents

the force of impact and careened laterally to the frozen Yellowstone River below, without breaking through the ice! The two postal clerks inside the car were seriously injured during the wild ride. Most other injuries resulting from this accident were minor.

Word of the accident reached Glendive, only 12 miles away, very quickly. Within minutes, medical help was on the way. Fortunately, there was a dirt road nearby, so ambulances were able to get fairly close to the accident site. The three-unit locomotive separated from the train during the derailment, so there was no source of steam for train heat in any of the cars. Even so, train heat dissipated slowly enough for passengers to await rescue in relative warmth inside the cars, none of which was severely damaged. Within a couple of hours, a rescue train reached the accident site and began hauling uninjured passengers to Glendive. Road switcher locomotives hauled the rear portion of the train backwards to a point near Miles City. There, a Milwaukee Road engine and crew handled those cars over its line to the Twin Cities, where the train arrived nearly a day late. A lack of train heat (the Milwaukee Road engines had no steam generators) and a lack of food in the diner for the extra day's journey resulted in some very cold and hungry passengers arriving in the Twin

Three diesel units and the first four cars of the eastbound *North Coast Limited* wait to be picked up by the Glendive wrecker on January 30, 1962. The dome coach is car *557*. In less than six months the same car would suffer another derailment, that one at Evaro. Coincidentally, the lead diesel unit here, No. 6701C, would also be involved in the Evaro accident. Note the position of the mail-dormitory car on the ice-covered Yellowstone River. The car literally popped out of the train from the force of the sudden stop and careened laterally to the frozen river below. Two postal clerks inside the car were seriously injured.
Bill Kuebler collection

The Vista-Dome North Coast Limited

Cities. The Stewardess-Nurse, Miss Joan Reitz, provided the passengers with extra sheets and blankets from the Pullman cars, and had children double up in berths so as to help them keep warm. Local residents in one small town on the Milwaukee Road line offered the train's crew and passengers some food, a welcome relief.

In the weeks following the accident, all locomotive units and cars in this train were repaired and returned to service. The train's crew included:

- Engineer Archie Marcotte
- Fireman M. Dawe
- Conductor Dan Collins
- Brakeman R. Jarding
- Brakeman B. Evers
- Stewardess-Nurse Joan Reitz

A detailed account of the Glendive derailment of train No. 26 appeared in the summer 1994 issue of the Northern Pacific Railway Historical Association (NPRHA) quarterly publication, *The Mainstreeter* (vol. 13 no. 3).

Train No. 25 Derails at Granite

At 10:18 p.m. on Friday, March 2, 1962, while traveling at 75–80 miles per hour, train No. 25 derailed on an eight-degree, left-hand curve immediately west of the west siding switch at Granite, Idaho. This curve was rated for 30 miles per hour. The train's three diesel units left the rails on this curve and slid to the top of a steep embankment. The first 11 of the following 12 cars derailed to the right, or outside, of the curve. The first two diesel units plunged over the steep embankment and into ice-covered Granite Lake, a dark, murky body of water situated some 140 feet below track level. The third unit also plunged over the embankment and came to rest at the edge of the lake. The first two cars went over the embankment and came to rest at precarious angles on the steep slope, and the remainder of the train's derailed cars came to rest in various positions, some completely overturned, on the ground that sloped gently away from the track and toward the steep embankment.

Engineer Jess Pruitt and Fireman Steve Renner were killed in the accident, and 138 passengers and crewmembers were injured, some seriously. Conductor Walter St. Clair was one of the less seriously injured. One member of the dining car crew narrowly escaped death by pure chance. Charlie Snodgrass, a Traveller's Rest waiter, retired to bed in the mail-dormitory car shortly after 10 P.M. A last minute trip to the restroom, however, saved his life. While he was out of his bunk, the derailment occurred. The mail-dormitory car was severely bent in the middle—right where Charlie's bunk was situated—as the roof of the car slammed against the end of the car ahead. The collapsed roof of his car and the intruding end of the water-baggage car crushed his top bunk. Had Charlie been in his bunk, he surely would have been killed. As it was, he was seriously and permanently injured, and the trip turned out to be his last in NP service.

Idaho Division Superintendent Norman Lorentzsen was notified within a few minutes of the accident that the Railway's telegraph line had been severed near Granite—an indication that a derailment may have occurred there. Since the only train in the vicinity of Granite at that time was No. 25, Superintendent Lorentzsen decided that a derailment of train No. 25 had, indeed, occurred and he immediately acted, calling for emergency rescue services. Railway executives noted and, later, formally lauded him for his prompt and effective response. Within minutes of the accident and in spite of bad weather, Mr. Lorentzsen was on his way to Granite by automobile. The rescue and clean-up operation turned out to be very extensive and challenging, and he spent most of the next several days at the site, supervising the operation.

Chapter 11: Accidents

The NP hired specially equipped divers to find the diesel units, at least one of which had careened into the lake with such momentum as to completely bury itself in the floor of the muddy lake. It took some time just to find the lead diesel unit. With great effort the NP eventually recovered the first two locomotive units and the bodies of the engine crew from the depths of Granite Lake. Several Caterpillar tractors with winches and three-inch steel cables, as well as two 250-ton wreckers, worked together to extricate the locomotive units against tremendous suction forces of the muddy lake bottom. In short, this accident was catastrophic. That the casualties were not far worse is a wonder.

One crewmember was a true heroine. Stewardess-Nurse Gladys Stewart, originally from Scotland, had retired for the night by the time of the accident. She was uninjured in the accident itself. Immediately after the accident happened, she went to work helping to remove passengers, some seriously injured, from the cars. In so doing, however, she suffered several serious injuries. In spite of her situation, her actions were both fast and effective. They went a long way toward minimizing further passenger injury and suffering in those critical moments following this very serious accident. NP President Robert Macfarlane lauded her efforts and brought them to the attention of NP employees across the system. (See the "Stewardess-Nurses" section in Chapter 12 for more details concerning Miss Stewart's actions.)

The ICC never officially determined the cause of this accident, in spite of an intensive investigation. Railway employees and officials, however, have pointed to one or the other of two likely causes. Generally, fellow enginemen at Parkwater (Spokane) engine terminal and other engine

F-9A No. 6700C and cars 402 and 428 lie askew following a high-speed derailment on the 8-degree curve at Granite, Idaho. The train did not quite make it to the high trestle (upper right) that crosses Granite Lake. The lake's ice-covered surface appears in the lower foreground. The first two diesel units are still submerged and buried in the floor of the muddy lake. March 3, 1962.
Al Bennett photo, Bill Kuebler collection

terminals tended to blame the train's brake system, which was said to be prone to poor braking action in snow and ice conditions such as existed that night in the vicinity of the accident. In contrast, NP officials tended to blame the engine crew for having exceeded posted speed limits and possibly for having lost awareness of their precise location with respect to the 30-mile-per-hour curve involved in the accident. Not surprisingly, evidence exists to support both viewpoints. Neither is likely to be conclusively disproved. There is also a third possibility, thus: Both the engineer and fireman just happened to doze off at the same critical moment, only seconds before the derailment occurred. Even though no evidence exists, or even could exist, to prove this third possibility conclusively, railroaders know very well that fatigue on the job is a frequent, dangerous menace that can strike the most concientious employee at the worst moment. Since this scenario can never be conclusively proved, only the evidence supporting the first two possible causes remains for consideration.

Like most diesel locomotives, the one involved in this accident had a speed recorder. Although the last 12 miles' worth of speed recorder tape was illegible (due to immersion in water), the preceding portion of the tape showed a consistent pattern of excessive speed at various places where speed limits were posted between Paradise and Cocolalla, just east of Granite. In the words of Road Foreman R. M. "Bud" Cain, supervisor of Parkwater engine crews at the time of this accident, "The tape showed that it was a series of errors for the entire trip."

Diner 462 and dome sleeper 312 wait to be picked up by the wrecker at Granite, Idaho, on March 3, 1962. Wrecker engineers had to be especially careful when picking up derailed passenger cars, so as not to cause them further damage. This tragic high-speed derailment resulted in the deaths of Engineer Jess Pruitt and Fireman Steve Renner. Miraculously, there were no other fatalities in this accident. NPRHA member Mike Tellinghuisen was a four-year-old passenger in one of the coaches on this train. Though uninjured in the accident, he still remembers the events of that night.
Al Bennett photo, Bill Kuebler collection

Chapter 11: Accidents

His is a compelling account, especially when considering some of the events that took place in the weeks prior to this accident. To his credit, Road Foreman Bud Cain made no less than 13 supervisory trips with the engineer (though not always with the same fireman) on trains No. 25 and No. 26 between January 1, 1962, and the night of the accident, a rather high number. He did this because Engineer Pruitt had spent the previous 14 years (prior to January 1962) on the Paradise-Trout Creek local freight and away from passenger operations. According to the Road Foreman, Engineer Pruitt's performance on his last supervised trip (February 26–27) was flawless. Train handling and speed control were excellent and in accordance with posted speed limits. If Pruitt had gotten rusty at passenger work, he had apparently worked it all out by the end of February. Thus, Road Foreman Bud Cain approved Pruitt for passenger service at that time. Pruitt's next trip was the one on which the accident occurred.

Sometime during this January-February period, though, Engineer Pruitt is alleged to have quietly announced to some other enginemen that he sought to beat fellow Engineer Dave Townsend's record running time from Paradise to Spokane with No. 25. The three engineers assigned to trains No. 25 and No. 26 when the accident happened were Dave Townsend, Paul Staeheli, and Jess Pruitt.

Dome coach 550 came to rest upright, but very close to the top of a steep embankment. Slumbercoach "Silver Rest" appears in the background, overturned and at the top of the embankment. The forward end of overturned Traveller's Rest lounge car 499 appears in the right foreground. March 3, 1962.
Al Bennett photo, Bill Kuebler collection

The Vista-Dome North Coast Limited

Townsend had been on this assignment for many years, and had set a running time record in 1958. It is possible, but by no means certain, that Pruitt was doing just that—trying to beat Townsend's record—on the night of March 2 and took unnecessary risks, now that he was unsupervised. Besides the legible portion of the speed tape, one other bit of evidence was very compelling: The train left Paradise 59 minutes late, but passed Sandpoint only 40 minutes late. Even more time had been made up when it reached Granite, according to the time the telegraph wires were knocked down by the derailment. Even though evidence at the accident site showed that Fireman Renner, also a qualified engineer, was running the locomotive when the accident happened, at least one engineman familiar with Pruitt speculated that Pruitt was "coaching" Renner in the art of top performance passenger train handling.

Those who tended to blame the brake system also had substantial supporting evidence. First, many engine crews believed that the electro-pneumatic brake system on the train was prone to malfunction, especially in winter weather when snow and ice could interfere with electrical connections between the cars, thus interfering with a brake application. Several engineers experienced problems with this controversial system during the few years that it was in use. (See Chapter 12 for more details on the electro-pneumatic brake system.) Second, the disc brakes in use on most of the lightweight cars were also prone to malfunctions, especially in certain winter weather conditions. The electro-pneumatic brake system, which was in use exclusively on trains No. 25 and No. 26, and the disc brakes, which were in use on all lightweight passenger cars in the NP's fleet, regardless of passenger train assignments, were separate and independent components of the train's brake system, but engine crews believed that winter weather could adversely affect both of these components.

There were two significant problems with disc brakes. The first was ice and snow build-up on the brake pads, virtually eliminating useful friction during braking. The second problem was untimely action from the anti-wheel slide devices.

As for the brake pads, the problem of snow and ice build-up was partially solved, beginning in the mid-1950s, by use of a steel-toed brake shoe during November through March each winter season. Although these specially equipped shoes caused excessive wear of the brake discs, they did help reduce the braking action problem. Even with the use of these "winter shoes," the problem was not completely eliminated and may have been a factor in the Granite accident.

The anti-wheel slide system installed on disc brake-equipped lightweight passenger cars was also controversial, and a possible factor. It was designed to prevent wheel sliding and resultant flat spots during heavy braking. This system was controlled by a "decelostat" on each axle of each passenger car equipped with disc brakes. (Budd cars came so equipped; Pullman-Standard cars came equipped with clasp brakes, but these were eventually replaced with discs at Como shops. By early 1963, all lightweight passenger cars on the NP, including the Pullman-Standard cars, had disc brakes.) When excessive deceleration was detected—an impending wheel slide—the decelostat would automatically command a temporary brake release on that axle, and a re-application of that brake when the impending slide condition subsided. Essentially, these were anti-lock brakes, although railroad personnel did not use that term but called this an "anti-wheel slide" system instead. During winter weather conditions, with snow and ice accumulations, these decelostats were thought by some enginemen to be prone to improper action whereby the device would cause a brake release on an axle even when a release was not appropriate. In these cases, deceleration of the train during braking was erratic and unpredictable. More than one engineer was surprised and embarrassed by this problem as his train rolled well beyond its proper spot at a station. Generally, most experienced passenger engineers learned to compensate for this, as best they could, by initiating brake applications sooner and thereby having to use less braking force. Engineer Pruitt, however, had been away from passenger operations for many years prior to 1962. Even so, Fireman Renner—who was running the locomotive at the time of the accident—had been in passenger service for several years and was familiar with decelostats and their effect on braking. Though it is understandable that Pruitt might have underestimated their effect, it is difficult to imagine that Renner made the same mistake.

Chapter 11: Accidents

Compelling evidence that the disc brakes played a role in this accident exists, although this evidence is not consistent system-wide. Several engineers east of Livingston who handled the ill-fated train reported problems. Engineer Emil Stumm and Fireman Leroy Sly, waiting to board No. 25 at Dilworth on March 1 (the same train that derailed at Granite on March 2), watched Staples Engineer Frank Clossen helplessly overshoot his spot at the Dilworth yard office by an entire train length! Engineer Stumm arrived at Jamestown later that night quite dissatisfied with the performance of the train's brakes. He reported this to his supervisor. Likewise, engineers on the Yellowstone Division—Hunter Picken at Dickinson was one of them—reported similar problems. Picken reported that the train's "retardation was erratic, sometimes less than desired" during stops. Road Foreman Frank Scobee met the incoming Forsyth engine crew upon their arrival at Billings with the ill-fated train. They, too, had sent a message ahead that reported "insufficient retardation" during brake applications. Scobee warned Engineer Archie McGuire, who handled the train from Billings to Livingston, to be extra careful. These engineers were highly experienced. Most of them were also highly respected. Thus, officials deemed their reports to be credible.

For whatever reason, though, the train's performance seemed to improve west of Livingston. The locomotive units were changed there, although that should have had little to do with disc brake performance on the train's cars. In any case, the engine crews who handled the train west of Livingston all reported satisfactory performance of the train's brake system. One of them was Engineer Bud Aldrich of Missoula, who handled the train from Missoula to Paradise. He, too, was highly experienced and respected. He reported that the brake system was not only satisfactory, but that it operated even better than usual. It is important to note that the weather conditions probably varied from one division to the next, a possible factor in these variances in braking performance.

All things considered, the exact cause of this accident remains undetermined. It may be that all of the possibilities considered here were contributing factors. Whatever the reason, train No. 25 entered a 30-mile-per-hour curve at Granite at something over 74 miles per hour, possibly as high as 80. Consequently, the three diesel units derailed on this curve. They and the following cars careened off the track and tangentially away from the right-of-way.

Finally, it is interesting to note that the NP discontinued use of the controversial electro-pneumatic brake system on trains No. 25 and No. 26. Railway records do not state the reason for this discontinuance, a rather unusual omission suggesting the probability that this decision resulted directly from the Granite accident. The NP officially took the system out of service on May 27, 1962, just over two months after the Granite accident. Shop personnel gradually removed all electro-pneumatic brake system components from locomotive units and cars during the two-year period following the May 1962 discontinuance. Disc brakes, however, remained in use.

Train No. 25 which derailed at Granite consisted of the following equipment:

- 6508A F-7A (destroyed)
- 6512B F-7B (destroyed)
- 6700C F-9A (destroyed)
- 402 Water-Baggage (destroyed)
- 428 Mail-Dormitory (destroyed)
- "Silver Rest" CB&Q Slumbercoach (destroyed)*
- 550 Dome Coach
- CB&Q 499 Traveller's Rest
- 593 Day-Nite Coach
- 586 Deluxe Day-Nite Coach
- 462 Dining Car
- 312 Dome Sleeper
- 370 8-6-4 Sleeper
- 314 Dome Sleeper
- 394 Sleeper-Observation-Lounge

* Slumbercoach "Silver Rest" was repaired by the Budd Company and placed back into service in late 1963. Other equipment shown as destroyed was scrapped, although freight F-9A no. 7007A was converted to passenger service and numbered 6700C in May 1964. Equipment not shown as destroyed was repaired and placed back into service.

The Vista-Dome North Coast Limited

The crew of train No. 25 included:

- Engineer Jess J. Pruitt
- Fireman Stephen J. Renner
- Conductor Walter St. Clair
- Stewardess-Nurse Gladys Stewart

A detailed account of the Granite derailment appeared in the winter 1988 NPRHA quarterly publication, *The Mainstreeter* (vol. 7 no. 1).

It is interesting to consider the challenges the NP faced in continuing to operate the *Vista-Dome North Coast Limited* following a major accident. Only a few protection cars were available to fill in for cars undergoing repair. These and other cars, some normally assigned to other NP trains and some borrowed from other roads, were pressed into service on trains No. 25 and No. 26. Fortunately, some of the NP cars that had been standing by as protection equipment for the *North Coast Limited* were at the west end of the system in early March 1962. As cars damaged in the Granite accident were repaired at NP's Como shops in St. Paul and Pullman's Calumet shops in Illinois, it took weeks to return to a normal operation. The following information is taken verbatim from two telegrams. One was from General Superintendent of Transportation E. S. Ulyatt in St. Paul to Tacoma Division Superintendent I. W. Brewer, and the other was from Superintendent Brewer to affected division personnel. It illustrates what can happen in the aftermath of just one derailment. The Granite derailment of No. 25 on March 2 meant that there was no train set in Seattle for the March 3 departure of train No. 26. The telegrams directed the operation of a make-up train No. 26 out of Seattle and show the effects to other trains of temporary reassignment of equipment.

March 3 1962

ACCOUNT DERAILMENT OF TRAIN 25 AT GRANITE IDAHO MARCH 2 WILL OPERATE TRAIN 26 FROM SEATTLE DATE TO BE MADE UP AS FOLLOWS:

GN 38 21 FOOT BAGGAGE AND 60 FOOT MAIL COMPARTMENT CAR.

GN 1260 4-7-3-1 SLEEPER TO BE USED AS CREW DORM AND PARTIAL SLUMBERCOACH.

LINE SC 26 GN 1173 16-4 SLEEPER IN PLACE OF SLUMBERCOACH.

LINE C260 NP 513 COACH.

HOLIDAY LOUNGE 493 FROM 408 AS TRAVELLERS REST.

LINE C-700 NP 505 COACH FROM NO 1 C-700 TO PASCO AND VESTIBULE WILL BE REAR ACCOUNT INSUFFICIENT TIME TO TURN CAR.

LINE C-261 NP 592 DAY-NITE COACH ON HAND SEATTLE.

NP 454 DINER ON HAND SEATTLE.

LINE 265 GN 1167 4-8-4 SLEEPER

LINE 266 NP 350 8-6-3-1 SLEEPER ON HAND SEATTLE.

LINE 267 Q305 4-4-4 DOME SLEEPER ON HAND SEATTLE.

LINE 269 Q483 OBSERVATION LOUNGE CAR ON HAND SEATTLE.

ARRANGE TO USE 1340 SERIES COACH ON TRAIN 2 IN THE SEATTLE-ST PAUL LINE TO REPLACE COACH 505

PORTLAND PASSENGERS WILL BE ACCOMMODATED IN COACH 512 AND REGULAR LINE SPACE ON SP&S NO 2 FROM PORTLAND DATE. COACH 512 SENT TO PORTLAND ON NO 460 THIS AM TO BE USED ON SP&S 2 FROM PORTLAND DATE.

HOLIDAY LOUNGE CAR NO 489 WILL ARRIVE SEATTLE ON TRAIN 1 MARCH 4.

HAVE COFFEE SHOP CAR NO 1680 ADDED TO TRAIN NO 2 FROM SEATTLE THIS PM MARCH 3 DEADHEAD TO YAKIMA OR PASCO TO PROTECT BREAKFAST ON TRAIN NO 1 ARRIVING SEATTLE MARCH 4.

TRAIN 26 FROM SEATTLE DATE WILL HAVE NO WATER BAGGAGE CAR AND ARRANGEMENTS SHOULD BE MADE TO HAVE TRAIN TAKE WATER WHEN NECESSARY ENROUTE.

GN 1085 IS USED AS LOUNGE CAR TRAIN 408 TODAY ONLY.

Chapter 11: Accidents

Train No. 26 Derails at Evaro

The Granite accident was still fresh in the minds of Railway personnel when, at 4:35 A.M. on Sunday, June 10, 1962, the eastbound *Vista-Dome North Coast Limited* derailed at high speed on a six-degree left-hand curve rated for 30 miles per hour, about a mile and a half east of Evaro, Montana. In terms of safety, though certainly not in terms of revenue, the year 1962 was a terrible one for the *North Coast Limited*, and for NP personnel across the system. Two disastrous, fatal accidents with NP's premier train in three months was almost unbearable. The NP's reputation for safety had been seriously hurt, and virtually every operating employee on the system was acutely aware of this dismal situation.

Unlike the Granite disaster, the cause of the Evaro derailment was readily apparent almost immediately after the accident. According to the ICC accident report, the engine crew, who handled train No. 25 from Missoula to Paradise the evening prior to the accident, had been drinking and partying at nearby Hot Springs during their Paradise layover, instead of resting. In the early hours of the next morning, when they reported for duty on train No. 26 at Paradise, the engineer and fireman were inebriated. According to both the ICC accident report and public news accounts, blood tests performed after the accident confirmed that the engine crew had been intoxicated when the accident occurred. To make matters worse, even though he may have rested in his room during the layover at Paradise, the rear brakeman assigned to this trip was not attending to all his duties in the moments just prior to the accident.

This derailment happened in mountain grade territory, just below the top of Evaro hill on the Rocky Mountain Division's Sixth Subdivision, which extended from DeSmet to Paradise via Dixon. Applicable rules required the crew to perform a running test of the air brakes prior to passing the summit of the mountain grade at Evaro. These rules required the rear brakeman to observe this test from the rear car's vestibule, and to signal for the test with the cab signaling system if necessary. Rules also required any member of the train crew, including the rear brakeman, to make an emergency brake application in the event the running test was not successfully conducted for any reason, or in the event the train began to accelerate out of control on a descending grade.

As the train climbed the steep grade between Arlee and Evaro, the engine crew fell asleep at the controls, and the rear brakeman fell asleep in the rear dome. The conductor was awake and alert, but by the time he realized what was happening with his train, and that the train was accelerating out of control down the hill from Evaro, it was too late for him to reach a brake valve in time to prevent an accident. Although he headed for the nearest vestibule as quickly as he could, the excessive swaying of the cars on the curves immediately west of the point of derailment prevented him and the head brakeman from reaching a brake valve before the derailment happened.

The train passed the summit at 54 miles per hour (instead of the usual 30, the speed limit imposed on all trains descending this mountain grade) and was accelerating—with the throttle wide open in "Run 8" position. No running brake test occurred, and the rear brakeman did not signal the engineer for a test. Acceleration continued on the descent and the train rapidly exceeded 80 miles per hour. By the time the train reached the six-degree curve at milepost nine, less than two miles east of Evaro, its speed was accelerating through 87 miles per hour! When one NP official first observed the telltale speed recorder tape less than an hour after the accident, he was dumbfounded. The indicated speed was so high and had increased so rapidly that he thought the speed recorder had malfunctioned. Railway and ICC officials later tested the speed recorder and found it to be accurate.

Tragically, the Evaro derailment resulted in the death of a three-year-old, Theresa Ann Dooms. The young girl was riding in the forward end of dome coach 552 in line C-260 and, in a freak manner, was buried in mud that had been scooped into the forward end of the car as it nosed over an embankment during the derailment. The girl suffocated in the mud. She would be the only passenger fatality

The Vista-Dome North Coast Limited

Just three months after the Granite derailment, train No. 26 derailed at 87 miles per hour near Evaro, Montana, on June 10, 1962. This accident resulted in the only passenger fatality on the *North Coast Limited* during its entire history of operation. These two photos show the cleanup operation underway.
Ron Nixon photos; Bill Kuebler collection

Chapter 11: Accidents

in the entire 70-year history of the train's NP operation. The accident also resulted in the injury of 247 other passengers, six Pullman porters, 13 dining car employees, and one coach attendant. The three trainmen and two enginemen received only minor injuries.

The derailment itself was spectacular. All four diesel units and the first 15 cars of the 17-car train derailed; several of these overturned. The four diesel units slid on their sides down an embankment for some 470 feet before coming to rest in a muddy ditch alongside a highway. Although damage to them and many of the cars was heavy, it would have been much worse had the ground not been so soft and muddy from the heavy rains that had fallen the night before the accident.

Once again, the train's Stewardess-Nurse got involved in rescue efforts. Miss Carole McLennan, who was in her roomette in car 265, the first car behind the diner, when the accident occurred, immediately went to work by helping people out of the derailed and heavily damaged cars and grouping the injured ones in one location, as much as was safely possible, so doctors could tend to them on the scene. (A more detailed account of her experience in this accident appears in the "Stewardess-Nurses" section of Chapter 12.)

In the following weeks court hearings were held, and in the end, the engine crew was found "not guilty of criminal intent." Even so, the engine crew was fired and would never again serve on the NP. It is possible that this accident resulted, indirectly, in yet another fatality. The road foreman of engines who supervised Missoula engine crews at the time of this accident committed suicide several months later.

The high speed of this derailment is evident by the long path the first two diesel units took while sliding on their sides before coming to rest by the distant tree. Overturned water-baggage car 405 partially obscures the rear pair of diesel units. June 10, 1962.
Al Bennett photo; Bill Kuebler collection

The Vista-Dome North Coast Limited

The consist of train No. 26 which derailed at Evaro reflected the heavy travel associated with the 1962 Seattle World's Fair. It also reflected the temporary shortage of equipment that had resulted from the Granite accident three months earlier, for there was no Slumbercoach involved in the Evaro derailment. Two 8-6-3-1 sleepers served in place of the Slumbercoach. With another extra 8-6-3-1 sleeper just ahead of the observation-lounge car, the train was unusually long, at 17 cars. The consist of No. 26 that derailed at Evaro was as follows:

- 6510A F-7A
- 6701B F-9B
- 6701C F-9A
- 6511A F-7A
- CB&Q 405 Water-Baggage (destroyed)
- CB&Q 479 Mail-Dormitory (destroyed)*
- 354 8-6-3-1 Sleeper (destroyed; operating in place of Slumbercoach)
- 353 8-6-3-1 Sleeper (destroyed; operating in place of Slumbercoach)
- 552 Dome Coach
- 592 Day-Nite Coach
- CB&Q 557 Dome Coach
- 503 Day Coach
- CB&Q 598 Day-Nite Coach
- 496 Traveller's Rest
- 461 Dining Car
- 362 8-6-3-1 Sleeper
- CB&Q 304 Dome Sleeper
- 368 8-6-4 Sleeper
- 307 Dome Sleeper
- 358 8-6-3-1 Sleeper (extra car)
- 394 Sleeper-Observation-Lounge

The crew of train No. 26 included the following personnel:

- Engineer Eldon E. Lynn
- Fireman Gerry Haines
- Conductor Fred L. O'Brien
- Brakeman H. E. Johnson
- Brakeman J. H. Geiger
- Stewardess-Nurse Carole McLennan

---

* Mail-dormitory car 479 was repaired by CB&Q and placed back into service a few months after the accident. Other equipment shown as destroyed was scrapped. All four locomotive units and the cars not shown as destroyed were repaired and returned to service. Also, the second diesel unit in this train is incorrectly shown as 6510B in the Vol. 7, No. 4 issue of *The Mainstreeter*; the correct number is 6701B as shown above.

Chapter 12

The Crew of the Vista-Dome North Coast Limited

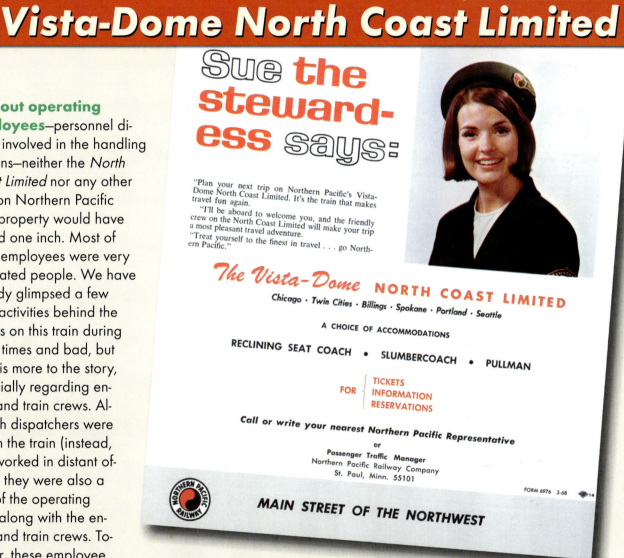

Without operating employees—personnel directly involved in the handling of trains—neither the *North Coast Limited* nor any other train on Northern Pacific (NP) property would have moved one inch. Most of these employees were very dedicated people. We have already glimpsed a few crew activities behind the scenes on this train during good times and bad, but there is more to the story, especially regarding engine and train crews. Although dispatchers were not on the train (instead, they worked in distant offices), they were also a part of the operating team along with the engine and train crews. Together, these employee groups carried the most responsibility for a safe, efficient operation. These people learned and developed their skills over many years, and the demands of their trades were formidable. This is necessarily so, because rail transportation is an inherently complex and unforgiving business, especially in the passenger department. And, there is yet another group of NP employees worth special consideration: the Stewardess-Nurses. They were a unique group, because they were associated only with the *Vista-Dome North Coast Limited*, and more closely so than any other group of employees.

187

The Vista-Dome North Coast Limited

A high-speed passenger train such as the *North Coast Limited* was a handful, requiring more than one person to effect a safe operation. Someone with a day job in an office can hardly relate to the locomotive engineer's daunting task of correctly executing 20 decisions per minute behind a throttle at 3 A.M., while ever-present fatigue plays havoc with the senses. The same is true regarding NP trainmen and dispatchers. Most were men of special character who had to possess a strong work ethic—and, perhaps enjoy a bit of good fortune now and then—in order to have a long, uneventful career. In this regard, NP operating employees were standouts in the transportation industry, suffering remarkably few exceptions in their ranks. Their combination of camaraderie, a "family" atmosphere on the job, and the necessarily high standards of professionalism was a remarkable achievement, something from which today's generation could learn much. The operating crew of the *Vista-Dome North Coast Limited*, NP's flagship train, is due some press, indeed. Furthermore, not only does a closer look at their jobs help us better to appreciate their accomplishments, it also provides a context for understanding who worked on this train and why they did. Railroad personnel often made career decisions for reasons a passenger or railfan might not appreciate or even expect. Before we consider engine crews, train crews, dispatchers, and the Stewardess-Nurses in more detail, however, we should briefly mention the entire spectrum of personnel involved in the operation of trains No. 25 and No. 26.

Depending on the season, up to 32 people operated and staffed each *Vista-Dome North Coast Limited* at any one time during its journey. The number of people working this train over six operating divisions was considerably larger, however, when including all the train and engine crew changes along the way. On a 14-car train in 1959 the entire crew included: the engineer and fireman; the trainmen (conductor, head brakeman, and rear brakeman); a baggage man; two postal clerks; three coach attendants; the Stewardess-Nurse; the Traveller's Rest crew (a cook, a waiter, and the waiter-in-charge); the dining car crew (the steward, three cooks, and six waiters); the Pullman conductor; five Pullman porters; and the Pullman observation-lounge attendant.

Some of the people who made the *Vista-Dome North Coast Limited* one of the world's finest trains.

Chapter 12: The Crew of the *Vista-Dome North Coast Limited*

Traveling electrician Larry Ryan poses for Stewardess-Nurse Joan Reitz at Livingston in 1961. He is making one of his usual trips from Missoula to Livingston and return. His maintenance skills and dedication to duty helped the NP achieve very high rates of in-service equipment reliability.
Joan Reitz photo

In addition to these essential personnel, an electrician rode the train between certain points *en route* as needed. One such electrician, a Missoula man, Larry Ryan, was noted for his exceptional skills in maintaining passenger car air-conditioning systems and for his dedication to duty. Throughout NP's vista-dome era, he would board train No. 26 at Missoula and ride it to Livingston, where he would get off, board train No. 25 about an hour later, and ride it back to Missoula. He did this almost every day. During these trips, he would troubleshoot any problems that occurred with the air-conditioning or electrical systems on the train and repair the equipment as necessary during stops at Missoula, Butte, or Livingston. In some cases, he repaired equipment in the cars while the train was moving. His efforts supplemented the routine maintenance programs at NP's Como shops and had a great deal to do with the NP's very high level of on-road equipment reliability. Conductor Warren McGee states:

> A serious air-conditioning problem on train 25 or 26, what with the dome cars in use, was something that could put a lot of gray hair on a conductor. One of the most difficult decisions a passenger conductor could ever face would be whether or not to set out a malfunctioning dome car, or any car, from train 25 or 26. That was something we didn't even want to think about! Fortunately, we rarely had such problems, and we can credit Mr. Larry Ryan of Missoula for much of our good record. And besides his electrical and mechanical skills, he was a true gentleman. I don't know a man on the NP who, if he knew anything about Larry Ryan, didn't highly respect him.

A traveling passenger representative would also be aboard the train on many occasions, observing and assessing the crew's performance, the condition of the equipment, and the overall operation, thus helping to assure the finest service possible. Ed Rowell, Northern Pacific Railway Historical Association (NPRHA) member and guest speaker at the Association's Bismarck convention in 1997, was a passenger agent and representative who frequently traveled aboard the train. Even G. Walter Rodine, head of NP's Passenger Traffic Department until his retirement in August 1963, would travel aboard the train on occasion and as inconspicuously as possible, spot-checking the quality of service.

Even though a large team of people helped make the *Vista-Dome North Coast Limited* the premier train that it was, throughout the remainder of this chapter we will focus on the operating team directly involved with handling the train: the engine crews, the train crews, and the dispatchers. We will also take a closer look at that unique group, the Stewardess-Nurses.

The Vista-Dome North Coast Limited

Engine Crews and Train Handling

The locomotive engineer was directly responsible for handling the locomotive and, therefore, the entire train. Although the conductor was technically the boss of the train, the two men were mutually responsible for its safe operation. In actual practice, rare was the occasion of disagreement between them about how the *Vista-Dome North Coast Limited* should be handled—"trains 25 and 26" to the crews, who rarely referred to passenger trains by their names. It was a first class operation all the way, and everyone knew it. With few exceptions, the only time an engineer on train No. 25 found himself sitting in a siding was when meeting train No. 26, and vice versa. The schedule was a fast one. Late arrivals at terminals meant explanations were due supervisors all the way up the ladder to St. Paul headquarters.

Therefore, whenever a train was late, as long as the crew had not received any train orders prohibiting making up the lost time, the engineer was free to do his best—within limits. Most speed limits were imposed by rules and special instructions. A speed-governing device on each diesel cab unit imposed the highest speed limit electrically and mechanically, so as to help keep the locomotive engineer from exceeding the 85 mile-per-hour speed limit shown on a placard in the cab. This speed governor had a shrill warning that sounded when the locomotive reached about 83 or 84 miles per hour. If the warning sounded, the engineer had about 10 seconds to apply the train's brakes and re-

Up against the speed governor... Paralleling Milwaukee's electrified line, train No. 25 races toward the late afternoon sun on May 23, 1957. Even when on-time, westbound NP passenger trains routinely achieve top speed between Bonner and Missoula, so as to arrive at the division terminal three or four minutes ahead of schedule. Here, at milepost 115 four miles east of Missoula, the westbound *North Coast Limited* is probably making at least 80 miles per hour, maybe even triggering an occasional chirp from the overspeed warning in the cab. The three-unit locomotive consists of F-7A 6501C, an unidentified F-3B (probably 6501B), and F-3A 6501A.
Ron Nixon photo; Bill Kuebler collection

Chapter 12: The Crew of the *Vista-Dome North Coast Limited*

duce speed. If the engineer ignored the warning and allowed the speed governor to fully activate, the governor would cause an automatic "penalty" brake application and idling of the engines. This "penalty" brake application (the term used by crews) would bring the train to a stop. Once begun, this action could not be interrupted by the engineer. To regain full control of his locomotive following a penalty brake application, an engineer had to reset a special control valve and then release the brakes, a process that took more than a few seconds. When making up lost time, some engineers reached speeds just high enough to "nudge" the speed governor without tripping it. Sometimes this happened because of a moment of inattention to speed, at other times engineers intentionally "nudged" the speed governor. A few engineers have told this author that they considered it an art to get as close as possible to the governor warning without tripping the device, when conditions permitted. On a few occasions in the mid- and late-1960s, while riding the locomotive cab on trains No. 25 and No. 26, this author witnessed speeds between Fargo and Jamestown that were just high enough to "nudge" the governor warning in the cab (about 83 miles per hour), causing an irregular beeping sound just as the engineer set some air to reduce speed a little.

Similar practices occurred on other operating divisions. In 1958, for example, Parkwater Engineer Dave Townsend established the best running time with No. 25 from Paradise to Spokane and took some pride in the fact that fellow enginemen tried in vain to break his record in the years to follow. (It is possible, though far from certain, that Engineer Jess Pruitt was trying to do just that—

Seconds before this picture was taken, Engineer Charlie Reinke "set the air" for his initial brake application. Train No. 25 approaches Missoula in 1954 at a good 75 miles per hour on this well elevated curve, which circumvents Mount Jumbo. Reinke "has a hold of 'em," locomotive engineer's jargon for assuring a definite brake application on all cars in the train by use of the automatic brake valve, followed by a well-timed reduction in throttle setting. The Missoula "spot" is one mile ahead, where precise stopping point leeway is very small. Reinke brings 49 years of experience in engine service to the task, so another perfect spot is probable.
Ron Nixon photo, Bill Kuebler collection

The Vista-Dome North Coast Limited

Some engineers dressed up for work. Art Willis, of Staples, was known for wearing a dress shirt, bow tie, and white cap whenever he worked in passenger service. He was also known for good train handling. In this view, he handles GP-9 No. 245 and three F-units on train No. 1 at Hawley, Minnesota, in March 1965. His next trip will be on trains 25 and 26. Road Foreman Paul Wagner, supervisor of Staples terminal enginemen, took this picture as Willis acknowledged a radio call from the conductor. Willis had several colorful quips and referred to road foremen as "wandering hogheads," instead of the more common term among enginemen: "traveling engineer." Art Willis entered engine service as a fireman in 1923 and was promoted to engineer in 1944.
Paul Wagner photo; Bill Kuebler collection

break Townsend's record—on the night he lost his life in the Granite derailment in March 1962.) Each engine district had certain engineers who were known to be particularly fast runners when making up lost time, although the diesel era tended to level the playing field somewhat as compared with the steam era. Apart from speed limits imposed by rules and speed governors, a diesel locomotive's top speed was more or less fixed by gear ratio, and for any given train, acceleration was determined by available horsepower and tractive effort—factors independent of who was running the locomotive. In contrast, a steam locomotive's performance was much more labor-intensive

One of Tacoma Division's best, Engineer James A. "Jimmy" Darker plies his trade in F-9A 6700A on train No. 25, April 8, 1963. This photo was taken inside Stampede Tunnel No. 3, just as the train reached the summit about midway through the tunnel. Darker's left hand grasps the transition lever. Although NP's F-units had automatic transition (changing electrical circuitry at various speeds) during this period, the transition lever was still used for dynamic braking. Darker is moving the handle from the "OFF" position to the "B" position, or to his right, to begin dynamic braking. From there, he can increase the amount of dynamic braking by moving the transition lever further right. As long as train speed is not too high at this point, he should be able to control the train on the long mountain grade descent with little or no use of the air brake system. Hired as a fireman in 1917, Darker was promoted to engineer in 1942.
Jim Fredrickson photo

Chapter 12: The Crew of the *Vista-Dome North Coast Limited*

Several years before he had enough seniority to hold passenger service on a regular basis, 45-year-old Engineer Fred J. "Fritz" Lewis was called out from the "chain gang" freight pool to handle train No. 1 on this day in 1951. Lewis's outstanding train handling ability was well known among Fargo Division enginemen and trainmen—and supervisors. Among other things, he was known for using minimal brake-pipe reductions during brake applications on streamlined passenger trains. One night, a road foreman forsook his seat to stand behind Lewis in the cab of No. 26 all the way from Berea to Dilworth (67 miles), in the supervisor's own words, "just to watch him and see how he could be so smooth and use such small reductions like that...It was fascinating to see, and I was humbled."
Bill Kuebler collection, courtesy of Esther Lewis

and dependent on the engine crew's abilities to work the engine to full capacity. Therefore, the only remaining method of establishing the best running time across an engine district in the diesel era was to perfect braking and train handling techniques.

Many passenger engineers had reputations as "fast runners" during the period 1954–70, but there were only a few among them who were also known for possessing exceptional train-handling skills. These engineers were both fast *and smooth*. They were highly respected by peers and road foremen, alike. During NP's vista-dome era, these enginemen included, among others: Pat Hannon and Frank "Pug" Pugleasa (St. Paul), Art Willis (Staples), Fred J. "Fritz" Lewis (Dilworth), Ed Ingstad (Jamestown), Stuart Farmer and Joe Sagmiller (Mandan), Hunter Picken (Dickinson), Herb Wurdeman (Forsyth), Barney Bassett and Bob Logan (Livingston), Bud Aldrich and Howard Burtch (Missoula), Bill Kuhn (Parkwater), George Ritter and M. J. "Mickey" O'Larey (Pasco), Jack Hodder, and Jimmy Darker (Seattle).

Engineer "Fritz" Lewis congratulates St. Paul Division Conductor Ray Lundberg at Fargo as the trainman begins the final trip of his 51-year railroad career. Lundberg's run on No. 2 is from Fargo to St. Paul, whereas Lewis is handling the train from Jamestown to Dilworth. It is August 1969, and Lewis himself will retire in just 16 months. Since trains 3 and 4 were discontinued in October 1967, the veteran engineer's trip pairings alternate between trains 25-2 and 1-26. Lewis hired out in engine service in 1922 and was promoted to engineer in 1941.
Bill Kuebler collection, courtesy of Esther Lewis

With dates-of-hire as firemen ranging from 1901 to 1941 (promotion to engineer followed as seniority permitted), several of these engineers retired early in the vista-dome era, whereas some of the others did not have enough seniority to work in passenger service regularly until late in this era.

It is interesting to note that there was no mandatory retirement age for locomotive engineers until 1959, when retirement at age 70 became mandatory. Therefore, prior to 1959, it was common for an engineer to retire with as many as 54 or 55 years of service on the Railway. In fact, when the "age-70 rule" went into effect in 1959, it forced five engineers at Parkwater to retire. Three of these five men had over 50 years of service, and all five represented an aggregate of 244 years in engine service on the NP! Engineer Walter Pansky at Mandan, who regularly worked in passenger service, was said to be over 80 years old—possibly a record—when he was forced to retire in 1959, although he seldom revealed his exact age to fellow railroaders. I met him in Fargo a few months before he died in about 1977. He told me then that he was 101 years old, which would have made him 83 when he was forced to retire in 1959.

It is important to put the subject of train handling in proper context. Engine crews felt a certain amount of pressure to maintain schedules and make up lost time. An on-time arrival in division terminals, especially with NP's flagship train, was paramount. It is in this environment that enginemen honed their skills and, on occasion, exceeded certain posted speed limits by a small margin. While officials neither condoned nor overtly permitted violations of rules or speed limits, it is also true that an engineer with a good reputation would not likely be called on the carpet for exceeding a posted speed limit by a few miles per hour—provided he had maintained a safe operation. As for the practical aspects of the matter, engine crews on each subdivision were well aware of which curves' speed limits could safely be exceeded and by how much. Engineers referred to this as "crowding curves." Some curves could safely be "crowded" while others could not; any engineer who hoped to turn in a good performance without compromising safety had best know which ones were which and just what the margin was for each curve.

Strict adherence to speed limits became a matter of greater concern, however, following the disastrous derailment of No. 25 at Granite in March 1962. Among road foremen, tolerance for an engineer exceeding speed limits, even slightly, narrowed. On-time performance of trains No. 25 and No. 26 remained high throughout the 1960s, but it is interesting to note that from 1962 to 1970, improvements to schedules and running times across the system resulted primarily from line changes and curve reductions, not from train handling factors. Even so, the human factor was still the most important one with regard to train handling and performance. The second most important factor, one closely associated with the first, was brake systems.

Brake Systems

A high-speed passenger train possesses an incredible amount of momentum. The only viable means of decelerating a streamlined, lightweight passenger train are gravity (on ascending grades) and brake systems. Rolling friction is negligible. On straight and level track, merely closing the locomotive's throttle has almost no effect on train speed. This author once witnessed a 13-car passenger train decelerate from 80 to 75 miles per hour while coasting along level track. The throttle was in *IDLE* and brakes were released, leaving only wheel-rail friction, roller bearings, and wind to resist the train's motion. It took nearly two miles to slow to 75 miles per hour!

As for handling NP trains No. 25 and No. 26 (or, any other trains for that matter), brake systems and the engine crew were very closely related, interdependent factors. Engineers who understood brake systems well were in the best position to perform well on the job. Some engineers developed reputations as "air brake experts" and even held informal classes in their homes for

Chapter 12: The Crew of the *Vista-Dome North Coast Limited*

younger enginemen who were studying for their air brake exams in preparation for promotion to engineer. One Idaho Division engineer, known for his air brake expertise, held many informal sessions in his home during the steam era. In these sessions he explained complicated air brake systems to younger men in a way they could understand. He was Jess Pruitt, none other than the engineer who lost his life in the Granite derailment of train No. 25 in 1962. One of Pruitt's air brake students was Glenn Staeheli, a man who, years later, became a road foreman of engines and then NP's system air brake supervisor.

All in a day's work... With grip and lantern in hand, the Tacoma Division rear brakeman who worked train No. 26 in from Seattle has just been relieved and heads for his layover hotel in Ellensburg. He will return to Seattle early the following morning on train No. 1. An Idaho Division train crew, including the relieving rear brakeman standing in the vestibule of car 391, will handle this train from Ellensburg to Spokane. It is late afternoon in this October 1964 photo.
Robert W. Johnston collection

The Vista-Dome North Coast Limited

Besides hand brakes (not used in normal passenger train operations), trains No. 25 and No. 26 actually had four brake systems during the 1950s and early 1960s: the independent brake, the automatic air brake system, the electro-pneumatic brake system (until May 1962), and the dynamic brake. I will list these systems and briefly summarize their essential features and characteristics below, and then I will discuss how NP engine crews used these systems, particularly on trains No. 25 and No. 26. Although they may seem rather lengthy and tedious in places, the following summaries cover only the essential features of each system as they relate to our story.

Independent Brake System
- Was referred to variously by engine crews as the "straight air," the "independent brake," or the "engine brake." All locomotives had this system.
- Controlled only the brakes on the locomotive. This system had to be used when running a locomotive "light" (without cars); it could also be used when the locomotive was handling cars.
- Was controlled by use of the independent brake valve in the locomotive cab, often referred to as the "straight air valve." The engineer controlled this valve by use of a handle about seven inches long on the engineer's brake control pedestal.
- Applied the locomotive brakes by a "straight" (direct and positive) application of air pressure to the locomotive's brake cylinders. Air pressure was directly proportional to movement of the independent brake valve, just as braking force in an automobile is directly proportional to brake pedal movement. This was a fast acting system; there was almost no delay from brake valve handle movement to brake application.
- Was not independent of other brake systems, in spite of its name, because the locomotive brakes could be activated by use of the automatic air brake system, the system that controlled the brakes on all the cars in a train.
- Could be overridden during an automatic air brake application. The engineer could depress the independent brake valve handle straight down about two inches, thus keeping the engine's brakes released during an application of the train's brakes.
- Was relatively easy to understand and use. It was easier to "spot" (precisely stop) a passenger train by use of this system as compared with the automatic air brake system.
- When used by itself to stop a train, caused slack action in the train as cars tended to run up against the braking locomotive and then roll back away from it when the locomotive stopped. Thus, it tended to cause rough handling; it could be jerky.

Automatic Air Brake System
- Required by Interstate Commerce Commission (ICC) regulations to be installed and operational on all trains, except when the electro-pneumatic brake system was in use on trains No. 25 and No. 26. (See summary of the electro-pneumatic system below.)
- Complex system that controlled all the brakes in a train; this included the brakes on each car and, through the independent brake system, on the locomotive. The automatic air brake system was not used when running a locomotive light (without cars).
- Functioned on the train essentially as follows: brakes were applied throughout the train by *reducing* air pressure in the train's brake pipe from a nominal value; brakes were released by *increasing* air pressure in the brake pipe back toward the nominal value. Brake pipe air was the

pressurized air extending through the train via piping on each car and hose couplings between cars. On NP passenger trains, nominal brake pipe air pressure was 90 pounds per square inch (p.s.i.) and 110 p.s.i. in mountain grade territory. The engineer used a "feed valve" in the locomotive cab to establish the nominal brake pipe pressure value on his train.

- Functioned on each car essentially as follows: compressed air was stored in the car's reservoir; a complex valve mounted on the car, known on the NP generally as a "triple valve," served as an interface between brake pipe air and air stored in the car's reservoir; during a brake application, as brake pipe air pressure decreased below the nominal value, the triple valve mechanically sensed this decrease and thereby allowed compressed air to flow from that car's reservoir, through the triple valve, and into the brake cylinders; compressed air in the brake cylinders pushed the brake shoes (via mechanical rigging) against that car's wheels or brake discs. During brake release, brake pipe air pressure increased back toward the nominal value. As a car's triple valve mechanically sensed this increase, it allowed brake cylinder air to exhaust to the atmosphere, releasing the car's brakes (this took only a few seconds), and it allowed brake pipe air to refill that car's reservoir until reservoir pressure equaled brake pipe pressure (this took longer).

- Designed to be a fail-safe system in the event the train accidentally parted at any coupling (known as a "break-in-two"). Breaking the air hose coupling between any two engine units or cars immediately released pressurized brake pipe air to atmosphere, causing an automatic emergency brake application on both parts of the train; hence, the term "automatic" in reference to this system.

- Required "charging" a train (initially) and "recharging" the train after each brake application and release. Each car's air reservoir had to be "charged" (filled) for use and "recharged" (refilled) after each brake application and release. To accomplish this, the triple valve on each car routed pressurized air from the brake pipe, through the triple valve, and into that car's reservoir until brake pipe and reservoir air were at equal pressures. This process normally began during each release of the train's air brakes and continued until brake pipe pressure reached nominal value. Recharging a train could take anywhere from a few seconds to several minutes, depending on the number of cars in the train and the amount of air needed to recharge each car. A passenger train normally recharged in less than a minute following a typical brake application and release.

- Limited the number of possible brake applications and releases in immediate succession before depletion of reservoir air on each car. Depletion could result in a runaway train. This meant that engineers had to have good judgment in when and how to use the train's brakes for planned stops or slow-downs; they had to think well ahead of the train and avoid situations that required multiple applications and releases in quick succession.

- Controlled in most situations by use of an air brake valve in the locomotive cab; crews called this the "automatic air brake valve" or "automatic brake valve." In spite of its name, the engineer manually operated this valve. The automatic brake valve was controlled by use of a handle about 10 inches long, located on the brake control pedestal in the locomotive cab, usually near the independent brake valve handle. The brake control pedestal was adjacent the engine control pedestal (which contained the throttle and other controls); both pedestals were in front of or to the side of the engineer's seat.

- Also controlled by use of an emergency valve on the fireman's side of the locomotive cab, or by use of an emergency valve in the vestibule of each passenger car (or by a valve in the caboose

The Vista-Dome North Coast Limited

on freight trains). This system could also be controlled by use of a special valve at the rear of the observation-lounge car on trains No. 25 and No. 26—the rear brakeman normally used this valve during back up movements at such places as St. Paul Union Depot (SPUD).

- Complex system, difficult for engineers to understand and master. Accurately spotting a train with this system was challenging.

- Involved substantial delay during a normal brake application or release. This delay was due to "pressure gradients" throughout the brake pipe as brake pipe pressure changed on the first car first, then the next car, and so on through the train. Several seconds elapsed between the first car's brake application or release, and the last car's (as much as almost two minutes on a 100-car freight train). On a passenger train, this delay was relatively short but not inconsequential.

- Tended to cause slack action in the train because of this delay. Excessive slack action could result in a break-in-two at one of the train's couplings, especially in the case of a long, heavy freight train. Passenger trains had less slack in them than freights trains—a break-in-two was rare on a passenger train—but, slack action could still be a factor in terms of smoothness. The engineer could counter this slack action during braking by judicious and skillful use of throttle, in effect keeping the train stretched by pulling against the braking action of the train with just the right amount of power and reducing that power as more and more cars' brakes applied from the front part of the train to the rear part. This method was known as "power braking."

Using the automatic brake system to spot a passenger train had significant advantages. When used skillfully, it resulted in a very smooth operation. It also resulted in a more efficient stop, because, while closely approaching a stopping point, a train's speed could be much higher than with use of the independent brake system. Use of the automatic brake system also had disadvantages, for it required good judgment and skill. Poor judgment could result in overshooting or undershooting a stopping point; poor skill could result in rough handling of equipment and, though rare with a passenger train, a break-in-two.

Electro-Pneumatic Brake System

- Special, combination air and electrical system. The NP used this system exclusively on trains No. 25 and No. 26 in 1952–53, and again from 1956 until 1962. No other NP trains used this system.

- Used most of the components of the automatic air brake system, plus other, special, components. Passenger diesel units and lightweight passenger cars required special hoses and electrical connections for this system.

- Required the engineer to use the automatic brake valve to control the train's brakes, but the valve functioned differently when used with this system as compared with the automatic air brake system.

- Functioned essentially as follows: movement of the automatic brake valve handle caused an immediate and "straight air" application (direct application) of brakes on all the cars in the train. Electrical connections and signals made this feature possible. When used with this system, the automatic brake valve functioned much like the independent brake valve.

- Involved no delays during brake applications and releases. All brakes on all cars in the train operated immediately and simultaneously with movement of the automatic brake valve handle in the locomotive cab.

- Found by engineers to be easy to use, once they got used to the system.

Chapter 12: The Crew of the *Vista-Dome North Coast Limited*

- Most efficient, fastest acting brake system available. When functioning properly, this system allowed the engineer to delay a brake application in any normal situation by several seconds.
- Controversial system (more on this in the text below). Some engineers thought it was unreliable and disliked using it. Eventually, the NP permanently removed it from service.

Dynamic Brake System

- Strictly an electrical system for braking a train with the locomotive.
- Installed only on certain locomotives; this system was an available option when ordering new diesel-electric locomotive units. All NP passenger F-units in the transcontinental pool had this system.
- Controlled by use of a "transition" lever in the locomotive cab. This lever was located on the control stand; on F-units the transition lever was near the throttle.
- Functioned essentially as follows: placing the transition lever in the dynamic brake range turned the traction motor (an electrical motor geared directly to the axle) on each axle of the locomotive into a generator driven by the rotation of the axle; electricity generated by each traction motor during dynamic braking was fed into resistor grids atop the locomotive unit and converted into heat, which dissipated into the atmosphere with the help of a large, roof-mounted fan. Thus, the train's kinetic energy was dissipated at the locomotive—the electrical equivalent of slowing an automobile mechanically by using a lower gear and allowing the motor to slow the vehicle. The engineer simply moved the transition lever further into the brake range to increase electrical resistance and, thus, the braking force. Braking force at any given speed was directly proportional to handle movement.
- Required time to set up for a brake application, because of complicated electrical switching that took place when the engineer selected this mode of braking.
- Tended to cause slack action just like that caused by use of the independent brake system. The engineer could not counter this slack action by use of the throttle; control interlocks prevented use of throttle when the dynamic brake was in use.
- Provided braking force that was directly proportional to the locomotive's speed, for any given position of the transition lever. This system was very ineffective at speeds below about 20 miles per hour; this system alone could not stop a train.

Locomotive engineers used the dynamic brake most often to control train speed on long or steep descents where the desired speed was in the 25-50 mile-per-hour range, especially in mountain grade territory. Engineers occasionally used it to slow from a medium speed to a lower speed. They normally did not use the dynamic brake at very high speeds, because doing so could easily result in an electrical overload of the system.

As noted in the above summary, an automatic brake valve was anything but automatic in terms of its use. The engineer manually handled the automatic brake valve. The automatic air brake system was a complex system, and it required of the engineer a great deal of skill, understanding, and experience. Some men were artists; others just got by.

Regarding train handling and air brake systems, a railroad tended to develop a system-wide culture among its engine crews. Road foremen taught certain techniques to the engineers they supervised, usually on the job. Firemen being promoted to engineers attended classes, also taught by a road foreman, who spent a high percentage of class time explaining brake systems and braking techniques. On the NP, a company air brake manual, which was given to all newly promoted engineers, formally set forth standard air brake procedures. The men behind most of these air brake procedures were George Ernstrom, NP's General Mechanical Superintendent from 1946 until 1956, and his successor, Jess Cannon. Cannon wrote many of the company's standard air brake procedures in his younger years, while he was a road foreman of engines. This got him some of the attention that later resulted in further promotion.

In addition to formal means of developing a system-wide culture, senior enginemen passed air brake techniques along to junior enginemen, usually on the job, when the junior men were firing for the older, more experienced ones. Thus, the NP developed its system-wide culture of air brake practices. It is important to note that these practices were not the same on all railroads, and some of the differences were significant.

One notable difference between railroads was in the choice for which brake system to use when stopping a passenger train at a precise point—called "spotting" a train. On a few railroads engineers typically used the independent brake to spot a passenger train, because the technique was quite easy to master. To do this, they would typically slow the train from some high speed to about 15 or 20 miles per hour using the automatic brake valve. Then they would release the train's brakes, creep into the station or toward the stopping point, and complete the stop using only the independent brake valve, precisely stopping the train with the engine brake. But, this spotting technique had a significant disadvantage: it tended to cause rough handling and jerking of the cars during the final moments of the stop, because of "slack action" throughout the train as its cars tended to push up against the locomotive during braking. Then, once the locomotive stopped, the cars tended to roll back away from the locomotive, so as to release the compression forces that had built up throughout the train. This sort of slack action could be quite noticeable and even uncomfortable to passengers.

It is interesting to note that NP's road foremen of engines were men promoted from the ranks of locomotive engineers. Thus, the men who supervised engineers and fireman had had plenty of experience in the same line of work. This was not the case on some other railroads. Road foremen on the Great Northern (GN), for example, were typically men promoted from the ranks of machinists. While they tended to have excellent understanding of mechanical and electrical equipment, they had little or no experience with train handling. This probably accounts for the train handling and air brake techniques that permeated the GN culture.

Use of the automatic air brake system to spot a passenger train at a scheduled stop went a long way toward faster running times across divisions, because an engineer could closely approach a stop or slow-down point at a much higher speed. Officials on the NP were very aware of the importance of this factor in an environment of competitive passenger train scheduling. (Recall that the NP's longer and tougher route placed it at a significant disadvantage to the GN.) Engineers on the NP liked the smoothness they could achieve with this technique. For them, it was a matter of professional pride. Though this braking technique was more challenging to master, NP engineers across the system preferred it and made almost all their stops with passenger trains by using the automatic brake valve. On trains No. 25 and No. 26, however, if the electro-pneumatic brake system was installed and operational, they would use that system (which involved using the same automatic brake valve), a system to which we now turn for a closer look.

Sometime in 1952, the NP equipped its passenger F-3s, F-5s, and F-7s with an electro-pneumatic brake system for use on trains No. 25 and No. 26. Passenger cars also required special equipment and connections for this system. The NP placed it in operation exclusively on trains No. 25 and No. 26 shortly after November 1952, when the *North Coast Limited* first consisted of all lightweight cars. Heavyweight passenger cars did not have electro-pneumatic brake connections. A complete, detailed description of how the electro-pneumatic brake system worked is beyond the scope of this book. Rather, it is important to understand the *effect* that it had on train handling and performance.

Chapter 12: The Crew of the *Vista-Dome North Coast Limited*

As mentioned in the brake system summaries, use of the automatic air brake system involved "pressure gradients" and tended to cause slack action. The electro-pneumatic brake system, however, did not have these undesirable characteristics. And, it functioned like a "straight air" system, making it much easier to spot a train accurately. In effect, the electro-pneumatic brake system combined the advantages of the independent brake system (quick response; simple "straight air" operation; easy-to-achieve accuracy) with all the advantages of power braking with the automatic air brake

Passenger Train Handling on the Northern Pacific

I began to discover the Northern Pacific (NP) train handling philosophy in an interesting way, even though at the time I was unaware that it was, in fact, system-wide. Although this incident did not involve the *Vista-Dome North Coast Limited*, it is representative of NP enginemen's passenger train handling techniques. Indeed, this incident could just as well have happened with trains No. 25 or No. 26, and it could have happened elsewhere on the NP. It happened one hot summer day in 1965 with train No. 2, the eastbound *Mainstreeter*, during its station stop at Fargo.

To put this incident in perspective, it occurred soon after I had witnessed several arrivals of Great Northern (GN) passenger trains at Fargo (an interesting city in which to live for a fan of these two excellent railroads). Few places afforded such close comparison of these two roads' passenger train operations. Typically, GN engine crews spotted passenger trains at the depot by using the independent brake valve. By the time of the NP incident, I had seen a number of GN arrivals that led me to believe that passenger trains always "crept" into the station and came to a very gradual stop.

Not so! On this day in June 1965, I had finally made my way down to the NP depot in time for No. 2's arrival there. (I was on foot and a long ways from home, the first time I visited NP property without an adult escort.) I looked to the west, watching for the train. As it finally came into view, cresting a short hill about a half-mile west, something looked different. The train appeared to be kicking up a thin cloud of dust—and moving fast! I was standing about 500 feet west of the depot and actually stepped back and away from the edge of the platform at the approach of this fast moving train, thinking it was going to blow through town without stopping. This scene was incredible to a young railfan who had never seen such action before.

As the lead F-unit rolled past me at what must have been at least 40 miles per hour (instead of 15 or 20 as I had been used to seeing), Engineer Lewis, who later befriended me, sat up there on his seat in the locomotive cab, appearing utterly relaxed as if nothing was wrong. His arms were folded across his chest, and he seemed oblivious to a requirement to stop his train just short of Broadway, about 300 feet east of the depot. According to an agreement between the NP and Fargo, passenger trains could not block Broadway during station work. I knew from past observations that this train was supposed to stop short of this street, the busiest one in downtown Fargo. "How could he get this train stopped in less than two city blocks?" I wondered. This was going to be interesting.

As the first cars in the train rolled past, I noticed an unusual sound (to me). Their brakes were squealing, something I'd never heard before on a passenger train. They seemed to be squealing in protest to preposterous demands for deceleration—and yet, everything was so smooth. In a moment of magic, the train just came to a smooth stop in its cloud of dust, just as the cars' brakes released. The cars did not surge back and forth; there was no apparent whiplash effect. Stunned, I looked toward Broadway, wondering if the engineer had overshot his spot. I had to go see for myself. As I got there, I was amazed to find Engineer Lewis standing there on the ground, next to his engine, which was perfectly spotted one foot short of Broadway. Lewis had one foot up on NP's new brick and stone centennial marker (1964 marked the 100th anniversary of the signing of the NP charter), casually taking in the sun as if nothing unusual had happened.

I mustered the courage to ask him how he had just stopped his train like that. The question seemed to perplex him. His response: "Whaddya mean? That's the way we always do it, sonny. It's no big deal." When I tried to explain to him what I had observed elsewhere, on "that other road," he just shrugged his shoulders and chuckled.

In later years, after the Burlington Northern (BN) merger, NP and GN passenger engine crews in the Fargo area mixed on various runs, and braking techniques became a point of discussion and, on some occasions, contention. While one former GN fireman, a qualified engineer, was running the locomotive, he attempted to spot a passenger train with the independent brake. His former NP engineer said to him, "Don't! That can be hard on the passengers. When you spot using the straight air like that, if anybody's standing up back there, either you'll make 'em dance or you'll knock 'em down!" When GN enginemen first observed the NP technique up close, some of them were shocked at such high-speed approaches and the accuracy achieved by the NP men.

Very similar and outstanding railroads, the GN and NP were, but their differences went well beyond paint schemes!

Incidentally, NP men were not above misjudgment in passenger train spotting. Although I never observed a GN passenger engineer overshoot a spot, I once observed an NP engineer overshoot his Fargo spot at Broadway with train No. 2. He overshot by nearly the full length of the first diesel unit, forcing pedestrians and automobiles to squeeze their way around the front of his engine during the next several minutes. He was angry with himself, and so embarrassed that he stood on the ground and apologized to pedestrians for having to walk around his engine.

The Vista-Dome North Coast Limited

system (smooth stops and no slack action). In the words of one NP road foreman of engines, "That electro-pneumatic brake system made an expert out of everyone."

On top of all that, it was by far the most efficient system available. It substantially improved train performance, because instantaneous response meant that an engineer could delay a brake application in any normal situation by anywhere from a few seconds to more than half a minute, depending on conditions. There were several factors for an engineer to consider when spotting a train: train speed; the number of cars in a train (there was a substantial difference between braking an 11-car train and a 14-car train); track gradient and curvature; rail condition (wet rail required earlier applications); weather conditions (snow and ice could adversely affect brake equipment and increase stopping distance); the type of brakes on each car and the number of cars in the train with disc brakes (disc brakes required a slightly earlier application than clasp brakes); and other factors. Generally, all other factors being equal, the length of time an engineer could delay his brake application with the electro-pneumatic system was slightly less at higher train speeds than at lower speeds, but it was substantial in all cases. Passenger engineers on the NP had several rules-of-thumb regarding this. For example: With a train of from 10 to 15 cars moving at 70 miles per hour on straight and level track, an engineer could delay a typical brake application by the distance equal to the length of his train. (On a 14-car train with three diesel units, that works out to about 1,350 feet and about 14 seconds.) Thus, the electro-pneumatic brake system permitted better running times across a division.

Depending on the territory, an NP engineer usually had to make several brake applications and releases to control his train during a typical trip. As mentioned earlier, a high-speed passenger train possesses an incredible amount of momentum, so merely closing the throttle had little or no effect on train speed on level grade. Thus, on any given trip, more air brake applications were necessary than one might think. For example, when on-time, the engineer on No. 26 would normally have to "set the air" (make a brake application) 17 times between Livingston and Billings, a gentle, de-

Legend of Engineer's Controls
1. Automatic Brake Valve
2. Full Release Selector Cock
3. First Service Position Clock
4. Pneumatic Control Switch (PC)
5. Safety Control Cock
6. Brake Valve Cutout Cock
7. Deadman's Foot Pedal
8. Rotair Valve (Selector)
9. Cab Heater Valve
10. Reverse Lever
11. Transition Lever
12. Speed Indicator
13. Horn Cords
14. Load and Transition Indicating Meter
15. Throttle Lever
16. Heater Switch
17. Windshield Wiper Valve
18. Equalizing Reservoir and Main Reservoir Air Gauge
19. Independent Brake Valve
20. Brake Pipe and Brake Cylinder Air Gauge
21. Bell Valve
22. Application Pipe and Supression Pipe Air Gauge (if used)
23. Engineer's Watch Receptacle
24. Wheel Slip Indicator
25. Dynamic Brake Warning Light

Chapter 12: The Crew of the *Vista-Dome North Coast Limited*

scending river grade. The seconds gained by use of the electro-pneumatic brake system, as compared with the automatic air brake system, on each of these occasions translated into minutes across the district, significantly improving running times.

In spite of all these advantages, the electro-pneumatic brake system was a controversial one. It was sometimes prone to malfunction and, in a few cases, mishandling by engineers who were not used to it. Mishandling resulted in a very rough ride for passengers, and malfunctions could result in much worse. Engineers have told this author that the system could malfunction at any time under any conditions, but it was more likely to malfunction in winter weather when snow and ice interfered with the electrical connections between the cars. Malfunctions included erratic and inconsistent retardation of the train, and in some cases complete failure of the system. One of the system's advantages could quickly turn into a serious drawback. A malfunction usually occurred in a way that tended to place the train in great jeopardy, because the brake application typically began rather close to the point where a speed restriction would apply and, thus, the engineer would discover the problem too late to take corrective action. When a malfunction with the electro-pneumatic system occurred, the engineer could convert over to the automatic air brake system, but the procedure required at least a few seconds, and in a moment of panic it might take even longer. Either way, this was precious time that the engineer did not have to spare.

One harrowing incident occurred in 1957, for example. Engineer Howard E. McGee was handling train No. 26 just west of Columbus, Montana, when the electro-pneumatic brake system failed during an application to reduce speed for a 40 mile-per-hour curve. McGee reacted immediately and correctly, maintaining his cool under great pressure. Even so, by the time he converted over to the automatic air brake system and began to reduce speed, the train had entered the curve at nearly 70 miles per hour and almost derailed. Had it done so, it would have careened into the Yellowstone River!

Howard McGee was an experienced and highly skilled engineer with an excellent reputation. But, what about enginemen who were less experienced? Was it asking too much of engine crews in the early 1950s to learn a new type of locomotive—the diesel-electric—as well as a new, electro-pneumatic brake system? Perhaps, but in any case, engineers in those days were not given the luxury of extensive formal classroom instruction on new locomotives and systems. Classroom time, with road foremen as instructors, was limited, and this time was usually given to firemen who were being promoted to engineers. Simulators, of course, were unheard of back then. Most learning occurred on the job, and to a great extent it was up to the individual engineman to educate himself by whatever means he could, usually with some help and guidance from the road foremen of engines assigned to his district. (Road foremen received specialized classroom instruction at the various locomotive factories and at the Westinghouse air brake factory.)

For whatever reason, the NP removed the electro-pneumatic brake system from its passenger F-3s, F-5s, and F-7s not long after it was first placed in operation in 1952, although some of the components were left in the cab units. A few years later, in April 1956, Jess Cannon became NP's General Mechanical Superintendent. One of his first decisions was to have the electro-pneumatic brake system re-installed on trains No. 25 and No. 26. Perhaps he believed that passenger engine crews had had enough time to familiarize themselves with diesel-electric locomotives and it was time to re-introduce this braking system. After all, improvement of schedule and running times was still a top priority on the NP; competition with rival GN was stiff. The electro-pneumatic brake system was the fastest acting system available, allowing the shortest possible lead points during *en route* brake applications.

In any case, the NP brought the electro-pneumatic brake system on all passenger F-3, F-5, and F-7 cab units back into service in 1956. The NP never installed master controls in its passenger F-9's cab and engine compartments, but the road did add special hose and cable connections to passenger F-9s in 1956. So, when an F-9 was one of the trailing units in a locomotive, with an F-3, F-5, or F-7 in the lead, the train's electro-pneumatic brake system was functional.

Then, on May 27, 1962, the NP permanently discontinued use of the electro-pneumatic brake system and began a program of removing system components from equipment. No NP documents (known to this author) state the reason for this sudden, permanent discontinuance. The fact that NP officials made this decision about two months after the Granite derailment of train No. 25—a derailment for which the ICC never determined the ultimate cause—suggests that NP officials suspected that the system might have been a factor in the accident. Regardless of that possibility, the system was a controversial one; many engine crews had complained about it over the years. By summer 1964, Livingston Shop and air brake personnel had removed all electro-pneumatic brake system components from *North Coast Limited* equipment.

As noted in the brake systems summary, the dynamic brake was strictly an electrical system. Most engineers did not use the dynamic brake to slow a passenger train, especially when beginning a slow-down at high speed, for high speed could easily cause an overload of the system. They did not use it at very low speeds, either, because it was ineffective at very low speed. Road foremen on the NP encouraged use of the dynamic brake system whenever it was feasible to use it, rather than the automatic air brake system, because the dynamic brake saved wear and tear on brake discs and shoes. Still, some engineers just didn't like using the system, especially the older men who had spent decades on steam locomotives, none of which had anything like a dynamic brake. Once engineers got used to it, however, they usually used it to control train speed on long descending grades, especially in mountain grade territory.

The engineman and brake systems, then, were the most important factors with regard to train handling and overall performance of the *Vista-Dome North Coast Limited*. An outstanding locomotive engineer made his mark by thoroughly understanding the equipment on his locomotive and train, exercising good judgment, being aware of his precise location and all relevant operating conditions, perfecting his braking techniques, developing a good "feel" for the train, and "staying ahead of the game"—thinking way ahead of the train. While watching many different enginemen ply their trades on this train over the years, one thing became clear to this author: the job of locomotive engineer on a high-speed passenger train was a busy one that demanded a great deal of knowledge and constant attention to duty.

Assignment to the North Coast Limited

From the perspective of a railfan, duty aboard the *North Coast Limited* might well be considered a special honor for an engineman. While there may be some truth to that, it was rarely a major consideration when weighing a career decision about whether or not to work on this train. Far more important to enginemen were the factors of pay, schedule, and working conditions. Furthermore, crew rotations often meant handling various passenger trains and not just the *North Coast Limited*. This subject is best understood in the context of engine districts, seniority, and union agreements.

The NP was divided into seven operating divisions, six of which handled the *North Coast Limited*. These were further divided into subdivisions. Generally, an engine district for main line passenger trains corresponded to a main line subdivision, covering about 100–150 miles. Each engine district had a home terminal and a distant (or layover) terminal. In some cases, engine crews' seniority rights covered only one district; these men never worked over adjacent districts. In other cases, as are noted in the accompanying table, engine crews had seniority rights over two or more adjacent districts. In all cases, though, the territory where a given engineman had seniority rights defined the limits of where he could work on the NP while maintaining his seniority. If an engineer moved from, say, the St. Paul Division out to, say, the Rocky Mountain Division, where he had no seniority rights, he would have to start at the bottom of the seniority roster there. This rarely occurred.

Chapter 12: The Crew of the Vista-Dome North Coast Limited

Therefore, enginemen (and trainmen) tended to live and work in a relatively small geographical area of the NP throughout their railroad careers.

The accompanying table shows the engine districts involved in handling trains No. 25 and No. 26, and other main line passenger trains. These districts did not change during the 1954–70 period, except for a few adjustments in mileage due to line changes.

Passenger Engine Crew Districts
(Mileage figures accurate as of June 1959)

District	Home Terminal	Distant Terminal	Mileage	Notes
St. Paul First Sub	St. Paul	Staples	141	1
St. Paul Second Sub	Staples	Dilworth	106	1
Fargo First Sub	Dilworth	Jamestown	97	1, 2
Fargo Second Sub	Jamestown	Mandan	108	1
Yellowstone First Sub	Mandan	Dickinson	100	3
Yellowstone Second Sub	Dickinson	Glendive	106	3
Yellowstone Third Sub	Glendive	Forsyth	124	3
Yellowstone Fourth Sub	Forsyth	Billings	102	3, 4
Livingston "East End"	Livingston	Billings	116	5, 6, 7
Livingston "West End"	Livingston	Butte/Helena	120/123	6, 7
Missoula "East End"	Missoula	Butte/Helena	120/119	7, 8
Missoula "West End"	Missoula	Paradise	71	7, 8, 9
Parkwater	Spokane	Paradise	187	10
Pasco "East End"	Pasco	Spokane	145	11
Pasco "West End"	Pasco	Yakima (firemen)	90	11, 12
		Ellensburg (engineers)	126	11, 12
Seattle	Seattle	Ellensburg (engineers)	124	12
		Yakima (firemen)	161	12

Notes:
1. Engine crews on the St. Paul and Fargo Divisions had seniority rights on only one district. They did not have rights on the other subdivision on their division.
2. Fargo First Subdivision engine crews' pay was based on 100 miles, the minimum mileage for pay purposes.
3. Engine crews on the Yellowstone division had seniority rights from Mandan to Billings/Laurel. Thus, they could exercise their seniority to work on any one of these four engine districts. The Yellowstone First Subdivision tended to attract the most senior men, because the home terminal, Mandan, was the largest city as compared with other home terminals. The Yellowstone Third Subdivision was the next most senior district, because of the longer mileage (thus, higher pay) and a comparatively easy river grade run. The Yellowstone Second Subdivision tended to be the most junior district on this division.
4. Forsyth freight engine crews worked Forsyth-Laurel Yard, a distance of 116 miles.
5. Livingston "East End" freight engine crews worked Livingston-Laurel Yard, a distance of 102 miles.
6. Livingston terminal engine crews could exercise their seniority to work on either the "east end" or "west end." Generally, the "west end" tended to attract the most senior men, because of the greater mileage and, thus, higher pay.
7. The Livingston and Missoula engine crew districts correspond to the old Montana and Rocky Mountain Divisions, respectively. The Montana Division extended from Billings to Butte/Helena, and the Rocky Mountain Division originally extended from Butte/Helena through Missoula to Paradise. In 1932, the Montana Division was eliminated and absorbed by the Yellowstone and Rocky Mountain Divisions. At that time, Livingston became the dividing point between the two divisions. Engine crew seniority districts remained the same after this change, however.
8. Missoula terminal engine crews could exercise their seniority to work on either the "east end" or "west end." Generally, the "east end" tended to attract the most senior men, because of the greater mileage and higher pay.
9. Mileage corresponds to routing over the Sixth Subdivision, from DeSmet to Paradise via Evaro and Dixon. Freight engine crews usually handled trains over the Fifth Subdivision, via St. Regis, a distance of 100 miles. Pay was the same for either route, because the minimum pay for a trip was based on 100 miles.
10. This territory was also known as "the Idaho East." Parkwater passenger engine crews did not have seniority rights west of Spokane. Parkwater freight engine crews handled trains from Yardley to Paradise, a distance of 183 miles. This district had the highest rates of pay on the NP, because of the mileage.
11. Pasco engine crews had seniority rights on both the "east end" and "west end." The east end tended to attract the senior men, because of the greater mileage and higher pay. Pasco west end freight engine crews handled trains from Pasco to Yakima.
12. The territory for passenger engineers and fireman differed, as shown. This was in accordance with union agreements reached shortly after trains No. 25 and No. 26 began operation in 1952.

The Vista-Dome North Coast Limited

An engineman's seniority—by far the most important factor in his railroad career—determined his career options. Upon exercising his seniority, however, he may still have had to qualify for particular types of service, such as passenger, gas electrics, snow plow, etc. As for passenger service, many enginemen preferred this line of work, because of the regular schedule and shorter hours per trip. It did not pay as well as some other types of service, but many men deemed the desirable work schedule to be worth the trade-off in pay, especially when compared with working in the main line freight pool (nicknamed "chain gang").

As one might expect, the NP sought to maximize employee productivity, whereas labor unions sought to maximize pay and obtain desirable work conditions. Some examples of passenger trip rotations on various engine districts illustrate the results of balancing these goals at the negotiating table. Trains appearing in the examples below include trains No. 1 and No. 2, No. 3 and No. 4, and No. 25 and No. 26. Trains No. 1 and No. 2 operated as *The Mainstreeter*, a St. Paul-Seattle secondary train that generally stopped at several smaller towns between terminals and carried several mail, express, and baggage cars in addition to coaches, a lounge, diner, and a sleeping car. Trains No. 3 and No. 4 originally operated as *The Alaskan* and made even more stops *en route* than trains No. 1 and No. 2. It carried fewer cars but had a similar make-up, depending on the year (no sleeping cars by the mid-1950s). When the NP curtailed the operation of trains No. 3 and No. 4 from a St. Paul-Seattle operation to a St. Paul-Glendive operation, the Railway officially discontinued use of the train's name. In 1959 the NP further curtailed trains No. 3 and No. 4 to a St. Paul-Mandan operation.

On the St. Paul Second Subdivision (Staples to Dilworth), a main line passenger engine crew's trip rotation in 1959 was as follows:

First Trip: Out on No. 3, 11-hour layover, back on No. 2, then 15 hours off.
Second Trip: Out on No. 1, 7-hour layover, back on No. 4, then almost 21 hours off.
Third Trip: Out on No. 25, 2-hour layover, back on No. 26, then almost 24 hours off.

Then this pattern was repeated. Four regularly assigned passenger engine crews were necessary to fill this work schedule.

The Fargo First Subdivision (Dilworth to Jamestown) had its own rotation for main line passenger engine crews in 1959 that looked like this:

First Trip: Out on No. 1, 7-hour layover, back on No. 26, then 26 hours off.
Second Trip: Out on No. 3, 12-hour layover, back on No. 4, then 25 hours off.
Third Trip: Out on No. 25, 13-hour layover, back on No. 2, then 21 hours off.

Then this pattern was repeated. This rotation involved a little more layover and off-duty time than the one for the St. Paul Second Subdivision, so this one required five assigned engine crews to fill the schedule.

Beginning in 1959 trains No. 3 and No. 4 operated only between St. Paul and Mandan, so districts west of Mandan had fewer regularly assigned passenger engine crews. A passenger engine crew's trip rotation on the Yellowstone Second Subdivision (Dickinson to Glendive) in late 1959, for example, was as follows:

First Trip: Out on No. 1, 6-hour layover, back on No. 2, then 21 hours off.
Second Trip: Out on No. 25, 11-hour layover, back on No. 26, then 24 hours off.

Then, this pattern was repeated. This required only three regularly assigned engine crews.

Chapter 12: The Crew of the *Vista-Dome North Coast Limited*

In addition to regularly assigned crews, each district had several engineers and firemen in the main line "chain gang" freight pool or on the "extra board" who were passenger-qualified. The nickname "chain gang" reflected the system of first-in, first-out crew rotation in the main line freight pool. The "extra board" consisted of enginemen unassigned to other duty, who were available to fill in for regularly assigned men laying off one or more trips. The extra board usually consisted of the most junior men in the district. Whenever a regularly assigned passenger man decided to lay off a trip due to illness or for personal reasons, someone either from the chain gang freight pool, or from the extra board, in that order of precedence, would replace him. Whenever a man from chain gang replaced a regularly assigned passenger engineer or fireman, union agreements required that it be the senior "available" chain gang man, where "available" meant that he was legally rested from his previous trip and was passenger-qualified.

Train routing determined some districts' trip assignments. These districts included the territory between Livingston and Missoula via Butte (trains No. 25 and No. 26), and the territory between Livingston and Missoula via Helena (trains No. 1 and No. 2).

Thus, assignments and rotations were determined by the scheduling of passenger trains over the relevant crew's district, and, to a lesser extent, by the labor unions' negotiated preferences. There was, however, one engine district worth special mention.

A most interesting example of labor union preference occurred at the Parkwater engine terminal. The passenger enginemen's home terminal was Spokane and their distant terminal was Paradise. Timetable scheduling made trip pairings of No. 26-No. 1 and No. 2-No. 25 more logical, but the Brotherhood of Locomotive Engineers (BLE) successfully negotiated a No. 26-No. 25 and No. 2-No. 1 arrangement instead, with separate engine crews assigned to each pairing. Parkwater engine crews did not rotate. This created the need for one more passenger engine crew in this district than would have been necessary with the more logical rotation. It also created a day job that enginemen deemed to be highly desirable, namely the "east end 2-1 assignment," which some engineers affectionately dubbed "the golden chair." This assignment involved a 3-hour run from Spokane to Paradise, departing Spokane at about 8:30 A.M. on train No. 2, followed by a 4-hour mid-day layover and then a 3-hour run back home on train No. 1, arriving Spokane at about 8 P.M. Furthermore, mileage accumulation on this subdivision (374 miles per round trip) was high enough to require three crews to work each pair of trains, because union agreements included a monthly mileage maximum for crews. So, after each round trip, a passenger engine crew had the next two days off.

Extra jobs were always welcome to the BLE and the other unions representing the various crafts, but the creation of this "east end 2-1" assignment was the major reason behind the BLE's efforts. The No. 26-No. 25 trip was certainly nothing special—unless one preferred the long (16-hour) daytime layover at Paradise that went with it. (Some men did prefer that.) But, the "east end 2-1" assignment almost always went to the three most senior passenger engine crews at Parkwater. Without a doubt, it was one of the best engine service jobs on the NP.

There were special cases of "lap mileage jobs" that sometimes resulted in some very young engineers handling trains No. 25 and No. 26. An example explains this best. Saint Paul Second Subdivision enginemen did not have seniority rights west of Dilworth, because that was Fargo Division territory. On the Winnipeg trains, however, which operated between Fargo and Winnipeg via Manitoba Junction and East Grand Forks, St. Paul Division engine crews ran all the way to Fargo, their layover terminal, and thus accumulated mileage off their district each time they worked between Dilworth and Fargo. The "Brotherhoods" (the BLE and the Brotherhood of Locomotive Firemen and Engineers (BLF&E), which represented firemen) decided to balance this off-district mileage equitably by allowing one Fargo Division engine crew from Dilworth to work main line passenger trains between Staples and Dilworth for one or two months each year, usually in the summertime. Staples served as the home terminal, even for these Dilworth crews. Trips always began and

The Vista-Dome North Coast Limited

ended at the home terminal. Since there was a commute to the home terminal at Staples involved, such lap mileage jobs tended to go to junior men. Dilworth Engineer Runyon Peterson was fond of the summertime passenger lap mileage job at Staples, because he owned a lake cabin midway between those points, which facilitated a fairly easy commute to work. He was, thus, able to hold this job as a very young man. On one occasion in the 1950s at Staples, Peterson was assigned to handle train No. 25 from there to Dilworth. The incoming engineer on No. 25 from St. Paul was a man nearly twice Peterson's age. The elder engineman asked Peterson where his engineer was, mistaking the young engineer for a fireman!

Once a man's seniority permitted passenger service, he still had to qualify for it. The most significant factor in passenger work was the high speed involved. Some men had difficulty getting used to it. Passenger engine crews also had to learn how to operate and make running repairs to steam generators and associated equipment. (See the sidebar story, "Do You Want Me To Slow Down?" in this chapter.) They also had to learn passenger train handling techniques and all the "spots," or specific stopping points at each scheduled stop. Spots for one train, such as the *North Coast Limited*, at a given station were not necessarily the same as for another passenger train at that station, due to variances in train makeup. Some spots were fairly simple; others were quite challenging. The following "spots" for trains No. 25 and No. 26 were known by engine crews in the relevant districts to be particularly challenging: No. 26 at Fargo, where there was a descending grade on high speed track with a very small range of serviceable stopping points (just a few feet tolerance either way); No. 25 at Glendive, because of a descending grade with a turnout just east of the depot; No. 26 at Livingston, because of a steep descending grade (1.8%); and both directions at Missoula because of a limited range of serviceable stopping points.

Some enginemen never qualified for passenger service, usually because of inability or discomfort in handling high speeds, or even in handling a train on a schedule. Veteran enginemen say that a good passenger engineer must mentally stay at least five miles ahead of his train at all times. In some respects, maintaining schedule was just as challenging as making-up time. According to the rules in effect on the NP and most other railroads, a regular train, a train authorized by timetable schedule, could arrive at a station early, but it could never *leave* the station early, whether or not scheduled to stop there. In the Employee's Timetable, times for regular trains were shown for most stations between the terminals, regardless of whether or not the train was scheduled to stop at those intermediate stations. These times were necessary because of the system of operating rules then in effect. At intermediate stations in single track territory, the time shown in the

On-time to the minute, Engineer Emil Stumm checks his watch as train No. 1 approaches Sanborn, North Dakota, at 65 miles per hour on a sunny afternoon in 1956. The cab unit is 6509C. When running on-time, an engineer has to be careful not to pass a station ahead of schedule. Stumm will handle train No. 26 back to Dilworth from Jamestown in the early hours of the following morning. The fireman on this trip is Glenn Hove.
Glenn Hove photo; Bill Kuebler collection

Chapter 12: The Crew of the *Vista-Dome North Coast Limited*

"Do you want me to slow down?"

The following story, told to me by retired Road Foreman of Engines Glenn Hove, graphically illustrates the great difficulties faced by Northern Pacific (NP) crews in harsh winter weather conditions. It also shows how they typically dealt with unusual circumstances with aplomb. This harrowing incident took place during the early morning hours of February 12, 1969, between Dilworth and Staples on train No. 26. Although Mr. Hove is quite modest about his part in the story, it is apparent that his actions, and those of the engineer involved, kept the eastbound *Vista-Dome North Coast Limited* from becoming a frozen hulk that fateful night.

—the Author

Ever since I had hired-out in 1947, passenger engineers had routinely run at about 83 miles per hour when making up lost time. On many occasions, they would do this even with a road foreman or trainmaster sitting in the cab with them. Seldom was anything said about it. It was just standard practice. After the Granite accident, however, things began to tighten on western divisions, and eventually on all of them.

I was an engineer at Dilworth on the Fargo Division, but by 1969 I had been promoted to Road Foreman of Engines at Staples. My boss in that job was Master Mechanic Rex Earl. One day early in 1969, when I was still fairly new to the job, Mr. Earl called me from his office at Mississippi Street in St. Paul to remind me that the NP was strictly enforcing the passenger train speed limit of 75 miles per hour. He instructed me to ride with all the passenger engineers working out of Staples in order to remind them of this speed limit. So, I did this. On each trip I stressed the importance of adhering to the 75-mile-per-hour speed limit, even though the line between Staples and Dilworth was all double track, well elevated on the curves, and able to accommodate speeds in the 80s. The 70-mile-per-hour curve just east of Frazee was about the only "slow" curve we had on the St. Paul Second Sub.

Then, on boarding No. 26 one night in Dilworth, I found that the heater hose between the engine and water-baggage car was broken off right where it left the engine. This heater hose, a small hose that carried steam, was attached directly to the larger water hose extending between the water-baggage car and the rear diesel unit. With the heater hose broken off, the water line was frozen solid.

I got a steam hose temporarily connected to the rear diesel unit's steam generator and strung back through the nose door of the trailing unit. With that, I tried to thaw the water hose, but we were well out of Dilworth and moving right along, and with the wind whipping around between the diesel unit and baggage car, and it being very cold, it was hopeless. Usually, when the water line between the engine and the water-baggage car froze, it froze only at the coupling, where the heater hose was not taped to the water hose. That metal coupling readily let the cold penetrate. In that case, it was relatively easy to thaw out the water line with a temporary steam hose, but in this case, with no heater hose effective at all, the entire water hose froze. So, I ran up to the front cab and, rather breathlessly, informed the engine crew that all the water we had for the steam generators was what we had on the engine: 466 gallons in the side tanks of each of the cab units and what was left in the 1200 gallon tank in the "B" unit. If we ran out of water, the entire train would freeze up. That would have been a real disaster, and I was obviously very worried! We were now in a race against time.

The engineer was a wizened little old fellow, very competent, but just days short of retirement. His name was Ray Edwards. He was a fine man, and I'm sure that, even though it was dark in the cab, Edwards had a twinkle in his eye as he asked me, "Do you want me to slow down?" I looked at the speedometer. It indicated 83 miles per hour. In my worry and excitement, I shouted my answer: "No, no . . . *No!*"

The steam generators started dying as we came through Wadena, about 17 miles west of Staples. I called ahead to Staples to instruct the carmen to be ready and waiting, and to water the middle unit first. That way, the water would flow from there to the side tanks on the front and rear units. At Staples, as the carmen were filling the units' water tanks, the incoming and outgoing firemen fired up the steam generators while I thawed out the water line and blocked in the water pump in the baggage car, in order to have a constant flow of water so the water line would not freeze again. We did not freeze up the train, but we came real close to doing just that. If we had, it would have been a real showstopper.

In 1969, No. 26 was scheduled to leave Dilworth at 2:47 A.M. and arrive Staples at 4:33 A.M., 1 hour, 46 minutes over the subdivision. That night we were running late and, according to my records, we left Dilworth at 5:30 A.M. and arrived Staples at 6:48 A.M. We covered the entire subdivision in one hour, twenty-eight minutes; that's 106.3 miles in 88 minutes!

In retrospect, I wonder if Rex Earl noticed that we obviously were not obeying the Company's speed limit. I doubt that I told him, although I may have told him about the broken heater hose, just to make sure it would be repaired at Mississippi Street.

It was rather cold in that windy space between the rear diesel unit and the water-baggage car . . .

Author's Note: National Weather Service archives show that the temperature in the Dilworth area (Fargo) in the early morning hours of February 12, 1969, was 14 degrees below zero. While balancing himself between the rear diesel unit and the water-baggage car, even though the rear unit provided some protection from the 80 mile-per-hour wind, the wind-chill factor would have been close to 70 or 80 degrees below zero. Though he was an engineman and, later, a road foreman in such cold climates, Glenn Hove made it through his entire railroad career without ever freezing up a passenger train, no small feat. Tough railroaders, these NP men!

employee's timetable applied not at the station sign or depot, but at the switch that would be used by an opposing, inferior train to enter the siding there. (The reason for this will be explained in the section covering dispatchers, below.) In double track territory, the time applied at the station sign.

Whether in single track or double track territory, though, the engineer of a scheduled train had to keep an eye on his watch, lest he get ahead of his schedule. Leaving a station early would constitute a serious rules violation and jeopardize the safety of the operation, because inferior trains cleared regular trains by reference to the regular trains' schedules. Some passenger engineers were so wary of getting ahead of their schedule that they intentionally ran a few minutes late, just so they would not have to look at their watches so often.

One trick of the trade involved attempting to arrive early at terminals and scheduled stops. To accomplish this when running on-schedule, some engineers tried to pass the leaving end siding switch at the last station prior to the terminal or scheduled stopping point at the highest possible speed, on-time to the minute, and run as fast as possible from there to the terminal or stopping point. This usually resulted in an early arrival at the scheduled stop, maximizing available time for station work there.

Learning all these procedures and tricks came with the territory of working in passenger service. Some men thoroughly enjoyed it; others did not. In any case, an engineman's career choices, in accordance with what his seniority would permit, were based primarily on the factors of work conditions and pay. The *Vista-Dome North Coast Limited* was but one passenger train that fit into this picture along with the others.

Train Crews

The phrase "train crew" technically refers to the conductor and brakemen, and excludes the engine crew. The boss of the *North Coast Limited*, as on any train, was the conductor. As the highest authority in the crew, he was responsible for a safe operation in accordance with all applicable rules. All other employees on the train answered to him and received instructions from him, including the locomotive engineer. The engineer was equally responsible for a safe operation, though, particularly as regards train handling as previously noted. Although the engineer and conductor coordinated their duties appropriately and usually had the same ideas about how the train should be operated, it did not leave a station until the conductor gave the highball. He also had the authority—and the means, via the cab signal cord or an emergency air brake valve in each car's vestibule—to stop the train at any time for any reason he deemed appropriate.

One of the most important duties of a conductor was to maintain awareness of his train's location and operating conditions. This was especially important with respect to meeting another First Class train, because overrunning a meeting point could easily result in a collision. (Here, the capitalized phrase "First Class" is an operating term that refers to a train's right over Second Class and inferior trains, and not a reference to the type of cars or accommodations on a passenger train. A First Class train is one that has right, by timetable authority, over all other trains, unless a train order specifies otherwise.) Ever since a disastrous head-on collision between trains No. 7 and No. 4 at Rapids, Montana, in 1902, NP company rules required all First Class trains meeting one another to be given a "positive meet," a train order which specified the location for the meet and, in some cases, which train was to take siding. Such a train order took precedence over timetable scheduling of meeting points. With this type of order, neither train could pass the train order meeting point until the other had arrived and the inferior train had entered the siding. Thus, there was no such thing as a "timetable meet" of First Class trains on the NP, a meet conducted by reference only to the

Chapter 12: The Crew of the *Vista-Dome North Coast Limited*

Two of NP's finest passenger conductors, Jimmy Quinn, left, of Livingston and Dan Collins of Glendive, pose for Stewardess-Nurse Joan Reitz at Billings, winter 1961. Conductor Collins has just turned train No. 25 over to Conductor Quinn, who will handle it to Butte. About a year after this photo was taken, Conductor Collins was working train 26 when it derailed near Glendive. Miss Reitz was the Stewardess-Nurse aboard that train. She and other Stewardess-Nurses had a high regard for both of these conductors.
Joan Reitz photo

timetable, without train orders. If a conductor held a meet order, the meet was surely at the front of his mind until the train order was safely fulfilled.

The conductor was also responsible for assuring that the train crew caught train orders wherever they were issued *en route*. This meant checking train order signals—"order boards" to the crews—along the way, so for this reason as well, constant awareness of the train's location was a must. Some conductors delegated the duty of catching one set of train orders to the head brakeman. By virtue of his post at the rear of the train, the rear brakeman always caught his own set of train orders. Three identical sets of orders were issued to each passenger train: one for the engine crew, one for the conductor and head brakeman, and one for the rear brakeman. Above all, the conductor and the engineer were mutually responsible for fully understanding and complying with all train orders and messages they held.

A passenger conductor had the added responsibilities of being aware of the passengers' assigned spaces, punching tickets, and collecting fares. As previously noted, the *Vista-Dome North Coast Limited* was a reserved-seat-only train, but exceptions were made on special occasions. When a passenger, traveling on an emergency basis, arrived at the train with neither a reservation nor a ticket, the conductor had the authority and means to sell that person a ticket on the spot, provided space was available on the train. That is why a few seats in each coach were designated for the conductor's discretionary use. On almost every trip, people traveling on an emergency basis filled some of these seats.

Passenger seats are one thing, but passengers are yet another, for they were free to roam from their assigned space. The conductor, therefore, had to develop a "sixth sense" about where passengers were, and who was assigned to which space. Most conductors began developing these skills back when they were passenger brakemen, who assisted the conductor with some of these duties. The better conductors had a way of "training" their brakemen without being condescending or pedantic about it. Everyone had to start somewhere, and the senior conductors were no exception. Some of them never forgot their days as passenger brakemen and wisely tailored their work habits to help the younger men learn the ropes.

Few things escaped the conductor's notice. Even as the crack *North Coast Limited* was pulling out of a station, for example, its conductor would usually watch for a late passenger wanting to board

211

and would stop the train for that grateful patron. This author witnessed one occasion when train No. 26 was departing Fargo about 1:50 A.M., and then stopped just in time to board a woman frantically running toward the train. Even though she was a coach passenger, she had to board a sleeping car in the middle of Broadway, east of the depot, and then walk forward through the train to her coach. Had the train traveled another two car lengths or so before her arrival on the platform, she probably would have missed the train. The conductor's decision was wise, for only two minutes were lost (easily recovered prior to Staples) in exchange for a very happy customer, who probably told two dozen people about the experience.

Perhaps most important of all was the conductor's responsibility to maintain a proper order for all his duties. The myriad of duties he faced often came into conflict, simultaneously demanding his attention. A good conductor learned to rank them on the basis of safety-first. This sometimes meant leaving the task of fare collection and ticket punching for a later time—and, therefore, having to find passengers who had headed for dome, lounge, or diner soon after boarding.

Before the start of every trip, the engineer and conductor carefully compared watches with a standard time clock and with each other. The lives of passengers and crew depended on accurate time keeping, and comparison of watches was not merely a tradition, it was required by a rule that was strictly enforced. Each crewmember's watch also had to be regularly inspected by one of the certified watch inspectors whose names were listed in each operating division's Special Instructions. These Special Instructions were part of an operating division's Employee's Timetable and consisted of a set of rules tailored to that division; they supplemented the Consolidated Code of Operating Rules. Every trainman (and engineman) had to carry current copies of his division's Employee's Timetable and Special Instructions, and these documents had to be readily available during the course of his work.

Passenger trainmen faced the same kinds of career decisions as did enginemen. Likewise, seniority determined career options. With sufficient seniority a conductor or brakeman could opt for passenger service. As with enginemen, such decisions were based primarily on pay, schedule, and working conditions.

One significant difference between passenger engine and train crews, however, was the length of their districts. Most passenger train crews operated over two subdivisions, or two engine districts, rather than one. Freight train crews covered the same district as did their engine crews. On most divisions a passenger train crew would work a trip out with two (or even three) different engine crews, and the trip back to the home terminal may or may not involve the same engine crews. The following table shows passenger trainmen's districts involved in the operation of trains No. 25 and No. 26 and other main line trains. These districts were the same during the entire 1954–70 period, except for a few slight adjustments in mileage due to line changes.

Chapter 12: The Crew of the *Vista-Dome North Coast Limited*

Passenger Train Crew Districts
(Mileage figures accurate as of June 1959)

District	Home Terminal	Distant Terminal	Mileage	Notes
St. Paul Division	St. Paul	Fargo	252	1
Fargo Division	Fargo	Mandan	200	1, 2
Yellowstone Division	Mandan	Glendive	206	3
	Glendive	Billings	225	3
Rocky Mountain, "Old Montana"	Billings	Butte/Helena	235/238	4
Rocky Mountain, Missoula	Missoula	Paradise/Butte	382	5
		Paradise/Helena	380	5
"Idaho East"	Spokane	Paradise	187	6
"Idaho West" (Pasco district)	Spokane	Ellensburg	271	6
Seattle	Seattle	Ellensburg	124	

Notes:
1. St. Paul and Fargo Division passenger train crews changed at Fargo, rather than Dilworth. Strangely, this arrangement did not involve compensatory lap-mileage for the Fargo Division crews, even though St. Paul Division passenger train crews worked the territory between Dilworth and Fargo. This unique situation dated back to before the 1900s, and, for some reason, the trainmen's union never decided to change it.
2. Passenger trainmen on both the First and Second Subdivisions of the Fargo Division had seniority rights over the entire division. Jamestown trainmen could bid for passenger work. Their home terminal became Fargo, however, as long as they were in passenger service, so relatively few Jamestown men did this. Jamestown freight train crews did not have this option, and remained on the Fargo Second Subdivision instead.
3. As with engine crews, trainmen (both freight and passenger) had seniority rights between Mandan and Billings (passenger) or Laurel Yard (freight).
4. Passenger trainmen who worked over this district were Livingston men from the "Old Montana" Division district. When working passenger service, however, these Livingston men would have to commute or move to Billings, the home terminal.
5. Missoula passenger trainmen had a unique "step off" agreement with the NP. According to this agreement, a trip began at Missoula on train No. 25. The train crew went to Paradise, then went east on No. 26 all the way to Butte, and then went back west on No. 25 to Missoula, where they would then "step off" at the end of the trip. They then had two days off. A similar agreement existed for trainmen working trains No. 1 and No. 2, whose eastern distant terminal was Helena. The high mileage shown for these trips reflects this "step off" arrangement.
6. Most Spokane passenger trainmen worked on the "Idaho East." Only one or two Spokane passenger train crews were assigned to the "Idaho West" district. The others working that district were Pasco crews whose home terminal was Spokane during the time they were in passenger service.

Passenger trainmen's trip rotations and schedules were determined in much the same way as were those for engine crews. The NP sought to maximize crew productivity, and the trainman's union sought to obtain the best possible work conditions.

Fargo Division passenger trainmen, for example, worked the following trip rotation between Fargo and Mandan in 1959:

First Trip: Out on No. 25, 12-hour layover at Mandan, back on No. 4; then 17 hours off.
Second Trip: Out on No. 1; 18-hour layover at Mandan, back on No. 2; then 12 hours off.
Third Trip: Out on No. 3; 11-hour layover at Mandan, back on No. 26; then 22 hours off.

Then they repeated this cycle. Five regular passenger train crews filled this schedule, each rotating through the same cycle. To complicate matters, Trains No. 3 and No. 4 operated only six days a week in 1959, so some "deadheading" (riding, but not working on a train in the course of duty) of crews was necessary to cover half a trip. Contrast the Fargo Division passenger trainmen's work schedules with the trip pairings for St. Paul Division passenger trainmen in 1959. Between St. Paul and Fargo, two train crews worked No. 1 and No. 2 repeatedly, on alternating days, thus:

Out on No. 1, 2-hour layover at Fargo, back on No. 2; next day off.

This job tended to go to the most senior St. Paul Division passenger trainmen, because it was a day job and paid quite well. Pay was based on mileage, and a round trip covered more miles than were covered by passenger train crews on most other divisions. Two other crews worked No. 25 and No. 26 repeatedly, every other night, in similar fashion:

Out on No. 25, 2-hour layover at Fargo, back on No. 26; next night off.

This was an all-night job, but it still tended to go to senior men, because of the high mileage, short hours (even shorter than the hours worked on trains No. 1 and No. 2), and regular schedule. Other St. Paul Division trainmen were assigned to No. 3 and No. 4 in similar fashion.

Thus, crew rotations, even on a given division, were often different for engine crews and trainmen. In some cases, freight (chain gang) trainmen were used to work a passenger trip or part of one. These fill-in trips went to available freight crews (those who were rested and passenger qualified), in order of seniority, just as with engine crews.

Before making their first pay trip in passenger service, trainmen were permitted to make one or two "student trips" without pay, to learn the ropes, and most did so. A trainman qualifying for passenger service also had the responsibility of being fitted with a passenger service uniform and was responsible for maintaining it in good, clean condition.

Generally, passenger service paid engine and train crews a rate about midway between yard service, on the low end, and scheduled locals (main line or branches), on the high end. Pay for chain gang freight service was also somewhere in the middle, but was usually a little higher than pay for passenger service, provided an employee did not lay off any trips. Passenger service still typically attracted senior men, mostly because of its regular schedule and shorter hours, very valuable items to a railroader with a family. A man regularly assigned to passenger service was not married to the telephone, as were men in chain gang. Passenger crews did not risk being called to duty during time off between trips. Also, the work itself was usually easier than other types of train service.

Clearly, several factors were involved in crew assignments, but in almost all cases, the name of the train was far less important to crews than other matters. All-in-all, passenger service was deemed a very good balance of pay and working conditions for engine and train crews, alike.

People Skills

Working in passenger service naturally brought NP trainmen face-to-face with the traveling public. These trainmen represented the NP to revenue passengers, probably more so than even ticket agents did, so "people skill" was a very important asset for conductors and brakemen. Some passenger service employees lacked a good attitude nonetheless. Every large group contains some "bad apples," and the NP was no exception. Some conductors, for example, worked the *North Coast Limited* and other passenger trains because they could, because they had the seniority, and not because they enjoyed passengers. A few trainmen were even discourteous. These men surely tarnished NP's service record to some extent, but for every one of them there were plenty of others who did their best to polish that record.

Chapter 12: The Crew of the *Vista-Dome North Coast Limited*

Not leaving these matters to chance, the NP issued a booklet to all employees working in passenger train service and required them to be familiar with its contents. Its title, appropriately, was "Special Rules and Instructions for Employees in Passenger Train Service." Under the title on the cover was the notation, "Safety First; Courtesy Always." The following remarks by NP Vice President C. H. Burgess are from the foreword to the booklet (revised to June 1, 1960):

Passengers are customers and patrons of the Company and the necessity of courtesy, tact, and consideration when dealing with them is ever present.

Burgess went on to quote from an item entitled, "You Are Important," thus:

A corporation may spread itself over the whole world . . . may employ over 100,000 men . . . yet the average person will form his judgment of the corporation through his contact with one individual. If this person is rude or inefficient, it will require a lot of courtesy and efficiency to overcome the bad impression. Every member of an organization, who, in any capacity, comes in contact with people, is a salesman. The impression he makes is an advertisement—good or bad. A spirit of courteous and inviting hospitality will go far toward creating the friendly feeling toward the Northern Pacific that is necessary if it is to receive the patronage to which it is entitled . . .

C. H. Burgess,
Vice President

Dispatchers

Hidden behind the scenes more than anyone were NP's dispatchers, yet they were some of the most important people involved with the *North Coast Limited's* operation. The safety of the train was as dependent on them as on anybody. Ron Nixon, who served as a Rocky Mountain Division dispatcher at Missoula, once wrote to this author, "Dispatching was absolutely the most hazardous and demanding job on the railroad. Just one small error or the overlooking of one train could kill people off." Jim Fredrickson, who served the NP as a Tacoma Division dispatcher for many years, tells the story of a senior dispatcher (having 27 years of service) who made the awful mistake of issuing a "lap order." A lap order is a train order that granted overlapping main track authority to opposing trains—a type of train order that dispatchers had to avoid at all cost. Without the added protection of automatic block signals, that lap order resulted in the head-on collision of two locals that killed two men and injured several. The 27-year veteran dispatcher went into shock upon realizing his mistake and its consequences. He was so distraught that he had to be supported by his two sons as he left his office on that fateful day. He never recovered from the shock; one year later, he died.

A full account of dispatching procedures and techniques is outside the scope of this book. As for the *North Coast Limited*, however, trains No. 25 and No. 26 were generally given priority over all other trains. At least one NP rules examiner used to say to dispatchers, "The *North Coast Limited* is our baby. Don't do anything to delay it." By rule, inferior trains, which included most main line freight trains because they operated as extras, had to clear the time of No. 25 and No. 26 by entering an appropriate siding. For opposing movements in single track territory, an inferior train had to clear trains No. 25 and No. 26 and other First Class trains by being off the main track at least five minutes before the superior train was due to leave that station. That is why station leaving times in single track territory, as shown in the Employee's Timetable, applied at the siding switch that an inferior train would use to enter the siding. (In railroad jargon, the term "leave" was a technical term used in rulebooks and employees timetables. It did not necessarily mean that a train stopped at the place in

The Vista-Dome North Coast Limited

Dispatcher Jim Fredrickson was a mere 27 years old when this photograph was taken of him at the "Mountain desk" in the Tacoma Union Station dispatcher's office in 1954. His territory includes the main line extending between Yakima and Auburn. He is assigned to "Second Trick" (4 p.m. to midnight) on this day, and traffic is typically heavy. Trains 25 and 26 are but two of many trains that have filled the day's train sheet stretched across his desk. A dispatcher had one of the most challenging jobs on the railroad. The safe and efficient operation of the *Vista-Dome North Coast Limited* greatly depended on good dispatchers, and Jim was known across the system as one of the best.
Jim Fredrickson collection

question. If a train actually passed through a place without stopping, in railroad operating terms it was still said to have "left" that place. Timetables showed "leaving times" for a regular train at most stations, even if that train was not scheduled to stop at them.) For following movements, an inferior train had to clear trains No. 25 and No. 26 and other First Class trains by the time the superior train was due to leave the next station to the rear where time was shown in the Employee's Timetable.

Except for positive meet orders between opposing First Class trains, and the occasional slow order for track work, trains No. 25 and No. 26 often crossed an entire division without receiving a single train order. Ron Nixon said, "We would usually just give them a clearance and turn them loose." A clearance was a form that listed all the train order numbers of those orders that were being issued to that train at that station. If there were no orders, the clearance so stated. That way, the crew would know with certainty that they held all train orders issued to them, if any. As for main track authority, the Employee's Timetable authorized the movement of trains No. 25 and No. 26 and all other regular trains.

One notable exception to the practice of not issuing unnecessary train orders to trains No. 25 and No. 26, however, occurred on the Tacoma Division. Freights 600 and 601, operating as extras, were "hot" trains; they were given very high priority. (Freight train numbers on the NP were not operational terms; they were used mainly by the traffic and marketing departments. Crews and dispatchers used these freight train numbers loosely in conversation, but not in official operating documents such as train orders. All freight trains so numbered, including 600, were referred to in train orders and other operational materials as "Extra [lead engine number] East" or "Extra [lead engine number] west," depending on direction of movement. Thus, operationally these hot freight trains were "extras.") On some occasions the dispatcher would do what in most cases was unthinkable—issue a wait order for No. 25 to take siding somewhere in the Yakima River canyon for eastbound freight 600! The wait point was usually Wymer or Umtanum, and the wait was only 10 or 15 minutes after the scheduled time. The dispatcher did this only when No. 25 was on-time. Under those conditions, if something happened to delay 600 prior to the meeting point, No. 25 could proceed after its wait time had expired. The order typically read something like this:

NUMBER 25 ENG 6512A TAKE SIDING AT WYMER
NUMBER 25 WAIT ON SIDING AT WYMER UNTIL 415AM
FOR EXTRA 7002D EAST

Chapter 12: The Crew of the *Vista-Dome North Coast Limited*

Train No. 25 received six train orders at Garrison on May 11, 1959, as indicated by this Clearance Form A. Six train orders was an unusually high number for this train, especially in double track territory (Garrison to Missoula). Most of these orders were slow orders, issued to all westward trains, concerning track repair at various points between Garrison and Missoula. Train order No. 512, also issued to all westward trains, stated that the westward siding at Bearmouth was blocked with cars. Order No. 215 was the only one of the six addressed exclusively to train No. 25 at Garrison. (See accompanying photo.)
Bill Kuebler collection

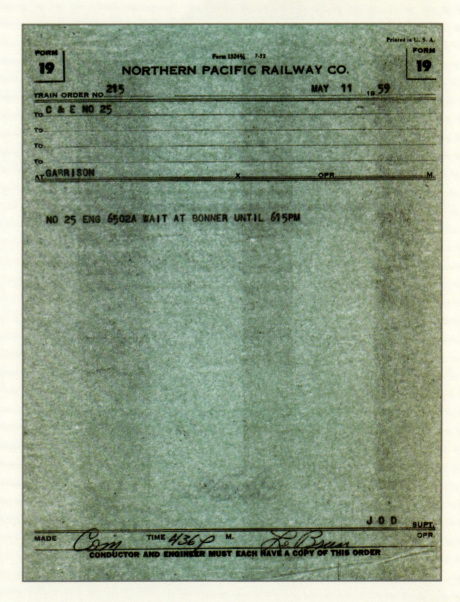

"C & E NO 25" in the address block means "Conductor and Engineer" of train No. 25. The body of the order restricts No. 25 at Bonner, where the train's scheduled leaving time was 5:53 p.m. This form of order, known as a "wait order," was a method by which a dispatcher could allow an inferior train to move further along the line before having to clear a superior train that was running late. In this case, train No. 25 was running a few minutes late because of several slow orders between Garrison and Missoula, and the dispatcher wanted to allow a westbound freight to make it into Missoula yard ahead of No. 25. The wait time (6:15 pm) probably expired shortly before the passenger train reached Bonner, so it probably never actually waited there. The initials "J O D" are for Rocky Mountain Division Superintendent J. O. Davies.
Bill Kuebler collection

217

The Vista-Dome North Coast Limited

Time to relax... Left-to-right: Tacoma Division dispatcher Jim Fredrickson, Stewardess-Nurse Marianne Osyp, former secretary to the Supervisor of Stewardess-Nurses Jean D. Parsons, and Roger Peck enjoy a few minutes of relaxation in the dining car on train No. 26, November 21, 1956. The car is one of the Pullman-Standard diners in the 450-series.
Jim Fredrickson photo

In this example train order, "Extra 7002D East" would be freight train 600. Ron Nixon once told this author that putting trains No. 25 or No. 26 in a siding for an extra on the Rocky Mountain Division (and presumably on most other divisions), except in emergency situations, would likely get a dispatcher fired. This sort of move on the Tacoma Division was very unusual.

At least three factors made this move feasible on the Tacoma Division. First, No. 25's schedule from Ellensburg to Seattle was not tight. Rather, it was designed to help effect an on-time arrival at the western terminus. A loss of only 10 or 15 minutes by No. 25 at the wait point could easily be made up by the time the train reached Seattle. Second, the engine and train crews involved were well known to the dispatcher, who in this case was Jim Fredrickson. He counted on them to handle this situation skillfully and efficiently, and so they did. Finally, the equipment in use was reliable. By the late 1950s, diesel-electric

The oldest and youngest members of this *North Coast Limited's* crew pose for the photographer at Seattle's King Street Station in April 1960. After 36 years with Pullman, half of them on NP's premier train, Porter G. W. Cain begins his last trip to Chicago. He and Stewardess-Nurse Marilyn Parsons are standing beside a dome sleeper just prior to boarding time.
NP Photo; collection of Marilyn Proctor

Chapter 12: The Crew of the Vista-Dome North Coast Limited

While traveling with their father aboard train No. 25 from Chicago to Seattle, Alan, 13, and Bruce Darr, 11, asked the train crew, "What's it like to sit in the 'driver's seat' of a three-unit diesel locomotive?" When their train arrived at Seattle's King Street Station on this date in May 1961, they found out. Engineer James A. "Jimmy" Darker welcomes the Darr boys to the cab of an F-9A as their escort, Stewardess-Nurse Joan Reitz, looks on. This photo appeared in the July-August 1961 issue of NP's employee magazine, "The North Coaster."
NP Photo; Joan Reitz Dolan collection

locomotives and even freight equipment did not break down very often.

It is interesting to note one other factor weighed in this decision—the hour of the operation. In the pre-dawn hours of the morning, passengers on train No. 25 were not likely to be awake and notice their relegation to a siding for a freight train. Still, this was a very unusual move. As it was, though, these meets were almost always pulled off without anything going wrong. In fact, everyone involved handled them so well that on some occasions the two trains would meet while the westbound passenger train was actually moving between siding switches, such was dispatcher Fredrickson's accurate figuring! In the vast majority of cases, however, dispatchers gave trains No. 25 and No. 26 priority over all other trains.

If No. 25 or No. 26 or any other regular train was running late, a dispatcher had the option of issuing a "run late" order, one designed to allow opposing (or preceding) inferior trains to move further along the line before having to clear the passenger train. An example:

TRAIN NUMBER 25 ENG 6504C RUN FIFTY MINUTES LATE GLENDIVE TO TERRY AND FORTY MINUTES LATE TERRY TO MILES CITY

This form of train order restricted the superior train by shifting its schedule between the stations specified to later times by whatever time increment was stated in the order. If the superior train ran up against its "run late" time, it could not make up any more time within the station limits of the order. When figuring "run late" times and station limits, dispatchers wanted to allow the superior train to make up time without forcing inferior trains to spend any more time in sidings

Dining car Steward Dick Carlson poses with two of his crewmembers alongside train No. 25 in 1961. Stewardess-Nurse Joan Reitz recalls the name of the waiter on the left as "Jake," but has forgotten the name of the one on the right. "Forty years can dim one's memory," she says. Even so, she remembers all three of these men as being "some of the nicest in the business."
Joan Reitz photo

The Vista-Dome North Coast Limited

Conductor Ernie Summers, right, and his head brakeman pose alongside a Day-Night coach on train No. 25 at Livingston in 1961. Ernie Summers was another conductor who was well liked by passengers and crewmembers alike. According to retired Livingston Conductor Warren McGee: "Ernie was a motorcycle nut. If you liked Harley-Davidsons, you were an instant friend of his! Come to think of it . . . there weren't too many railroad conductors in those days who were motorcycle enthusiasts."
Joan Reitz photo

than was necessary. So, it was a balancing act. Most dispatchers favored trains No. 25 and No. 26 in these cases and gave them enough leeway to make up as much lost time as possible, even at the expense of restricting inferior trains that were otherwise of very high priority.

When it came to meeting other First Class trains, trains No. 25 and No. 26 were usually given priority, regardless of the timetable conferring directional superiority to eastward trains over westward ones of the same class. As examples, over the years No. 25 usually met No. 2 near Anoka (double track, St. Paul First Subdivision), Beaver Hill or Hodges (single track, Yellowstone Second Subdivision), and again at Alfalfa or Toppenish (single track, Idaho Third Subdivision). These trains did not meet on the Rocky Mountain Division due to different routing via Helena and Butte. Even though No. 2 was the eastbound train and, therefore, superior by timetable direction, dispatchers usually put No. 2 in the siding for No. 25 when the meet was in single track territory, especially when both trains were on-time. On the other hand, when trains No. 26 and No. 1 met, dispatchers usually put No. 1 in the siding. Over the years the meeting points for trains No. 26 and No. 1 were typically at Sprague (single track, Idaho Second Subdivision) and Lehigh (single track, just east of Dickinson). Depending on the year and timetable schedule, trains No. 26 and No. 1 sometimes also met at Logan on the Rocky Mountain Division.

There were exceptions to the usual practices described above. Perhaps more than any other job on the railroad, dispatching required a great deal of sound judgment. Even within the confines of a well-defined, strict code of operating rules—confines which were further narrowed by the expectations of management—there was a good deal of flexibility for dispatchers. No two days on the job were exactly alike. In many unusual instances, and even normal ones,

This Pullman Conductor worked the *North Coast Limited* during most of the period from the late 1940's until the end of Pullman sleeping car operations in 1969. Stewardess-Nurse Joan Reitz remembers only his first name, "Oscar." She took this photo of him standing beside a dome sleeper and sleeper-observation-lounge car 483 in 1961. This is train No. 25 at Livingston.
Joan Reitz photo

Chapter 12: The Crew of the *Vista-Dome North Coast Limited*

Steward Frank Houska, right, was one of the senior stewards on the NP when he posed for this picture alongside a Pullman Conductor at Livingston in 1961. Houska, who was also an instructor in NP's Dining Car Department, was known among waiters for emphasizing proper procedure and paying close attention to details. The car behind the two men is Budd diner no. 459.
Joan Reitz photo

some rather amazing mental gymnastics took place at a dispatcher's desk.

Operation of the *Vista-Dome North Coast Limited* was labor intensive in more ways than one!

In this May 1966 publicity photo, advertising models pose in Traveller's Rest Lounge car 496. The Stewardess-Nurse uniform is a new design that Stewardess-Nurse Supervisor Joan Reitz helped develop a few months earlier. It replaced the original uniform dating from 1955 and modified slightly in 1957. Some of these murals were damaged in the June 1962 derailment of this car at Evaro, Montana, but Como Shop personnel were able to restore artist Edgar Miller's work remarkably well. Close observation, however, reveals a spot where two adjacent panels don't quite "match."
NP publicity photo; Bill Kuebler collection

The Vista-Dome North Coast Limited

One of the "extras" on the *North Coast Limited*... Santa charms a young traveler aboard a vista-dome on train No. 26 near East Auburn, December 24, 1954. Waino Hannus, a clerk at the Auburn depot, plays a very convincing Santa. He boarded the train at Seattle and after visiting all of the children on the train, got off at East Auburn where he greeted some 400 boys and girls from local schools who had responded to an invitation from the NP.
Jim Fredrickson photo

The conductor makes a general observation of his train and watches the depot platform for "runners"—late arriving passengers running to catch the train. The westbound *Vista-Dome North Coast Limited* is just leaving Butte on April 28, 1958. This view shows mail-dormitory car 427, dome coach 559, and "Day-Nite" coach 591.
Montague Powell photo; Bill Kuebler collection

On April 28, 1958, dome sleeper 313 operates in sleeping car line 256 as the westbound *North Coast Limited* departs Butte, Montana, on-time at 3:49 p.m. Standard sleeping cars 367 and 358 are operating in lines 255 and 257, respectively. Coincidentally, car 358 was originally named "Butte."
Montague Powell photo; Bill Kuebler collection

Chapter 12: The Crew of the *Vista-Dome North Coast Limited*

Stewardess–Nurses

Stewardess-Nurses were a unique and highly successful addition to the crews of the *Vista-Dome North Coast Limited*. In contrast to dispatchers, Stewardess-Nurses were some of the most visible—and certainly the most eye-catching—personnel involved in the operation of trains No. 25 and No. 26. They were unique in that all other employees who worked aboard trains No. 25 and No. 26 served on other trains as well, at one time or another. But the Stewardess-Nurses were the only NP employees to be hired exclusively for, and to serve exclusively on, the *Vista-Dome North Coast Limited*. While that fact, alone, distinguishes this group of NP employees, there were other things about these classy ladies worthy of our regard. They were in a special category. Indeed, the history of the *Vista-Dome North Coast Limited* would have been very different without them.

By every measure, the NP's Stewardess-Nurse program was successful, even outstanding. These young women were very attractive and had outgoing personalities. They were professional. They dressed in sharp, spiffy uniforms specially designed for this service. They contributed substantially to an atmosphere of friendliness aboard the train. Over the train's PA system, they called attention to and described points of interest along the "Scenic Route." Most of all, they were immensely helpful to passengers with special needs, especially medical needs. In some cases, passengers with illnesses and even ambulatory passengers traveled on trains No. 25 and No. 26; with a highly qualified Stewardess-Nurse aboard, these passengers received the special care and attention that only a Registered Nurse could give. Several other railroads also had Stewardesses (the Chicago and North Western (C&NW), the Santa Fe, and the Baltimore and Ohio (B&O), as examples), but not all of them were Registered Nurses, so NP's concept was still rather novel, particularly in the Pacific Northwest. It made the *Vista-Dome North Coast Limited* a unique, outstanding train in that region; no other streamliner there had Stewardess-Nurses. There were even passengers who choose the *Vista-Dome North Coast Limited* in lieu of its competition particularly because it carried a Stewardess-Nurse. In short, the program turned out to be a superb public relations move by the NP, and then some.

Inauguration of Stewardess-Nurse Service

In January 1955, Miss Lila Brekke received a call at her home in St. Louis. The caller identified himself as "Walt Rodine of the Northern Pacific Railway," and he explained that the NP was starting a new Stewardess-Nurse program on its premier transcontinental passenger train. He asked her if she would consider applying for the position of Supervisor of Stewardess-Nurses, and invited her to an interview. Miss Brekke had been a Stewardess-Nurse on the C&NW, and later on the B&O, so she had several years of experience in that line

Lila Brekke, the NP's first supervisor of Stewardess-Nurses

Geraldine Yanta, second supervisor

Elaine Rath third supervisor

Charlotte Hanes fourth supervisor

Karen Laumbach fifth supervisor

Joan Reitz sixth supervisor

The Vista-Dome North Coast Limited

of work. She agreed to an interview with Mr. Rodine in Chicago. He interviewed a number of other candidates as well, but Miss Brekke made the most favorable impression on him. He offered her the job, and she gratefully accepted.

By early February, the NP had moved Miss Brekke, all her household belongings, and her automobile by rail out to Seattle, where the Railway provided her an office: Suite 1620 in Smith Tower. The NP permitted her to hire one personal secretary. In the event a Stewardess-Nurse had to miss a trip on short notice, the road allowed the secretary to fill in as a Stewardess (the secretary was not a Registered Nurse), a practice that lasted only until 1958. During the next several months after her arrival in Seattle, Miss Brekke developed NP's Stewardess-Nurse program from scratch. First, she placed ads in nursing journals, newspapers, and magazines around the country, calling for job applicants. Then she wrote a Stewardess-Nurse manual (66 pages), aided by input from various other NP departments. With help from NP's Public Relations Department, she also wrote the "commentaries," initially a 13-page script to be read by the Stewardess-Nurse over the train's PA system, calling attention to points of interest *en route*. With help from the Passenger Traffic Department, she also wrote a "Question and Answer guide" for Stewardess-Nurses to use; it covered questions that passengers frequently asked, mostly technical ones about the train.

While doing all these things, Miss Brekke interviewed well over a hundred job applicants. From these she selected and trained a staff of 10 Stewardess-Nurses. Applicants had to meet certain requirements, including the following:

Education:	Registered Nurse with at least one year experience
Age:	22 to 27 years
Height:	5′3" to 5′7" (measured in stocking feet)
Weight:	115 to 135 pounds (in proportion to height)
Marital Status:	Single (not widowed or divorced)

Nona Whittendale   Patricia Thompson   Margery Delano   Emma Siddall   Barbara Chirstensen

Joelle Zabel   Kathleen St. Germain   Viola Barish   Eileen McGough   LaVaugnh Jurgensen

These photos of NP's first group of Stewardess-Nurses appeared in the July-August 1955 issue of NP's employee magazine, "The North Coaster."

Chapter 12: The Crew of the *Vista-Dome North Coast Limited*

Additional requirements included "good sound health" and "very good vision . . . glasses cannot be worn while on the train." Without exception, Miss Brekke personally interviewed applicants, one at a time, before hiring them. All five of her successors, in turn, continued this practice throughout the Stewardess-Nurse program.

Finally, after four months of intense work developing the Stewardess-Nurse program, Miss Brekke had her first cadre of 10 Stewardess-Nurses, trained and ready to go. On Wednesday, June 1, 1955, Miss Nona K. Whittendale stepped aboard train No. 26 at Seattle's King Street Station. She was the first Stewardess-Nurse to work a trip. When she stepped aboard, Stewardess-Nurse service on the *Vista-Dome North Coast Limited* officially began.

One Stewardess-Nurse served aboard each *North Coast Limited* train. The 10 Stewardess-Nurses on staff were known among NP employees affectionately as "Sues." Passengers and crew, alike, gave the generic name "Sue" to each and every Stewardess-Nurse in informal conversation, although NP regulations required the crew to address her formally as "Miss [last name]." The name "Sue" originated in NP advertising. "Hello! I'm Sue, your Stewardess-Nurse," proclaimed more than one NP ad above a photo of one of these smiling ladies. Miss Lila Brekke, however, knew them simply and affectionately as "my girls." (When applied to a young woman in those days, the term "girl" was usually one of endearment and respect; even the Stewardess-Nurses referred to each other with the term.)

According to the qualifications standards, all Stewardess-Nurses had to be single and not previously married. (Airline stewardesses faced the same restriction; they finally challenged this employment practice with a class action lawsuit in 1970 and won the case.) It was not unusual for a young, attractive Stewardess-Nurse to opt for marriage during her service on the NP and, thus, have to resign. Consequently, turnover was high. Average length of service for all the NP Stewardess-Nurses was just under 12 months. Total length of service ranged from as little as two months to as high as twenty-nine months. But, marriage was not the only thing that contributed to a high turnover rate. Dissatisfaction with pay and benefits was a factor, as well, for some of them. In an April 2001 interview with the author, Lila Brekke Kravetz stated,

> No sooner had I hired the first ten when I found that I was busier than ever trying to hire more—to replace those who were leaving. I had all I could do at times just to keep ten on staff. I could understand those who wanted to get married, but my big concern was for the others who were leaving. Although they just *loved* the job and hated to leave, I learned that for some it was because of pay and benefits. Even if they liked the work, they still had to pay their bills. You know . . . one thing the NP never established at the beginning was some kind of a plan for giving the girls a raise. On the B&O we were given raises. But on the NP, as Supervisor my hands were tied; I couldn't give them one, even though they deserved it. What they needed was a union, but our western passenger traffic manager, the man in Seattle, warned us that anyone who tried to form a union would be fired. Besides all that, I suppose some of my girls left just because they were young and didn't know for sure what they wanted to do . . .

The year 1962 was unique in that it had, by far, the highest turnover rate. Average length of service for Stewardess-Nurses hired between September 1961 and September 1962 was a mere seven and one-half months. There are two likely explanations for this phenomenon. First, travel aboard the *Vista-Dome North Coast Limited* was very heavy that year, because of the Seattle World's Fair. Perhaps some Stewardess-Nurses were "burned out" from the stresses of dealing with such heavy loads. Second, there were three major derailments in close succession that year. Perhaps these tended to scare away some Stewardess-Nurses. (Some who were hired in the months following those accidents have told me that the Supervisor of Stewardess-Nurses spent a great deal of time during

The Vista-Dome North Coast Limited

the interview stressing the safety of rail travel.) It is possible that both of these items were factors. The turnover rate for Stewardess-Nurses settled back down toward a normal level in 1963.

By the time the NP changed the Stewardess-Nurse program to a Stewardess program in January 1967, eliminating the Registered Nurse requirement, the list of Stewardess-Nurses, past and present, had grown to 120 names. (See the roster of Stewardess-Nurses.)

The Stewardess-Nurse Manual included the following interesting paragraph, which constituted a formal job description that remained in effect during all 12 years of the Stewardess-Nurse program:

DUTIES: Our Stewardesses distinguish themselves by their friendly, courteous service to our patrons. Their duties include the following:

1. Add to the comfort and enjoyment of all travelers by assisting passengers with train connections and schedules.
2. Supervising cleanliness of equipment.
3. The Stewardess enlightens *North Coast Limited* passengers by means of the Public Address System concerning services aboard the train and scenic and historical areas enroute.
4. A Stewardess must be a public relations expert.
5. Caring for accident cases, either major or minor; also other emergencies that might arise.
6. Assisting mothers with babies and small children.
7. Caring for unaccompanied children.
8. Assisting aged and infirm persons, and administering to those who are invalided or who become ill enroute.

Those first 10 Stewardess-Nurses, and all who followed them, soon found out that the job wasn't all fun and glory. It was a great deal of hard work! Before long, one of the first 10 coined a phrase that all the other "Sues" immediately adopted. It became a motto for all Stewardess-Nurses: "We *walk* from Seattle to Chicago and back on every trip." There was a lot of truth to that saying. The Stewardess-Nurses worked long, hard days, and spent most of them on their feet, walking back and forth throughout some 10 to 12 cars—and in high heels that made walking aboard a moving train a real chore.

The following three Stewardess-Nurses were involved in the three derailments that occurred with the *Vista-Dome North Coast Limited*, all in 1962.

Joan Reitz was in the derailment of train No. 26 near Glendive on January 29, 1962.

Gladys Stewart was in the derailment of train No. 25 at Granite on March 2, 1962.

Carole McLennan was in the derailment of train No. 26 near Evaro on June 10, 1962.

Numbers tell a story here. A single journey from the forward end of the first dome coach to the rear of the Pullman observation lounge car was exactly 1,020 feet on a 14-car train, even slightly more, allowing for the twists and turns of the aisle in some of the cars. With four domes in each train, there were also 28 steps to climb and descend. It was not unusual for these ladies to make up to 30 or so passes through the train on a trip from Seattle to Chicago. Assuming one trip into each dome section per pass, that

Chapter 12: The Crew of the *Vista-Dome North Coast Limited*

works out to some 840 steps to climb and 30,600 feet of distance—almost six miles—to walk. One way. After a two-day layover in Chicago, they repeated the performance on the westbound trip. Upon arrival at Seattle, they enjoyed a well-deserved four-day break before their next trip. In most cases, though, the Stewardess-Nurse was exhausted at the end of a six-day round trip and needed a few days off.

Then there were those duties requiring extra effort—like boarding passengers confined to stretchers by lifting them in through the swing-open type egress window on the 8-6-4 and dome sleeping cars. There were pregnant women who went into labor aboard the train, colic babies, elderly men with heart conditions, and patients on their way to the Mayo clinic in Rochester, Minnesota, who needed injections *en route*. There were heart attacks aboard the train and, in at least one case, even an abandoned baby in a restroom. The list goes on. In between all these exciting activities were the PA announcements, questions about the train and route to answer, and general conversation with passengers. That the Stewardess-Nurses maintained an excellent attitude, nonetheless, and smiles on their faces, is proof of their outstanding character and stamina. Supervisor Lila Brekke had obviously developed excellent hiring practices. They set the standard used by her five successors, and those standards worked. In spite of trials, tribulations, and some complaints about a lack of raises, most Stewardess-Nurses left the service reluctantly, usually because they were getting married or wanted to return to hospital work. Surely a Registered Nurse had to show a love for people and for this kind of work in order to become a *North Coast Limited* Stewardess-Nurse. Not least, she also had to have a good sense of humor. Indeed, most of them did. (See "Sue's Vignettes".)

The Ultimate Test

At no time did the NP better realize the most important facet of Stewardess-Nurse service than in those critical moments immediately following a serious accident with the train. Safety aboard the train was emphasized during Stewardess-Nurse training. It was not unusual for a passenger to smash a finger in an end door, or slip and fall down a set of dome or vestibule steps and the like, so the Supervisor advised the Stewardess-Nurses to treat injuries promptly, ask the conductor to call for a medical doctor to meet the train at the next stop if the Stewardess-Nurse deemed it necessary, and write a full report for every incident. Each Stewardess-Nurse completed a mandatory trip report at the end of every trip. In addition to that procedure, the Stewardess-Nurse manual stated a general, catch-all requirement thus: "The Stewardess-Nurse must be ready at all times for any emergency situation that might arise." That statement notwithstanding, it is interesting that the possibility of a major derailment or collision with the train itself was rarely a subject of much discussion at job interviews or even during Stewardess-Nurse training, except during the period right after the derailments in 1962, not surprisingly.

Still, accidents with the train happened. Some of them were comparatively minor; others were disastrous. On more than one occasion, a Stewardess-Nurse was on the ground, without a coat and in temperatures well below freezing, tending to an injured or dying motorist who had just been struck by the train. In 1961, train No. 26 struck an auto at nearly 70 miles per hour, at a grade crossing near Warm Springs, west of Butte. Two elderly men were in the auto. Former Stewardess-Nurse Joan Reitz Dolan, who was working aboard that train, commented some 40 years later, "I remember it like yesterday, how those two men were literally torn right out of their boots when we hit them. In fact, when I got to the site after we backed up, I noticed that the men were separated from their boots by several yards, and yet their boots were still tied . . ."

The ultimate test came with a major derailment. The Glendive, Granite, and Evaro derailments in 1962 occurred within a few weeks of each other, and they involved three different Stewardess-Nurses. In the accident near Glendive: Joan Reitz. At Granite: Gladys Stewart. And, at Evaro: Carole McLennan. Each of these Stewardess-Nurses performed admirably in a time of crisis. Joan Reitz, for example, went into action immediately after the Glendive derailment, ascertaining the number and nature of injuries, tending to the injured and gathering them together to the extent possible, until doctors arrived on the scene. She was in the first dome-sleeper behind the diner when the derailment occurred. She gave the following account to the author in April 2001:

> I looked out one of the aisle windows and saw the mail car pop out of the train. It was actually airborne and landed on the frozen river down below track level. I thought it would break through and take on water, but it didn't. My first thought was about the mail clerks inside that car. I knew they were injured right then and there, and badly. My next thought was a frightening question: "Where there any passengers between cars that separated?" I prayed there weren't any. When my car came to a sudden halt, I began working my way forward right away, to get to those injured. Thankfully, no passengers had been between cars at the moment of the accident, a near miracle because it happened right when the first dining car service began, at about five o'clock.

Carole McLennan's account of the Evaro accident contains both similarities and notable differences from the one above. One significant difference was that the Evaro accident occurred while almost every person on the train was asleep. Except for the fact that this included the engine crew, that was the good news. Nobody was between cars. The bad news was that her train was traveling nearly 90 miles per hour when it derailed, twice the speed of the train in the Glendive accident. Her account as given to me in April 2001:

> I was only half-asleep in my roomette on the car right behind the diner. It was just beginning to get light outside. All of a sudden I woke up—not because of any noise, but because it was suddenly quiet. The rapid clickety-clack suddenly stopped—*just like that*! And yet we were still moving! It was weird. My car was actually momentarily airborne. What may have been only a split second seemed like an hour. We came down with a crash. I can still hear the sounds of rocks hitting the bottom of the car, the twisting of steel rails, and strangely enough, I could even hear the crunch of wooden ties. My room was right above a set of wheels.
>
> When everything stopped, I put on my night coat—I was still in my pajamas and slippers—and got out on the ground. Most of the cars were separated from each other. I began working my way forward, toward the most heavily damaged cars, trying to help people out of their cars as I went along. A lot of them came out through smashed windows. There was glass, mud, and junk everywhere. With help from all the porters, the Pullman conductor, the train conductor, and the brakemen, we managed to get everyone to a safe place, grouping those injured in one place as much as we could do so safely. That train conductor was just wonderful, the way he handled the situation. We must have used every sheet, pillow, and blanket on the train . . .
>
> The *real* heroes that day were two people who pulled up in a pickup on the highway next to the track, right away—they may have even seen the derailment happen. They went right to work climbing up into those cars and helping people out of them. They had to use rope to climb into some of those cars, because of the steep angle on that mountainside . . .

A few hours after the Evaro accident, a man from *The Missoulian* newspaper interviewed Miss McLennan. The June 11, 1962, edition quotes her as saying, "You know, the gal [Stewardess-Nurse Gladys Stewart] who passed us going west last night is the one who was on that train that went into Granite Lake a couple months ago."

When the ill-fated No. 26 stopped at Spokane on the night of June 9, 1962, there, on an adjacent track, was train No. 25 with Gladys Stewart aboard. She had been on train No. 25 when it derailed at

Chapter 12: The Crew of the *Vista-Dome North Coast Limited*

Granite on March 2, 1962. This author spent several years trying to track her down for an interview. (Tracking down former Stewardess-Nurses can be a difficult task when one does not know their married names.) Upon finally obtaining a phone number to her last known residence in April 2001, I called to learn from her nephew that she had passed away only a few months earlier. Thus, the interview would never be. Even so, the following account of Gladys Stewart's outstanding performance in a time of crisis at Granite, Idaho, in March 1962, is informative, even fascinating. Miss Stewart was nicknamed "Scotty" by her family, friends, and fellow "Sues," because she was from Scotland and spoke with a heavy Scottish accent. Former Stewardess-Nurse Joan Reitz Dolan, who became a Supervisor of Stewardess-Nurses in 1963, had the following to say in an April 2001 interview with the author:

> That accident in Idaho was *really* serious. I shudder every time I think of it or see photos of it. But of all the Stewardess-Nurses the NP ever had, I don't think there could have been a better one to be involved in that accident than "Scotty." She was our very best, a girl with more energy than anyone I ever saw. She was very outgoing and personable. Most of all, she was professional and had an excellent nursing background.
>
> That night she was on the ground, in her pajamas, helping passengers to a safe place and tending to the injured. All she had for shoes were those high heels we had as part of our uniform. They were no good in snow and rocks, so she just took them off and went about her work in stocking feet, not slowing down for a minute nor complaining. She stepped on glass and strips of metal everywhere . . . cut her feet and legs very badly. She had scars for the rest of her life.
>
> Her actions were so effective, and she was fast. By the time rescue personnel arrived at the scene, Scotty already had everything organized and under control. They were amazed.
>
> Then, as if the accident weren't enough, she arrived in Spokane hours later only to learn that her mother was dying from an illness, back in Scotland. So, she had to go there right away. It was a great disappointment that the NP would not let her fly back to Seattle—they made her take a bus—nor would they even help her out with airfare from Seattle to Scotland. We didn't make much money in those days. Before Gladys got to Scotland, her mother died. Besides that, Gladys was pretty much on her own getting there. After all she did for the Railway at Granite, it would have been a nice gesture to help her out. Even so, she was a true heroine. All of us thought so highly of her before, and even more so after that accident. I miss her dearly . . .

Given the "family atmosphere" typical among NP employees and supervisors across the system, it really was unusual and disappointing that NP officials did not help Miss Stewart in her time of personal tragedy. Not every NP officer was in favor of the Stewardess-Nurse concept, and this may have had some bearing on the situation. In fact, some supervisors and executives on the NP were very much against the idea of having young women on the crew of a passenger train. President Macfarlane and Passenger Traffic Manager G. Walter Rodine in St. Paul, however, were not among them, for both of these men strongly supported the concept. And, Macfarlane himself was Scottish. Miss Stewart was Scottish. In retrospect, it is probable that Macfarlane and Rodine simply did not know about Miss Stewart's personal tragedy and would have helped her had they known about it. This author suspects that one or more mid-level supervisors in the Passenger Department, at Seattle, chose to do nothing about the situation even though they knew about it, keeping that knowledge to themselves.

In spite of these issues, Miss Stewart's performance that night in Idaho did not go unnoticed. President Macfarlane had this to say in his column in the March 1962 issue of *The Tell Tale*, a magazine issued by the road's Department of Safety and Fire Prevention:

The Vista-Dome North Coast Limited

    Typical of the Northern Pacific crew, Gladys Stewart, Stewardess-Nurse, was a tower of strength. Although unhurt in the derailment itself, she suffered numerous bruises and cuts as she helped passengers from the cars, directed the removal of others and attended to their injuries in a most sympathetic and professional manner. Police Chief George Elliot of Sandpoint praised her quick work in organizing rescue and first aid operations. Her conduct under such trying circumstances will long be an inspiration to those whom she aided and to us of Northern Pacific. We are proud to claim her as one of us.

When this photograph was taken on April 19, 1962, repairs to dome sleepers 312 and 314 following the Granite derailment of March 2 were not quite complete. Thus, this train is missing one dome sleeper. Train No. 26 ascends Bozeman pass at milepost 133 near Chestnut, with a 12-car consist that includes 8-6-4 sleeper 371, dome sleeper 308, and sleeper-observation-lounge 390 at the rear of the train. Grading is under way for a one-mile line relocation to make room for I-90 in Rocky Canyon. The Stewardess-Nurse aboard this train is Miss Gladys Stewart, who had just returned to work after recovering from injuries received in the Granite derailment.
Warren R. McGee photo

230

Chapter 12: **The Crew of the** *Vista-Dome North Coast Limited*

Stewardess-Nurse Service Ends

In January 1967, Stewardess-Nurse Supervisor Joan Reitz resigned to marry. Her superiors did not handle the situation well, for they did not use the usual protocol in announcing her replacement. Besides that, for nearly 12 years the NP had placed only a Registered Nurse (and, since Miss Lila Brekke, a former NP Stewardess-Nurse as well) in the Supervisor position, but in this case Passenger Traffic Manager F. G. Scott in St. Paul decided to fill Miss Reitz's position with one of the Seattle office secretaries, instead. (Passenger Traffic Manager G. Walter Rodine retired in August 1963. Mr. Scott was promoted to replace him and thus moved from Seattle to St. Paul at that time.) It did not take long for most of the Stewardess-Nurses to decide that they did not want to answer to a supervisor who was not a Registered Nurse. Within a few days of the announcement regarding Miss Reitz's replacement, all but one of the Stewardess-Nurses handed in their resignations, much to the chagrin of Mr. Scott and other NP officials.

The last Registered Nurses hired for the Stewardess-Nurse program were Linda McAllister, Betty Mullen, and Barbara Zepp. They joined the NP in November and December 1966. When nine of the 10 Stewardess-Nurses resigned in late January 1967, the Stewardess-Nurse program suddenly ended. The NP soon replaced it with a Stewardess program, but valuable, professional nursing skills were no longer available to the traveling public aboard the *Vista-Dome North Coast Limited*.

Sidetracked Sues

As of this writing, only five of the 120 *North Coast Limited* Stewardess-Nurses (plus one secretary to the supervisor) are known to this author to be deceased. Many of the others stay in touch with each other. Moreover, one of the former secretaries to the Supervisor of Stewardess-Nurses, Audrey Simpson Honegger, has been a central point-of-contact for many of the former "Sues." In fact, as late as August 2001, a large number of them convened in the Seattle area for a reunion, and in recent years some have gathered together for birthdays and other special occasions. Until several years ago, Audrey Honegger edited and published a newsletter for all former Stewardess-Nurses called *Sidetracked Sues*, the unofficial title that the entire group bestowed upon itself and by which these women are still known today. Although the newsletter has been discontinued, many of these women still count each other as close friends with a unique bond. Given the short average tenure of a Stewardess-Nurse, and the number of years that have passed since those days, the fact that they maintain a strong camaraderie and group identity is quite remarkable. Surely it indicates the pride, sense of accomplishment, and uniqueness of being a *North Coast Limited* Stewardess-Nurse. Finally, it is interesting to note that every former Stewardess-Nurse I've contacted thus far, without exception, has said that her time with the NP was absolutely delightful, fun, and most memorable. Almost every one has said, "Those were good days for me."

Sue's Vignettes

For NP's Stewardess-Nurses, work aboard the *Vista-Dome North Coast Limited* was always challenging, often tiring, but it was also fascinating. There was seldom a dull moment. Events aboard the train, in the Stewardess-Nurse office in Seattle, and at their layover hotel in Chicago were sometimes sad, sometimes amazing, and sometimes quite funny. Most of the Stewardess-Nurses had a lot of spunk and a great sense of humor, and were able to see

> **NOTE**
>
> For ease of reference to the Stewardess-Nurse roster, only the maiden names of former Stewardess-Nurses and Supervisors are shown.

The Vista-Dome North Coast Limited

the funny side of things whenever possible. At the same time, many of them realized that they were in a unique position and took advantage of it, as we shall see . . .

Several former "Sues" and Supervisors provided the author the following comments and vignettes in April 2001:

Will I make it? Will I be attractive enough? I had just had my lower teeth ground down more evenly, in order to look my best. I was a nurse, but how would I be as a stewardess? I was nervous, wondering why I had put myself in this position of possible rejection. Then the word came down . . . I was accepted! Hooray!

Barbara A. "Babs" Bidstrup

My girls were the cream of the crop, because I had so many to choose from when hiring. They came from all around the country. I was really proud of them and fortunate to have them.

Lila Brekke,
Supervisor

Our home base was Seattle. We parked along the railroad tracks there, leaped over rails in high heels and our green suit (after checking in with our Supervisor at Smith Tower) to pick up paperwork that told us who was aboard, how many unaccompanied children we had, etc. . . . We said goodbye to people detraining at all the main depots (we stood at the top of the escalator in the St. Paul Union Depot). Likewise, we greeted people as they got on, so often we were the first ones off and the last ones on, except for the conductor and porters who hauled up the step boxes.

Mary B. Pearson

No two trips were ever the same . . . Many times I would be in the last car of the train only to get a call to take care of a problem all the way at the front of the train, and this could go on all day. It involved a tremendous amount of walking. I was all over the train, back and forth, back and forth . . .

Margie Keller

I distinctly remember having several teenage school groups aboard going to various activities such as Girls and Boys State, who came with medication that needed to be administered by injection. We were allowed to do that if they had their own equipment (syringes, etc) and an MD's order. These kids would not have been able to travel with their group, minus the RNs aboard.

Sydney Tally

Chapter 12: The Crew of the *Vista-Dome North Coast Limited*

I always wanted to be a stewardess . . . I even interviewed with an airline, TWA. But then I was encouraged to check with the Northern Pacific, as they had Stewardess-Nurses. When I told the sisters in the local Catholic hospital where I was working that I wanted to be a Stewardess for the NP, they didn't want me "wasting my training being a Stewardess" . . . so they prayed for guidance for me. They even tried to find a nice fellow for me to marry, anything to keep me from going to the NP. This fellow and I dated . . . but I still went to the NP. Well, that "nice fellow" surprised me in May '58 by buying a ticket on my run from Chicago to Seattle! He gave me a diamond ring and said he was willing to wait 'til I was "tired of riding the rails." It took me only until August to decide to quit. After receiving my diamond, the train crew began teasing me . . . they'd put on their sunglasses whenever I'd walk through the cars.

Mary Hamilton

One of our Sues, Joanne Peduzzi, was and still is one of the funniest human beings I've ever known. We nicknamed her "Peduzz." I remember to this day that morning when she reported for work. It was a cold winter morning, and she came in all dressed up in her Sue uniform to pick up her trip papers. She had on nylons, but over them she had white Bobbi socks and *red* tennis shoes. I was kidding her about her attire, and she said she was a cheerleader and proceeded to do a little cheerleader routine by my desk. Just as "Peduzz" leapt into the air, saying "Rah Rah NP!" Mr. [F. G.] Scott walked out into our section from his office. When he came to the door just in time to see her in mid-air, she had her back to him and never saw him. I was sure he was going to have a coronary right there on the spot! He gave her a dirty look and immediately turned around and went back into his office . . . I don't think he ever said a word about it. On board the train, however, "Peduzz" was the perfect picture of propriety and professionalism. I know the crews really liked her.

Audrey Simpson,
secretary to the Supervisor

We had a gentleman aboard who was . . . a stretcher patient. He had a family member traveling with him to give personal care (since we did not normally do that). Well, as we pulled out of St. Paul and I was evaluating the care he would need from me, he did not have either a bedpan or a urinal—things he decidedly needed. Now, the little black medical bags that we carried housed a variety of things, but not urinals or bedpans! With the help of the dining car crew, several plastic milk jugs, and sanitary napkins and tape that we did carry in our black bags, I was able to make a functioning, if not state of the art, urinal and bed pan!

Sydney Tally

I grew up in a railroad family . . . My *North Coast Limited* experiences renewed these warm memories and I felt right at home. I loved the variety of the seasons and never grew tired of the ever-changing scenes out the windows of the *North Coast Limited* as we clickity-clacked up over the Cascades, over the Rockies, and then out across the prairies . . . I enjoyed watching calves and foals grow up into cows and horses as I checked in on familiar scenes every 10 days.

Barbara "Babs" Bidstrup

The Vista-Dome North Coast Limited

In June 1958 Gerry Yanta was the person who hired me, as she was Supervisor then. I went up to Chicago to visit my sister, Mary, a Stewardess-Nurse, on her layover there and Gerry was there at the time. To my surprise, I was unknowingly interviewed in a casual conversation and was called about a month later and asked if I was interested in joining the Sues. My sister's apartment mate, one of the other Sues, had resigned. Her name was Glenda Canada, so I got her place in that apartment. I had been the Infirmary nurse at the time, at the Illinois Braille and Sight Saving School in Jacksonville, my hometown . . . I resigned and put all my worldly belongings in my new little Ford Victoria Hardtop and $300 in my pocket and headed for the big city—Seattle! I had not a care in the world.

Rita Hamilton

"What's the ring for Sue? (Alias, Miss Hamilton) Those Montana batter flapjacks were great . . . but what's the ring for Sue? And . . . WHERE's ROCKY?"

Comments to Mary Hamilton, on a comment card as filled out by passenger Jon Herrington aboard train No. 26 on June 28, 1958, who had apparently mistaken the NP for "that other road."

One night I had a gentleman who fell down the dome steps and crushed his foot. I told the conductor and asked that a note be dropped off to have an MD meet the train in Fargo. (The NP had contracts with certain MD's in major cities along the line who would take care of the train crews and were supposed to meet the trains if one of the Sues requested it). Well, the train crew told me that they would wire the local vet, instead, since that is whom they all went to instead of the contract MD!

Stewardess-Nurse,
name withheld by request

As a Stewardess Nurse, I spent two days on the *North Coast Limited*, two in Chicago, two on the train returning, and then four days in Seattle. At the other end of the road, in Chicago, we Stewardess-Nurses stayed at the Palmer House. I felt so grown up and sophisticated. Once I saw Mort Sahl, a very popular entertainer of the time, at the Palmer House. I wrote home gloating about this. Mom wrote back saying, "That was nice. We had Bob Hope visit us here in Laramie at the Field House." Another time I wrote home about seeing a ticker tape parade for some well-known high politician in the Chicago area. Mom wrote back, "That was nice. President Kennedy was here to visit us in Laramie at the Field House."

Barbara "Babs" Bidstrup

We always had the same room at the Palmer House in Chicago—it was 2141W. There were always two of us to a room, since we overlapped on two-day layovers.

Mary B. Pearson

Chapter 12: The Crew of the *Vista-Dome North Coast Limited*

We always worked with the same two dining car crews, one going east and the other going west, because their Chicago layover was only one day; ours was two . . . My dining car crew on No. 26 was the best, as far as I was concerned. Those guys were so good to me. We'd sit and chat in the dining car after closure and rehash the day and all the amusing stories we had accumulated. My crew on No. 25 included Dining Car Steward Ray Pelletier and Head Chef Don Welligrant, Jr. They were gems also. Ray was a hoot! He liked to have a little vodka and orange juice after hours and loved to tell stories. I really hated to be out of line, when I got time off etc., because these guys were really great to work with, and they were so respectful of me.

Rita Hamilton

Author's note: "Out of line" was Stewardess-Nurse jargon for being out of sequence on the Stewardess-Nurse trip schedule, which happened whenever a Stewardess-Nurse needed a day off and another filled in for her. They were free to trade trips as they wished, provided they covered all the trips.

On one trip I was out of line, filling in for another Sue. We covered for each other when neccessary. With short notice that I had to work this particular trip, I had barely enough time to jump into my uniform and get to King Street for the departure. Not wanting to be late for work, I hurried. I just barely made it. *Whew!* Was I relieved! And then . . . the train derailed near Glendive.

Joan Reitz

Had a young mother in the Slumbercoach—up front in the train, where the hot water was the *hottest* . . . The train lurched around a curve, and she spilled some scalding water on the baby's arm . . . The baby's arm was badly blistered but the mother wouldn't let anyone touch this screaming baby. She wanted the train stopped and a Jehovah's Witness to say some prayers over the baby, over a telephone. I had rolled up my pajama legs, slipped into my green uniform raincoat (as was procedure), stepped into shoes, and was out of my roomette in record time, moving quickly through all the coaches up to the Slumbercoach—with my hair up in rollers (the fashion at that time). On my way back, after talking with the mother and seeing the burned baby, another mother said to her little girl, who was awake and watching me come down the aisle, "That's Sue, our Stewardess Nurse" The little girl replied, "Oh no it's not! Our Stewardess nurse is *pretty*."

Mary B. Pearson

We often had passengers who were headed to Chicago for conventions, so we would sometimes run into them as we made it to our room at the Palmer House. Since we were still in uniform, we were easily identified and most of the passengers were sure we remembered them. So we all learned that the smile stayed on the face until we were firmly behind our hotel room door! Well, after one really tough trip that included three people who smashed their fingers in the doors between cars . . . and the last night spent up with a surfeit of young mothers in coach, all who were sure their children were seriously ill, I was stumbling to my room when I noticed two people coming toward me who looked vaguely familiar. On went the smile. I courteously asked if they had been comfortable in their accommodations and were looking forward to their stay in Chicago. They gave me rather weird looks but answered politely. Imagine my chagrin when I entered my room and noted the advertisement for Peter Lind Hayes and Mary Ford who were appearing in the Empire Room—*that* was who I had just greeted!

Sydney Tally

The Vista-Dome North Coast Limited

The Pullman porters watched over us like fathers and would do anything for us.

Joelle Zabel

I certainly got to know the passengers well, especially if we were together for the full two-and-a-half-day trip. They became like family. In the summer it could get very busy at times. Children running up and down the aisles and hanging from the dome steps could be a bit trying. We sometimes jokingly referred to them as "house apes."

Margie Keller

Cars destined for Portland were switched out of the train at Pasco in the middle of the night on the westbound trip. The trainmen would walk through the train earlier in the evening and advise passengers to be sure to be in their proper places, so as to be in the right car for that switching move. Well, one night a man and his wife had a spat. She threw him out of their Pullman room. Somehow, he ended up in the wrong car. Later, there he was, in the middle of the night, standing on the Pasco platform in his pajamas with nowhere to go. I wonder what she thought when she realized that she had, in effect, thrown him right off the train . . .

A former "Sue"

I remember being wakened by an urgent knock on my roomette door in the middle of the night. A trembling, breathless messenger was calling on me . . . a gentleman was down in a forward car. I threw on my raincoat over my nightgown, grabbed my bag and followed my midnight caller swiftly through the swaying cars filled with sleeping people. He led me to a man lying on his back and not breathing. I could not feel a pulse. I opened his airway and breathed into his mouth. He regurgitated . . . Even so, I could see that he was mottled blue and white, dead and beyond my help. He must have been traveling alone, as none of the anxious bystanders knew him. I told the conductor, and he arranged to have a hearse meet us at the next station. I stayed with the gentleman through his removal from the train and helped with the inevitable paper work that followed. Everyone was very comforted by having a nurse aboard—except me!

Barbara "Babs" Bidstrup

Those dreaded PA announcements! I was *never* in the right place at the right time when I had to make one of those. Sometimes the PA system didn't work. When it did work, the crews would make fun of us, sometimes right while we were trying to make our announcement, trying to get us to laugh over the PA system. I didn't like PAs. I'd much rather be mingling with the passengers or warming baby bottles.

Joelle Zabel

One of the biggest surprises we had on that job was the extreme change in weather that could occur on a trip. We'd leave Seattle in mild, misty fifty-degree weather. The next day we'd step out at Livingston where it was twenty degrees below zero. Then we'd get to Chicago and it would be fifty degrees again.

Sydney Tally

Chapter 12: The Crew of the *Vista-Dome North Coast Limited*

The only real problem with the uniform that I recall was their coats. The ones they had with their uniforms were just not heavy enough for the extreme cold. Later, we added linings to those coats, but that still wasn't enough . . . Many of those poor girls would be right there on the platform at every stop, sometimes even without their coats so the uniform could be seen better, and they'd be freezing and smiling, smiling and freezing . . .

Lila Brekke,
Supervisor

The thing I remember most was all the fun I used to have with the crew. One night I went to my roomette, got undressed, and pulled my bed down, looking forward to reading the book I was lost in. I got the book out and, sure enough, the crew had torn out the next chapter. Of course, they were in the hallway laughing hysterically. Another time, I again got ready for bed, and when I started to pull down the shade, this skeleton went flying past my window, back and forth. Of course, it was the crew with this paper thing on a long string—nearly gave me a heart attack!

Patricia Heppner

If someone was really sick (!), we could get the conductor to send a message ahead and have a doctor meet the train. I have been known to head up the main street to a drug store to get Kaopectate or some such over the counter drug (in Bozeman, Montana, I think)—with the conductor knowing he couldn't leave without me.

Mary B. Pearson

One of our girls, Wilma Macklin, had to go get some medicine at a local pharmacy. She was left standing on the platform at Livingston. The train left without her . . . She ended up on an airplane to Fargo, where she re-joined her train. Boy, was *that* train crew surprised to see her!

Rita Hamilton

Fortunately, I didn't have any medical emergencies aboard the train, but for some reason an elderly man and his constipation problem always comes to mind. He was very preoccupied with his problem . . . don't know what he wanted me to do about it, but my expert medical advice was, *prunes!*

Joelle Zabel

The Vista-Dome North Coast Limited

We had Red Skelton aboard the train. Well, as a fun prank, Mr. Skelton wanted to be the dining car steward for an entire meal seating. So, he discreetly asked the steward if he could do it, and the steward went along with it! It was the last dinner seating. The steward equipped Mr. Skelton with his steward's jacket, gave him a quick course in procedures, and turned him loose. As passengers came into the diner, "Steward" Skelton greeted them and showed them to their seats. Some of them gave him a quizzical look, as though they felt they should know him from somewhere, but they couldn't quite figure it out. As Mr. Skelton took their orders, the real steward (now out of his uniform jacket) stood a ways back but close enough to hear them, and copied them down for the waiters. This went on for the entire dinner seating and none of those passengers knew that Red Skelton had been their steward.

Joan Reitz

To travel the world was my dream from childhood . . . The Seattle World's Fair drew many people from around the world, so we had many international passengers aboard the train in 1962. This presented me a unique opportunity. Some families would invite me to visit them if I ever got to their part of the world. They would supply me with their addresses or phone numbers, which I carefully saved. One family of five from Australia stands out in my memory . . . They decided to travel the world as a family. Part of their trip was riding the *North Coast Limited*, which led to their fervent invitation to me to visit them if I ever got to Australia. Eventually I got there and my "Aussie family" hosted me for a month, taking me to see all the sights in their vicinity around Sydney and on weekend trips to Melbourne and Canberra. I have kept in touch with them through all these years . . . they truly became a part of my extended family. Other families I met on the train, from New Zealand, Singapore and Bangkok, also shared their homes with me as I later traveled around the world for a year. Thus, after a year and a half on the NP, the available money had finally matched up with my desire to travel the world, so I left Stewardess-Nursing to take off and accomplish my dream.

Barbara "Babs" Bidstrup

Vista-Dome North Coast Limited Stewardess-Nurses

This is a complete roster of all the Stewardess-Nurses on the Northern Pacific Railway (NP), their supervisors, and the secretaries to the supervisors. Following several months of program development by the first supervisor, Miss Lila Brekke, and several weeks of training for the first Stewardess-Nurses, the program officially began on June 1, 1955, and ended on January 31, 1967, when Stewardesses were no longer required to be Registered Nurses.

Names are in chronological order by date of hire. Each listing will show maiden name, dates of service, and hometown when known. In some cases, dates are approximate; these are indicated by "ca." One Stewardess-Nurse left the service and returned later; separate service dates will be shown for each time in service. Entries for those known by the author to be deceased are shown in italics.

The author is indebted to former secretary to the supervisor, Audrey Simpson Honegger, and former Stewardess-Nurse Supervisor, Joan Reitz Dolan, for compiling this roster.

Chapter 12: The Crew of the Vista-Dome North Coast Limited

Supervisors of Stewardess-Nurses	Service Dates as Supervisor	Hometown
Lila Brekke	February 1, 1955–May 31, 1958	Frost, MN
Geraldine Yanta	*June 1, 1958–February 28, 1959*	*St. Paul, MN*
Elaine Rath	March 1, 1959–September 30, 1960	Mott, ND
Charlotte Hanes	October 1, 1960–May 31, 1963	Colorado Springs, CO
Karen Laumbach	June 1, 1963–November 30, 1963	Lake City, IA
Joan Reitz	December 1, 1963–January 31, 1967	Lancaster, PA

Secretaries to the Supervisor	Service Dates	Hometown
Jean D. Parsons	Ca. March 1955–March 1956	Billings, MT
Deloris Pederson	April 1956–April 1957	Kent, WA
Agnes Sharkey	*May 1957–October 1958*	*Hoboken, NJ*
Audrey Simpson	November 1958–October 1961	Billings, MT
Nicki H. Anderson	October 1961–?	Olympia, WA
Mary Ann Hines	(Unknown)	(Unknown)
Sharon Thompson	(Unknown)	(Unknown)
Roberta Livingston	(Unknown)	Bremerton, WA
Marlene Saunders	December 1965–January 1967	Seattle, WA

Stewardess-Nurse	Stewardess-Nurse Service Dates	Hometown
1. Nona K. Whittendale	May 12, 1955–July 5, 1957	Seattle, WA
2. Shirley Ulricksen	May 12, 1955–July 18, 1955	(Unknown)

(Note: Due to her very short time on the NP, Miss Ulricksen's photo did not appear in NP's employee magazine, "The North Coaster," as one of the original 10 Stewardess-Nurses.)

Stewardess-Nurse	Stewardess-Nurse Service Dates	Hometown
3. Patricia Thompson	May 12, 1955–January 18, 1956	Wellington, Ontario, Canada
4. Margery Delano	May 12, 1955–June 15, 1956	Wincester, MA
5. *Emma Siddall*	*June 6, 1955–March 3, 1956*	*Portland, OR*
6. Barbara Christensen	June 6, 1955–May 28, 1956	Minneapolis, MN
7. Joelle Zabel	June 7, 1955–June 3, 1956	Seattle, WA
8. Kathleen St. Germain	July 12, 1955–August 3, 1956	St. Paul, MN
9. Viola Barich	July 13, 1955–July 15, 1957	Roslyn, WA
10. Eileen McGough	July 14, 1955–July 19, 1956	Seattle, WA
11. Lavaughn Jurgensen	July 14, 1955–December 22, 1956	Seattle, WA
12. Kathleen Ahern	January 3, 1956–February 5, 1957	Kent, WA
13. Elaine Rath*	February 20, 1956–August 16, 1957 November 1958–February 28, 1959	Mott, ND
14. Edonna Furo	May 16, 1956–August 15, 1957	Minneapolis, MN
15. *Geraldine Yanta**	*May 16, 1956–May 31, 1958*	*St. Paul, MN*
16. Patricia Poole	June 18, 1956–January 19, 1957	Vancouver, B.C., Canada
17. Sylvia Davis	July 2, 1956–September 26, 1958	Juneau, AK
18. Marianne Osyp	July 16, 1956–December 20, 1956	Vancouver, B.C., Canada
19. Beverly MacDonald	December 3, 1956–November 6, 1957	Worcester, MS
20. Irene Jenkin	January 7, 1957–January 8, 1958	Calgary, Alberta, Canada
21. Madelon George	January 14, 1957–May 20, 1957	Los Angeles, CA
22. Shari Fain	January 16, 1957–May 6, 1958	Walla Walla, WA
23. Carol Ann Bell	May 9, 1957–October 5, 1959	Everett, WA
24. Lorain Nygaard	June 10, 1957–February 10, 1958	Columbus, ND
25. Ruth Halverson	June 22, 1957–February 11, 1958	Cottonwood, MN
26. Jacqueline McLeod	July 26, 1957–December 4, 1957	South Dakota
27. Irma Weberling	August 6, 1957–May 15, 1958	Lewiston, ID

*Denotes Stewardess-Nurse who later served as a supervisor.

The Vista-Dome North Coast Limited

Stewardess-Nurse	Stewardess-Nurse Service Dates	Hometown
28. Barbara Person	October 22, 1957–December 13, 1958	Naselle, WA
29. Glenda Canada	December 1, 1957–June 16, 1958	Memphis, TN
30. Patricia F. Heppner	December 7, 1957–April 20, 1958	Lake City, MN
31. Joann Peduzzi	January 18, 1958–June 10, 1960	Trafford, PA
32. Judith Marker	February 3, 1958–June 20, 1959	Puyallup, WA
33. Mary (Mari) Hamilton	March 23, 1958–August 5, 1958	Jacksonville, IL
34. Rita Hamilton	June 9, 1958–September 9, 1959	Jacksonville, IL
35. Molly Herley	June 24, 1958–June 30, 1959	Everett, WA
36. Wilma Macklin	July 21, 1958–September 1, 1959	Folsom, CA
37. Mary Petri	September 23, 1958–June 28, 1959	Tacoma, WA
38. Marilyn Sanden	September 29, 1958–December 7, 1959	(Unknown)
39. Janet Gotz	December 26, 1958–September 12, 1959	Marshfield, WI
40. Joann Serwold	February 17, 1959–March 31, 1960	Poulsbo, WA
41. Mary Stevenson	March 1, 1959–May 30, 1960	Pataskala, OH
42. Doris Podhorn	June 16, 1959–June 15, 1960	Alton, IL
43. Patricia Collins	July 1, 1959–August 1, 1960	Pittsburgh, PA
44. Helen Cobb	September 1, 1959–September 3, 1960	Jacksonville, IL
45. Helen Martin	September 1, 1959–March 6, 1960	Cairo, IL
46. Joan Holecek	September 16, 1959–December 4, 1960	Berwyn, IL
47. Marilyn Fritts	September 16, 1959–December 3, 1960	Norristown, PA
48. Marilyn Parsons	February 19, 1960–April 30, 1961	Dubuque, IA
49. Ann Gallager	March 1, 1960–July 22, 1960	(Unknown)
50. Charlotte Hanes*	May, 1960–September 30, 1960	Colorado Springs, CO
51. Marjorie Keller	May 19, 1960–July 18, 1961	Cataldo, ID
52. Mary Lou Cascadden	May 22, 1960–April 30, 1962	St. Clair, MI
53. Elizabeth Ramsey	July 11, 1960–October 25, 1961	Walnut, AR
54. Karen Walt	*July 16, 1960–October 11, 1962*	*Duluth, MN*
55. Janet Sparks	July 20, 1960–October 14, 1961	Olive Hill, KY
56. Kathleen Deleury	August 22, 1960–June 1, 1961	Van Nuys, CA
57. Joan Reitz*	September 13, 1960–April 11, 1962	Lancaster, PA

(Note: Miss Reitz left the Stewardess-Nurse service in April 1962 and went into nursing in the private sector. In December 1963 she was hired back as Supervisor of Stewardess-Nurses to replace Karen Laumbach.)

Stewardess-Nurse	Stewardess-Nurse Service Dates	Hometown
58. Patricia Lawlor	November 17, 1960–December 20, 1961	Clinton, IA
59. Anita Dinatale	November 18, 1960–December 23, 1961	Donora, PA
60. Sally Omar	April 17, 1961–June 7, 1962	Ross, ND
61. Donna Lee Thompson	May 17, 1961–June 16, 1962	Fargo, ND
62. Gladys Stewart	*July 5, 1961–August 6, 1962*	*Keith, Banffshire, Scotland.*
63. Mary B. Pearson	September 18, 1961–February 11, 1963	St. Paul, MN
64. Barbara Brown	October 2, 1961–March 5, 1962	Courtland, NY
65. Barbara Bidstrup	*November 4, 1961–January 17, 1963*	*Laramie, WY*
66. Joyce Tarabokia	December 4, 1961–January 29, 1962	New Jersey
67. Carole McLennan	January 16, 1962–August 17, 1962	Mundelein, IL
68. Mary Markle	March 12, 1962–July 4, 1962	Elkins, WV
69. Joanne Olson	March 19, 1962–August 8, 1962	Bellingham, WA
70. Flavia Jones	March 23, 1962–August 21, 1962	Sequim, WA
71. Nancy Renshaw	April 11, 1962–October 30, 1962	Clarkston, WA
72. Sydney Tally	June 1, 1962–August 24, 1963	Leesburg, FL
73. Hilda Garber	June 18, 1962–October 12, 1963	Cheverly, MD
74. Betty Foster	*July 9, 1962–November 28, 1963*	*(Unknown)*
75. Julie Antonioni	August 2, 1962–February 3, 1963	(Unknown)

*Denotes Stewardess-Nurse who later served as a supervisor.

Chapter 12: The Crew of the *Vista-Dome North Coast Limited*

Stewardess-Nurse	Stewardess-Nurse Service Dates	Hometown
76. Mary Bergin	August 3, 1962–May 3, 1963	(Unknown)
77. Glenis Nielsen	August 6, 1962–January 31, 1964	Grandview, WA
78. Roseanne Ruder	September 24, 1962–April 28, 1963	Worthington, MN
79. Joanne Reczuch	September 26, 1962–July 9, 1963	Chicago, IL
80. Lois Shirley	October 12, 1962–November 7, 1963	Homestead, PA
81. Carol Lovelett	December 3, 1962–June 27, 1963	Dupree, SD
82. Elizabeth Horvath	January 16, 1963–November 17, 1964	Indiana
83. Karen Laumbach*	January 24, 1963–May 31, 1963	Lake City, IA
84. Maureen Halle	April 13, 1963–February 26, 1964	Niles, IL
85. Kay Troutwine	April 16, 1963–January 15, 1964	Crown Point, IN
86. Susan Rathburn	June 20, 1963–?	(Unknown)
87. Marifran Kelly	June 25, 1963–January 4, 1964	Seattle, WA
88. Lucille Mitrovitch	July 20, 1963–September 12, 1964	Masury, OH
89. Judith Seaton	August 7, 1963–August 4, 1964	Victor, IA
90. Joan Clink	Ca. September 1963–Ca 1965	Chippewa Falls, WI
91. Marlys Johnson	November 13, 1963–September 1965	Seattle, WA
92. Carol Farquhar	January 6, 1964–June 22, 1964	Methuen, MA
93. Elizabeth Cline	March 3, 1964–?	Ft. Wayne, IN
94. Barbara Walters	August 14, 1964–November 5, 1964	Pennsylvania
95. Anne Philiben	January 6, 1964–January 30, 1965	Bensonville, IL
96. Mary Ann Lyman	August 21, 1964–May 28, 1965	Seattle, WA
97. Patricia Prchlik	September 9, 1964–1966	Knox, IN
98. Mary Lou Boland	November 3, 1964–?	Toronto, Ontario, Canada
99. Shirley E. Nelson	December 7, 1964–?	Winnipeg, Manitoba, Canada
100. Cheryle Eyerly	January 7, 1965–June ?	Livingston, MT
101. Delores Correll	April 1965–September 1966	Lenoir, ND
102. Sharon Spencer	May 29, 1965–?	La Cañada, CA
103. Susan Conlon	July 1965–?	Portland, OR
104. Kathleen O'hara	July 1965–?	Lackawanna, NY
105. Norma Irene Brown	(Unknown)	(Unknown)
106. Carol Conant	(Unknown)	Illinois
107. Margaret Munis	November 8, 1965–July 11, 1966	Bakersfield, CA
108. Norma Aldrich	December 1965–Ca. 1966	Seattle, WA
109. Margaret Champlin	Ca. January 1966–Ca. December 1966	Nashville, TN
110. Dorothy MacArthur	Ca. March 1966–Ca. December 1966	North Surrey, B.C., Canada
111. Gail Holmes	Ca. March 1966–Ca. March 1967	Butte, MT
112. Kathleen Bishard	Ca. May 1966–Ca. January 31, 1967	Columbus, OH
113. Sharon Johnson	Ca. May 1966–Ca. January 31, 1967	Elkhorn, WI
114. Marie Antush	Ca. June 1966–Ca. January 31, 1967	Tacoma, WA
115. Lavonne Schuster	Ca. June 1966–Ca. January 31, 1967	Shell Lake, WI
116. Julie Waterstreet	July 14, 1966–March 13, 1967	Sacramento, CA
117. Carol Fendrick	Ca. July 1966–Ca. January 31, 1967	Meridian, ID
118. Linda Mcallister	November 1966–Ca. January 31, 1967	Greenville, SC
119. Betty Sue Mullen	November 1966–Ca. January 31, 1967	Lacy, WA
120. Barbara Zepp	December 1966–Ca. January 31, 1967	(Unknown)

*Denotes Stewardess-Nurse who later served as a supervisor.

The Vista-Dome North Coast Limited

 Kathleen Ahern
 Norma Aldrich
 Julie Antonioni
 Marie Antush
 Carol Bell
 Mary Bergin
 Barbara Bidstrup
 Kathleen Bishard
 Mary Lou Boland

 Barbara Brown
 Norma Brown
 Glenda Canada
 Mary Lou Cascadden
 Elizabeth Cline
 Joan Clink
 Helen Cobb
 Patricia Ann Collins
 Carol Conant

 Susan Conlon
 Delores Correll
 Sylvia Davis
 Kathleen Deleury
 Anita diNatale
 Cheryle Eyerle
 Shari Fain
 Carol Farquhar
 Carol Fendrick

 Betty Foster
 Marilyn Fritts
 Edonna Furo
 Ann Gallagher
 Hilda Garber
 Madelon George
 Janet Gotz
 Maureen Halle
 Ruth Halverson

 Mary Hamilton
 Rita Hamilton
 Patricia Heppner
 Molly Herley
 Joan Holecek
 Gail Holmes
 Elizabeth Horvath
 Irene Jenkin
 Marlys Johnson

 Sharon Johnson
 Flavia Jones
 Marjorie Keller
 Marifran Kelly
 Patricia Lawlor
 Carol Lovelett
 Mary Ann Lyman
 Dorothy MacArthur
 Beverly MacDonald

Chapter 12: The Crew of the *Vista-Dome North Coast Limited*

Wilma Macklin	Judith Marker	Mary Margaret Markle	Helen Martin	Linda McAllister	Jacqueline McLeod	Lucille Mitrovich	Betty Mullen	Margaret Munis
Shirley Nelson	Glenis Neilsen	Lorain Nygaard	Kathleen O'Hara	Joanne Olson	Sally Omar	Marianne Osyp	Jeanne Parsons	Marilyn Parsons
Mary Pearson	Anne Philiben	Doris Podhorn	Patricia Poole	Patricia Prchlik	Elizabeth Ramsey	Susan Rathburn	Elaine Rath	Joanne Reczuch
Nancy Renshaw	Roseanne Ruder	Marilyn Sanden	La Vonne Schuster	Judith Seaton	Joann Serwold	Lois Shirley	Janet Sparks	Sharon Spencer
Mary Stevenson	Sydney Tally	Donna Thompson	Kay Troutwine	Karen Waly	Julie Waterstreet	Irma Weberling		

The Vista-Dome North Coast Limited

The Day Cupid "Ran the Train"...

Perhaps the most unusual and noteworthy event ever to occur on the *Vista-Dome North Coast Limited* occurred on train No. 26, about 45 minutes before its departure from Seattle on April 15, 1958, when Conductor James C. Taylor and Miss Lorain Nygaard were married in the train's observation-lounge car. Miss Nygaard had served as a Stewardess-Nurse on the *North Coast Limited* from early 1957 until the wedding. (The NP required Stewardess-Nurses to be single.) The trainmen's union, the Order of Railway Conductors and Brakemen, published a monthly news magazine, *Conductor & Brakeman*. The cover of the May 1958 issue and its lead article featured the on-train wedding.

The pair had met while working aboard the train—Conductor Taylor worked between Seattle and Ellensburg. For this special occasion, an altar was set up at the rear of the lounge, and Rev. Stanley Holman of Seattle conducted the ceremony. Family and friends, including off-duty Stewardess-Nurses in uniform, attended. A congratulatory telegram from NP President Robert S. Macfarlane arrived just before the ceremony. The NP's chief executive wrote:'"May your journey through life together be as smooth as a journey aboard the Vista-Dome North Coast Limited where, I am told, you first met. Mrs. Macfarlane joins me in extending sincere congratulations and in wishing you much happiness."

After the ceremony a reception was held in the train's dining car, where the dining car crew served up a beautiful four-tiered wedding cake. Then the newlyweds rode the train from Seattle to East Auburn, where they disembarked and began their honeymoon trip to California. Conductor Taylor (retired) and his wife, Lorain, attended the NPRHA's 1998 convention in Tacoma, where both participated in the popular "NP Vets Panel," answering questions from an audience of about 150 conventioneers and telling stories of their time on the Railway.

Bill Kuebler collection; courtesy James C. and Lorain Taylor

Part 4
HIGHBALL INTO HISTORY

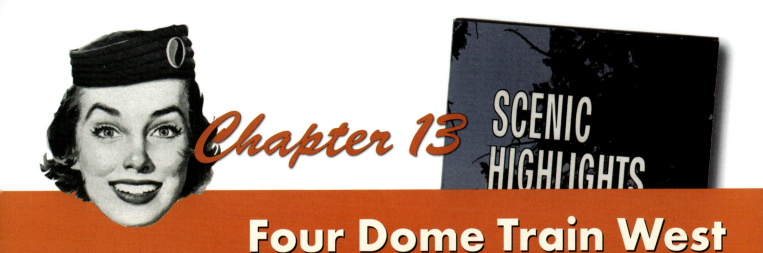

Chapter 13
Four Dome Train West

Now that we have seen some of the things "behind the scenes" in the operation of the *Vista-Dome North Coast Limited*, let's return to 1959 and our journey to Seattle and back to Chicago . . .

WESTBOUND - 1st Day - Commentary No. 4
15 minutes after leaving Minneapolis (8:00 p.m.)

Good evening! This is your Stewardess Nurse, Miss Hamilton.
   On behalf of the train crew* may I welcome those of you who joined us at the Twin Cities. We are glad to have you aboard the Vista-Dome NORTH COAST LIMITED and we want you to have an enjoyable trip...Please let us know* if we may be of help to you.
   May I tell you something about the facilities on our train* that are available to you. The Vista-Dome seats* are for your enjoyment* at no extra cost. Dome seats are not reserved. Please be careful when using the stairway in the dome cars...and remember there is a step down* to the aisle from your dome seat.
   The dining car* is located in the center of the train. Meal times* except breakfast* will be announced over the public address system. Just ahead of the diner* and behind the last coach* is the Traveller's Rest buffet-lounge car. A la carte meals and light snacks are served here* from 7 a.m. until 10 p.m.. The observation-lounge car* at the rear of the train* provides magazines and stationery for standard Pullman passengers. Beverage service is available from 7 a.m. until midnight.
   All of the many facilities available on the train* are described in our "Train Service Guide" booklet. If you would like a copy* I'll be glad to give you one.
   Our time will change at Mandan* North Dakota* when we enter the Mountain Time Zone* during the night. Passengers who are going beyond Mandan* should turn their watches back* one hour. I'll repeat that ...Passengers who are going beyond* Mandan* should turn their watches back* one hour tonight.
   Thank you and good night!

*Denotes breath pauses, while giving the commentaries. If a breath pause is not necessary for you, please pause for a moment. A period, of course, always denotes a breath pause.

"FOUR DOME TRAIN WEST". Thus proclaims the large neon sign from the roof of the Northern Pacific (NP) St. Paul commissary building nearby. In keeping with that slogan our four-dome train is due to head west. We have just stepped aboard the observation-lounge car. In moments, a grand journey will resume as our four F-units shoot eight gray-blue streams of diesel exhaust skyward in an effort to accelerate our train up Westminster Hill. Ahead of us are scenes and events that will firmly

247

The Vista-Dome North Coast Limited

This large neon sign atop NP's St. Paul commissary proudly advertised the best overland transport that money could buy during the period 1954–1970. The NP coach yard is visible in the background of this 1968 photo.
Bill Kuebler collection

Chapter 13: "Four Dome Train West"

Four F-units—6704A, 6510A, an unidentified F-7B, and 6703A—power 14 cars westbound up the 2.2% gradient of Homestake Pass in August 1959. This is the only grade crossing on the 19-mile climb between Whitehall and Homestake (except for one right at Homestake), and it is located near milepost 48, below Spire Rock. The forward part of the train stretches around a seven-degree curve. Most curves in this territory are even sharper, at twelve degrees.
Ron Nixon photo; Bill Kuebler collection

WESTBOUND - 2nd Day - Commentary No. 1
At Myers (about 9 a.m.)

Good morning: This is your Stewardess-Nurse, Miss Hamilton.
  Will you please check your watches* for the correct Mountain Standard Time.
  The correct time is now _____ a.m..
  We are now following the Yellowstone River in Montana. The valley of the Yellowstone* is rich in history and pioneer lore...Many indian battles were fought here...all the way from Glendive to Livingston. In a few minutes* we will pass the station of Custer. It was about 40 miles south of here that General George Custer* made his famous last stand.
  You will also be interested* in history to be made. During the summer of 1962* Seattle will present a world's fair, known as "Century 21."* The theme will be, "Man in the Space Age."* We suggest you plan on attending this unusual event* traveling on the Vista-Dome NORTH COAST LIMITED.
  Before you reach your destination* we would like to know your impression of our train. I'll be glad to give you a comment card* designed for this purpose, if you'd like. Just fill it out and return it to me, or drop it in a mail box...No postage is required.
  Thank you!
  *Denotes breath pauses, while giving the commentaries. If a breath pause is not necessary for you, please pause for a moment. A period, of course, always denotes a breath pause.

The Vista-Dome North Coast Limited

With less than a mile to go before stopping at the Missoula depot, the engineer on No. 25 has the air set and his 12-car train under control. This is high-speed double track territory, and a great deal of momentum is being dissipated here. Mount Sentinel (to the right in this view) and Hell Gate Canyon are now behind the train. Ahead, beginning at DeSmet, lies the Rocky Mountain Division's Sixth Subdivision, noted for the Coriacan Defile and the Jocko and Flathead River valleys. Anybody care to turn the clock back to May 1956 and experience this scene in real life?
Ron Nixon photo; Lorenz P. Schrenk collection

WESTBOUND - 2nd Day - Commentary No. 2
About 15 minutes prior to arrival Billings (10:15 a.m.)

Hello! This is your Stewardess-Nurse, Miss Hamilton.
   In about 15 minutes we will arrive in Billings.
   This is a headquarters city* for companies having important oil interests in Montana* North Dakota* and northern Wyoming. You can see evidence of this oil activity shortly* as we pass three oil refineries. On our right* just before we enter the city* is the refinery of the Carter Division* of the Humble Oil and Refinery Company. A little farther on* and to the left* you can see the Conoco refinery. The Farmer's Union refinery* which is the oldest in the state* is at Laurel* 15 miles west of Billings.
   Located in a productive agricultural region* Billings is the largest livestock feeding center* between the Twin Cities* and the Pacific Northwest.
   Billings is also a gateway to Yellowstone National Park. During the Park season* buses make daily trips over the spectacular* Red Lodge High Road* to take visitors to the Silver Gate entrance* or to the east entrance* via Cody, Wyoming.
   Thank you for your attention, and enjoy your morning!

*Denotes breath pauses, while giving the commentaries. If a breath pause is not necessary for you, please pause for a moment. A period, of course, always denotes a breath pause.

Chapter 13: "Four Dome Train West"

implant themselves in our long-term memories. We may acquire all the more memories should we wisely exchange a little sleep for consumption of nighttime railroading. Yes, all five of our senses are about to be fed a continuous 38-hour travel experience like no other. Any number of years from now, long after 1959, we might be able to tell the story to our grandchildren, but it is hard to imagine how we would describe all the anticipation and excitement of this journey.

After calling his second and final "All Aboard!," Conductor Lundberg waives a highball to Engineer Kath. The rear brakeman closes the steps and bottom door of the rear car's vestibule and assumes his position for the upcoming running brake test. Porter Bob Durham is responsible for closing the vestibule door on the Portland dome sleeper just ahead of the observation-lounge car, but he has already correctly guessed that we wish to observe this departure from its vestibule. He leaves the top door open on both sides of the car and steps aside for us. Before we realize it, our train has begun moving. It is another smooth start.

Train No. 25 reaches the point where the 2.2% descending grade of Evaro hill begins to subside on this four-degree curve, located one and a half miles east of Arlee. This May 1957 edition of the *Vista-Dome North Coast Limited* includes 8-6-4 sleeper 369, dome sleeper 311, 8-6-3-1 sleeper 362, and dome sleeper 305. Passengers on this train are enjoying one of the most scenic segments of the journey from Chicago to Seattle.
Ron Nixon photo; Bill Kuebler collection

After accelerating to about 20 miles per hour, Kath sets about seven or eight pounds of air. The rear brakeman observes the disc brake plunger on his car and quickly waives a highball to Lundberg, who answers and relays it to the head end. Kath releases the brakes and accelerates our train up Westminster Hill. Crew coordination is impressive; there is hardly any deceleration with this maneuver, and passengers do not even notice it.

It is difficult to give up our vestibule spot for a dome seat, the comfort of the later notwithstanding, for the noise and motion are always a great show here. Throughout the rest of our trip, we will be back in this vestibule on

> **WESTBOUND - 2nd Day - Commentary No. 3**
> As train leaves Greycliff (about 11:30 a.m.)
> (**Stewardess-Nurse be sure to look and see from which side of the train the mountains may be seen, before giving the commentary. This will change as the train changes direction.)
>
> Hello! This is your Stewardess-Nurse, Miss Hamilton.
>   This afternoon* we will be traveling through the American Rockies. We can see some of the mountains to our **right/left.** These are called the Crazy Mountains...some of the peaks rise to an elevation of 11,000 feet* and they are in view from the train* for many miles. We can look forward to a scenic ride today-I hope you will enjoy it.
>   Be sure to pick up your copy of* our "Scenic Guide" booklet* from the folder rack in your car. It describes many interesting points* that can be soon from the train.
>   Thank you!
>
> *Denotes breath pauses, while giving the commentaries. If a breath pause is not necessary for you, please pause for a moment. A period, of course, always denotes a breath pause.

several occasions. A few scenes from this perch will be particularly memorable during our westbound trip:

- Clicks and clacks magnified to loud pops by the walls of a long, rocky cut.
- Metallic explosions of switch frogs under the trucks, seemingly all the louder at night.
- The snap of the string on Brakeman Gregory Belland's arm as he catches train orders at Buffalo, North Dakota, in the middle of the night. (The order tersely states that we're meeting No. 26 up ahead, at Peak. No. 26 will take siding.)
- The *whumph* of a grade crossing taken at 80.

This boarding sign directs *North Coast Limited* **passengers to their train at Seattle's King Street Station in 1955.**
Jim Fredrickson photo

Chapter 13: "Four Dome Train West"

Diesel units 6510A, 6513B, and 6508C wait to depart Seattle's King Street Station with ten cars in April 1966. Two cars will be added to this train at Pasco.
Ron Nixon photo; Bill Kuebler collection

- The distant Nathan P-3 Air Chime on the lead F-unit, to us a half-step lower in pitch than what motorists ahead of our train hear as they wisely trade seconds of time for their lives.

- The whiny squeal of disc brakes slowing us for the station stop at Glendive, as we descend the grade east of the depot with incredible momentum in the early morning light; accompanying this is an occasional cyclic hiss from the car's brake cylinder as the anti-wheel slide devices do their thing. Has Dickinson Engineer Hunter Picken factored in the moisture on the rail? Indeed he has. Our stop is right on the money—and on time.

> **WESTBOUND - 2nd Day - Commentary No. 4**
> 15 minutes before arrival at Livingston (about 12:05 p.m.)
>
> Hello! This is your Stewardess-Nurse, Miss Hamilton.
>   In 15 minutes we will arrive in Livingston. Just before we enter the city* we cross the Yellowstone River* for the last time on our trip west.
>   Captain Clark of the Lewis & Clark Expedition* camped at the site of the present city* on the return from the Pacific Northwest.
>   The original entrance to Yellowstone Park* is located 50 miles south of Livingston at Gardiner. Northern Pacific, incidentally* was the first railroad to serve a national park* and began its Yellowstone Park train service* in 1883. During the Park season* buses make connections with our train* to take visitors on scheduled tours of the Park.
>   We are now in an area known for its dude ranches* which are becoming increasingly popular as vacation spots. Many of them arc located between Billings* and Missoula.
>   About 45 minutes after the train leaves Livingston* we will cross the Gallatin Mountain range* and then arrive at Bozeman* oldest town in Montana on the Northern Pacific,* and home of the Montana State College. Then, about 40 minutes later* we will pass through* Three Forks* where the Jefferson* Madison* and Gallatin Rivers merge to form the Missouri River. The scenery this afternoon is lovely* and we hope you will enjoy it.
>   Thank you and good afternoon!
>
> *Denotes breath pauses, while giving the commentaries. If a breath pause is not necessary for you, please pause for a moment. A period, of course, always denotes a breath pause.

The Vista-Dome North Coast Limited

Eastbound *North Coast Limited* passengers enjoy afternoon daylight views of the scenic and unique Yakima River canyon, whereas the westbound *North Coast* is scheduled to operate through this territory in the morning hours before sunrise. Train No. 26 follows the winding course of the Yakima River at milepost 13, between Bristol and Thorp, Washington, on April 27, 1965. F-9A No. 6500C was rebuilt from a wrecked F-7A in 1955 and will soon be renumbered 6703C.
Both photos by Jim Fredrickson

Chapter 13: "Four Dome Train West"

WESTBOUND - 2nd Day - Commentary No. 5
As train leaves Whitehall (about 2:40 p.m.)

Good afternoon! This is your Stewardess-Nurse, Miss Hamilton.
   The correct Mountain Standard Time is _____ p.m..
   We are now beginning the ride up the eastern slope of the Continental Divide. We will cross the Divide at Homestake* at an altitude of 6,328 feet-the highest point on our route.
   From the point where we cross the Divide* rivers flowing east eventually reach the Atlantic Ocean* chiefly through the Gulf of Mexico. River flowing to the west* reach the Pacific Ocean through the Columbia River.
   As we begin the descent of the western side of the Divide-about an hour from now-you will get your first view of Butte* on the mountain slopes north of Silver Bow Valley.
   Butte has long been known* as the "richest hill on earth." The shafts of its underground mines extend a mile into the earth. More copper* and silver* have been produced there than in any other district* in the world. The Montana School of Mines is located at Butte.
   Thank you for your attention!

*Denotes breath pauses, while giving the commentaries. If a breath pause is not necessary for you, please pause for a moment. A period, of course, always denotes a breath pause.

- The unconquerable impulse to pull one's head back into the vestibule as we meet a sided eastbound freight at Hoyt, Montana, on a sunny morning; its brakeman on the ground waves a highball to our rear brakeman after "looking us over" for dragging equipment.
- The way passengers walking through to the next car stop momentarily to watch us watch the train, perhaps envious of our opportunity, probably uncomprehending of our peculiar fascination.

Train No. 26 descends the 19-mile 2.2% grade of Butte mountain, about two miles west of Spire Rock, on June 28, 1955. The rear portion of this 13-car train is just crossing Bridge 52 over Big Pipestone Creek. The 500 foot long steel bridge was built in 1902 to replace a wooden one. Ron Nixon is riding the rear cab unit from Butte to Livingston this morning. He will get off the train at Livingston and then ride the rear cab of No. 25 back to Butte this afternoon. Several publicity photos such as this one will result from these two rides.
Ron Nixon photo; Bill Kuebler collection

The Vista-Dome North Coast Limited

A dome coach gets another window wash at Livingston in August 1963.
Alfred Butler photo; Bill Kuebler collection

Train No. 26 moves eastward onto CB&Q trackage in the early morning light before backing into SPUD for an on-time arrival in July 1964. Before the train backs in, the rear brakeman will move from the vestibule to the rear of car 390, so as to handle the air brake valve there for the reverse movement. Just ahead are dome sleeper 305 and 8-6-4 sleeping car 371. An 8-6-3-1 sleeper is in car line 265, just behind the Budd diner.
Bill Kuebler collection

Chapter 13: "Four Dome Train West"

Train No. 26 highballs through Oregon, Illinois, on October 11, 1955, with a pair of CB&Q E-8s in the lead. The 450-series dining car is the only car in this train that has been given the new VISTA-DOME NORTH COAST LIMITED slogan. Soon, all domes, diners, and lounge cars will have the slogan. Sleeper-observation-lounge car 390 wears the narrow stripe. Throughout most of the 1953–1967 period, however, it wore the wide stripe. The car ahead of it is dome sleeper 305.
William A. Raia collection

WESTBOUND - 2nd Day - Commentary No. 6
About 25 minutes after leaving Butte (about 4:20 p.m.)

Hello again! This is your Stewardess-Nurse.
   If you look to the left of our train* you can see the huge smokestack of* Anaconda Company's copper smelter.
   Built in 1919, it still retains the title* of the "largest smokestack in the world". Some are taller* but none can compare for sheer massiveness. It stands 585 feet high*...the inside diameter is 60 feet at the top* and 76 feet at the bottom*...the walls are 22 and one-half inches thick at the top* and 67 inches at the bottom.
   It took seven million acid-proof bricks to build it. A black mastic coat was applied to the top 150 feet* in 1955. This was the first major repair work of the stack* since it was built.
   We are about seven and one-half miles from this huge landmark.
   Thank you!

*Denotes breath pauses, while giving the commentaries. If a breath pause is not necessary for you, please pause for a moment. A period, of course, always denotes a breath pause.

The Vista-Dome North Coast Limited

The eastbound *Vista-Dome North Coast Limited* arrives Chicago Union Station on-time at 1:45 p.m. on a bright day in March 1960. Bringing up the rear of the train are dome sleeper 312 (car line 266), 8-6-3-1 sleeper 355 (car line 267), and sleeper-observation-lounge 390. Dome sleeper line 268 is not being operated in this off-season, 12-car consist.
Bill Kuebler collection

- Speaking of passengers . . . the way most of them seem to experience this train, seeing but not always observing, hearing but not understanding, gripping the Pullman handrails without touching, confusing diesel talk for meaningless noise. Thank God for them. They are the revenue producers who make this train possible.
- The way the brakeman deftly swings the step box from platform to vestibule and climbs aboard at the exact instant the train begins moving. He has done this a thousand times before.

Then there is the dome. There is too much to see from this perch to be deeply engaged in conversation with fellow passengers. By day, we do our best to be sociable without missing the action outside; by night, we enjoy having the dome to ourselves, one of the privileges of riding in the first class section of this train. (In contrast, several coach passengers ride in their dome sections throughout the night.) The following scenes become permanent memories of vista-dome travel:

Chapter 13: "Four Dome Train West"

EASTBOUND - 1st Day - Commentary No. 1
Immediately after leaving East Auburn

Good afternoon...and welcome aboard the Vista-Dome NORTH COAST LIMITED.
   This is your Stewardess-Nurse, Miss Anita DiNatale.
   The train crew and I are here* to help make your trip enjoyable. Please let us know* if we may be of assistance to you.
   Our train has several facilities* which can add to your travel pleasure. Vista-Dome seats are available* for both coach* and Pullman passengers. These are for your enjoyment at no extra cost...and* they are not reserved. Please be careful when using the stairways* in the dome cars...and remember, there is a step down* from your dome seat to the aisle.
   The dining car is located in the center of the train. Meal times* except breakfast* will be announced over the public address system.
   The Traveller's Rest buffet-lounge car* is located just ahead of the diner* and behind the last coach. Here you can order a la carte meals* light snacks or beverages* from 7 a.m. until 10 p.m.. In this car you will also find magazines* post cards* and a mail box...you may also purchase postage stamps* from the attendant.
   For standard Pullman passengers* the observation-lounge car at the rear of the train* provides magazines and writing material. Beverage service is available* from 7 a.m. until midnight.
   All of these, and other facilities on the train* are described in our "Train Service Guide" booklet. If you would like a copy* I'll be glad to give you one.
   This afternoon we will follow the Green River* through the Cascade Mountains. At about 2:50 p.m.* you can see construction in progress* on the Howard A. Hansen dam* which will be completed some time in 1962. At about 3:30 p.m.* we will cross the summit of the Cascades* at Stampede Tunnel, at an elevation of 2,852 feet.
   As we emerge from the two-mile-long tunnel, you can see a lovely waterfall, if you look to the left* and rear of the train.
   We invite you to make use* of the services and facilities on the train. Make yourselves comfortable...and we hope you have a pleasant trip.
   Thank you!

*Denotes breath pauses, while giving the commentaries. If a breath pause is not necessary for you, please pause for a moment. A period, of course, always denotes a breath pause.

EASTBOUND - 1st Day - Commentary No. 2
10 minutes before arrival at Ellensburg (4:30 p.m.)

Hello! This is your Stewardess-Nurse, Miss Ann Gallagher.
   In about 10 minutes* we will arrive in Ellensburg* an attractive city in the Kittitas Valley. At 5:45 p.m.* we will stop at Yakima* the well-known city which is named* for the Indian tribe of the same name*; it means "Black Bear". The Yakima valley* comprising nearly half-a-million acres of irrigated land* is famous for its fruits and vegetables* which are distributed to all parts of the country.
   Before you reach your destination* we would like to have your impressions of the services* aboard the Vista-Dome NORTH COAST LIMITED...suggestions for improving our service* are welcome. I'll be glad to give you a comment card* designed for this purpose. You can either return the completed card to me* or drop it ire a mail box...no postage is required.
   Thank you!

*Denotes breath pauses, while giving the commentaries. If a breath pause is not necessary for you, please pause for a moment. A period, of course, always denotes a breath pause.

- The deep *whoosh* of four F-units, headlight out, rolling a fast eastbound freight somewhere west of Fargo on double track at night . . . didn't get the engine number; the lighted number box on the lead diesel unit was but a split-second streak on our dome window.

- The rumble of Valley City's vast steel viaduct under our train at night, the town's lights stretched out below us and to the south.

- The challenge of trying to identify all the cars ahead of us, merely by the telling patterns of lighted and unlighted windows, as the train rounds curves at night.

- The mesmerizing figure eight of the F-7's gyrating white Mars light, as boxcars' shadows do a corresponding movement across the side of the elevator next to them.

- The Badlands near Medora, with the buttes a fiery red in the rays of dawn's early light.

- The endless series of long, sweeping curves along the wide, bluff-lined Yellowstone River valley, reached just after 6:00 A.M., westbound, and followed for the next 6 hours and 15 minutes.

- The magnificent Bridger range, seen continuously at various angles all the way from Big Timber to Welch, a distance of 139 miles; total elapsed time between these points: 3 hours, 10 minutes. This range remains in continuous view longer than any of the other 27 ranges.

The Vista-Dome North Coast Limited

- The beautiful Jefferson River canyon, where we negotiate some rather tight curves sandwiched between the river on our left and limestone mountains on our right. Across the river, the Milwaukee Road's longer, more sweeping curves give away the fact that the junior road was built some 20 years after the NP line.

- The climb up Homestake Pass; curves here are so sharp—most are 12 degrees—that, at one point (milepost 52), we look across a gulch and are momentarily surprised by the sight of four Loewy green F-units rolling the opposite direction across a high steel trestle, realizing after a few seconds that they are pulling our train around a horseshoe curve.

- The walls in Tunnel 3 on Butte mountain, close enough to reach out and touch were our dome window not in the way.

- Skones trestle on the west side of Homestake Pass; this trestle is situated on a 12-degree curve from which we look out over a valley and the city of Butte some 800 feet below our elevation.

- On tangent track, the way the cars ahead roll through a slight dip in the tracks, each car bouncing slightly, front end and then back end, through the train in monkey-see-monkey-do fashion, car after car, until ours finally reaches the dip. It turns out to be seen more than felt. But, what if one had been in mid-vestibule at that precise moment?

- The gorgeous view of the Bitterroot Range along the Clark Fork River between Paradise and Noxon, made all the more scenic by the setting sun. In this author's

---

EASTBOUND - 1st Day - Commentary No. 3
Prior to arrival at Pasco (about 7:20 p.m.)

Good evening: This is your Stewardess-Nurse, Miss _____
We are now approaching the Tri-Cities area-Richland* Kennewick* and Pasco. These cities are located* at the southern end of the great* Columbia Basin Irrigation Project. Key feature of this* is the gigantic Grand Coulee Dam* which will eventually furnish water* to irrigate a million acres of land.
Richland is located five miles to our left. This is the home of the famous* Hanford Atomic Energy Project* established during World War Two* and now operated for the Atomic Energy Commission* by the General Electric Company. With establishment of the Hanford Atomic Energy* and the Columbia Basin Irrigation Projects* this area has witnessed a tremendous increase in population. In 1940* about 6,000 persons lived in the area. Today the population exceeds 61,000.
After passing through Kennewick* we will cross the Columbia River* and arrive in Pasco. East of the station* is Northern Pacific's* "Push Button" freight classification yard* which stretches along the main track* for a distance of four miles.
At Pasco* cars with passengers from Portland* will be added to our train. If you plan to step off the train during our stop here* please do not attempt to board again* until the train is re-assembled. A station announcement will be made* when the train is ready for re-loading.
Thank you for your attention!

*Denotes breath pauses, while giving the commentaries. If a breath pause is not necessary for you, please pause for a moment. A period, of course, always denotes a breath pause.

EASTBOUND - 2nd Day - Commentary No. 1
15 minutes after leaving Butte (about 8 a.m.) (DO NOT GIVE IN PULLMANS)

Good morning: This is your Stewardess-Nurse, Miss (last name) _____
The correct Mountain Standard time is _____.
**If you'll look out the window* to the right and rear of the train* you'll get a magnificent view of Butte, known as the "Richest Hill on Earth". Beneath the streets of this city* lie 9,000 miles of mining tunnels* with shafts as deep as 5,000 feet. In recent years* open pit operations* have been started in this area. More copper* and silver has been produced from these mines* than any other district in the world* as well as a substantial percentage* of zinc used in the United States.
**We are beginning to climb* the western slope of the Continental Divide. At Homestake* where we cross the Divide, the flow of the rivers changes. Those flowing east* enter the Atlantic Ocean* by way of the Gulf of Mexico* and those flowing west* reach the Pacific Ocean through the Columbia River. When we reach the top of the Divide* we will be at the highest altitude of the trip*- 6,328 feet.
In the literature racks in your car* you will find timetables* and information about the country you will see* from the train windows. This literature is for your use.
Thank you and enjoy your morning!

*Denotes breath pauses, while giving the commentaries. If a breath pause is not necessary for you, please pause for a moment. A period, of course, always denotes a breath pause.

Chapter 13: "Four Dome Train West"

> **EASTBOUND - 2nd Day - Commentary No. 2**
> Leaving Logan (about 9:50 a.m.)
>
> Hello: This is your Stewardess-Nurse, Miss (last name)
>   We are now traveling through the American Rockies. If you will look out the window to the right* you will see the Madison Mountains...and to the left are the Bridger Mountains.
>   In approximately 15 minutes* we will arrive in Bozeman. This is the oldest established town in Montana* on our routes* and the home of Montana State College. After leaving the city* we will go through* the 3,000-foot-long Bozeman Tunnel. This tunnel cuts through a mountain pass* that Sacajaweah* the Indian maiden* pointed out to Captain Clark* on the Lewis and Clark expedition.
>   In about an hour from now* our train will arrive in Livingston. Mount Livingston* in the Absarokee (Ab-sor-key) Range* will be visible to our right.
>   Gardiner* 50 miles south of Livingston* is the original entrance* to Yellowstone National Park. Northern Pacific, incidentally* was the first railroad to serve a national park* and began its Yellowstone Park train service* in 1883. During the Park season* buses make daily connections with our trains* to take visitors on scheduled tours of the Park.
>   We are now in the heart of the Rocky Mountain dude ranch country. Many dude ranches are located along our route* near Missoula, Bowman, Livingston and Billings.
>   We will be traveling through the American Rockies* the rest of the morning. I hope you'll enjoy the ride.
>   Thank you for your attention!
>
> *Denotes breath pauses, while giving the commentaries. If a breath pause is not necessary for you, please pause for a moment. A period, of course, always denotes a breath pause.

> **EASTBOUND - 2nd Day - Commentary No. 3**
> 20 minutes before arrival Billings.
>
> Good afternoon! This is your Stewardess-Nurse, Miss (last name)
>   In 20 minutes we will arrive in Billings. This is the headquarters city* for companies having important oil interests* in Montana* North Dakota* and northern Wyoming. You can see evidence of the oil activity shortly. The refinery of Farmers Union Oil Company is at Laurel, 15 miles west of Billings. Conoco's refinery is on our right* as we leave the Billings station* and the Carter Division of the Humble Oil and Refinery Company* has one on the eastern edge of the city* to the left.
>   Located in a productive agricultural region* Billings is the most important* livestock feeding center* between the Pacific Coast and the Twin Cities.
>   This is also another gateway to Yellowstone Park. Buses make connections here with our trains* taking Park visitors over either* the Red Lodge High Road, or to the East entrance* via Cody, Wyoming.
>   We are interested in your impression of the services* aboard the Vista-Dome NORTH COAST LIMITED. I will be glad to give you a card* on which you can write your comments. You may either return the completed card to me* or drop it in a mail box...no postage is required.
>   Thank you!
>
> *Denotes breath pauses, while giving the commentaries. If a breath pause is not necessary for you, please pause for a moment. A period, of course, always denotes a breath pause.

opinion, this segment of our journey justifies the "Scenic Route of the *Vista-Dome North Coast Limited*" slogan on NP boxcars more than any other segment. This is highly debatable, however; the candidate territories are many.

- The fun of working the following math problem: How fast are we traveling if the semaphore blade reaches horizontal at the precise instant the 11th car (first dome sleeper) reaches the signal? Answer: 75 miles per hour, plus or minus. Semaphore and milepost timing confirm this; signals are fairly consistent.

- The oddly combined senses of accomplishment and disappointment as the train slowly rolls to a stop at King St. Station at precisely 7:30 A.M. On time.

Other items during this trip will forever linger in our minds. The curious and erratic movements of one vestibule relative to its mate, for example, accompanied by those wonderfully loud noises there of high speed travel over jointed rail and switches. Even smells—or rather, *the* smell—is memorable. Yes, this train has a strangely cool and pleasant smell that is unique. Is it caused by upholstery, steel, the air-conditioning system, or some combination of these?

Along the way, we mentally note the places where we meet our eastbound counterpart: just outside Aurora on the "Q" in mid-afternoon; Peak, North Dakota just after midnight; Greycliff, Montana, at mid-day; and Spokane, about 10:40 P.M. While watching the middle two meets from the vestibule, brakemen inform us that these meets are quite dependable, as both trains are usually on

The Vista-Dome North Coast Limited

time. Even though employee timetables establish eastward trains as superior to westward ones of the same class, dispatchers usually put No. 26 "in the hole" (crew lingo for "in the siding") at Peak and Greycliff for operational reasons, and thereby give advantage to the westward train because of grade conditions. At both Peak and Greycliff, No. 25 is on an ascending grade. Peak is at the top of "Oriska Hill," a five mile one percent grade, and Greycliff is on a gentler river grade. The meet at Spokane is in double track territory, or more accurately, on the passenger station tracks. There, dining car crews exchange waves and sign language before retiring to bed, an informal greeting that has become a tradition.

> **EASTBOUND - 2nd Day - Commentary No. 5**
> About 10 minutes before arrival at Glendive (at town of Marsh or about 5:00 p.m.)
>
> Hello! This is your Stewardess-Nurse.
>   In about 10 minutes* we will arrive in Glendive. We are now riding* through the center of the Williston Basin* which gained public attention with discovery of oil in 1951.* Derricks and producing wells may be seen* on both sides of the train. The Williston Basin is large* extending all the way from Central Montana* to as far east as Mandan, North Dakota. And from South Dakota* north into Canada.
>   The area around Glendive* and eastern Montana* was once a range for great buffalo herds. Today* livestock raising and irrigated farming* arc carried on extensively here.
>   We are interested in your impression of the services* aboard the Vista-Dome NORTH COAST LIMITED. I will be glad to give you a card* on which you can write your comments. You can either return the completed card to me* or drop it in a mail box...no postage is required.
>   Thank you for your attention!
>
> *Denotes breath pauses, while giving the commentaries. If a breath pause is not necessary for you, please pause for a moment. A period, of course, always denotes a breath pause.

Then, there are those nuances peculiar to Pullman travel:

- A peek out the window at Mandan in the middle of the night reveals the incoming Fargo Division rear brakeman walking past your window to the depot, and then to the crew's layover hotel, with lantern and grip in hand. He does not see you; he does not appear to sense your presence even, but you see him. The same scene will take place again tomorrow night 1,317 miles west, at Ellensburg, but with a different brakeman. And, in all probability, those two brakemen have never even heard of each other. It is a big railroad.

- In the middle of the night something wakes us, or rather nothing—the lack of motion and its accompanying soft noises. Are we stopped? No. A raise of the shade reveals that we are moving at 15 miles per hour through a slow order in the middle of nowhere. Looks maybe like the desert of eastern Washington. With cheek against window, a peak ahead across a curve reveals that the Portland dome coach appears still to be in our train. Must be east of Pasco, then. Back to sleep.

- You dream of a pleasant journey aboard a domeliner only to wake up and find yourself on a pleasant journey aboard a domeliner.

> **EASTBOUND - 2nd Day - Commentary No. 6 (Summer)**
> As train approaches Sentinel Butte (about 6:05 p.m.)
>
> Good evening! This is your Stewardess-Nurse, Miss (last name)
>   We are now in the famous* North Dakota Badlands. Just ahead of us is Sentinel Butte. This town was named* for the 620-foot butte on our right* which was used as a lookout by army scouts* during the Indian Wars. To the left* you may see the irregular shaped, doubled-crested butte* known as the Camel's Hump.
>   You will notice* as we ride along* that the rocks and buttes have strange and weird colors. This has been caused by burned out* lignite coal beds.
>   In half an hour we will go through Medora* headquarters for the Theodore Roosevelt* National Memorial Park. As a young man* "Teddy" Roosevelt lived in this region* and operated a cattle ranch near Medora. The town was founded* by the Marquis (Markey) De Mores (Moray) and named after his wife.
>   The Marquis (Markey) built a meat packing plant here* which was destroyed by fire*-except the chimney* which is still standing.
>   When we arrive in Mandan this evening* we will enter the Central Standard Time zone...and your watches should be turned* ahead one hour. I'll repeat that. When we arrive in Mandan* you should turn your watches ahead one hour.
>   Thank you and a pleasant good night.
>
> *Denotes breath pauses, while giving the commentaries. If a breath pause is not necessary for you, please pause for a moment. A period, of course, always denotes a breath pause.

Chapter 13: "Four Dome Train West"

EASTBOUND - 3rd Day - Commentary No. 1
Leaving Winona Junction (about 8:05 a.m.)

    Good morning: This is your Stewardess-Nurse, Miss Peduzzi.
    We are now following the Mississippi River-along the east bank* on the Wisconsin side. Our train follows the river all the way from St. Paul* to Savanna, Illinois-a distance of nearly 300 miles.
    The bluffs and interesting rock formations*...the color and beauty of the surrounding area* makes this an enjoyable ride* at every season of the year.
    This region is rich in history. The upper Mississippi* was the route of early explorers-Father Hennepin and Marquette* Joliet* Radisson* and many others. Following them* came the fur traders, soldiers and settlers.
    Some of the towns we will ride through this morning* were early French forts* or military posts-Trempealeau and Prairie Du Chien (Sheen), for example. The decisive battle of the Black Hawk War* took place near Victory, Wisconsin.
    In about three hours* we will pass by the Savanna Military Ordnance Depot. You can see the buildings on both sides of the track.
    Thank you and I hope you enjoy the morning ride.

*Denotes breath pauses, while giving the commentaries. If a breath pause is not necessary for you, please pause for a moment. A period, of course, always denotes a breath pause.

EASTBOUND - 3rd Day - Commentary No. 2
10 minutes before arrival at Chicago Union Station

Hello again* This is your Stewardess-Nurse, Miss Peduzzi.
    In about ten minutes we will arrive in the Chicago Union Station.
    Speaking for the entire crew* I hope our services have contributed toward making your trip enjoyable and that you* and your friends* will soon be back with us* on the Vista-Dome NORTH COAST LIMITED.
    Thank you and Good-Bye.

*Denotes breath pauses, while giving the commentaries. If a breath pause is not necessary for you, please pause for a moment. A period, of course, always denotes a breath pause.

- Dancing with a sink for a partner as you shave at 70 miles per hour in your private washroom. Motion in lightweight equipment is quite manageable nonetheless.

- Awakening just before sunrise, yet feeling *refreshed* (how could five hours of sleep be sufficient?) and just sitting there on the edge of your bed, looking out your window at the spacious, colorful fields for which nearby Belfield was named. Twenty-five hours later you do the same thing but, instead, are greeted by the pre-dawn beauty of Lake Easton and the Cascades and Stampede Tunnel and . . . floating in mid-air while crossing the high viaduct between Stampede and Lester.

    Finally, at Seattle's King Street Station we ponder the return trip. Will it be the same? No, not exactly. The scenery is the same, yes, but it will look different when seen from the opposite direction, under different lighting conditions. Eastbound, we'll see the Cascades in bright afternoon daylight and the mountains west of Paradise in moonlight at 2 A.M., should we care to be up at that hour. The sun will rise on the Clark Fork River valley as we leave Missoula, and it will set on western North Dakota's vast prairies, a likely place for a fabulous light show from towering thunderstorms ahead of our train. The sun will rise again in Minnesota's lake country east of Little Falls. Perhaps only the high speed run from St. Paul to Chicago will seem the same as on the westbound trip, except that the Mississippi River will be on our right this time.

    Approaching Chicago, we only begin to appreciate what has just transpired on this round trip. Indeed, for the past several days we have experienced the best interstate transportation that money can buy in 1959. One is hard pressed to identify the finest moments aboard this train. Surely the 91-hour round-trip diet of the finest in United States railroading is all palatable, even addictive. One thing is certain, however. The worst moment of the entire journey, only minutes away, will be our last over-the-shoulder look at the 14-car train, now a little dusty, as it sits on track 22 at Chicago. This time, it will be facing the bumper.

Chapter 14

The Vista-Dome North Coast Limited in Action: A Photo Gallery

Photographed from the rear platform of a freight train's caboose, train No. 26 kicks up a cloud of snow at the east siding switch, Waco, Montana. The sleeper-observation-lounge is car 393, formerly "Spokane Club". February 1960.
Ron Nixon photo; Gary Wildung collection

The Vista-Dome North Coast Limited

Train No. 26, led by F-3A 6504A, an F-3B, and F-9A 6700C, arrives Livingston in March 1958 with 13 cars.
Ron Nixon photo; Gary Wildung collection

Train No. 25 is serviced at Livingston on June 28, 1955. Note the water hose connected to dome coach 551.
Ron Nixon photo; Gary Wildung collection

Chapter 14: The Vista-Dome North Coast Limited in Action: A Photo Gallery

Train No. 26 stops at Livingston on June 28, 1955. *Top*: Dome coach 558 and Day-Nite coach 590 are operating in Portland-Chicago lines C-262 and C-263, respectively. *Bottom*: Cars 499 (Traveller's Rest), 455, 368, and dome sleeper 308 are four of the thirteen cars in this consist. The train is all buttoned up and will depart in just moments.
Both photos: Ron Nixon; Gary Wildung collection

The Vista-Dome North Coast Limited

The eastbound *Vista-Dome North Coast Limited* emerges from Bozeman Tunnel. Equipment includes diesel units 6510C, an F-9B, and 6507C, and cars 402, 427, 554, 599, and 556. June 1957 photo.
Ron Nixon photo; Gary Wildung collection

Priority freight B-603 has taken siding to clear No. 26 near Bozeman in 1958. Sleeper-observation-lounge car 483 has the wide white stripe, but soon it will have a narrow one. (See Appendix)
Ron Nixon photo; Bill Kuebler collection

Chapter 14: The Vista-Dome North Coast Limited in Action: A Photo Gallery

Train No. 25, led by F-7A No. 6508C, leaves double track and enters Centralized Traffic Control territory at Bozeman in March 1958. The train is just accelerating away from its station stop, but the depot is not easily visible behind the telegraph poles in the distance.
Ron Nixon photo; Gary Wildung collection

The Vista-Dome North Coast Limited

Train No. 25 rolls briskly across the Madison River bridge at milepost 5 on the Rocky Mountain Division's Second Subdivision, one and a half miles east of Three Forks. The four-unit locomotive consists of 6510C, 6509C, 6552B, and 6513C. This photo was made in the summer of 1965.
Ron Nixon photo; Gary Wildung collection

(facing page)   Dome sleeper 305 is destined for Seattle as it rolls past the photographer near Lime Spur in June 1959. Lime Spur is in the Jefferson River canyon, 27 miles west of Logan.
Ron Nixon photo; Gary Wildung collection

Chapter 14: The Vista-Dome North Coast Limited in Action: A Photo Gallery

The Vista-Dome North Coast Limited

The eastbound *Vista-Dome North Coast Limited* along the Jefferson River, near milepost 29. June 1955.
Ron Nixon photo; Gary Wildung collection

(facing page)   The westbound *Vista-Dome North Coast Limited* climbs the 2.2% grade near milepost 48, between Pipestone and Spire Rock, in August 1959. This is the same train that appears in the photo on page 249. The consist of this train includes cars 587 (right foreground), 556, and 599.
Ron Nixon photo; Bill Kuebler collection

Chapter 14: The Vista-Dome North Coast Limited in Action: A Photo Gallery

273

The Vista-Dome North Coast Limited

Westbound on Butte mountain between Pipestone and Spire Rock, November 1954. Most of the long ascent lies ahead of the train. The gradient is 2.2%, compensated. "Compensated" means that the gradient is decreased just enough on curves to offset the added resistance of the curvature. While compensation helps ascending trains, it works against descending trains with brakes continuously applied. A descending train tends to slow down on curves due to the reduced gradient *and* the added resistance of the curvature. In territory like this, it is impractical, even unsafe, for an engineer to compensate for this by releasing air brakes on a descending train. Minor adjustments with the dynamic brake can be made, however, permitting a more uniform speed during descent. (See Chapter 12 for details concerning these brake systems.)

The same train passes the mile board east of Spire Rock. This line is a seemingly endless series of reverse curves as sharp as this one, at 12-degrees. Cars in this view include dome coaches 552 and 553, followed by diner 457, 8-6-4 sleeper 368, dome sleeper 311, and 8-6-3-1 sleeper 352.

Chapter 14: The Vista-Dome North Coast Limited in Action: A Photo Gallery

About five minutes later the train negotiates yet another sharp curve, this one between Spire Rock and Welch. Between the foot of the grade (west of Whitehall) and the summit at Homestake, a distance of 19 miles, this train will negotiate 79 curves!

Passing the east siding switch at Welch. The summit is now only six miles ahead.
All four photos: Ron Nixon; Gary Wildung collection

275

The Vista-Dome North Coast Limited

Train No. 26 descends Butte mountain between Pipestone and Spire Rock on November 2, 1954. The rear five cars are diner 452, 8-6-4 sleeper 367, dome sleeper 309, 8-6-3-1 sleeper 362, and sleeper-observation-lounge 394. The NP is yet to receive the last one or two of its ten new dome sleepers from Budd. Their delivery is but days away and will allow two dome sleepers to operate in each train.
Ron Nixon photo; Gary Wildung collection

Cars 371, 304, and 350 are probably rolling at 75 miles per hour or faster in this view of Train No. 25 near Bonner in September 1959.
Ron Nixon photo; Gary Wildung collection

Chapter 14: The Vista-Dome North Coast Limited in Action: A Photo Gallery

Train No. 25 climbs the 2.2% grade near Tunnel No. 3, about midway between Welch and Homestake, in July 1966. The A-A-B-A locomotive consists of 6506C, 6503A, 6552B, and 6507A. Cars visible in the bottom view include, from left to right, 589, 554, 587, 599, and 499. A Slumbercoach is behind car 499.
Both photos: Ron Nixon; Gary Wildung collection

The Vista-Dome North Coast Limited

The eastbound *Vista-Dome North Coast Limited* passes between semaphores on Rocky Mountain Division's "racetrack," a nickname given by crews to the 69-mile, high-speed double track line between Garrison and Missoula. In this magnificent view, NP's finest rolls up the Clark Fork River valley near Turah, about 12 miles east of Missoula, in late April 1959. The sleeper-observation-lounge is car 390. Judging from sun angle, this train is running several hours late, as the schedule calls for it to pass this spot at about 5:30 a.m. Today, I-90 has displaced the river further to the south and eliminated many of the trees in the center of this view.
Ron Nixon photo; Bill Kuebler collection

Chapter 14: The Vista-Dome North Coast Limited in Action: A Photo Gallery

279

The Vista-Dome North Coast Limited

F-7 A-B-A set No. 6510 handles Train No. 25 four miles east of Missoula in May 1954. The engine crew has visors down as the 11-car train heads toward the late afternoon sun. A fast 45-hour schedule for the *North Coast Limited* has been in effect for about a year and a half, but vista-dome service is still three months away. Note the placement of the eastward block signal, due to the location of Milwaukee Road's main line just to the right of NP's eastward main.
Ron Nixon photo; Gary Wildung collection

Train No. 25 is serviced at Missoula in May 1955. When dome window washing was moved to Livingston later in 1955, special wash rigs enabled carmen to do the job without having to walk atop the cars. Following dome coach 559 are coach-buffet-lounge 496 and diner 454. Judging from the prism glass windows on its non-vestibule end, the car ahead of 559 must be "Deluxe Day-Nite" coach 586 or 587.
Ron Nixon photo; Gary Wildung collection

Chapter 14: The Vista-Dome North Coast Limited in Action: A Photo Gallery

*The view from Mt. Jumbo...*The westbound *Vista-Dome North Coast Limited* approaches Missoula in May 1958. From front-to-rear on the train (right-to-left), the cars in view are 558, 594, 554, and 497. Appearing to the south of the train are U.S. Highway 10, then the Clark Fork River, and just beyond that, the Milwaukee Road. Today, I-90 is located where the truck farm appears in the lower foreground.
Ron Nixon photo; Bill Kuebler collection

The Vista-Dome North Coast Limited

Train No. 25 passes DeSmet, 6.6 miles west of Missoula, in August 1958. These interlocking signals govern eastward movements from the Fifth Subdivision, via St. Regis, and the Sixth Subdivision, via Evaro and Dixon, to the double track line that extends from here east to Garrison. A westward "19-order" signal at the depot appears above the third diesel unit, indicating that No. 25 is catching train orders here as it passes. That may explain why the fireman is not visible on his side of the cab, for he has probably just caught the engine crew's set of orders from the right cab door's open window. The lead unit, 6508A, was destroyed in the Granite derailment in March 1962.
Ron Nixon photo; Gary Wildung collection

Chapter 14: The Vista-Dome North Coast Limited in Action: A Photo Gallery

Riding the dome in Seattle-Chicago sleeper line 268 on the Tacoma Division, April 1962. *(Top)* East of Lester, the Cascades are spectacular in this mid-afternoon view. The dispatcher has decided to run No. 26 up the westward main track from Lester to Stampede, probably to get the passenger train around a slower freight. On the double track between Lester and Stampede, and between Martin and Easton, both main tracks had signals and circuits designed for traffic in either direction. A T-shaped signal mast can be seen just ahead of the train; each signal on it governs westward trains on the respective main track. Similar signal masts govern eastward trains on this line. *(Bottom)* About two hours later, the train follows the banks of the Yakima River near Hillside. The consist includes a CB&Q "Rest"-series Slumbercoach, a Lewis and Clark Traveller's Rest lounge car (behind the first dome), and a Pullman-Standard 450-series dining car (in front of second dome) operating in place of a shopped Budd diner.
Jim Fredrickson photos

The Vista-Dome North Coast Limited

The eastbound *Vista-Dome North Coast Limited* looks resplendent as it rolls through the upper Jefferson River canyon in this June 1958 scene. Its 14-car summer season consist includes two dome coaches and two dome sleepers. Sleeping car 357 and dome sleeper 312 appear in the lower foreground. They are operating in Portland–Chicago car lines 267 and 268, respectively.
Ron Nixon photo; Gary Wildung collection

Chapter 14: The Vista-Dome North Coast Limited in Action: A Photo Gallery

The westbound *Vista-Dome North Coast Limited* follows the curves of the Mississippi River in the territory "where nature smiles for 300 miles." Two CB&Q E-8s are powering this train from Chicago to St. Paul. The 15-car summer season consist includes a Slumbercoach positioned just ahead of the first dome coach. During most of 1961, the NP exchanged the dome sleeping cars' places in the train lineup with those of the standard sleeping cars, as seen here. This photo was taken near Savanna on July 3, 1961.
Tom Gildersleeve photo; Bill Kuebler collection

The eastbound *Vista-Dome North Coast Limited*, powered by F-5A 6506C, F-3B 6502B, and F-7A 6509A, emerges from Stampede Tunnel No. 3 at Martin, Washington, in April 1961. This is territory where annual snowfall is measured in feet rather than inches. At this point No. 26 leaves single track CTC territory and enters double track ABS territory. The NP installed CTC between Martin and Stampede in 1958.
Jim Fredrickson photo

The Vista-Dome North Coast Limited

Train No. 26 has just left Ellensburg as it heads for the long, sweeping curves of the Yakima River Canyon only a few miles ahead. Dome sleeper 304, 8-6-3-1 sleeper 482 (out of its usual position behind the diner), and sleeper-observation-lounge 392 bring up the rear of the train on this sunny day in July 1966. The Slumbercoach is operating between the diner and Traveller's Rest lounge car. This train is also carrying two extra coaches, probably because of a prolonged airline strike that occurred during the summer of 1966.
Bill Kuebler collection

The sun has just set as train No. 25 prepares for departure from St. Paul Union Depot on September 24, 1967. Providing 5,000 horsepower for the 12-car train this evening are diesel units 6703C, 6511B, and 6700B.
Matt Herson photo

Chapter 14: The Vista-Dome North Coast Limited in Action: A Photo Gallery

Train No. 25 climbs the 2.2% grade of Evaro hill, about one mile east of Nagos, on June 27, 1955. Marent Trestle, highest on the NP main line at 225 feet, is a mile and a half ahead of this train. In this view, footings from the long-gone O'Keefe trestle remain visible inside the sweeping curve and fill which replaced the original alignment decades earlier. It is about 6:30 p.m. While passengers with reservations for the second seating are enjoying dinner in the diner, many others have found a "grandstand" seat in one of the four vista-domes.

Ron Nixon photo; Gary Wildung collection

The Vista-Dome North Coast Limited

Dome sleeper 310 gets its windows washed at Livingston during this ten-minute stop of the eastbound *Vista-Dome North Coast Limited* in September 1969. Up ahead, enginemen and switchmen are exchanging diesel units.
Jim Fredrickson photo

In a view from the rear cab unit, train No. 25 snakes around reverse curves at milepost 133 in Rocky Canyon on June 28, 1955. Bozeman Tunnel is five miles behind the train. Note the accumulation of sand deposited by ascending trains along the eastward main track. According to photographer Ron Nixon, "There were some swell rainbow trout in Rocky Creek right alongside the track here."
Ron Nixon photo; Bill Kuebler collection

288

Chapter 14: The Vista-Dome North Coast Limited in Action: A Photo Gallery

Train No. 26 gets underway at Seattle on July 16, 1969. The photographer is standing on the Team Track platform between Lander and Horton Streets. Dome sleeper 305 (foreground) follows immediately behind "Lounge-in-the-Sky" dome sleeper 378. Shop forces did an excellent job, recently, of painting these dome sleepers—except for the upside-down NP Monad on car 305's right flank. But don't tell anybody!
Rick Leach photo

A heavy rain has just fallen on Missoula, leaving a rainbow stretched across the sky as Train No. 25 prepares for departure, only minutes away. This 15-car train includes a "Day-Nite" coach in the 581–585 series, between the two dome coaches.
Alfred Butler photo; Bill Kuebler collection

The Vista-Dome North Coast Limited

It is mid-afternoon in May 1963 as the eastbound *Vista-Dome North Coast Limited* moves up a steady one percent grade near Covington, Washington. The ten-car train is lead by F 3A No. 6501A and includes a CB&Q Slumbercoach (third car in the train) and two dome sleepers. Prior to late 1961, one dome sleeper was assigned to Portland service. The mail-dormitory car is No. 430, the second mail-dormitory to carry that number. It is an ex-C&NW car purchased and rebuilt by the NP to replace a car destroyed in the derailment at Granite, Idaho, in March 1962. At Pasco, cars arriving there from Portland will lengthen this train to 13 cars.

Warren Wing photos; Bill Kuebler collection

Chapter 14: The Vista-Dome North Coast Limited in Action: A Photo Gallery

Dome sleeper 310 and sleeper-observation-lounge car 393 are the twelfth and thirteenth cars of this eastbound *Vista-Dome North Coast Limited*. The train is passing milepost 99, sixteen miles east of Livingston, on November 24, 1955. The "Vista-Dome North Coast Limited" slogan has just recently been applied to the observation car, and soon it will be applied to the dome sleepers as well.
Warren McGee photo

Train No. 25 approaches the west end of the upper Jefferson River canyon, near milepost 30, in August 1958. Powering the train are F-3A 6502A, an unidentified F-9B, and F-3A 6504A. The tiny town of Cardwell lies just over a mile ahead of the train. Pat Huntley, father of well known television news anchor Chet Huntley (retired from NBC in 1970), was an NP telegrapher and agent for many years and lived with his family in the Cardwell depot when son, Chet, was born there. Famous NP photographer Ron Nixon and Chet Huntley were life-long friends; both were graduated from Whitehall High School in 1929. Whitehall is seven miles west of Cardwell.
Ron Nixon photo; Gary Wildung collection

The Vista-Dome North Coast Limited

The *Vista-Dome North Coast Limited* is powered by a pair of CB&Q E 8s making 85 miles per hour near Naperville, Illinois, November 2, 1956. The last three cars in this 12-car train are 8-6-3-1 sleeping car 360, dome sleeper 306, and sleeper-observation-lounge car 390. This handsome domeliner is destined for King Street Station in Seattle, exactly 2,290 miles ahead of the train.
Bill Kuebler collection

Epilogue

The *Vista-Dome North Coast Limited* was overland travel at its finest. For a brief 15-year period on the Northern Pacific Railway (NP), one could get from Chicago to Seattle and back, or travel to intermediate points, quickly and in luxury and comfort aboard this train, with a penthouse view of the Northwest's finest scenery. It was an all too brief chapter in the history book of American railroading. Those days are gone forever. Modern day special excursions have attempted to give us a taste of it, but they are mere shadows of the past. As for Amtrak, well, it just isn't the same as NP service and equipment. Times have changed. Borrowing lines from a popular song, retired NP dispatcher, Jim Fredrickson, puts it this way: "Those were the days, my friend. We thought they'd never end." Those words convey a rather deep and profound truth. Yes, we thought those days were here to stay, and those of us who thought so were badly mistaken. Even when "the handwriting was on the wall" in the 1960s, many of us either didn't notice or looked the other way. Paradoxically, one constant is that we humans have difficulty facing change.

The essential facts about the *Vista-Dome North Coast Limited* are plentiful. Questions about the "what" are relatively easy to answer. More difficult are the questions about the "So what?" and the "Why?" What is the significance of NP's *Vista-Dome North Coast Limited*? Why was it so short lived? Will such a train ever return?

Perhaps an answer to the first question begins to emerge when we contrast the rough and tough beginnings of the NP with the train we have considered here. The great dream of men in the mid-1800s who envisioned a northern transcontinental railroad, one moving raw materials and goods and people to and fro between Lake Superior and Puget Sound, was definitely realized by the mid-1900s. The "people" component of that dream was realized nowhere better than in Northern Pacific's trains No. 25 and No. 26. Imagine what men like NP's first president, Josiah Perham, or America's 16th President, Abraham Lincoln, would have thought had they been able jump into the future and travel from Chicago to Seattle aboard NP's domeliner! In short, the *Vista-Dome North Coast Limited* was an amazing achievement in transportation. But, it was even more than that. It was also a remarkably successful (profitable) long-distance passenger train, even in an era when people were turning to other modes of transportation in ever increasing numbers.

That brings us to the second question. Why was its operation so brief in duration, then? Well, there was a merger, yes (and then Amtrak), but could such a train have lasted longer anyway? (Its operation by Amtrak ended less than a decade after the Burlington Northern (BN) merger in 1970.) Did it have to disappear as quickly as it did? Many analysts would say yes, that its rapid demise was inevitable. Although it is easy to lay all blame for its demise at the feet of past railroad managements and leave it at that, more thoughtful analysts cite the modern American traveler's penchant for independence and hurry as primary causes for the train's rapid demise. Independence—a status that Americans value more than almost anything—is realized nowhere more than in the private automobile. In the early 1950s, a typical family could barely afford one car; now the average American family has three. Apart from its practical utility, the automobile is firmly entrenched as an icon of independence and freedom. As for hurry, Americans seem always to be in one, and it's getting worse by the day. Comedian Steven Wright notes this with his quip, "I want a microwave fireplace in my home. That way, I can relax in front of it for an entire evening in just ten minutes." Do more in less time—that seems to be our practice, if not our motto. One result of this urge to do ever more in less time: major airlines have grown and prospered beyond their wildest dreams. The fleet of aircraft at one major airline, American Airlines, has quadrupled in the last 30 years. On any given weekday, there are about 2,000 flight arrivals or departures at Chicago's O'Hare airport alone—in the city that once boasted passenger train service of comparable capacity. Time is money, we are told. And after all, when one prefers to be there in person, 600 miles per hour *is* much faster than 70 miles per hour.

The Vista-Dome North Coast Limited

Indeed, American freedom and independence—and speed—have been maximized in the transportation arena. But, this all comes with a price. One easily overlooked aspect of this price is a certain kind of ignorance. We now have a new and rather large category of young Americans, people who have seen both the east and west coasts of the United States but have never seen the continental divide. Some Americans don't even know what a continental divide is. Once, it was inconceivable for a person to have been to New York *and* Los Angeles without ever having seen a farm in between, or an oil well or a mountain pass or the Mississippi River. Today, the notion hardly surprises us, what with the popularity of airline travel. And, this is to say nothing about the continuing pollution and fatal accident rates associated with the private automobile—quite a price, indeed. Amazingly, Americans seem willing to continue paying this price. It is now clear that, regardless of the decisions of past railroad managements, our society itself is what doomed the *Vista-Dome North Coast Limited* as we knew it. Ironically, the same American society that produced that train brought about its rapid disappearance by turning to other modes of transportation in huge numbers.

And yet . . . other analysts insist that the crack domeliner's rapid demise was not inevitable. Moreover, some think it will, or ought to, return, even if in an updated version. Their argument is rather compelling, even to non-railfans. The limitations and shortcomings of today's superhighways and airlines are painfully obvious now. Heavy trucks quickly turn newly resurfaced interstate highways into dangerously rough roads. Eight or 10 lanes seem inadequate to handle all the traffic in so many cities. Drunk drivers still kill fellow citizens in huge numbers. More recently, we have "road rage" to face. We even have "air rage." Airline passengers have grown tired of delays and poor treatment, even to the point of becoming cynical—and violent toward airline crewmembers (a Federal offense, incidentally). Entire books have been published compiling jokes and cartoons poking fun at air travel. How many passengers have been left stranded in today's airport terminals because of weather that would not have even fazed the *Vista-Dome North Coast Limited* decades ago? What price, progress? That the *Vista-Dome North Coast Limited* made a profit for as long as it did says something, too. True, freight trains produced the vast majority of NP's traffic revenue, but maybe there's more room for a train like this in today's or tomorrow's American free market (such as we have) than one would think.

Given the right conditions, could a *North Coast Limited* return to the rails someday? Of course, the "right conditions" would have to, or at least ought to, include a market sufficient to support the operation, a matter of lengthy debate. But, even if there were such a market, would the operation really be the *North Coast Limited*? Would the train warrant the title, or be worthy of it? After all, the standard set back in the 1950s is rather difficult to exceed or even meet. It is doubtful that the types of passenger cars depicted in this book will once again be produced in equal or better form. Although several former NP vista-domes continue to operate after all these decades, they are not in regular Amtrak service and probably never will be again. It is interesting to note, however, the reputation these cars have with their private owners and users. Several who are maintaining them in running condition insist that these former NP cars, and others like them, put Amtrak's more modern equipment to shame, particularly in terms of quality of construction and overall design. This doesn't surprise most of us who have ridden both types of equipment. To be sure, no railroad passenger car has since been constructed that provides a better view than the one had from one of the 24 dome seats in a 1954-vintage Budd vista-dome. As for quality of construction, the accidents that occurred at Glendive, Granite, and Evaro in 1962 are instructive. It is remarkable that there were as few casualties as there were, and that most of the equipment involved in those accidents was repaired and returned to service. Has modern Amtrak equipment faired as well in serious accidents?

Epilogue

Alas, in spite of all these compelling arguments, and for whatever reason, even today's cynical American travelers prefer the freedom and independence of the automobile, or the fleeting expedience of air travel, over safe, luxurious rail travel. We will probably never again see the *Vista-Dome North Coast Limited* as we knew it—if at all. In all probability, the name and the train have both passed into history forever.

Perhaps, then, the NP's *Vista-Dome North Coast Limited*, and precious few other trains like it, represent America's best, a peak of sorts, in the transportation industry. The *Vista-Dome North Coast Limited* was a vehicle of unsurpassed quality as well as aesthetic appeal. It was certainly a train on the cutting edge of technology. In the railroad industry, at least, it represented the best in human performance. The train and its NP operation demonstrate what can result from an excellent work ethic, dedication, ingenuity, and careful attention to the details and complexities of a transportation enterprise—and, a willingness to let the bottom line be less than ideal on occasion. This is neither a call nor praise for a money-losing, anti-business philosophy. Indeed, the point of business in a capitalist nation is to earn money. But, in so doing, let an enterprise's decision makers also consider a few other things that are just as important, such as customer service, convenience, and especially safety—words that should be synonymous with public transportation. Today's airlines could learn much from yesterday's railroads, especially the NP.

All these issues are worthy of much discussion and debate, and they are not easily settled. The very least that can be said, though, is that the Northern Pacific Railway left an impressive railroad technology and lore. Its premier passenger train of the modern era, the *vista-dome* era, is now permanently ensconced in the historical record as "one of the world's *extra fine* trains." About that description there is no doubt. And, its aesthetic appeal is still unsurpassed. There is much about the train to commend to our regard, and to that of future generations should they ever be wise enough to look back and see how it was done.

More than one vehicle rolled up and down the *Main Street of the Northwest*. Each of them had a purpose, whether it be a car carrying lumber or people or coal, or an engine pulling combinations of these. Some of these conveyances were more interesting than others, but among those that lasted fewer years than it takes a person to reach adulthood, none captured the hearts and minds of so many for so long as the *Vista-Dome North Coast Limited*.

Northern Pacific Railway Historical Association

Individuals with an interest in the Northern Pacific Railway (NP)—whether as rail fans, veterans, modelers, collectors or historians—should consider joining the Northern Pacific Railway Historical Association (NPRHA).

Dues are very reasonable and entitle members to receive the high-quality NPRHA quarterly, *The Mainstreeter*, as well as a one-photo-per-month wall calendar. *The Mainstreeter* is also sold in various hobby shops located in NP territory. Members may purchase back issues from the NPRHA. The Association convenes each summer in one of the major cities along the NP's route, and each convention is a fun-packed, four-day event focusing exclusively on the "Main Street of the Northwest." For details about upcoming events and how to join this fine organization, consult the latest issue of *The Mainstreeter* or write to:

NPRHA

P.O. Box 2937

Kirkland, WA 98083-2937

http://www.nprha.org

Appendix

Modeling the Vista-Dome North Coast Limited

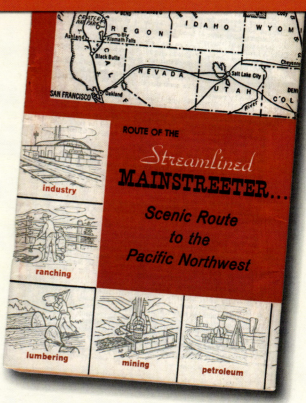

Though this appendix provides information relevant to modeling the locomotive and cars of the *Vista-Dome North Coast Limited*, it is not a "how to" section. Modeling procedures and techniques are outside the scope of this book. Rather, certain prototypical details are presented for each piece of equipment, so as to give the modeler a better idea of how the model should look when complete. The year 1959 is the reference point, with brief comments about changes that occurred before and after that year included where fitting. Thus, information is presented for each piece of equipment that appeared in the 1959 edition of the train.

Locomotive

The task of accurately modeling NP's passenger diesels is very challenging, regardless of what year is chosen. Many changes occurred to NP's passenger F-unit fleet over the years. Some units were converted from passenger to freight service and vice versa, and renumbered accordingly. Only two conversions occurred during 1959, and they are not shown in the roster for June of that year (see Chapter 7). Passenger F-9A no. 6703A (1st) was converted to freight service and renumbered 7051A in November 1959, and freight F-3B no. 6006B, originally a passenger unit, was converted back to passenger service and renumbered 6551B in December. Two more freight F-3Bs, also originally passenger units, were converted back to passenger service and renumbered 6552B and 6553B in 1960 and 1962, respectively. Beginning in 1964, several 7000-series freight F-9s were converted to 6700-series passenger locomotives as older passenger units were traded in on new freight power.

Besides all these conversions and renumbering, NP's passenger F-units changed appearance in lettering and external features. In a few cases, individual units changed in unusual ways or were destroyed in accidents. (See Chapter 11.) Rather than account for all these features and changes during the entire vista-dome era, a concise table of pertinent data for June 1959 is presented below. For a complete and detailed roster, refer to

The Vista-Dome North Coast Limited

NP's Passenger F-unit Fleet in 1959: A Brief Look at Some Details

"Loewy" Scheme	Color Data (NP Scheme No. 8211098):
Dark Green	Duco #254-57926 (Dupont Dulux #88-9008)
Light Green	Duco #254-57927 (Dupont Dulux #88-11736)
White	Duco 254-1 (Dupont White Enamel #88-508)
Locomotive Black	Dupont Dulux #88-762

Note: These color codes are no longer in use. See NPRHA's quarterly, *The Mainstreeter*, Vol. 12, No. 4 (Fall 1993), pages 22-24, for information regarding current custom paint formulas for these colors.

1. Locomotives sets were broken up and intermixed by 1960.
2. Large white engine numbers with letter suffixes appeared on the rear of only the cab units. Large numbers did not yet appear at the rear of B-units; they were added in 1961. F-7B no. 6550 was never given a "B" suffix on the large number at the rear of the unit. All units had small (3-inch) white numbers near the lower forward end. These numbers were Roman style on most F-3s, Gothic on newer models. Cab unit nose heralds (all F-unit models) gradually changed from NORTHERN PACIFIC to NORTHERN PACIFIC RAILWAY. between early 1957 and 1961.
3. All cab units had two portholes on each side.
4. Most cab units had Nathan P-3 Air Chime horns. One or two F-3As may still have had standard EMD-applied Leslie horns in 1959. "Firecracker" style radio antennas and "Radio Equipped" slogans did not begin appearing on cab units until late 1962.
5. F-3B nos. 6500B-6509B and F-7B nos. 6510B-6513B had only two portholes on each side and an F-7 style louver in place of the middle porthole. Boosters 6550-6551B (and 6552B-6553B later), 6700B, and 6701B had three portholes on each side and no louvers.
6. F-3A and F-3B grilles: All units had phase-I, "chicken wire" style grille. F-3B grilles, however, had two horizontal bars with large white NORTHERN PACIFIC metal letters affixed.
   F-5A grilles: Horizontal grilles painted dark green to match, same as F-7A units.
   F-7 grilles: All were horizontal grilles painted dark green to match. F-7Bs had metal NORTHERN PACIFIC letters affixed directly to the grille.
   F-9 grilles: Farr grilles painted dark green to match, but on rare occasions appeared as plain aluminum (stainless steel). Metal NORTHERN PACIFIC letters affixed directly to F-9B grilles.
7. All cab units had lift rings and most cab units had front end M.U. cables by 1959.
8. Top headlight: Single large figure-8 oscillating type, white with moveable red filter, on all F-3, 5, and 7 cab units. All F-9As had two small sealed beam type lights, white above red, and the entire light unit moved so the light beam described a circular pattern.
   Bottom headlight: Single large reflector on all F-3 and F-5 cab units. Twin sealed beam lights positioned vertically on all F-7As and positioned horizontally on all F-9As. (The following F-7As' lower headlights were changed to horizontal position in the mid-1960s: 6510A, 6511A,C, and 6512A.)
9. F-3 fans: Four high, roof mounted 36-inch radiator fans with a winterization cover around the rear fan. Two rectangular screened openings instead of forward dynamic brake roof fan.
   F-5A fans: Same as F-3s, except four low fans instead of high ones.
   F-7 fans: Four low radiator fans plus a forward, 36-inch dynamic brake roof fan. Winterization hatch around the rear roof fan.
   F-9 fans: Same as F-7s, except forward fan (dynamic brake) was a 48-inch fan.
10. A vertical row of grab irons was added to the right side of the nose on cab units, behind the number boards, during the period 1959-1961. F-3 cab units were given anti-slip treads across the top of the nose, beginning in 1947-48. All later model cab units were either delivered with these treads or were given the treads shortly after delivery.
11. A steam generator exhaust appeared on the roof, near the rear of all passenger F-units.

Northern Pacific Railway Diesel Era: 1945-1970, by Schrenk and Fry (Golden West Books). For details regarding changes in painting and lettering, appliances, and physical appearance during the 1947-1970 period, refer to *Northern Pacific Color Pictorial, Volume 3*, by Kuebler (Four Ways West Publications).

All cars regularly assigned to the *Vista-Dome North Coast Limited* were 85-foot cars, except for certain water-baggage cars (73-foot cars) that had been converted from 200-series baggage cars, as noted below. Each car in the train was equipped with inside diaphragms, including the water-baggage car. Budd cars and Pullman-Standard cars built in 1954 or later were delivered equipped with disc brakes. Older Pullman-Standard cars originally had clasp brakes with cylinders mounted outside the trucks, but these were gradually replaced with disc brakes during the period 1956-1962. Details for each type of car follow:

Appendix: Modeling The Vista-Dome North Coast Limited

Water-Baggage

The position of the words "Northern Pacific" on the letter board was unusual. A baggage door, with the word "Pacific" toward the end of the car on each side, split the two words. The space available for the "Pacific" was not the same on both sides, either. The word barely fit on the 'B' end, left side, but ample room was available at the "A' end for the lettering on the right side. Until 1958, there were two car numbers on each side, centered above the trucks. In fact, this was true of all cars in the "Loewy" scheme, except as noted below for the mail-dormitory car and Budd dining car. Beginning in 1958, as cars were repainted, the number at one end on each side was eliminated. Which end on which side depended on the type of car, and there were a few inconsistencies. After this change, the water-baggage car had a number at the"'B' end on the right side, and at the 'A' end on the left side. Unlike the 200-series baggage cars, this one had end skirts, but it lost its center skirt by 1953. Although car 405 was owned by the CB&Q, there were no ownership letters in the upper corners on this car. They were probably never added with the Loewy paint scheme because the word PACIFIC on either side would interfere, especially on the car's left side where available space for the lettering was insufficient to accommodate the ownership letters as well. On the 1947 pre-Loewy scheme, the words NORTHERN PACIFIC both appeared between the baggage doors, because the lettering was a little smaller and more compact in that scheme.

Part of the end skirt at the rear (B-end) of water-baggage 400 was missing when the car was photographed at Seattle in July 1974. Note the position and spacing of the lettering, and the difference between the nearest baggage door and each end of the car. The A-end, or forward end, is where the water tanks were located.
Rick Leach photo

299

The Vista-Dome North Coast Limited

From 1962 to 1967, the NP converted several 73-foot lightweight baggage cars, originally numbered in the 200-series, to water-baggage cars. These were numbered 406-411 following conversion. Other than the newly assigned equipment numbers, these cars retained the same paint scheme. The words NORTHERN PACIFIC were positioned between the side doors on these cars. These cars had no skirts or end skirts.

Mail-Dormitory

The window arrangement on this car was unique. The NP was the only road with cars built to this particular floor plan, although other roads had similar cars. Lettering was typical for NP equipment in the Loewy scheme, with a couple of exceptions. First, the car number at the A (forward) end could not be positioned above the center of the forward truck because of the pocket doors. An open door would hide the car's number from view, so the number was positioned further forward, midway between the door and the end of the car on each side. Second, just aft of the pocket doors and below the white stripe were the words "UNITED STATES MAIL" equally spaced above the words "RAILWAY POST OFFICE". These words were lettered in dark green to match the top half of the car, rather than in white. After 1958, car numbers appeared only at the B (rear) end of the car on each side instead of at both ends, except for car 429 and (in the 1960's) car 427, which had the number at the A end on each side rather than at the B end. Car 479 (renumbered from 430 in 1954) had CB&Q ownership letters in the upper corners.

Following the 1962 Granite derailment that destroyed car 428, the NP purchased Chicago and North Western baggage-dormitory no. 9301 and converted it to a mail-dormitory car. This car was built by American Car and Foundry and assigned number 430. It had a distinctive appearance unlike the original NP mail-dormitory cars, including a different window arrangement.

Left side of the mail-dormitory car 429, May 26, 1972. This was how this car appeared after 1958, when the number at the B-end on this side was eliminated.
Bill Kuebler collection

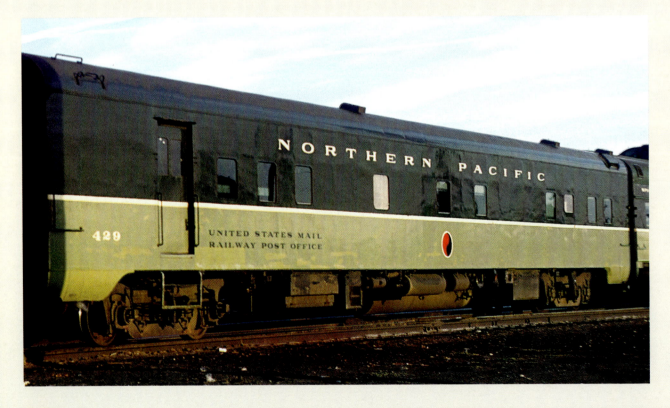

Appendix: Modeling The Vista-Dome North Coast Limited

Mail-dormitory 426 at Livingston on June 28, 1955. Prior to 1958, this car had equipment numbers at both ends on each side.
Ron Nixon photo; Bill Kuebler collection

Slumbercoach

Slumbercoach operation on the *Vista-Dome North Coast Limited* began in late November 1959 and continued through 1970. The Slumbercoach was the only car regularly assigned to the train that was not painted in the Loewy two-tone green paint scheme. Instead, it was unpainted stainless steel with black lettering. Numbers and lettering appeared on various letterboards, because of the plentiful use of fluting and corrugation.

Slumbercoaches lettered for Northern Pacific carried both numbers and names of Scottish lakes, or "Lochs." The Loch's name appeared on a letterboard on each side of the car, centered on the car about midway the windows and the bottom of the car side. The length of this letterboard varied according to the number of letters in the name. The car's number appeared on a small letterboard on each side of the car, centered over the forward truck. A slightly taller letterboard appeared at the same level as the other two, just ahead of the vestibule. This one displayed the word "Slumbercoach" in script-like font. This letterboard also contained a small window with integral lighting; this window displayed the car line number, "SC-25" or "SC-26". The Northern Pacific road name appeared on a large letterboard near the top of the car side, just behind the rear-most upper level window. A small letterboard appeared just below and behind the road name, and an identical small letterboard appeared near the forward upper corner of the car. These small letterboards displayed the word PULLMAN. The two cars lettered for Northern Pacific but owned by the CB&Q (cars 335 and 336, purchased second hand in 1964 and sold to CB&Q in March 1965) had CB&Q ownership letters in the upper corner just ahead of the vestibule, instead of the word PULLMAN.

Slumbercoaches were equipped with outside swing hanger trucks and all the other modern features common to Budd equipment of the day. The roof was fluted like those on the dome cars, except that the fluting extended further down the side of the car, below the roof, to a level between

The Vista-Dome North Coast Limited

Slumbercoaches 325–334 had small PULLMAN letterboards in both upper corners on each side of the car. Slumbercoaches 335 and 336 were owned by CB&Q and lettered for Northern Pacific, so they had CB&Q ownership letters in the rear corner letterboards. "Loch Rannoch" (car 334) was photographed at Chicago on July 13, 1968, and "Loch Awe" (car 336) was photographed at Chicago in July 1973.
both photos: William A. Raia collection

that of the upper and lower windows. Instead of metal planking used on the dome cars, the Slumbercoach had corrugated sides extending from just below the main-level windows to the bottom of the car side. Slumbercoaches lettered for Northern Pacific had no skirts, except for a short one directly under the vestibule. This car was designed to operate with the vestibule to the rear.

Dome-Coach

Some notable features of the vista-dome cars included the fluted roof and metal planks and strips below the white stripe. There was a center skirt, but only below the dome section; this accommodated the lowered main level under the dome and helped to hide some of the water and lavatory piping under this car. A potable water inlet was located on each side at the forward end of this skirt. Two large cooling fans for the air conditioners were easily seen under the rear coach section on the right side, and two large battery boxes on the opposite side, slightly further forward. A small exhaust hood was located on the car's right side, above the rear prism glass window (men's restroom).

Painting and lettering was typical for the Loewy scheme, except that the "VISTA-DOME NORTH COAST LIMITED" name was included. It appeared on both sides of this car. This slogan was added to all dome cars, Traveller's Rest lounge cars, diners, and observation lounge cars between October 1955 and April 1956. No other *North Coast Limited* cars had this slogan. When the 450-series diners were displaced to the *Mainstreeter* in early 1958, they retained the slogan; the Budd diners that displaced them came painted with it. Use of this slogan was consistent from 1956 until 1970.

The car number on dome coaches originally appeared at both ends, centered above each truck. After 1958, the number appeared above only the forward truck, except for dome coach 557, which had its number above only the rear truck, and car 559, which retained two numbers on each side during

Dome Coach 556 at Chicago on March 22, 1969. Prior to 1958, this car had two equipment numbers on each side. The numbers were positioned directly above truck centers.
William A. Raia collection

The Vista-Dome North Coast Limited

most of its career. Cars 557 and 558 have small ownership letters, CB&Q, near the upper corners at each end of the car. Car 559 also has small ownership letters in the same locations, thus: SP&S RY CO

Day-Nite Coaches

Cars 586 and 587 had no center skirts. Cars 588-599 did have center skirts until about 1952, when they were permanently removed. All Day-Nite coaches had end skirts, however, but the end skirts opposite the vestibule end on cars 586 and 587 were very short, about half as long as those on the older Day-Nite coaches. The end skirts under the vestibule were the same length on all Day-Nite coaches. Car 586 was in the 1962 Granite accident. Following repairs to this car after that accident, the non-vestibule end skirts were longer than they were earlier.

All Day-Nite coaches had 14 three-foot windows on each side, plus "prism" type windows for the dressing rooms and lavatories. Cars 586 and 587 had the dressing rooms and lavatories at the end opposite the vestibule, whereas cars 588-599 had them at the same end as the vestibule. Coach seat windows were three feet long with about 16 inches spacing (including the seals) between them on cars 586-599, slightly greater figures than on day coaches in the 500 series. Cars 586 and 587 had outside swing hanger trucks. Other differences between the newer and older cars include the roof mounted air vents. Cars 588-599 had protruding vents near each end, but cars 586 and 587 had nearly flush vents mounted lower on the roof, just above the car side, giving these two cars a more streamlined and modern appearance. Also, the top vestibule Dutch-door window on the newer cars was a little shorter, closer to a square shape, whereas the door windows on the older cars were vertically longer.

Painting and lettering was in accordance with the standard Loewy scheme. Some time beginning in 1958, only the number above the truck at the end opposite the vestibule appeared on each

"Day-Nite" Coach 597 is on stand-by status, serving as a protection car for trains 25 and 26 at Seattle in February 1970. This car, identical to the others in series 588–599, was painted and lettered for SP&S and numbered 300 until it was sold to the NP in 1954.
Rick Leach photo

side of the car; prior to then, two numbers appeared on each side as on the other cars. Although car 597 was formerly SP&S 300, it was sold to the NP in 1954, so it did not have SP&S ownership letters in the upper corners. Cars 598 and 599 had CB&Q ownership letters in the upper corners.

Some Day-Nite coaches were temporarily painted silver underneath, including the trucks, but this was due to service on the CB&Q between Chicago and Denver. This leasing arrangement occurred during the 1960s and was infrequent. The silver was definitely not part of NP's standard Loewy paint scheme, so the cars' underbody equipment and trucks were usually repainted upon return to the NP. Few cars were ever given this treatment. Cars 593, 595, and 598 were three cars in this series temporarily painted this way.

Day Coach

The window arrangement on day coaches in series 500-517 was the most notable difference between them and day-nite coaches 588-599. While there were still 14 passenger seat windows on each side, these were slightly shorter, at 2'-6" in length, and they were spaced less than 12" apart. At the non-vestibule end were two extra windows on each side, one pair for the smoking lounge and the other pair for the aisle around the lounge. Painting and lettering details were the same as for the Day-Nite coaches. External mechanical features were the same as for Day-Nite coaches 588-599. The NP owned all coaches in series 500-517; thus, no ownership lettering appeared on any of these cars.

This view shows two extra windows for the aisle around the smoking room on day coach 514. This car was photographed at Seattle in April 1971.
Rick Leach photo

The Vista-Dome North Coast Limited

Traveller's Rest Buffet-Lounge

The window arrangement on this car was unique and the most notable external feature. The words "LEWIS AND CLARK" were positioned above the words "TRAVELLER'S REST" on each side of the car, in white lettering, about midway between the white stripe and the bottom of the car side. On the car's right side, these words were at the forward end, just behind the vestibule, and on the left side, they were at the rear end. Car 497 was an exception. On its left side these letters appeared at the forward end during part of its career, just behind where the vestibule would have been if there had been one. It is interesting to note that the word "Traveller's" is normally spelled with one "l", but the NP spelled it with two, presumably because that is how Lewis and Clark spelled it in their journals. This spelling also permitted equal spacing in the two-line name on the outside of the car.

The Traveller's Rest car operated with the lunch-counter end (half-vestibule end) forward. Center skirts were removed from cars 494-499 in about 1952, three years before the car's conversion, but they did have end skirts the same length as those on other 1947 cars. There was a radio antenna extending part way along the roof, positioned slightly forward of the mid-point. These cars also had the VISTA-DOME NORTH COAST LIMITED slogan since late 1955 or, depending on the car, early 1956. They retained the slogan for the remainder of their NP service. Until 1958, car numbers were at both ends as usual; since then, the number appeared only at the forward end on the left side, and at the rear end on the right side. Car 499 had CB&Q ownership markings in the upper corners.

This view of the right side of Traveller's Rest 498 shows a vestibule door and a row of windows along the aisle of the lunch counter section. There is no vestibule door on the opposite side. This photo of train No. 26 was taken during its brief stop at Ellensburg in September 1970.
Bill Kuebler collection

Appendix: Modeling The Vista-Dome North Coast Limited

> **Note**
> NP painting diagrams for the Budd dining car are unavailable as of this writing. A painting diagram for dining cars 450-455 is provided, instead. Reference to painting diagrams for other Budd equipment will guide the modeler with respect to fluting and side paneling on the Budd diners.

Budd Dining Car

Although this car could have been oriented in either direction, it was almost always oriented with the kitchen end, or "A" end, forward. This convention for dining car orientation aided servicing of the car at St. Paul and points enroute. Some NP trainmen believed that dining cars tended to ride a little better when oriented this way, because the kitchen end of dining cars was considerably heavier than the other end.

These cars had many external features in common with the dome cars, including fluting on the roof, metal planking below the white stripe, and outside swing hanger trucks. While this car had no vestibule, it did have one small service door on each side. The service door on the car's right side was near the forward end of the aisle around the kitchen, and the left side service door was at the pantry, just forward of the steward's desk area. Roof features included a five-pole radio antenna near the forward end and large covered openings near the antenna, two on the right side and one on the left, for ventilation of the kitchen and its equipment. Other large covered openings appeared at the bottom left side of the roof, one at the forward end, the other just aft of the pantry service door. Small flush mounted vents were located at various places low on the side of the roof.

Painting and lettering were typical for the Loewy scheme. These cars were delivered with only one equipment number on each side of the car, one over the forward truck on the car's left side, the

Dining car 459, November 1968. Budd dining cars entered *North Coast Limited* service in early 1958 with only one equipment number on each side of the car. This was how they appeared during their entire NP careers.
Bill Kuebler collection

The Vista-Dome North Coast Limited

other over the rear truck on the car's right side. A builder's photo of car 463 shows the round journal covers painted silver, but the NP usually painted these the same as the rest of the trucks. Car 458 had CB&Q ownership markings in the upper corners.

8-6-4 Sleeper

Sleeping cars 367-372 were designed to operate with the vestibule end, or "A" end, forward.

These cars had many of the same external features as Deluxe Day-Nite coaches 586 and 587. These included short end skirts on the non-vestibule end, outside swing hanger trucks, a vestibule door window shorter vertically than those on the 1947-48 cars, and nearly-flush air vents mounted low on the sides of the roof. Two hinged egress windows were a distinctive feature on this car. One was the window for the rearmost double bedroom (D), the other was the side aisle window approximately opposite bedroom D's egress window. These two egress windows had a distinctive narrow stainless steel frame with rounded corners. Although the dome sleepers had similar egress windows with frames painted dark green to match the car, the frames on the egress windows of cars 367-372 were not painted to match. The reason for this is unknown.

Lettering was standard Loewy scheme, except that there was slightly inconsistent spacing and positioning of the road name on the letter board within this group of cars. Differences appear to be very minor. After 1958 the car number appeared only above the rear truck on each side, the end opposite the vestibule. The word PULLMAN appeared in white lettering about midway between the white stripe and the bottom of the car side, just behind the vestibule. This indicated the contractual arrangement between NP and Pullman as described in Chapter 4. None of these six cars had CB&Q or SP&S ownership letters; the NP owned all six.

Builder's photo showing the right side of car 370, October 26, 1954. The appearance of these cars was unchanged during their NP careers, except for the elimination of the forward equipment number in 1958.
Pullman-Standard photo; Bill Kuebler collection

Appendix: Modeling The Vista-Dome North Coast Limited

Dome Sleeper

Dome sleeping cars were designed to be operated with the vestibule to the rear. This end of the car was the "B" end.

Dome sleepers had a unique look, because of the four low windows for the duplex single rooms. These were under the dome on the car's right side. Their location, extending through and thus interrupting the white stripe, forced placement of the VISTA-DOME NORTH COAST LIMITED slogan downward. This slogan was normally positioned on the middle of the three metal planks in the light green area. That was its position on the car's left side, but it was positioned on the bottom plank on the right side of dome sleepers. The 20-inch diameter NP monad in the middle of the slogan, however, was up at its normal position, centered on the middle plank on both sides of the car. The four windows and lowered slogan on the right side were the most distinctive external feature of this car. An exhaust hood was positioned on the right side, above the window for duplex single room F. Windows on the left side of the car were well spaced, since all but the forward two accommodated the long aisle extending along the side of the car. A prism glass window for the restroom was on the car's right side, main level, just aft of the duplex single rooms. Lavatory drainpipes extended vertically downward under the various rooms, some pipes more easily visible than others. Other than these distinctive features, dome sleepers were essentially identical to dome coaches, including the use of outside swing hanger trucks, and center skirts under the dome section.

Painting and lettering were typical for the Loewy scheme, except for the slogan on the right side, as noted above. Also, the word PULLMAN appeared at the usual place on each side, just ahead of the vestibule. Ownership letters appeared in the upper corners, "SP&S RAILWAY CO" on car 306, and "CB&Q" on cars 304 and 305. Since 1958, only one car number appeared on each side; it appeared at the end opposite the vestibule, centered over the forward truck. Prior to 1958, a number was centered over both trucks on each side.

Dome sleeper 313's right side, February 1970.
Rick Leach photo

The Vista-Dome North Coast Limited

Lounge-in-the-Sky Dome Sleeper

Lounge-in-the-Sky dome sleepers operated on the NP from spring 1967 until the Burlington Northern merger in 1970. These cars differ in appearance from that of unmodified dome sleepers in only three ways: the tables and seats in the dome section as previously described in Chapter 8; the car number; and the two prism glass windows for the buffet, where duplex single rooms E and F had been.

8-6-3-1 Sleeper

These sleeping cars were designed to operate with the vestibule end, or "A" end, forward.

At first glance, this car might appear to have had the same window arrangement as the 8-6-4 sleeper, but it did not. Even though the basic floor plan was almost the same, minor differences in room spacing existed, and there was a window for the porter's section, which the 1954 cars did not have. Also, the restroom's prism glass window at the vestibule end was on the left side of these cars; it was on the right side of the 8-6-4 cars.

Due to these differences, the windows for the double bedrooms and compartment were shaped and positioned a little differently than the corresponding windows on the newer cars. A careful modeler should check photos and closely compare the older sleepers with the newer ones. Other external differences were similar to those regarding the coaches; the 350-series cars had protruding roof vents, a longer end skirt at the non-vestibule end, and inside hanger trucks.

Painting and lettering were typical for Pullmans in the Loewy scheme. Ownership letters for the SP&S (366) and CB&Q (480-482) cars and the small PULLMAN lettering just behind the vestibule were the same as described for other cars. Only one equipment number appeared on each side after 1958; it appeared only at the non-vestibule end of these sleeping cars.

The right side of Pullman-Standard 8-6-3-1 sleeping car 361, November 1961.
Slide courtesy Northern Pacific Railway Historical Association

Appendix: Modeling The Vista-Dome North Coast Limited

Observation-Lounge Car

Again, the *North Coast Limited* cars were unique. No other streamlined observation cars had precisely the same window arrangement or floor plan, although some observation cars on other roads were similar in appearance to the NP cars.

The glass plates in the rear observation windows were not curved to match the curve of the car. They were flat plates, set furthest into the car at the middle of each window. Extra grab irons and steps were positioned just aft of the rear truck, and another large grab iron was on each end skirt at the rear of the car. Marker lights were permanently built into the upper car sides near the round end. Each light was fixed in a streamlined, teardrop shaped case, red always showing to the rear. No red Mars lights were permanently installed in these cars as on GN observation cars. The CB&Q, however, did attach a Mars light just above the rear coupler when handling this train between St. Paul and Chicago. This light was removed from the car at St. Paul on westbound trips.

These observation-lounge cars had a lighted, rectangular tail sign on the rear end of the car. On cars 390-393 and 483, these signs were changed so that the NP logo included the word "RAILWAY", beginning in about 1958. Car 394 retained the older style sign throughout its NP career.

Except for the white stripe, painting and lettering were typical for the Loewy scheme, including use of the VISTA-DOME NORTH COAST LIMITED slogan after late 1955. One notable exception to the standard Loewy scheme for passenger cars was the wide white stripe that appeared on at least two of these observation-lounge cars. This is cause for some digression.

Sleeper-Observation-Lounge car 394, July 30, 1961. This was the only car in this group that retained the original "Northern Pacific" tail sign for its entire *North Coast Limited* career. The other five cars were updated with the "Northern Pacific Railway" tail sign, beginning in about 1958. Only cars 390 and 483 are known to have worn the wide white stripe, the latter of these two cars only during the period of 1956–58.
Bill Kuebler collection

The Vista-Dome North Coast Limited

A question lingers as to which cars had this wide stripe and for how long. All evidence available to this author as of this writing (August 2002) indicates that at least two cars, but probably no others, had the wide end stripe. According to photographic evidence, car 390 had it for almost its entire NP career, but did not have it for a short period of time in about 1954-55. Car 483 had the wide stripe during the period 1956-58, but apparently reverted back to the continuous narrow stripe in about 1958 or 1959 and had the narrow stripe for the remainder of its career. No conclusive photographic evidence known to this author shows any other cars with the wide stripe. All known photos of cars positively identified as nos. 391-394 show them with the narrow stripe.

One explanation for this recognizes that the NP (and Raymond Loewy) originally intended the scheme to have the wide stripe. Standard painting diagrams of the era show this to be true. But, after first seeing a car painted this way, NP officials may have decided that it did not look very appealing and, on short notice, ordered use of a continuous narrow stripe. The reason for car 390 carrying the wide stripe for so long while the other cars did not is unclear. Given this inconclusive evidence, this author recommends that modelers wishing to use the wide stripe during the 1956-1967 period choose car number 390. Those using the narrow stripe should choose any one of the other five cars.

Car 483 had CB&Q ownership letters at each end of the car, on both sides. The rear ones were positioned immediately below and just ahead of the built-in markers.

Car 390, March 1960. This car wore the wide white stripe, seen in this view, during most of the period 1953–67.
Bill Kuebler collection

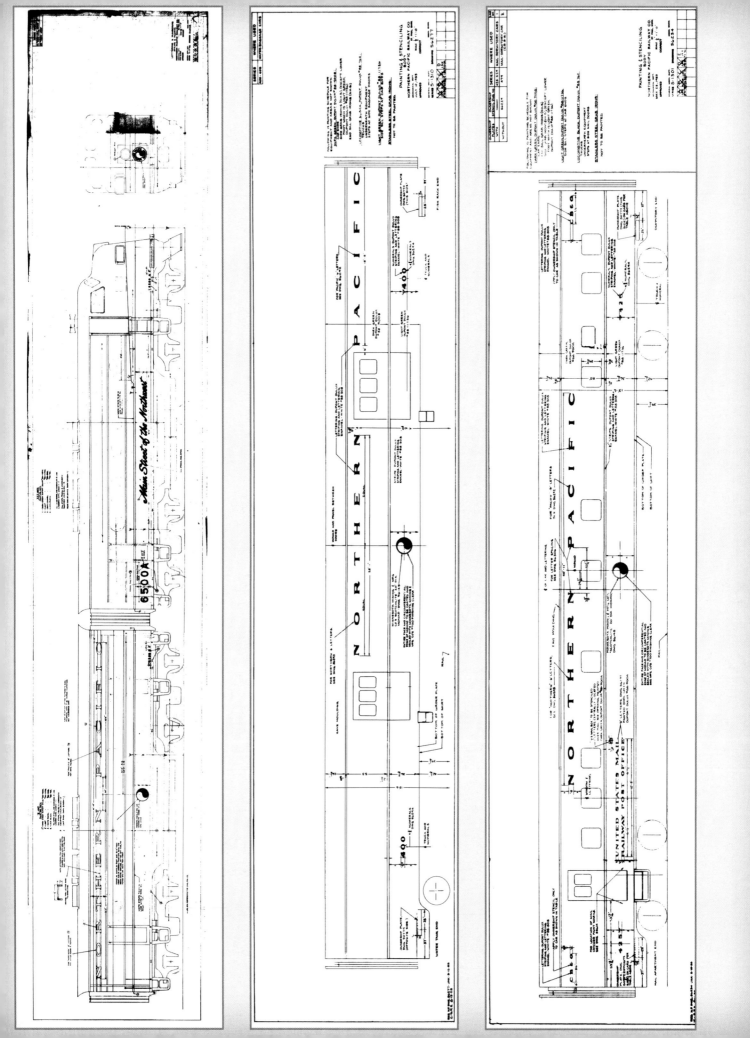

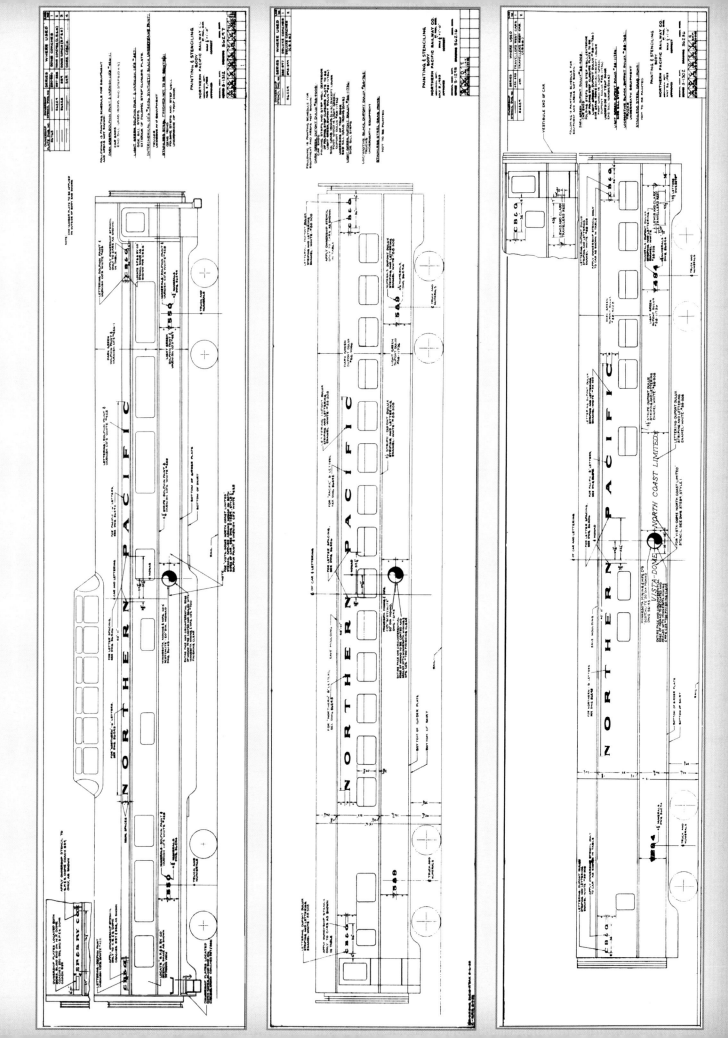

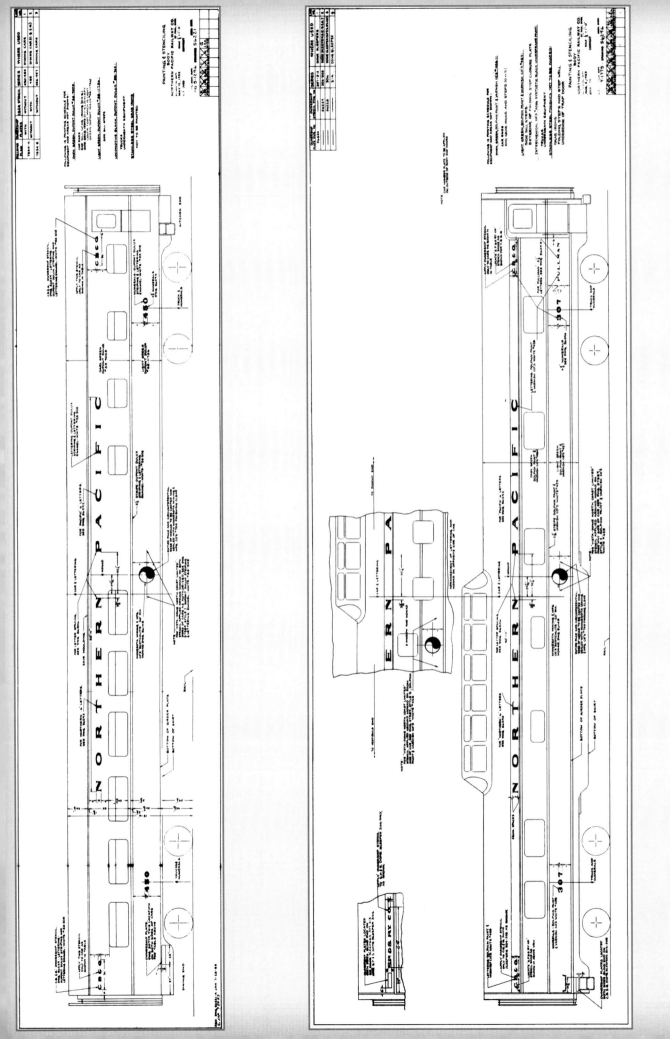

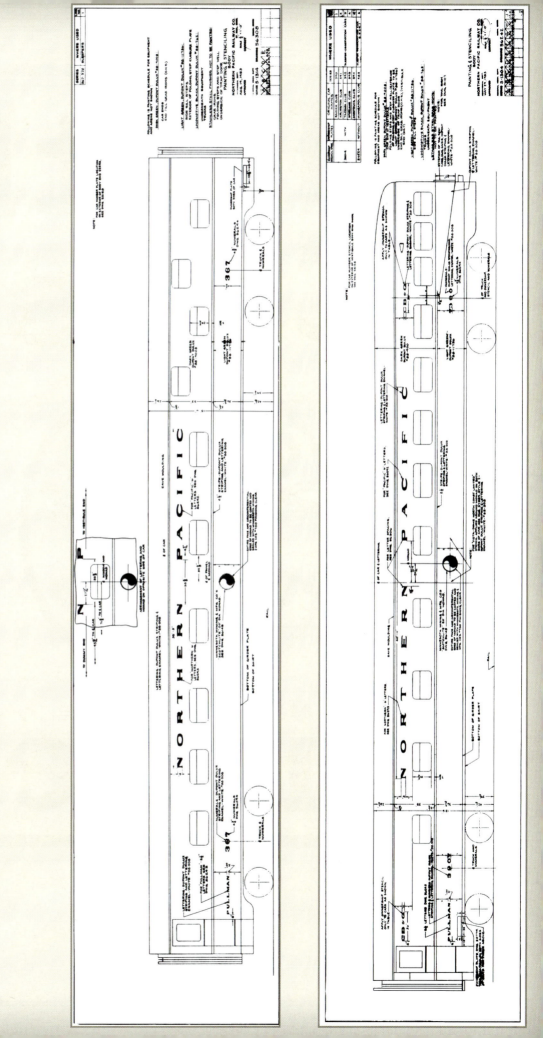

Bibliography

The following books and magazine articles contain information about the *Vista-Dome North Coast Limited* or its equipment:
1. *Northern Pacific Diesel Era: 1945–1970* by Lorenz P. Schrenk and Robert L. Frey (Golden West Books, 1988).
2. *Northern Pacific Color Pictorial, Volume 1* by Joseph W. Shine (Four Ways West, 1994).
3. *Northern Pacific Color Pictorial, Volume 2* by Joseph W. Shine (Four Ways West, 1995).
4. *Northern Pacific Color Pictorial, Volume 3* by William R. Kuebler, Jr. (Four Ways West, 1998).
5. *Northern Pacific Color Pictorial, Volume 5* by John F. Strauss, Jr. (Four Ways West, 2001).
6. *NP Color Guide to Freight and Passenger Equipment* by Todd Sullivan (Morning Sun Books, 1995).
7. *Dining Car Line to the Pacific* by William A. McKenzie (Minnesota Historical Society Press, 1990).
8. *The Northern Pacific Railway of McGee and Nixon* by Richard Green (Northwest Shortline, 1985).
9. *The Pacific Northwest Railroads of McGee and Nixon* by Richard Green (Northwest Shortline, 1997).
10. *Burlington Northern Passenger Cars* (Vol. 1) by Charles A. Rudisel (C.A.R. Publications, 1974).
11. *The Official Pullman-Standard Library, Volume 3*, by W. David Randall and William M. Ross (Railway Production Classics, 1987).
12. *The Passenger Car Library, Volume 3*, by W. David Randall (RPC Publications Inc., 2000)
13. "Northern Pacific *Likes* Passengers" by William D. Middleton, December 1959 *Trains*, pp. 32–40.
14. "*North Coast Limited*: A Venerable Name Provides the Finest in Service" by Arthur Dubin, August 1963 *Trains*, pp. 28–45.
15. "The All-American Railroad" by David P. Morgan, December 1985 *Trains*, pp. 28–36.
16. "Tomorrow's Trains Today on Yesterday's Tracks" by Donald M. Steffee, September 1970 *Trains*, pp. 36, 41–43.
17. "Landscape of Memory" by Fred Matthews, August 1994 *Passenger Train Journal*, pp. 32, 42–43.
18. "Rocky Mountain Division" by Donald Sims, July 1977 *Rail Classics*, pp. 16–23.
19. "Great Passenger Trains Series: The *North Coast Limited*" by Donald Sims, March 1980 *Railroad Modeler*, pp. 12–19.
20. "Northern Pacific Diesel Paint Schemes" by Todd Sullivan, September-October 1982 *Prototype Modeler*, pp. 16–21.
21. "Was This the Greatest Streamliner?" by Fred Matthews, November 1981 *Passenger Train Journal*, pp. 20–27.
22. "Club Cars of the Limited" by Ron Palmquist, March 1978 *Rail Classics*, pp. 48–57.
23. "Northern Pacific F Units" by Jeff Wilson, November 1993 *Model Railroader*, pp. 112–118.
24. "Trains of Note" by Karl Zimmerman, April/May 1976 *Passenger Train Journal*, pp. 14–19.
25. "Northern Pacific Sleeper-Observation," November 1968 *Railroad Model Craftsman*, pp. 38–39.
26. "Northern Pacific Lightweight Sleeper - 1948," February 1969 *Railroad Model Craftsman*, pp. 38–39.
27. "Alfred Langley, NP Engineer" transcribed by Hal Riegger, January/February 1999 *Vintage Rails*, pp. 80–86.
28. *The Mainstreeter*, quarterly journal of the Northern Pacific Railway Historical Association (NPRHA), various issues, July 1981 to present. Note: The Winter 2001 (Volume 20, No. 1) and Spring 2001 (Volume 20, No. 2) issues of *The Mainstreeter* contain feature articles about the *Vista-Dome North Coast Limited*, consisting of material drawn from this book.
29. *The Northern Pacific* by Dale Sanders (Hundman Publishing Company, 2002).

Sources

The following notes provide the reader information about the most important sources used by the author. In the process of writing this volume, however, I consulted so many sources that it is simply not possible to list (or, even remember) every one of them. While it is true that some of the sources listed below are not available to the general reader, I believe that the others listed are sufficient as a starting point for anyone interested in further research into the subject of this book.

As a matter of record, I will also show sources that are in my personal collection. I began collecting ephemera related to the Northern Pacific (NP) in 1964, and photos and slides in about 1968. Correspondence with NP employees and veterans across the system began in about 1968. In the years since, this collection of audio, visual, and paper material has grown substantially. In fact, much of the information in this book came from my collection.

Sources are listed according to their relevant chapter or appendix. Interviews with various NP employees and veterans provided important material used in more than one chapter. To simplify listing, these sources are listed below under the heading, "Northern Pacific Employees and Veterans."

Most of the NP's corporate records are currently archived at the Minnesota Historical Society in St. Paul, Minnesota. Files and subfiles cited for the various chapters below refer to these archives.

Finally, even though material came from these various sources, a great deal of the contents of this book resulted from the author's personal experience aboard the *Vista-Dome North Coast Limited*. Much of this experience came when I was a young lad. I freely admit that I was too immature (at age eight!) to record in proper form all pertinent facts, names, and dates as they happened. Even so, a good number of my experiences from that time, and over the next several years, still stand out vividly in memory, including many details, such was the impact they had on me at the time. To the extent possible, I have given facts, names, and dates in the text where appropriate.

Chapter 1

Some of the material for this chapter came from NP's Advertising and Publicity Department files. These included various files from groups A-2 through A-57 and A-117 through A-182. Some material came from the President's files of the NP—an extremely extensive and comprehensive set of records. In this group, I consulted subfiles 349A, 349A-78, and 349A-81 for information regarding passenger train service; streamline type trains, and fast train service between Chicago and Seattle. I also consulted subfiles 1112 and 1703 covering trips of prominent people on NP trains and NP passenger train schedules during the period 1947-69.

The Vista-Dome North Coast Limited

Chapter 2
Other than interviews with NP veterans, most of the material for this chapter came from the President's subject files and from the author's personal collection. In the President's files I consulted subfiles 103-4, 214, 349A, 349A-78, 349A-81, 391-99 and 523A-7. I also consulted subfile 1852-2. In my personal collection, I consulted NP's public timetables published during the period 1954–69. I also drew material from various newspaper clippings on file, most from various issues of the *Fargo Forum* and *Minneapolis Tribune* from the period 1955–69. To the extent possible, I checked this material for accuracy by consulting NP records, as shown here. I also consulted NP annual reports to stockholders for various years during the period 1954–69. The December 1959 issue of *Trains* Magazine ("Northern Pacific Likes Passengers," by William D. Middleton, pp. 32–40) is an excellent source of information regarding NP's Passenger Traffic Department in general, and the *Vista-Dome North Coast Limited* operation in particular. Another excellent source is the August 1963 issue of *Trains* ("North Coast Limited: A Venerable Name Provides the Finest in Service," by Arthur Dubin, pp. 28–45).

Chapter 3
Some of the material in this chapter came from NP's Advertising and Publicity Department files A-117 through A-182. Information regarding the choice of train numbers (No. 25 and No. 26) came from Kurt Armbruster, who had previously interviewed Mr. Mossman of the NP. Information related to the Duke Ellington interview was drawn from an issue of *Cadence* magazine (a magazine for jazz aficionados), clipping on file. For material related to Raymond Loewy, I consulted the fall 1986 issue of the Northern Pacific Railway Historical Association (NPRHA) quarterly publication, *The Mainstreeter* (vol. 5 No. 4), "Raymond Loewy and His Influence on the Northern Pacific," by L. P. Schrenk, pp. 7–9. Some of the material related to Raymond Loewy was drawn from interviews with former NP Vice President of Operations Norman Lorentzsen, which I conducted during May–June 1990. All information related to the scenery on the NP and Great Northern (GN) Railways comes from the author's personal experience riding both the *North Coast Limited* and the *Empire Builder* across their respective Railway lines, as well as interviews with several people who had ridden as passengers aboard those trains a number of times during the period 1954–70. One person I interviewed, the late John J. Hogan, made at least one round-trip per year between Seattle and Fargo on each of those two trains during the period 1953–70. His perspectives were particularly interesting.

Chapter 4
Material in this chapter was drawn from NP equipment listings and public timetables from the period 1954–68, in the author's collection. The book, *Palace Car Prince: A Biography of George Mortimer Pullman*, by Liston E. Leyendecker (University Press of Colorado, 1992) is an excellent source of information about the Pullman and Pullman-Standard Car companies. I consulted retired Como Shop veterans Don Kjellberg, Frank Palewitcz, Bob Bjorklund, and Leo Rafferty for most of the information concerning maintenance of *North Coast Limited* equipment. I also consulted the following sub files in the President's subject files: 103-4, 349A, 805-35, 805-70, 805-94, 1703, and 1852-2.

Chapter 5
I drew most of the information in this chapter from my personal experience riding with engine and train crews. I also drew information about the physical profiles of the six NP operating divisions involved in the operation of trains No. 25 and No. 26 from track profiles (blueprints showing grades, curves, rail weights, dates of laying, and ballast type) in my collection. Public timetables and NP Employee's Timetables from the various operating divisions are excellent sources of information as well. Information about train servicing came from the NP employee's manual, "Special Rules and Instructions for Employees in Passenger Trains Service" (revised to June 1, 1960) in my collection, as well as from my personal experience observing *North Coast Limited* operations on the various divisions. Interviews with a great number of NP veterans across the system, including NP officers, supplemented these sources.

Chapter 6
Almost all of the material in this chapter came from the author's personal experience riding aboard the *Vista-Dome North Coast Limited*. A specially-designed calculator that accounts for inflation or deflation and calculates equivalent dollar-value between any two past years came in handy for figuring costs of various modes of transportation during the 1959 journey from Chicago to Seattle.

Chapter 7
Material regarding cost and weight of *North Coast Limited* equipment came from NP's Authorization for Expenditure (AFE) files, as well as equipment listings and diagrams in the author's collection. Specific AFE files included the following: 5042-46, 5002-47, 5082-53, 5018-54, 5081-54, 5091-54, and 5108-57. Most of the information regarding F-unit lettering and numbering schemes came from the author's personal observation of this equipment during the 1960s, supplemented by locomotive equipment listings and drawings in the author's collection, and interviews with former NP Mechanical Department officers and locomotive engineers. *Northern Pacific Railway Diesel Era: 1945–1970*, by Lorenz P. Schrenk and Robert L. Frey (Golden West Books, 1988) is an excellent source of material regarding all NP diesel locomotives. The volume contains a detailed history of the purchase and operation of NP's diesel locomotives, plus a complete locomotive roster and locomotive diagrams.

Information regarding speeds and train handling came from the author's personal observation during locomotive cab rides over a period of several years, beginning in 1966. Train assignment and fuel and water consumption data came from NP's Mechanical Department files, specifically from the diesel locomotive subject files DP-11 and DL-20-22, and from files in the collection of the late Glenn Staeheli, former NP Road Foreman of Engines and General Air Brake Inspector. (Mr. Staeheli was a long-time member of the National Railway Fuel and Operating Officers organization. His knowledge of air brake systems and fuel consumption was extensive.)

Car line assignment data came from various equipments listings, public timetables, and correspondence between division superintendents and division personnel, and between the passenger traffic department and Railway employees, all in the author's personal collection. Most of these items (except the public timetables) originally came from numerous sources, usually from NP veterans who had collected them during their railroad careers. Former Tacoma Division dispatcher, Jim Fredrickson, and former NP Passenger Representative Ed Rowell were sources of many of these items.

Bibliography

Almost all of the material contained in the "walk-through" of *North Coast Limited* cars, described in this and the following chapter, came from the author's personal experience aboard the train. Generally, whenever I traveled aboard the train, usually in the Pullman section, I would walk through the entire train and make mental or written notes about each of the cars. Reference to equipment floor plans contained in the author's collection supplemented these notes. I also consulted correspondence in the files of several former NP passenger conductors, as well as the NP employee's manual, "Special Rules and Instructions for Employees in Passenger Trains Service" (revised to June 1, 1960), for information about seat assignments in the coach section of the train.

Dining Car Line to the Pacific, by William A. McKenzie (Minnesota Historical Society Press, 1990) is an excellent source of information regarding NP dining car operations. The volume contains an excellent history of dining car service on the NP, including many of the road's official recipes.

Chapter 8

Almost all of the material in this chapter came from the author's personal experience riding aboard trains No. 25 and No. 26 on dozens of occasions as a guest of Fargo Division trainmen. In most cases I rode with the rear brakeman. Those trips provided my first opportunities to experience travel in Pullman cars (which I did again as a paying passenger on several occasions), and to observe the duties of the rear brakeman. I also made some trips with St. Paul Division trainmen—affording me an opportunity to learn about backing maneuvers in St. Paul's Union Depot (SPUD). Reference to NP's *Air Brake Rules and Special Instructions* (June 1, 1955 edition) supplemented these experiences. Fargo Division Conductor Arnold Lorentzsen kept a record of his service on passenger trains, noting any celebrities that happened to be passengers on his train. I also consulted several issues of NP's magazine, *The North Coaster* (the Passenger Traffic Department published this magazine every other month until the late 1960s). Several of these issues document celebrities who traveled aboard trains No. 25 and No. 26. In April 2001, I consulted with about a dozen former NP Stewardess-Nurses and two former Stewardess-Nurse supervisors, who provided valuable information that appears both in this chapter and in Chapter 12.

Chapter 9

Most of the material regarding consist evolution and seasonal changes came from extensive analysis of photographic evidence contained within the author's collection. Photographers Ronald V. Nixon, Warren R. McGee, and Jim Fredrickson made many of these images. Equipment listings in public timetables are a good source of information regarding equipment and car lines, but the reader should use caution when referring to these sources, because they do not always reflect actual practice, even during the time period a given timetable was in effect. Deviations from what is shown in public timetables occurred on more than a few occasions. I also consulted dispatchers' records of train movements (trainsheets) for information regarding consists. Most of these were in the collections of Ron Nixon and Jim Fredrickson. Information regarding the dome sleeper leasing arrangement came from several sources; among these were NP's Presidents files (103-4, 805, 1852), *Burlington Northern Passenger Cars* (vol. 1), by Charles A. Rudisel (C. A. R. Publications, 1974), photographs in the author's collection, and interviews with NP Como Shop employees. The following web site contains information regarding NP dome sleeper leasing: http://www.trainweb.org/web_lurker.

Chapter 10

Material in this chapter came from the following sources: Correspondence between NP's Passenger Traffic Department and Tacoma Division Superintendent and personnel; communication with former NP Passenger Traffic Representative Ed Rowell (1970); correspondence between John Strauss and the author (1999–2000); Dispatcher's Records of Train Movements from the St. Paul and Tacoma Divisions; and the author's personal recollections and notes.

Chapter 11

Information in this chapter came from the following three general sources: Interstate Commerce Commission (ICC) accident reports; NP corporate records; and a great number of interviews and conversations with NP employees and veterans during the period 1968–2000. Specifically, I consulted ICC Railroad Accident Investigation Report No. 3948 (Granite, Idaho) and Ex Parte No. 229 (Evaro, Montana). In the NP corporate records I consulted NP President's files 349A-81, 490, and 1703. I also consulted the Mechanical Department file DL-21, as well as the personnel records of most of the enginemen and trainmen involved in the accidents. A microfilm index in the NP archives at the Minnesota Historical Society in St. Paul, Minnesota, provides access to personnel records by employee surname and an individual file number. Information on the NP's Budd disc brake conversion program for Pullman-Standard cars came from AFE files 5009-59, 5004-60, and 5016-62. But the majority of material in this chapter came from interviews and conversations with NP employees and veterans, many of whom were closely associated with the employees involved in the accidents. This association was either as fellow enginemen or trainmen, or as supervisors. Others whom I interviewed were directly involved in cleanup operations following a derailment. All these names are listed under "Northern Pacific Employees and Veterans." Information regarding makeup train operations following the Granite accident came from the files of NP dispatcher Jim Fredrickson.

Chapter 12

Almost all of the information in this chapter came from the author's personal experience riding on trains No. 25 and No. 26, and from interviews and conversations with NP employees and veterans across the system, whose names will be listed separately at the end of these notes. The material in the Stewardess-Nurse section of this chapter came from interviews and correspondence with about two-dozen former Stewardess-Nurses, two former Stewardess-Nurse supervisors, and a former secretary to the supervisor, during April and May 2001. A great deal of detailed information about the electro-pneumatic brake system came from Mr. Don Angle, former NP locomotive engineer and General Air Brake Inspector, who provided me excerpts from several air brake manuals in his collection.

Chapter 13

The author drew upon personal experience aboard trains No. 25 and No. 26, and from NP Employee's Timetables of the era, for this chapter.

The Vista-Dome North Coast Limited

Northern Pacific Employees and Veterans

A great number of NP employees and veterans provided insights regarding the operation of NP trains No. 25 and No. 26, and I have drawn heavily from them. Admittedly, I do not remember all those who have in some way helped with this book, but I believe it is important to list as many names here as I can recall. Collectively, these are my most important sources. Names appear in alphabetical order. Along with each name are the individual's job title(s) held while working on the NP and the general time frame(s) during which interviews or conversations relating in some way to the subject of this book (or observations of them while they were on-duty aboard trains No. 25 and No. 26) took place.

Don Angle, locomotive engineer, Rocky Mountain (Old Montana) Division; General Air Brake Inspector; 1993–2000.
Bill Arnold, dispatcher, Fargo Division; 1967–1970, 1979.
Gregory P. Belland, brakeman/conductor, Fargo Division; 1966–1971.
Harold Belland, locomotive engineer, Fargo Division; 1966–1972.
Al Bennett, locomotive engineer, Idaho Division; 1968–1970, 1987–1996.
Robert Bjorklund, carman, Como Shops; 1981.
R. M. 'Bud' Cain, locomotive engineer, Rocky Mountain Division; Road Foreman of Engines, Tacoma and Idaho Divisions; 1988–2000.
Jack Christensen, locomotive engineer, Tacoma Division; Road Foreman of Engines, St. Paul Division; 1988–2001.
Frank Clossen, locomotive engineer, St. Paul Division; 1964–1968.
Kenneth Dahl, conductor, Fargo Division; 1965–1970.
James A. Darker, locomotive engineer, Tacoma Division; 1969, 1982.
Owen Dawson, carman and wrecker engineer, Fargo Division; 1987–1991.
Bernard Delmore, conductor, Fargo Division; 1966–1970, 1980–1982.
Benny Empting, conductor, Fargo Division; 1964–1967.
Arthur Fiedler, Jr., locomotive engineer, Tacoma Division; Road Forman of Engines, Fargo Division; 1966–1969, 1992–2000.
Jim Fredrickson, dispatcher, Tacoma Division; 1988–2001.
Al Gomer, dispatcher, Yellowstone Division; 1995–1996.
Gene Gossett, locomotive engineer, Fargo Division; 1968–1969, 1987–2000.
Robert Gruman, locomotive engineer, Yellowstone Division; 1994–2001.
Glenn Hove, locomotive engineer, Fargo Division; Road Foreman of Engines, St. Paul and Rocky Mountain Divisions; 1996–2000.
Percy Jellison, locomotive engineer, Fargo Division; 1965–1971, 1996–2000.
Robert Jones, dining car steward; 1969.
Don Kjellberg, car foreman and shop superintendent, Como Shops; 1988–2001.
C. J. 'Dusty' Knoll, trainman/conductor, Yellowstone Division; 1968–1971, 1994–2000.
Leonard Kuhn, locomotive engineer, Idaho Division; 1990–1992.
Ben Layton, locomotive engineer, Fargo Division; 1966–1970, 1974–1977.
Fred J. Lewis, locomotive engineer, Fargo Division; 1964–1993.
Robert Logan, locomotive engineer, Rocky Mountain (Old Montana) Division; 1996–2000.
Normal M. Lorentzsen, trainman, Fargo Division; Trainmaster, Lake Superior and Rocky Mountain Divisions; Superintendent, Rocky Mountain and Idaho Divisions; NP Vice President of Operations; 1988–1990, 1992–2001.
Robert Marden, locomotive engineer, St. Paul Division; 1968–2001.
Warren R. McGee, trainman/conductor, Rocky Mountain (Old Montana) Division; 1968–1970, 1979–2001.
Elmer Nelson, locomotive engineer, Rocky Mountain (Old Montana) Division; 1968–1969.
Floyd R. Nelson, locomotive engineer, St. Paul Division; 1997–2000.
Ronald V. Nixon, telegrapher-dispatcher, Rocky Mountain Division; 1973–1989.
Fred L. O'Brien, conductor, Rocky Mountain Division; 1999–2000.
Frank Palewicz, paint shop foreman, Como Shops; 1991–1993.
Walter Pansky, locomotive engineer, Yellowstone Division; 1969, 1977.
E. N. Peters, trainman/conductor, Idaho Division; 1993.
Roy P. Peterson, locomotive engineer, Fargo Division; 1965–2001.
Runyon C. Peterson, locomotive engineer, Fargo Division; 1967–2001.
Hunter M. Picken, locomotive engineer, Yellowstone Division; 1968–1969, 1976–1979.
Leo Rafferty, carman, Como Shops, 1981, ca. 1991–1992.
Robert Robideau, conductor, Fargo Division; 1966–1970.
Francis Scobee, locomotive engineer, Tacoma Division; Road Foreman of Engines, Yellowstone Division; 1998–2000.
Leroy Sly, locomotive fireman and engineer, Fargo Division; 1965–1971.
Charlie Snodgrass, dining car/Traveller's Rest waiter; 1993.
Frank L. Soare, locomotive engineer, Yellowstone Division; 1968–1969, 1976, 1989.
Glenn A. Staeheli, locomotive engineer, Idaho Division; Road Foreman of Engines, Tacoma and Fargo Divisions, 1970–1995.
Bill Stumpf, locomotive engineer, Yellowstone Division; 1968–1969, 1990–2001.
Don Welligrant, Jr., dining car chef; 1969.
Arthur Willis, locomotive engineer, St. Paul Division; 1968–1970, 1981–1983.
Jack Zelinski, brakeman, Fargo Division; 1970, 1996–1998.

Note: A number of former Stewardess-Nurses, Stewardess-Nurse supervisors, and a secretary to the supervisor, provided a great deal of valuable information for this book, most of it appearing in Chapter 8. Their names appear in the main text.

Index

A

A. C. Gilbert (American Flyer toy trains), 8–9
Accidents and derailments
  consists of, 174, 181, 186
  Evaro derailment (No. 26), 9, 92, 181, 183–186, 221, 282, 287, 294–295
  Glendive derailment (No. 26), 9, 174–176, 211, 235, 294–295
  Granite derailment (No. 25), vii, 9, 77, 92, 176–182, 282, 290, 294–295, 300
  historical sources for, 319–321
  safety-related issues and, 171–174
Actual consists, 165–167. See also Consists
Advertisements
  billboards, 3, 5
  boarding signs, 252
  camera shooting tips, 265
  crew, 187–188
  drum heads, 3
  menu covers, 44
  neon signs, 3, 247–248
  on-line, 5–6
  pamphlets, flyers, and handbills, 3–4, 7, 15, 23, 29, 39, 44, 49, 101, 149, 165, 171, 187–188, 247, 265, 297
  print media, 6
  radio, 6
  route guide, 15
  on steel deck girder bridges, 3
  television, 6
  timetables. See Scheduling and train servicing; Timetables and time folders
  wall calendars, 3
Ahern, Kathleen, 239, 242
"Air Brake Rules and Special Instructions," 321
Aircraft, Boeing, 7, 19
Alaskan, The, 54, 193, 206, 210, 213
Aldrich, Bud, 181, 193
Aldrich, Norma, 241–242
"Alfred Langley, NP Engineer" (Vintage Rails, January/February 1999), 319
"All-American Railroad, The" (Trains, December 1985), 319
American Airlines, 293
American Car and Foundry, 290, 300
American Flyer toy trains (A. C. Gilbert), 8–9
Amtrak, 94, 293–295
Anderson, Nicki H., 239
Angle, Don, vii, 321–322
Antennas, radio, 298
Antonioni, Julie, 240, 242
Antush, Marie, 241–242
Arlee, 251
Armbruster, Kurt, 320
Arnold, Bill, 322
Assignments
  of crews
    description of, 204–210
    districts, 205–213
  of locomotives, 54
Auburn and Auburn Depot, 17, 222
Automatic brake systems, 196–198

B

Badlands, 118, 262
Baggage cars (Pullman-Standard)
  200-series NP, 59
  baggage-mail, 182
  water-baggage. See Water-baggage cars (Pullman-Standard)
Baldwin DRS 4-4-15 switchers, 81
Baltimore and Ohio railway. See B&O (Baltimore and Ohio) railway
Barich, Viola, 239
Bassett, Barney, 193
Batten, Barton, Durnstein & Osborn, Inc., 80
Baurer, W. A., 172
Beach, Phillip, vii
Bearmouth, 217
Bell, Carol Ann, 239, 242
Belland, Gregory P., 322
Belland, Harold, 322
Bennett, Al, 178, 322
Bergin, Mary, 241–242
Bidstrup, Barbara A. (Babs), 232–234, 236, 238, 240, 242
Big Pipestone Creek, 255, 272, 274, 276
Big Timber, 259
Billboard advertisements, 3, 5
Billings, 5, 18, 30, 32, 49, 154, 211, 250, 261
Bishard, Kathleen, 241–242
Bismark, 5
Bitteroot Range, 260–261
Bjorklund, Robert (Bob), 320, 322
BLE (Brotherhood of Locomotive Engineers), 207–208
BLF&E (Brotherhood of Locomotive Firemen and Engineers), 207–208
BN (Burlington Northern) railway, merger of, ix, 3, 9, 25, 127, 163, 201, 293, 310
B&O (Baltimore and Ohio) railway, 222, 224
Boarding signs, 252
Boeing aircraft, 7, 19
Boland, Mary Lou, 241–242
Bonner, 276
Borup Loop, 21
Box cars, 17
Bozeman, Bozeman Pass, and Bozeman Tunnel, 18, 124–125, 229, 253, 261, 268–269, 288
Brake systems and brake system crews
  automatic systems, 196–198
  dynamic systems, 199–204
  electro-pneumatic systems, 198–199
  independent systems, 196
  overviews of, 194–196
Brekke (Kravetz), Lila, 223–224, 231–232, 237–239
Brewer, I. W., 182
Bridges, advertisements on, 3
Bristol, 254
Broadway Limited, 19, 21, 26
Brockelbank, William, 6
Brotherhood of Locomotive Engineers (BLE), 207–208
Brotherhood of Locomotive Firemen and Engineers (BLF&E), 207–208
Brown, Barbara, 240, 242
Brown, Norma Irene, 241–242

Budd Rail Diesel Cars
  diner. See Diner cars (Budd)
  dome. See Dome cars (Budd)
  factory of, 5, 26
Burgess, C. H., 172, 215
Burlington Northern Passenger Cars, Vol. 1, 319, 321
Burlington Northern railway. See BN (Burlington Northern) railway, merger of
Burtch, Howard, 193
Business cars, executive, 154
Butler, Alfred, 256, 289
Butte, 4, 12–13, 16–17, 20, 29, 52, 61, 172, 189, 211, 222, 255, 260
Butte Mountain, 274, 276

C

Cain, G. W., 218
Cain, R. M. (Bud), vii, 178–179, 322
California Zephyr, 8
Camera shooting tip pamphlets, 265
Canada, Glenda, 240, 242
Cannon, Jess, 200, 203
Car lines. See Lines (car)
Cardwell, 119, 290
Carlson, Dick, 219
Cars
  baggage (Pullman-Standard)
    200-series NP, 59
    baggage-mail, 182
    water-baggage. See Cars, water-baggage
  box, 17
  club, sleeper-observation-buffet-lounge, Club 4-1 (Pullman-Standard). See Cars, sleeper
  coach, day (Pullman-Standard)
    500 NP, 57, 82–85, 165, 305
    501 NP, 57, 82–85, 165, 305
    502 NP, 57, 82–85, 165, 168, 305
    503 NP, 57, 82–85, 165, 186, 305
    504 NP, 57, 82–85, 165, 305
    505 NP, 57, 82–85, 165, 168–169, 182, 305
    506 NP, 57, 82–85, 165, 168–169, 305
    507 NP, 57, 82–85, 165, 305
    508 NP, 57, 82–85, 165, 305
    509 NP, 57, 82–85, 165, 305
    510 NP, 57, 82–85, 165, 305
    511 NP, 57, 82–85, 165, 168–169, 305
    512 NP, 57, 82–85, 165, 182, 305
    513 NP, 57, 82–85, 165, 168, 182, 305
    514 NP, 57, 82–85, 165, 305
    515 NP, 57, 82–85, 165, 305
    516 NP, 57, 82–85, 165, 168–169, 305
    517 NP, 57, 82–85, 165, 305
    description of, 8, 50, 57, 82–85, 162–163
    modeling information for, 305
  coach, Day-Nite/Deluxe Day-Nite (Pullman-Standard)
    300 SP&S/597 NP, 60, 70–78, 84, 165, 168–169, 304–305
    581 NP, 289
    582 NP, 289
    583/489 NP (Holiday conversion), 170, 289

323

The Vista-Dome North Coast Limited

Cars (continued)
    584 NP, 21, 289
    585 NP, 289
    586 NP (Deluxe), 9, 71–78, 84–86, 168, 170, 181, 280, 304
    587 NP (Deluxe), 4, 9, 71–78, 84–86, 168–170, 272–273, 277, 280, 304
    588 NP 71–78, 8, 12, 70–78, 84–86, 165, 169, 304
    589 NP, 8, 70–78, 84–86, 165, 168–169, 174, 277, 304
    590 NP, 70–78, 84–86, 165, 169–170, 267, 304
    591 NP, 12, 70–78, 84–86, 165, 169, 222, 304
    592 NP, 70–78, 84–86, 165, 168, 186, 304
    593 NP, 70–78, 84–86, 165, 168, 170, 181, 304–305
    594 NP, 20, 70–78, 84–86, 165, 168–169, 281, 304
    595 NP, 70–78, 84–86, 165, 169–170, 304–305
    596 NP, 70–78, 84–86, 165, 169–170, 304
    598 CB&Q, 70–78, 84–86, 165, 168, 186, 304–305
    599 CB&Q, 70–78, 84–86, 165, 168, 170, 277, 304
    description of, 23, 40, 45, 50, 57, 70–78, 85–86, 149–150, 162–163
    modeling information for, 304–305
coach, dome-coach/Vista-Dome (Budd). See Cars, dome
coach, Slumbercoach (Budd)
    325 NP (Loch Sloy), 158–159, 302
    326 NP (Loch Leven), 156, 158, 169, 302
    327 NP (Loch Lomond), 158, 174, 302
    328 NP (Loch Ness), 158, 169, 302
    329 NP (Loch Tarbet/ex-T&P Southland), 158, 170, 302
    330 NP (Loch Katrine/ex-B&O Restland), 158, 302
    331 NP (Loch Long/ex-B&O Sleepland), 158, 302
    332 NP (Loch Lochy/ex-B&O Thriftland), 158, 170, 302
    333 NP (Loch Tay/ex-NYC 10800), 158, 302
    334 NP (Loch Rannoch), 158, 302
    335 CB&Q (Loch Arkaig/ex-NYC 10802), 158, 301–302
    336 CB&Q (Loch Awe/ex-NYC 10803), 158, 301–302
    description of, xi, 9–10, 27, 57, 149, 155–158, 162–163, 166, 277, 285–286
    modeling information for, 301–303
    Silver series (CB&Q pool), 156–157, 169, 179, 181
coffee shop, 182
consists of, 149–170. See also Consists
costs of, 50
delivery dates of, 50
diner (Budd)
    400-455 NP, 307
    455 NP, 267, 307
    458 CB&Q, 9, 21, 94–100, 168–169, 174, 307–308
    459 NP, 9, 94–100, 168–170, 221, 307
    460 NP, 9, 94–100, 168–170, 307
    461 NP, 9, 94–100, 168, 170, 186, 307
    462 NP, 9, 94–100, 178, 181, 307
    463 NP, 9, 94–100, 307–308
    description of, 10, 46, 94–100, 124, 154, 162–163
    modeling information for, 307–308
diner, diner-lunch (Pullman-Standard)
    450 NP, 8, 124
    450-series NP, 257, 283
    451 NP, 8, 124
    452 NP, 8, 124, 276
    453 NP (rebuilt), 8, 124
    454 NP, 8, 124, 182, 280
    455 NP (CB&Q), 8, 124
    456 NP, 8, 124
    457 NP, 8, 124, 150, 274
    description of, 4, 10, 162–163
diner, Lewis & Clark Traveller's Rest Buffet-Lounge (Pullman-Standard)
    494 NP, 8–9, 12, 86–94, 168–170, 306
    495 NP, 8, 168–169, 306
    496 NP, 8, 21, 86–94, 168, 186, 221, 280, 306
    497 NP, 8, 168–169, 281, 306
    498 NP, 8–9, 86–94, 168–170, 174, 182, 306
    499 CB&Q, 8–9, 86–94, 168, 173, 179, 181, 267, 277, 306
    description of, 4, 10, 21–22, 39–40, 50, 57, 63–64, 74, 86–94, 140, 149–151, 154–155, 162–163, 221, 283, 286
    modeling information for, 306
diner, sleeper-observation-buffet-lounge, Club 4-1 (Pullman-Standard). See Cars, sleeper
disc brakes on, 298
dome, dome-coach/Vista-Dome (Budd)
    549 NP, 9, 50, 63–71, 74, 78–81, 168–170
    550 NP, 5, 9, 12, 27, 60, 63–71, 78–81, 165, 168, 179, 181
    551 NP, 6, 9, 63–71, 78–81, 168–169, 266
    552 NP, 5, 9, 63–71, 78–81, 168, 182, 186, 274
    553 NP, 4, 9, 63–71, 78–81, 150, 168–170, 274
    554 NP, 9, 63–71, 78–81, 168–169, 174, 268, 277, 281
    555 NP, 9, 63–71, 78–81, 154, 168–170
    556 NP, 9, 56, 63–71, 78–81, 168–170, 268, 303
    557 CB&Q, 9, 20, 63–71, 78–81, 168, 170, 174, 185–186, 303–304
    558 CB&Q, 4, 9, 63–71, 78–81, 168–169, 267, 281, 304
    559 SP&S, 9, 63–71, 78–81, 168–169, 222, 268, 280, 303–304
    description of, 23, 50, 63–71, 78–81, 94, 149–150, 162–163, 225
    modeling information for, 303–304
dome, sleeper 4-4-4 (Budd)
    304/380 CB&Q, 4, 9, 110–125, 134–136, 159, 162, 168, 186, 276, 286, 309
    305 CB&Q, 4, 9, 110–125, 134–136, 153, 162, 168–169, 174, 182, 251, 270–271, 289, 309
    306 SP&S, 9, 110–125, 134–136, 168, 170, 292, 309
    307/375 NP, 4, 9, 110–125, 134–136, 153, 162, 168, 170, 186
    308/376 NP, 9, 110–125, 134–136, 162, 168–169, 267
    309 NP, 9, 110–125, 134–136, 162, 168–169, 276
    310 NP, 9, 110–125, 134–136, 162, 168–170, 174, 288, 291
    311/377 NP, 9, 110–125, 134–136, 150, 162, 168–170, 251, 272
    312/378 NP, 9, 110–125, 134–136, 160, 168–169, 178, 181, 258, 284, 289
    313 NP, 162, 9, 31, 56, 110–125, 134–136, 168–169, 222, 309
    314/379 NP, 9, 50, 110–125, 134–136, 155, 168–170, 181
    conversions, Lounge-in-the-Sky, 9, 136, 152–153, 155, 159, 161
    description of, 21, 23, 27, 50, 57–58, 94, 110–125, 134–136, 152–155, 161–163, 218
    modeling information for, 309
dome, sleeper Lounge-in-the-Sky (Budd)
    375/307 NP, 4, 9, 110–125, 134–136, 153, 162, 168, 170, 186
    376/308 NP, 9, 110–125, 134–136, 162, 168–169
    377/311 NP, 9, 110–125, 134–136, 150, 162, 168–170, 251
    378/312 NP, 9, 110–125, 134–136, 160, 168–169, 178, 181, 258, 289
    379/314 NP, 9, 50, 110–125, 134–136, 155, 168–170, 181
    380/304 CB&Q, 4, 9, 110–125, 134–136, 159, 162, 168, 186, 276, 286
    descriptions of, 9, 136, 152–153, 155, 159, 161
    modeling information for, 310
executive business, 154
historical sources for, 319–321
lines. See Lines (car)
locomotives. See Locomotives
lounge, coffee shop, Cars, coffee shop
lounge, Holiday Lounge (Pullman-Standard)
    487 NP (conversion), 21
    488 NP (conversion), 21
    489 NP (conversion), 21, 170, 182, 289
    490 NP (conversion), 21
    491 NP (conversion), 21
    493 NP, 182
    conversion of, 21
    description of, 10
lounge, Lewis & Clark Traveller's Rest Buffet-Lounge (Pullman-Standard). See Cars, diner
lounge, sleeper-observation-buffet-lounge, Club 4-1 (Pullman-Standard). See Cars, sleeper
mail-dormitory (American Car and Foundry)
    9301 C&NW/430 NP, 290, 300
    modeling information for, 300–301
mail-dormitory (Pullman-Standard)
    425 NP, 8, 60–63, 165, 168–169
    426 NP, 8, 60–63, 168–169, 301
    427 NP, 8, 60–63, 168–170, 222, 268, 300
    428 NP, 8, 12, 60–63, 168, 170, 177, 181, 300
    429 NP, 8, 60–63, 168, 174–185, 300
    430/479 CB&Q, 8, 60–63, 168, 170, 186, 300

Index

Cars *(continued)*
    440 NP (conversion), 160
    441 NP (conversion), 160
    442 NP (conversion), 160
    443 NP (conversion), 160
    444 NP (conversion), 160
    conversions of, 160
    description of, 8, 10, 43, 50, 57, 60–63, 160, 162–163
    modeling information for, 300–301
  Mars lights on, 311
  mechanical refrigerator, 500 N.P.M.X., 17
  modeling information for, 297–312. *See also* Modeling information
  numbering of (line vs. equipment), 56–57
  observation, sleeper-observation-buffet-lounge, Club 4-1 (Pullman-Standard). *See* Cars, sleeper
  schematics of, 58, 60, 63, 73–74, 85–86, 94, 102, 110, 125, 136, 314–318
  sleeper, 8-6-3-1 all-room (Pullman-Standard)
    350 NP (Detroit Lakes), 8, 57, 125–133, 182, 276
    351 NP (Billings), 8, 57, 125–133, 310
    352 NP (Fargo), 8, 57, 125–133, 150, 169, 274, 310
    353 NP (Walla Walla), 8, 57, 125–133, 186, 310
    354 NP (Missoula), 8, 31, 57, 125–133, 168, 186, 310
    355 NP (Bismark), 8, 57, 125–133, 169, 258, 310
    356 NP (Aberdeen), 8, 57, 125–133, 310
    357 NP (Brainerd), 8, 57, 125–133, 168, 170, 284, 310
    358 NP (Butte), 8, 57, 125–133, 145, 168, 170, 186, 222, 310
    359 NP (Valley City), 8, 57, 125–133, 168, 310
    360 NP (Pasco), 8, 57, 125–133, 292, 310
    361 NP (Helena), 8, 57, 125–133, 169, 310
    362 NP (Jamestown), 8, 57, 125–133, 168, 185–186, 251, 276, 310
    363 NP (Dickenson), 8, 57, 125–133, 310
    364 NP, 160, 169, 310
    366 SP&S (Portland), 8, 57, 125–133, 169, 310
    480 CB&Q (Chicago), 8, 57, 125–133, 310
    481 CB&Q (Savannah), 8, 57, 125–133, 169–170, 310
    482 (Dubuque), 4, 8, 57, 125–133, 149, 286, 310
    description of, 8, 10, 25, 41, 50, 57–58, 102–109, 125–133, 136, 149–153, 162–163
    modeling information for, 310
  sleeper, 8-6-4 (Pullman-Standard)
    367 NP, 9, 56–57, 78, 102–109, 125–133, 168–169, 276, 308
    368 NP, 9, 56–57, 78, 102–109, 125–133, 150, 168, 186, 267, 274, 308
    369 NP, 9, 56–57, 78, 102–109, 125–133, 168, 170, 251, 308
    370 NP, 9, 56–57, 78, 102–109, 125–133, 168–169, 181, 308
    371 NP, 9, 56–57, 78, 102–109, 125–133, 168, 170, 174, 229, 256, 276, 308
    372 NP, 4, 9, 56–57, 78, 102–109, 125–133, 168–169, 308

    description of, 8, 10, 25, 41, 50, 57–58, 102–109, 125–133, 136, 149–153, 162–163, 308
    modeling information for, 308
  sleeper, 10-6 all-room (Pullman-Standard)
    365 NP, 160, 169
    modeling information for, 308–310
  sleeper, dome 4-4-4 (Budd). *See* Cars, dome
  sleeper, dome Lounge-in-the-Sky (Budd). *See* Cars, dome
  sleeper, mail-dormitory. *See* Cars, mail-dormitory
  sleeper, sleeper-observation-buffet-lounge, Club 4-1 (Pullman-Standard)
    390 NP (Rainier Club), 8, 10, 18, 136–145, 149, 168, 170, 229, 256–258, 278–279, 292, 311–312
    391 NP (Arlington Club), 8, 10, 31, 136–145, 153, 168, 170, 195, 311–312
    392 NP (Tacoma Club), 8, 10, 42, 136–145, 168–169, 311–312
    393 NP (Spokane Club), 8, 10, 136–145, 168, 174, 265, 291, 311–312
    394 NP (Montana Club), 4, 8, 10, 136–145, 168, 181, 186, 276, 311–312
    483 CB&Q (Minneapolis Club), 8, 10, 56, 168–169, 182, 220, 268, 311–312
    description of, 10, 50, 57–58, 136–145, 150, 154, 162–163
    modeling information for, 311–312
  sleeper, Slumbercoach (Budd). *See* Cars, coach
  Slumbercoach (Budd). *See* Cars, coach
  Traveller's Rest Buffet-Lounge. *See* Cars, Lewis & Clark Traveller's Rest Buffet-Lounge (Pullman-Standard)
  Vista-Dome (Budd). *See* Cars, dome
  water-baggage (Pullman-Standard)
    200-series, 300
    400 NP, 8, 12, 58–60, 165, 168–169, 299
    401 NP, 8, 58–60, 166, 168, 170
    402 NP, 8, 58–60, 168, 177, 181, 268
    403 NP, 168–170
    404 NP, 8, 58–60, 168–170
    405 CB&Q, 8, 58–60, 169, 174, 185–186, 299
    406 NP (conversion), 300
    407 NP (conversion), 300
    408 NP (conversion), 300
    409 NP (conversion), 300
    410 NP (conversion), 300
    411 NP (conversion), 300
    description of, 4, 10, 50, 55, 57–60, 162–163
    modeling of, 299–300
    weights of, 50
Carson, Johnny, 119
Cascadden, Mary Lou, 240, 242
CB&Q (Chicago, Burlington, and Quincy) railway
  California Zephyr, 8
  cars of
    coach (Pullman-Standard), 70–78, 84–86, 165, 168, 170, 186, 277, 304–305
    diner (Budd), 9, 21, 94–100, 168–169, 174, 307–308
    diner-lunch (Pullman-Standard), 8, 124

    dome sleepers (Budd), 4, 9, 110–125, 134–136, 153, 159, 162, 168–169, 174, 182, 186, 251, 270–271, 276, 286, 289, 309
    dome-coach/Vista-Dome (Budd), 4, 9, 20, 63–71, 78–81, 168–170, 174, 185–186, 267, 281, 303–304
    mail-dormitory (Pullman-Standard), 8, 60–63, 168, 170, 186, 300
    sleeper-observation-buffet-lounge (Pullman-Standard), 8, 10, 56, 168–169, 182, 220, 268, 311–312
    description of, 29, 31, 39–45, 53–56, 99–100
  Empire Builder, handling of, 15
  Vista-Dome North Coast Limited, handling of, 15
Centralized Traffic Control (CTC), 269, 285
Champlin, Margaret, 241
Chicago, 5–6, 12, 24–47, 92, 96, 135, 142, 157, 168, 218, 258, 263, 302–303, 319
Chicago and North Western railway. *See* C&NW (Chicago and North Western) railway
Chicago, Burlington, and Quincy railway. *See* CB&Q (Chicago, Burlington, and Quincy) railway
Christensen, Barbara, 239
Christensen, Jack, 322
Chronology, consist changes, 162–163
City of Miami, 161–163
Clark Fork River and valley, 18, 118, 260–261, 278–281
Cline, Elizabeth, 241–242
Clink, Joan, 241–242
Clossen, Frank, 181, 322
"Club Car of the Limited" (Rail Classics, March 1978), 319
Club cars (Pullman-Standard). *See* Sleeper cars (Pullman-Standard)
C&NW (Chicago and North Western) railway, 15, 222
Coach cars (Budd)
  dome-coach/Vista-Dome. *See* Dome cars (Budd)
  Slumbercoach
    325 NP (Loch Sloy), 158–159, 302
    325 NP (Lock Sloy), 158–159, 302
    326 NP (Loch Leven), 156, 158, 169, 302
    327 NP (Loch Lomond), 158, 174, 302
    328 NP (Loch Ness), 158, 169, 302
    329 NP (Loch Tarbet/ex-T&P Southland), 158, 170, 302
    330 NP (Loch Katrine/ex-B&O Restland), 158, 302
    331 NP (Loch Long/ex-B&O Sleepland), 158, 302
    332 NP (Loch Lochy/ex-B&O Thriftland), 158, 170, 302
    333 NP (Loch Tay/ex-NYC 10800), 158, 302
    334 NP (Loch Rannoch), 158, 302
    335 CB&Q (Loch Arkaig/ex-NYC 10802), 158, 301–302
    336 CB&Q (Loch Awe/ex-NYC 10803), 158, 301–302
    description of, xi, 9–10, 27, 57, 149, 155–158, 162–163, 166, 277, 285–286
    modeling information for, 301–303

Coach cars (Budd) *(continued)*
    Silver series (CB&Q pool), 156–157, 169, 179, 181
Coach cars (Pullman-Standard)
    day
        500 NP, 57, 82–85, 165, 305
        501 NP, 57, 82–85, 165, 305
        502 NP, 57, 82–85, 165, 168, 305
        503 NP, 57, 82–85, 165, 186, 305
        504 NP, 57, 82–85, 165, 305
        505 NP, 57, 82–85, 165, 168–169, 182, 305
        506 NP, 57, 82–85, 165, 168–169, 305
        507 NP, 57, 82–85, 165, 305
        508 NP, 57, 82–85, 165, 305
        509 NP, 57, 82–85, 165, 305
        510 NP, 57, 82–85, 165, 305
        511 NP, 57, 82–85, 165, 168–169, 305
        512 NP, 57, 82–85, 165, 182, 305
        513 NP, 57, 82–85, 165, 168, 182, 305
        514 NP, 57, 82–85, 165, 305
        516 NP, 57, 82–85, 165, 168–169, 305
        517 NP, 57, 82–85, 165, 305
    description of, 8, 50, 57, 82–85, 162–163
    modeling information for, 305
    Day-Nite/Deluxe Day-Nite
        300 SP&S/597 NP, 60, 70–78, 84, 165, 168–169, 304–305
        581 NP, 289
        582 NP, 289
        583/489 NP (Holiday conversion), 170, 289
        584 NP, 21, 289
        585 NP, 289
        586 NP (Deluxe), 9, 71–78, 84–86, 168, 170, 181, 280, 304
        587 NP (Deluxe), 4, 9, 71–78, 84–86, 168–170, 272–273, 277, 280, 304
        588 NP 71-78, 8, 12, 70–78, 84–86, 165, 169, 304
        589 NP, 8, 70–78, 84–86, 165, 168–169, 174, 277, 304
        590 NP, 70–78, 84–86, 165, 169–170, 267, 304
        591 NP, 12, 70–78, 84–86, 165, 169, 222, 304
        592 NP, 70–78, 84–86, 165, 168, 186, 304
        593 NP, 70–78, 84–86, 165, 168, 170, 181, 304–305
        594 NP, 20, 70–78, 84–86, 165, 168–169, 281, 304
        595 NP, 70–78, 84–86, 165, 169–170, 304–305
        596 NP, 70–78, 84–86, 165, 169–170, 304
        598 CB&Q, 70–78, 84–86, 165, 168, 186, 304–305
        599 CB&Q, 70–78, 84–86, 165, 168, 170, 277, 304
    description of, 23, 40, 45, 50, 57, 70–78, 85–86, 149–150, 162–163
    modeling information for, 304–305
Cobb, Helen, 240, 242
Cody, 261
Coffee shop cars, 182
Collins, Dan, 211
Collins, Patricia Ann, 240, 242
Color schemes
    Loewy, 8, 10–11, 19–22, 72, 88, 127–128, 143–145, 160, 298–299, 301, 305, 307, 309–311

pre-Loewy, 126, 143
Columbia River, 260
Commentaries
    eastbound
        day 1 (commentary no. 1), 41, 259
        day 1 (commentary no. 2), 45, 259
        day 1 (commentary no. 3), 47, 260
        day 2 (commentary no. 1), 260
        day 2 (commentary no. 2), 261
        day 2 (commentary no. 3), 261
        day 2 (commentary no. 5), 262
        day 2 (commentary no. 6, summer), 262
        day 3 (commentary no. 1), 263
        day 3 (commentary no. 2), 263
    westbound
        day 1 (commentary no. 4), 247
        day 2 (commentary no. 1), 249
        day 2 (commentary no. 2), 250
        day 2 (commentary no. 3), 252
        day 2 (commentary no. 4), 253
        day 2 (commentary no. 5), 255
        day 2 (commentary no. 6), 257
Como Shops, 24–26, 84–94, 124, 189, 221, 289, 320
Compensated gradients, 274
Conant, Carol, 241–242
Conductor & Brakeman, 244
Conlon, Susan, 241–242
Consists
    actual, 165–167
    for cars. *See also* Cars
        dome sleepers (Budd), 160–161
        Slumbercoaches (Pullman-Standard), 155–158
    changes of
        chronology of, 162–163
        seasonal, 158–160
    of derailed trains. *See also* Accidents and derailments
        Evaro derailment (No. 26), 186
        Glendive derailment (No. 26), 174
        Granite derailment (No. 25), 181
    description of, 10, 149–155, 165
    lines (car), description of, 56–58. *See also* Lines (car)
    North Coast Limited (No. 25 and No. 26), 168
    Vista-Dome North Coast Limited (No. 25 and No. 26), 169–170
Continental Divide, 255
Corican Defile, 250
Correll, Delores, 241–242
Costs, cars, 50
Covington, 290
Crews
    advertisements of, 187–188
    assignments of
        description of, 204–210
        districts, 205–213
    brake system
        automatic, 196–198
        dynamic, 199–204
        electro-pneumatic, 198–199
        independent, 196
        overviews of, 194–196
    dispatchers, 215–221
    electricians, 189
    engine, 190–194
    historical sources for, 319–321

overviews of, 187–189
people skills of, 214–221
Stewardess-Nurses (Sues), 223–244. *See also* Stewardess-Nurses (Sues)
traffic handling, 190–194, 201
train crews
    description of, 210–214
    districts, 205–213
Crosby, Bing, 119
CTC (Centralized Traffic Control), 269, 285
Cunneen, John, 144
Custer, George Armstrong, 249

D

Dahl, Kenneth (Kenny), 170, 322
Darker, James A. (Jimmy), 192–193, 219, 322
Darr, Alan, 219
Darr, Bruce, 219
Davies, J. O., 172, 217
Davis, Sylvia, 239, 242
Dawson, 140
Dawson, Owen, 322
Day coach cars. *See* Coach cars (Pullman-Standard)
Day-Nite/Deluxe Day-Nite coach cars (Pullman-Standard). *See* Coach cars (Pullman-Standard)
Delano, Margery, 239
Deleury, Kathleen, 240, 242
Delivery dates, cars, 50
Delmore, Bernard, 322
Deluxe Day-Nite coach cars (Pullman-Standard). *See* Coach cars (Pullman-Standard)
Denver and Rio Grande Western railway. *See* D&RGW (Denver and Rio Grande Western) railway
Denver Zephyr power units, 39
Derailments. *See* Accidents and derailments
DeSmet, 52, 250, 282
DeWitt, C. T., 172
Dickinson, 32
Diesel locomotives. *See* Locomotives
Dilworth, 32, 193, 207–209
DiNatale, Anita, 240, 242, 259
Diner cars (Budd)
    400-455 NP, 307
    455 NP, 267, 307
    458 CB&Q, 9, 21, 94–100, 168–169, 174, 307–308
    459 NP, 9, 94–100, 168–170, 221, 307
    460 NP, 9, 94–100, 168–170, 307
    461 NP, 9, 94–100, 168, 170, 186, 307
    462 NP, 9, 94–100, 178, 181, 307
    463 NP, 9, 94–100, 307–308
    description of, 10, 46, 94–100, 124, 154, 162–163
    modeling information for, 307–308
Diner cars (Pullman-Standard)
    diner-lunch
        450 NP, 8, 124
        450-series NP, 257, 283
        451 NP, 8, 124
        452 NP, 8, 124, 276
        453 NP, 8, 124
        453 NP (rebuilt), 8, 124
        454 NP, 8, 124, 182, 280
        455 NP (CB&Q), 8, 124

Index

Diner cars (Pullman-Standard) *(continued)*
  456 NP, 8, 124
  457 NP, 8, 124, 150, 274
  description of, 4, 10, 162–163
  Lewis & Clark Traveller's Rest Buffet-Lounge
  494 NP, 8–9, 12, 86–94, 168–170, 306
  495 NP, 8, 168–169, 306
  496 NP, 8, 21, 86–94, 168, 186, 221, 280, 306
  497 NP, 8, 168–169, 281, 306
  498 NP, 8–9, 86–94, 168–170, 174, 182, 306
  499 CB&Q, 8–9, 86–94, 168, 173, 179, 181, 267, 277, 306
  description of, 4, 10, 21–22, 39–40, 50, 57, 63–64, 74, 86–94, 140, 149–151, 154–155, 162–163, 221, 283, 286
  modeling information for, 306
  sleeper-observation-buffet-lounge, Club 4-1. *See* Sleeper cars (Pullman-Standard)
Dining Car Line to the Pacific, 319, 321
Disc brakes, cars, 298
Disney, Walt, 119
Dispatchers, 215–221
District assignments, crew, 205–213
Dixon, 282
Dome cars (Budd)
  dome-coach/Vista-Dome
    549 NP, 9, 50, 63–71, 74, 78–81, 168–170
    550 NP, 5, 9, 12, 27, 60, 63–71, 78–81, 165, 168, 179, 181
    551 NP, 6, 9, 63–71, 78–81, 168–169, 266
    552 NP, 5, 9, 63–71, 78–81, 168, 182, 186, 274
    553 NP, 4, 9, 63–71, 78–81, 150, 168–170, 274
    554 NP, 9, 63–71, 78–81, 168–169, 174, 268, 277, 281
    555 NP, 9, 63–71, 78–81, 154, 168–170
    556 NP, 9, 56, 63–71, 78–81, 168–170, 268, 303
    557 CB&Q, 9, 20, 63–71, 78–81, 168, 170, 174, 185–186, 303–304
    558 CB&Q, 4, 9, 63–71, 78–81, 168–169, 267, 281, 304
    559 SP&S, 9, 63–71, 78–81, 168–169, 222, 268, 280, 303–304
    description of, 23, 50, 63–71, 78–81, 94, 149–150, 162–163, 225
    modeling information for, 303–304
  sleeper 4-4-4
    304/380 CB&Q, 4, 9, 110–125, 134–136, 159, 162, 168, 186, 276, 286, 309
    305 CB&Q, 4, 9, 110–125, 134–136, 153, 162, 168–169, 174, 182, 251, 270–271, 289, 309
    306 SP&S, 9, 110–125, 134–136, 168, 170, 292, 309
    307/375 NP, 4, 9, 110–125, 134–136, 153, 162, 168, 170, 186
    308/376 NP, 9, 110–125, 134–136, 162, 168–169, 267
    309 NP, 9, 110–125, 134–136, 162, 168–169, 276
    310 NP, 9, 110–125, 134–136, 162, 168–170, 174, 288, 291
    311/377 NP, 9, 110–125, 134–136, 150, 162, 168–170, 251, 272
    312/378 NP, 9, 110–125, 134–136, 160, 168–169, 178, 181, 258, 284, 289
    313 NP, 162, 9, 31, 56, 110–125, 134–136, 168–169, 222, 309
    314/379 NP, 9, 50, 110–125, 134–136, 155, 168–170, 181
    conversions, Lounge-in-the-Sky, 9, 136, 152–153, 155, 159, 161
    description of, 21, 23, 27, 50, 57–58, 94, 110–125, 134–136, 152–155, 161–163, 218
    modeling information for, 309
  sleeper Lounge-in-the-Sky
    375/307 NP, 4, 9, 110–125, 134–136, 153, 162, 168, 170, 186
    376/308 NP, 9, 110–125, 134–136, 162, 168–169
    377/311 NP, 9, 110–125, 134–136, 150, 162, 168–170, 251
    378/312 NP, 9, 110–125, 134–136, 160, 168–169, 178, 181, 258, 289
    379/314 NP, 9, 50, 110–125, 134–136, 155, 168–170, 181
    380/304 CB&Q, 4, 9, 110–125, 134–136, 159, 162, 168, 186, 276, 286
    descriptions of, 9, 136, 152–153, 155, 159, 161
    modeling information for, 310
Dooms, Theresa Ann, 183, 185
Dormitory cars
  American Car and Foundry. *See* Mail-dormitory cars (American Car and Foundry)
  Pullman-Standard. *See* Mail-dormitory cars (Pullman-Standard)
D&RGW (Denver and Rio Grande Western) railway, 8
Drum head advertisements, 3
Dubin, Arthur, 319–320
Dubois, Bob, 144
Durham, Bob, 251
Durr, Duane, 83
Duties, Stewardess-Nurses (Sues), 223, 226
Dynamic brake systems, 199–204

E

Earl, Rex, 209
East Auburn, 222
Eastbound commentaries, 41–47, 259–263. *See also* Commentaries
Easton, 283
Edwards, Ray, 209
Egan, Pat, vii
Electric locomotives, CG-1 type, 19
Electricians, 189
Electro-Motive Division (EMD) diesel locomotives. *See* Locomotives
Electro-pneumatic brake systems, 198–199
Ellensburg, 79, 91, 160, 195, 259, 262, 285, 306
Ellington, Duke, 22, 119, 320
EMD (Electro-Motive Division) diesel locomotives. *See* Locomotives
Empire Builder, 8–9, 12–13, 15, 17, 24–26, 29, 110–112, 120, 200–201, 320
Employees, operating. *See* Crews
Empting, Benny, 322
Engine crews, 190–194
Engines. *See* Locomotives

Equipment vs. line numbers, 56–57
Ernstrom, George, 200
Evaro, 18, 183–186, 221, 251
Evaro derailment (No. 26), 9, 92, 183–186, 221, 282, 287, 294–295, 300
Executive business cars, 154
Eyerly, Cheryl, 241–242

F

Fain, Shari, 239, 242
Fargo, 30, 32, 119, 170, 193, 212–214
Fargo Forum, 320
Farmer, Stuart, 193
Farquhar, Carol, 241–242
Fendrick, Carol, 241–242
Fiedler, Jr., Arthur, 322
Firecracker radio antennas, 298
Flathead River valley, 18, 250
Flyer advertisements, 3–4, 7, 15, 23, 29, 39, 44, 49, 101, 149, 165, 171, 187–188, 247, 265, 297
Ford, Tennessee Ernie, 119
Forsyth, 32
Foster, Betty, 240, 242
Fredrickson, Jim, 5–6, 69, 72, 141, 151–153, 192, 215–216, 218–219, 252, 254, 283, 285, 288, 320–322
Frey, Robert L., 319–320
Fritts, Marilyn, 240, 242
Furo, Edonna, 239, 242

G

Gallagher, Ann, 240, 242, 259
Garber, Hilda, 240, 242
Gardiner, 253
Garrison, 217, 278–279, 282
Geiger, J. H., 186
George, Madelon, 239, 242
Gershwin, George, 43
Gilbert, A. C. (American Flyer toy trains), 8–9
Gildersleeve, Tom, 285
Glacier National Park, 17
Glendive, 9, 32, 174–176, 205–206, 211, 235, 249, 253, 262, 294–295, 300
Glendive derailment (No. 26), 9, 174–176, 211, 235, 294–295, 300
GN (Great Northern) railway
  baggage-mail cars of, 182
  Empire Builder, 8–9, 12–13, 15, 17, 24–26, 29, 110–112, 120, 200–201, 320
Gomer, Al, 322
Gossett, Gene, 322
Gotz, Janet, 240, 242
Grand Coolee Dam, 260
Granite and Granite Lake, 9, 77, 92, 176–182, 282, 290, 294–295, 300
Granite derailment (No. 25), vii, 9, 77, 92, 176–182, 282, 290, 294–295, 300
Graves, Charlie, 4
Great big baked potato, 97
Great Northern Pictorial, 13
Great Northern railway. *See* GN (Great Northern) railway
"Great Passenger Trains Series: The North Coast Limited" (Railroad Modeler, March 1980), 319
Green, Richard, 319
Green River valley, 18, 118, 259
Greycliff, 124, 261–262

Grilles, locomotive, 298
Gruman, Robert, 322

H

Haines, Gerry, 186
Halle, Maureen, 241–242
Halverson, Ruth, 239, 242
Hamilton, Mary, 42, 233–234, 240, 242
Hamilton, Rita, 41–42, 45, 47, 93–94, 234–235, 237, 240, 242, 247–250, 252–253, 255
Handbill advertisements, 3–4, 7, 15, 23, 29, 39, 44, 49, 101, 149, 165, 171, 187–188, 247, 265, 297
Hanes, Charlotte, 223, 239–240
Hannon, Pat, 193
Hannus, Waino, 222
Harding, Caroll Rede, 25
Harve, 17
Headlights, locomotives, 298
Hell Gate Canyon, 250
Hepper, David, vii
Heppner, Patricia F., 237, 240, 242
Herbert, M. R., 188
Herley, Molly, 240, 242
Herson, Matt, 154, 286
Hillside, 283
Hines, Mary Ann, 239
Hodder, Jack, 193
Hogan, John J., 320
Holecek, Joan, 240, 242
Holiday Lounge cars. *See* Lounge cars (Pullman-Standard)
Holman, Stanley, 244
Holmes, Gail, 241–242
Holy Cross Central School of Nursing, 94
Homestake and Homestake Pass, 12, 18, 249, 260, 275, 277
Hope, 52
Hope, Bob, 234
Horvath, Elizabeth, 241–242
Houska, Frank, 43, 95–96, 99, 221
Hove, Glenn, vii, 208–209, 322
Hoyt, 255
Huntley, Chet, 119, 291
Huntley, Pat, 291

I

IC (Illinois Central) railway
  City of Miami, 161–163
  Panama Limited, 161–163
  South Wind, 161–163
ICC (Interstate Commerce Commission), 11, 32, 53, 177, 183, 196, 321
Illinois Braille and Sight Saving School, 94
Illinois Central railway. *See* IC (Illinois Central) railway
Independent brake systems, 196
Ingstad, Ed, 193
Inside tours
  of cars. *See also* cars
    coach, 63–86
    diner and lounge, 86–100
    mail-dormitory, 60–63
    sleeper, 101–143
    water-baggage, 58–60
  commentaries. *See* Commentaries
  of consists, 149–167. *See also* Consists
  of locomotives, 49–56. *See also* Locomotives

menus, 44, 94–100
overviews of, 39–47
Interstate Commerce Commission (ICC), 11, 32, 53, 177, 183, 196, 321
Interstate-90 (I-90), 278–279, 281

J

J. P. Morgan & Co., 25
Jacko River valley, 18
Jake (waiter on No. 25), 219
Jamestown, 30, 32, 61, 193, 208
Jefferson River Canyon and valley, 20, 150, 253, 260, 270–271, 284, 291
Jellison, Percy, 322
Jenkin, Irene, 239, 242
Jocko River valley, 250
Johnson, H. E., 186
Johnson, Marlys, 241–242
Johnson, Sharon, 241–242
Johnston, Robert W., 195
Jones, Flavia, 240, 242
Jones, Robert, 322
Jurgensen, LaVaughn, 239

K

Kalmbach, A. C., 39, 124–125
Kath, Art, 46–47, 55–56, 251–252
Keller, Marjorie (Margie), 232, 236, 240, 242
Kelly, Marifran, 241–242
Kennedy, J. F. K., 19, 92, 155, 234
Kennewick, 260
King Street Station, Seattle, 53, 218–219, 252–253, 261, 292
KING-TV (Channel 5), 6
Kjellberg, Don, 26, 320, 322
Kluender, Clarence, 188
Knoll, C. J. (Dusty), 322
Kroenke, Robert G., 188
Kuebler, Jr., William R. (Bill), ix–xiii, 8–9, 12, 16–18, 20, 25, 31, 35, 39, 42, 44, 46, 52, 56, 58–63, 65–69, 72, 75–80, 83–84, 87–91, 93, 95–96, 98–99, 103–109, 111–125, 128–133, 135, 137–140, 142–143, 145, 149–150, 154, 156–157, 172, 175, 177–178, 184, 190–193, 208–209, 217, 221–222, 244, 248–249, 251, 253, 255–256, 258, 272–273, 278–279, 281, 285–286, 288–289, 292, 298, 300–301, 306–308, 311–312, 319
Kuhn, Bill, 193
Kuhn, Leonard, 322

L

Lake Easton, 263
Lake Pend Oreille, 52
"Landscape Memory" (Passenger Train Journal, August 1994), 319
Laumbach, Karen, 223, 239–241
Lawlor, Patricia, 240, 242
Layton, Ben, 322
Leach, Rick, 70, 82, 86, 127, 134, 173, 289, 299, 304–305, 309
Leach, S. W., 173
Leslie horns, 298
Lester, 283
Lewis & Clark Traveller's Rest Buffet-Lounge. *See* Diner cars (Pullman-Standard)
Lewis, Esther, 193
Lewis, Fred J. (Fritz), 170, 193, 201, 322
Lewis, Jerry, 119

Leyendecker, Liston E., 320
Lime Spur, 270–271
Lincoln, Abraham, xi, 293
Lines (car)
  255, 57, 124–125, 151–152, 158, 162–163, 222
  256, 57, 134, 151, 162–163
  257, 57, 106, 124, 151–152, 158, 162–163, 222
  258, 57, 106, 149, 151, 158–160, 163
  259, 56–57, 106
  265, 57, 124, 151–152, 162–163, 182, 185, 256
  266, 57, 151, 162–163, 182, 256
  267, 57, 124, 151–152, 158, 162–163, 182, 256, 283
  268, 57, 151, 158–160, 163, 283–284
  269, 57, 182
  C-250, 56–57, 64, 78
  C-251, 57, 73–74, 81, 85–86
  C-252, 57, 79, 81
  C-253/700, 57, 81–83, 158, 162, 182
  C-254, 57, 76, 81, 86, 158, 162
  C-255, 94, 102
  C-256, 81
  C-257, 81
  C-258, 81
  C-259, 81
  C-260, 57, 182
  C-261, 57, 73–74, 86, 182
  C-262, 57
  C-263/800, 57, 82, 158, 163, 267
  C-264, 57, 86, 158, 162
  description of, 56–58
  equipment numbers
    cars. *See* Cars
    vs. line numbers, 56–57
  listing (1959) of, 57
  SC-25, 57
  SC-26, 57, 182
Little Falls, 263
Livingston, 4, 31–32, 49, 60, 144, 171, 173, 189, 249, 253, 255–256, 261, 266–267, 280, 287, 291
Livingston, Roberta, 239
Locomotives
  assignments of, 54
  Denver Zephyr power units, 39
  diesels (EMD (Electro-Motive Division))
    754 (demonstrator), 8
    6500 set, 8
    6500A, 8, 49–56
    6500B, 8, 50–56, 298
    6500C, 50–56, 254
    6501 set, 8
    6501A, 8, 50–56, 190, 290
    6501B, 8, 50–56, 174, 186, 190, 298
    6501C, 8, 50–56, 190
    6502 set, 8
    6502A, 8, 50–56, 291
    6502B, 8, 50–56, 298
    6502C, 8, 50–56
    6503 set, 8
    6503A, 8, 50–56, 277
    6503B, 8, 50–56, 298
    6503C, 8, 50–56
    6504 set, 8
    6504A, 8, 50–56, 291
    6504B, 8, 50–56, 298

Index

Locomotives (continued)
  6504C, 8, 50–56, 219
  6505 set, 8
  6505A, 8, 50–56, 166
  6505B, 8, 50–56, 298
  6505C, 8, 50–56
  6506A, 8, 12, 50–56, 151, 170
  6506B, 8, 12, 50–56, 298
  6506C, 8, 12, 50–56, 277
  6507A, 8, 50–56
  6507B, 8, 50–56, 166, 298
  6507C, 268, 277
  6508A, 181, 282
  6508B, 8, 50–56, 298
  6508C, 151, 170, 253, 269
  6509A, 285
  6509B, 8, 50–56, 151, 298
  6509C, 208, 270
  6510 set, 280
  6510A, 186, 249, 253, 298
  6510B, 8, 50–56, 170, 186
  6510C, 166, 268, 270
  6511A, 186, 298
  6511B, 8, 50–56, 286
  6511C, 298
  6512A, 170, 174, 297
  6512B, 8, 50–56, 181
  6513A, 8, 50–56, 250
  6513B, 8, 50–56
  6513C, 8, 50–56, 170, 270
  6550B, 8, 50–56, 298
  6551B/6006B, 8, 50–56, 297–298
  6552B, 270, 298
  6553B, 298
  6700A, 50–56, 170, 192
  6700B, 50–56, 279, 286
  6700C, 177, 181, 266
  6701A, 50–56
  6701B, 50–56, 170, 186, 298
  6701C, 50–56, 174–175, 186
  6702A, 50–56
  6703, 254
  6703A, 250, 286
  6703A/7051A, 50–56, 297
  6704A, 50–56, 249–250
  7007A, 181
  color schemes of, 298
  F units (general), 8, 10, 50–56, 192, 202, 247–249, 297–298
  F-3 units, 8, 10, 50–53, 190, 200–204, 266, 290–291, 298
  F-5 units, 8, 10, 50–53, 200–204, 285, 298
  F-7 units, 8, 10, 50–53, 55, 190, 200–204, 249, 254, 269, 280, 285, 298
  F-9 units, 8, 10, 50–53, 124, 170, 192, 254, 266–267, 291, 297–298
  firecracker radio antennas on, 298
  grilles of, 298
  headlights on, 298
  in-car illustrations of, 69
  Leslie horns on, 298
  Nathan P-3 Air Chime horns on, 298
  diesels (other)
    E-8s, 39, 46, 254, 285, 292
    FP-7As, 54
    GP-7s, 54
    GP-9s, 54, 192

  electric, CG-1 type, 19
  historical sources for, 319–321
  model designations of, 51
  modeling of, 297–312. See also Modeling information
  numbering schema of, 51
  schematics of, 314
  shovelnoses, 39
  switchers (Baldwin DRS 4-4-15), 81
Loewy colors, 8, 10–11, 19–22, 72, 88, 127–128, 143–145, 160, 298–299, 301, 305, 307, 309–311
Loewy, Raymond, 8, 19–22, 26, 72, 88, 127–128, 141, 143–145, 320–321
Logan, 20, 270–271
Logan, Robert (Bob), 193, 322
Logos, schematics of, 318
Lorentzsen, Norman M., ix, xii, 110, 172, 176, 320, 322
Lounge cars (Pullman-Standard)
  Holiday Lounge (Pullman-Standard)
    487 NP (conversion), 21
    488 NP (conversion), 21
    489 NP (conversion), 21, 170, 182, 289
    490 NP (conversion), 21
    491 NP (conversion), 21
    493 NP, 182
    conversion of, 21
    description of, 10
  Lewis & Clark Traveller's Rest Buffet-Lounge (Pullman-Standard). See Diner cars (Pullman-Standard)
  sleeper-observation-buffet-lounge, Club 4-1. See Sleeper cars (Pullman-Standard)
Lounge-in-the-Sky cars (Budd). See Dome cars (Budd)
Lovelett, Carol, 241
Lundberg, Ray, 45–46, 144, 193, 251–252
Lyman, Mary Ann, 241–242
Lynn, Eldon E., 186

M

MacArthur, Dorothy, 241–242
MacDonald, Beverly, 239, 242
Macfarlane, Robert S., 8, 18–19, 22, 27–28, 88, 244
Macklin, Wilma, 240, 243
Madison River bridge, 270
Mail-dormitory cars (American Car and Foundry)
  9301 C&NW/430 NP, 290, 300
  modeling information for, 300–301
Mail-dormitory cars (Pullman-Standard)
  425 NP, 8, 60–63, 165, 168–169
  426 NP, 8, 60–63, 168–169, 301
  427 NP, 8, 60–63, 168–170, 222, 268, 300
  428 NP, 8, 12, 60–63, 168, 170, 177, 181, 300
  429 NP, 8, 60–63, 168, 174–185, 300
  430/479 CB&Q, 8, 60–63, 168, 170, 186, 300
  440 NP (conversion), 160
  441 NP (conversion), 160
  442 NP (conversion), 160
  443 NP (conversion), 160
  444 NP (conversion), 160
  conversions of, 160
  description of, 8, 10, 43, 50, 57, 60–63, 160, 162–163

  modeling information for, 300–301
Mainstreeter, The, 8, 10, 15, 17–18, 54, 84, 154, 158, 167, 171–173, 192–193, 206–208, 213–214, 220
Maintenance-related issues, 23–28
Mandan, 262
Mantle, Mickey, 71
Marden, Robert, 322
Marent Trestle, 287
Maris, Roger, 71
Marker, Judith, 240, 243
Markey, 262
Markle, Mary Margaret, 240, 243
Mars lights, 311
Martin, 283, 285
Martin, Dean, 11, 119
Martin, Helen, 240, 243
Matthews, Fred, 319
McAllister, Linda, 231, 241, 243
McGee, Howard, 49, 203
McGee, P. R. (Pat), 172
McGee, Warren R., vii, 4, 49, 81, 172, 189, 291, 319, 321–322
McGough, Eileen, 239
McGuire, Archie, 181
McKenzie, William A., 319, 321
McLennan, Carole, 185–186, 226–230, 240
McLeod, Jacqueline, 239, 243
Mechanical refrigerator cars, 17
Media advertisements, 6
Menk, Louis W., 8
Menus and menu covers, 44, 94–100
Mergers, ix, 3, 9, 25, 127, 163, 201
Middleton, William D., 319–320
Milages, track, 29
Miles City, 61
Miller, Edgar, 50, 88–89, 92, 221
Milwaukee Road railway, Olympian Hiawatha, 8–9, 12–13, 29, 110, 166, 190
Minneapolis, 46, 109
Minneapolis Tribune, 320
Minnesota Historical Society, 319, 321
Minnesota lake country, 17
Mission, 4
Mississippi River, 285
Missoula, 17, 31, 118, 172, 189–191, 250, 263, 278–280, 282, 289
Mitrovitch, Lucille, 241, 243
Model designations, locomotives, 51
Model Railroader, 319
Modeling information
  for cars, 298–318. See also Cars
  coach (day), 305
  coach (day-nite), 304–305
  coach (dome-coach), 303–304
  coach (slumbercoach), 301–303
  dining (Budd), 307–308
  dining (Traveller's Rest buffet-lounge), 306
  dome (dome-coach), 303–304
  dome (sleeper), 309
  mail-dormitory, 300–301
  observation-lounge, 311–312
  overviews of, 298
  sleeper (8-6-3-1), 310
  sleeper (8-6-4), 308
  sleeper (dome), 309
  sleeper (Lounge-in-the-Sky dome), 310
  sleeper (slumbercoach), 301–303

Modeling information *(continued)*
    water-baggage, 299–300
  for locomotives, 297–298. *See also* Locomotives
  for Loewy color scheme, 298
  overviews of, 297–298
  schematics for, 58, 60, 63, 73–74, 85–86, 94, 102, 110, 125, 136, 314–318
Morgan, David P., 17, 319
Morgan (J. P. Morgan & Co.), 25
Mossman, Richard, 15, 320
Mount Sentinel, 250
Mt. Jumbo, 281
Mullen, Betty Sue, 231, 241, 243
Munis, Margaret, 241, 243

N
Nagos, 287
Names and name changes, 1–20
Naperville, 292
Nathan P-3 Air Chime horns, 253, 298
National Weather Service, 209
Neilsen, Glenis, 241, 243
Nelson, Bill, 99
Nelson, Elmer, 322
Nelson, Floyd R., 322
Nelson, Shirley E., 240, 243
Neon sign advertisements, 3, 247–248
New Haven railway, 160
New York Central railway, Twentieth Century Limited, 26
Nixon, Ronald V. (Ron), vii, 12–13, 16–18, 20–21, 27, 31, 166–167, 184, 190–191, 215, 218, 249–251, 253, 255, 265–282, 284, 287–288, 291, 301, 319, 321–322
"North Coast Limited: A Venerable Name Provides the Finest in Service" (Trains, August 1963), 319–320
North Coaster, The, 219, 321
North Pacific Railway Historical Association (NPRHA), 320
Northern Pacific Color Pictorial, Vols. 1, 2, 3, 5, 298, 319
"Northern Pacific Diesel Paint Schemes" (Prototype Modeler, September-October 1982), 319
"Northern Pacific F Units" (Model Railroader, November 1993), 319
"Northern Pacific Lightweight Sleeper" (Railroad Model Craftsman, February 1969), 319
"Northern Pacific Likes Passengers" (Trains, December 1959), 319–320
Northern Pacific Railway Diesel Era: 1945–1970, 298, 319–320
Northern Pacific Railway Historical Association (NPRHA), vii, 61, 119, 127, 176, 178, 182, 189, 244, 296, 298, 310, 319
Northern Pacific Railway of McGee and Nixon, The, 319
"Northern Pacific Sleeper-Observation" (Railroad Model Craftsman, November 1968), 319
Northern Pacific, The, 319
NP Color Guide to Freight and Passenger Equipment, 319
Numbering schema
  line vs. equipment, 56–57
  of locomotives, 51

Nygaard (Taylor), Lorain, vii, 239, 242, 244

O
O'Brien, Fred L., 186, 322
Official Pullman-Standard Cars, The (Vol. 1), 319
O'Hara, Kathleen, 241, 243
O'Keefe Trestle, 287
O'Larey, M. J. (Mickey), 193
Olson, Joanne, 240, 243
Olympian Hiawatha, 8–9, 12–13, 29, 110, 166, 190
Omar, Sally, 240, 243
On-line advertisements, 5–6
Operating employees. *See* Crews
Order of Railway Conductors and Brakemen, 244
Oscar (Pullman Conductor on No. 25), 220
Osyp, Marianne, 218, 239, 243

P
Paar, Bill, 99
Pacific Car and Foundry Company, 17
Pacific Northwest Railroads of McGee and Nixon, The, 319
Palace Car Prince: A Biography of George Mortimer Pullman, 320
Palewicz, Frank, 320, 322
Palmer House, 94, 232–238
Palmquist, Ron, 319
Pamphlet advertisements, 3–4, 7, 15, 23, 29, 39, 44, 49, 101, 149, 165, 171, 187–188, 247, 265, 297
Panama Limited, 161–163
Pansky, Walter, 194, 322
Paradise, 18, 191
Parsons, Jean D., 218, 239, 243
Parsons, Marilyn, 240, 243
Pasco, 81, 253, 260, 290
Passenger Car Library, The, 319
Passenger Train Journal, 319
Peak, 262
Pearson, Mary B., 232, 234–235, 237, 240, 243
Peck, Roger, 218
Pederson, Deloris, 239
Peduzzi, Joann (Peduzz), 233, 240, 263
Pelletier, Ray, 235
Pennsylvania Railroad, Broadway Limited, 19, 21, 26
Perham, John, 293
Person, Barbara, 240
Peters, E. N., 322
Peterson, Jerry, 49
Peterson, Roy P., 170, 322
Peterson, Runyon C., 208, 322
Petri, Mary, 240
Philiben, Anne, 241, 243
Picken, Hunter M., 181, 193, 253, 322
Pipestone and Big Pipestone Creek, 255, 272, 274, 276
Podhorn, Doris, 240, 243
Poole, Patricia, 239, 243
Prchlik, Patricia, 241, 243
Pre-Loewy color and numbering schemes, 126, 143
Presley, Elvis, 119
Print media advertisements, 6
Proctor, Marilyn, 218

Prototype Modeler, 319
Pruitt, Jess J., 176, 179–180, 182, 191, 195
Pugleasa, Frank (Pug), 193
Pullman Company shops (Calument, Illinois), 24–26
Pullman, George Mortimer, 320
Pullman-Standard
  cars of
    baggage. *See* Baggage cars (Pullman-Standard)
    coach. *See* Coach cars (Pullman-Standard)
    diner. *See* Diner cars (Pullman-Standard)
    Holiday Lounge. *See* Lounge cars (Pullman-Standard)
    Lewis & Clark Traveller's Rest Buffet-Lounge (Pullman-Standard). *See* Diner cars (Pullman-Standard)
    mail-dormitory. *See* Mail-dormitory cars (Pullman-Standard)
    sleeper. *See* Sleeper cars (Pullman Standard)
    water-baggage. *See* Water-baggage cars (Pullman-Standard)
  company shops of, 24–26

Q
Quinn, Jimmy, 144, 211

R
Racetrack, The, 278–279
Radio advertisements, 6
Radio antennas, firecracker, 298
Rafferty, Leo, 320, 322
Raia, William A., 53, 81, 96, 159, 257, 302–303
Rail Classics, 319
Railroad Model Craftsman, 319
Railroad Modeler, 319
Railway Post Office (R.P.O.), 61–63
Railways
  Amtrak, 94, 293–295
  BN (Burlington Northern), merger of, ix, 3, 9, 25, 127, 163, 201, 293, 310
  B&O (Baltimore and Ohio), 222, 224
  CB&Q (Chicago, Burlington, and Quincy)
    California Zephyr, 8
    description of, 29, 31, 39–45, 53–56, 99–100
    Empire Builder, handling of, 15
    Vista-Dome North Coast Limited, handling of, 15
  C&NW (Chicago and North Western), 15, 222
  D&RGW (Denver and Rio Grande Western), 8
  GN (Great Northern), Empire Builder, 8–9, 12–13, 15, 17, 24–26, 29, 110–112, 120, 200–201, 320
  IC (Illinois Central)
    City of Miami, 161–163
    Panama Limited, 161–163
    South Wind, 161–163
  Milwaukee Road, Olympian Hiawatha, 8–9, 12–13, 29, 110, 166, 190
  New Haven, 160
  New York Central, Twentieth Century Limited, 26
  Pennsylvania Railroad, Broadway Limited, 19, 21, 26

Index

Railways (continued)
  SP (Southern Pacific), 25
  SP&S (Spokane, Portland, and Seattle), The Streamliner, 15
  UP (Union Pacific), 160
  WP (Western Pacific), California Zephyr, 8
Ramsey, Elizabeth, 240, 243
Randall, W. David, 319
Rapids, 210
Rath, Elaine, 94, 223, 239, 243
Rathburn, Susan, 241, 243
Raymond Loewy & Associates, 8, 19–22, 26, 69, 72, 88, 127–128, 140–141, 143–145, 320–321
Reczuch, Joanne, 241, 243
Refrigerator cars, mechanical, 17
Reid, Archie, 46, 55–56
Reinke, Charlie, 191
Reitz (Dolan), Joan, 176, 189, 211, 219–221, 223, 226–231, 235, 238–240
Renner, Stephen J. (Steve), 176, 180, 182
Renshaw, Nancy, 240, 243
Repairs, running, 24, 27
Riegger, Hal, 319
Ritter, George, 193
Robideau, Robert, 322
Robinson, Palton, 188
Robinson, R. H. (Robbie), 41, 188
Rocky Creek, 288
"Rocky Mountain Division" (Rail Classics, July 1977), 319
Rodine, G. Walter (Walt), 79, 189, 223–224, 231
Roskraft, Ivan G., 46, 188
Ross, William M., 319
Route commentaries. See Commentaries
Route guide advertisements, 15
Rowell, Ed, 189, 320–321
R.P.O. (Railway Post Office), 61–63
Ruder, Roseanne, 241, 243
Rudisel, Charles A., 319, 321
Running repairs, 24, 27
Ryan, Larry, 189

S

Safety-related issues, 171–174
Sagmiller, Joe, 193
Sahl, Mort, 234
Sanborn, 208
Sanden, Marilyn, 240, 243
Sanders, Dale, 319
Santa Claus, 222
Saunders, Marlene, 239
Savanna, 149
Scenic route highlights
  advertising about, 247
  commentaries about. See Commentaries
  descriptions of, 247–263
  overviews of, 247, 251
  photograph gallery of, 265–292
  place names of
    Arlee, 251
    Auburn and Auburn Depot, 17, 222
    Badlands, 118, 262
    Bearmouth, 217
    Big Timber, 259
    Billings, 5, 18, 30, 32, 49, 154, 211, 250, 261
    Bismark, 5
    Bitteroot Range, 260–261
    Bonner, 276
    Borup Loop, 21
    Bozeman, Bozeman Pass, and Bozeman Tunnel, 18, 124–125, 229, 253, 261, 268–269, 288
    Bristol, 254
    Butte, 4, 12–13, 16–17, 20, 29, 52, 61, 172, 189, 211, 222, 255, 260
    Butte Mountain, 274, 276
    Cardwell, 119, 290
    Chestnut, 229
    Chicago, 5–6, 12, 24–47, 92, 96, 135, 142, 157, 168, 218, 258, 263, 302–303, 319
    Clark Fork River and valley, 18, 118, 260–261, 278–281
    Cody, 261
    Columbia River, 260
    Continental Divide, 255
    Corican Defile, 250
    Covington, 290
    Dawson, 140
    DeSmet, 52, 250, 282
    Dickinson, 32
    Dilworth, 32, 193, 207–209
    Dixon, 282
    East Auburn, 222
    Easton, 283
    Ellensburg, 79, 91, 160, 195, 259, 262, 285, 306
    Evaro, 18, 183–186, 221, 251
    Fargo, 30, 32, 119, 170, 193, 212–214
    Flathead River valley, 18, 250
    Forsyth, 32
    Gardiner, 253
    Garrison, 217, 278–279, 282
    Glacier National Park, 17
    Glendive, 9, 32, 174–176, 205–206, 211, 235, 249, 253, 262, 294–295, 300
    Grand Coolee Dam, 260
    Granite and Granite Lake, 9, 77, 92, 176–182, 282, 290, 294–295, 300
    Green River valley, 18, 118, 259
    Greycliff, 124, 261–262
    Harve, 17
    Hell Gate Canyon, 250
    Hillside, 283
    Homestake and Homestake Pass, 12, 18, 249, 260, 275, 277
    Hope, 52
    Hoyt, 255
    Jacko River valley, 18
    Jamestown, 30, 32, 61, 193, 208
    Jefferson and Jefferson River, 253, 260
    Jefferson River Canyon and valley, 20, 150, 253, 260, 270–271, 284, 291
    Jocko River valley, 250
    Kennewick, 260
    King Street Station, Seattle, 53, 218–219, 252–253, 261, 292
    Lake Easton, 263
    Lake Pend Oreille, 52
    Lester, 283
    Lime Spur, 270–271
    Little Falls, 263
    Livingston, 4, 31–32, 49, 60, 144, 171, 173, 189, 249, 253, 255–256, 261, 266–267, 280, 287, 291
    Logan, 20, 270–271
    Mandan, 262
    Marent Trestle, 287
    Markey, 262
    Martin, 283, 285
    Miles City, 61
    Minneapolis, 46, 109
    Minnesota lake country, 17
    Mission, 4
    Mississippi River, 285
    Missoula, 17, 31, 118, 172, 189–191, 250, 263, 278–280, 282, 289
    Mount Sentinel, 250
    Mt. Jumbo, 281
    Nagos, 287
    Naperville, 292
    Paradise, 18, 191
    Pasco, 81, 253, 260, 290
    Peak, 262
    Pipestone and Big Pipestone Creek, 255, 272, 274, 276
    Rapids, 210
    Rocky Creek, 288
    Seattle, 5–6, 11–12, 25–40, 52–61, 70, 77, 92, 124–127, 134–135, 153, 160–169, 195, 218–219, 252–253, 289, 291–292, 304, 319
    Sheep Mountain, 4
    Silver Bow valley, 16, 52
    Skones Trestle, 16
    Spire Rock, 249, 255, 272, 274–276
    St. Paul, 5, 11, 24, 29, 32, 42–43, 54, 58, 65, 85, 92, 142, 150–151, 156, 165, 169–170, 190, 205–206, 208
    St. Regis, 282
    Stampede Pass, 17, 21, 151, 283
    Stampede Tunnels (Nos. 2, 3, 4), 152–153, 192, 259–260, 263, 277, 285
    Staples, 32, 207–209
    Tacoma, 5–6, 17, 216
    Thorp, 254
    Three Forks, 253, 270
    Tri-Cities, 260
    Turah, 18, 278–279
    Umtantum, 216
    U.S. Highway 10, 281
    Valley City, 259
    Waco, 265
    Welch, 259, 275, 277
    Westminster Hill, 252
    Windsor, 140
    Wymer, 216
    Yakima and Yakima River, 254, 259, 283, 285
    Yellowstone National Park, 261
    Yellowstone River, 18, 124, 249, 259
Scheduling and train servicing
  historical sources for, 319–321
  timetables and time folders, 3–4, 7, 29–30, 171, 320–321
Schematics
  of cars, 58, 60, 63, 73–74, 85–86, 94, 102, 110, 125, 136, 314–318
  of locomotives, 314
  for modeling, 58, 60, 63, 73–74, 85–86, 94, 102, 110, 125, 136, 314–318
Schrenk, Lorenz P., vii, 8–9, 27, 166–167, 250, 298, 319–320

Schuster, La Vonne, 241, 243
Scobee, Francis (Frank), vii, 181, 322
Scott, F. G., 6, 231, 233
Seafair, Seattle, 6
Seasonal consist changes, 158–160. *See also* Consists
Seaton, Judith, 241, 243
Seattle, 5–6, 11–12, 25–40, 52–61, 70, 77, 92, 124–127, 134–135, 153, 160–169, 195, 218–219, 249, 252–253, 289, 291–292, 304, 319
Seeinbright, F. L., 172
Serwold, Joann, 240, 243
Sharkey, Agnes, 239
Sheep Mountain, 4
Shepherd, Eugene M., 46, 188
Shine, Joseph W., 319
Shirley, Lois, 241, 243
Shovelnoses, 39
Siddall, Emma, 239
Sidetracked Sues, 231
Signs
　boarding, 252
　neon, 3, 247–248
Silver Bow valley, 16, 52
Simpson (Honegger), Audrey, 231, 233, 238–239
Sims, Donald, 319
Skelton, Red, 238
Skones Trestle, 16
Sleeper cars (Budd)
　dome. *See* Dome cars (Budd)
　Slumbercoach. *See* Coach cars (Budd)
Sleeper cars (Pullman-Standard)
　8-6-3-1 all-room
　　350 NP (Detroit Lakes), 8, 57, 125–133, 182, 276
　　351 NP (Billings), 8, 57, 125–133, 310
　　352 NP (Fargo), 8, 57, 125–133, 150, 169, 274, 310
　　353 NP (Walla Walla), 8, 57, 125–133, 186, 310
　　354 NP (Missoula), 8, 31, 57, 125–133, 168, 186, 310
　　355 NP (Bismark), 8, 57, 125–133, 169, 258, 310
　　356 NP (Aberdeen), 8, 57, 125–133, 310
　　357 NP (Brainerd), 8, 57, 125–133, 168, 170, 284, 310
　　358 NP (Butte), 8, 57, 125–133, 145, 168, 170, 186, 222, 310
　　359 NP (Valley City), 8, 57, 125–133, 168, 310
　　360 NP (Pasco), 8, 57, 125–133, 292, 310
　　361 NP (Helena), 8, 57, 125–133, 169, 310
　　362 NP (Jamestown), 8, 57, 125–133, 168, 185–186, 251, 276, 310
　　363 NP (Dickenson), 8, 57, 125–133, 310
　　364 NP, 160, 169, 310
　　366 SP&S (Portland), 8, 57, 125–133, 169, 310
　　480 CB&Q (Chicago), 8, 57, 125–133, 310
　　481 CB&Q (Savannah), 8, 57, 125–133, 169–170, 310
　　482 (Dubuque), 4, 8, 57, 125–133, 149, 286, 310
　　description of, 8, 10, 25, 41, 50, 57–58, 102–109, 125–133, 136, 149–153, 162–163
　　modeling information for, 310
　8-6-4
　　367 NP, 9, 56–57, 78, 102–109, 125–133, 168–169, 276, 308
　　368 NP, 9, 56–57, 78, 102–109, 125–133, 150, 168, 186, 267, 274, 308
　　369 NP, 9, 56–57, 78, 102–109, 125–133, 168, 170, 251, 308
　　370 NP, 9, 56–57, 78, 102–109, 125–133, 168–169, 181, 308
　　371 NP, 9, 56–57, 78, 102–109, 125–133, 168, 170, 174, 229, 256, 276, 308
　　372 NP, 4, 9, 56–57, 78, 102–109, 125–133, 168–169, 308
　　description of, 8, 10, 25, 41, 50, 57–58, 102–109, 125–133, 136, 149–153, 162–163, 308
　　modeling information for, 308
　10-6 all-room
　　365 NP, 160, 169
　　modeling information for, 308–310
　mail-dormitory. *See* Mail-dormitory cars (Pullman-Standard)
　sleeper-observation-buffet-lounge, Club 4-1
　　390 NP (Rainier Club), 8, 10, 18, 136–145, 149, 168, 170, 229, 256–258, 278–279, 292, 311–312
　　391 NP (Arlington Club), 8, 10, 31, 136–145, 153, 168, 170, 195, 311–312
　　392 NP (Tacoma Club), 8, 10, 42, 136–145, 168–169, 311–312
　　393 NP (Spokane Club), 8, 10, 136–145, 168, 174, 265, 291, 311–312
　　394 NP (Montana Club), 4, 8, 10, 136–145, 168, 181, 186, 276, 311–312
　　483 CB&Q (Minneapolis Club), 8, 10, 56, 168–169, 182, 220, 268, 311–312
　　description of, 10, 50, 57–58, 136–145, 150, 154, 162–163
　　modeling information for, 311–312
Slumbercoach cars (Budd). *See* Coach cars (Budd)
Sly, Leroy, 181, 322
Smith, Earl, 69
Snodgrass, Charlie, 176, 322
Soare, Frank L., 322
South Wind, 161–163
Southern Pacific railway. *See* SP (Southern Pacific) railway
SP (Southern Pacific) railway, 25
Sparks, Janet, 240, 243
"Special Rules and Instructions for Employees in Passenger Train Service," 320–321
Spencer, Sharon, 241, 243
Spicer Drive generators, 64
Spire Rock, 249, 255, 272, 274–276
Spokane, Portland, and Seattle railway. *See* SP&S (Spokane, Portland, and Seattle) railway
SP&S (Spokane, Portland, and Seattle) railway
　cars of
　　Day-Nite/Deluxe Day-Nite coach (Pullman-Standard), 60, 70–78, 84, 165, 168–169, 304–305
　　dome sleepers (Budd), 9, 110–125, 134–136, 168, 170, 292, 309
　　dome-coach/Vista-Dome (Budd), 9, 63–71, 78–81, 168–169, 222, 268, 280, 303–304
　The Streamliner, 15
SPUD (St. Paul Union Depot), 43, 53–54, 92, 140–143, 154, 247–248, 254, 286, 321
St. Claire, Walter, 176, 182
St. Germaine, Kathleen, 239
St. Mary's College, 94
St. Paul, 5, 11, 24, 29, 32, 42–43, 54, 58, 65, 85, 92, 142, 150–151, 156, 165, 169–170, 190, 205–206, 208
　Como Shops, 24–26, 84–94, 124, 189, 221, 289, 320
St. Paul Union Depot (SPUD), 43, 53–54, 92, 140–143, 154, 247–248, 254, 286, 321
St. Regis, 282
Staeheli, Glenn A., vii, 195, 320, 322
Staeheli, Paul, 179
Stampede Pass, 17, 21, 151, 283
Stampede Tunnels
　No. 2, 152
　No. 3, 192, 259–260, 263, 277, 285
　No. 4, 153
Staples, 32, 207–209
State Historical Society of North Dakota, 6
Steel deck girder bridges, advertisements on, 3
Steffee, Donald M., 319
Stevenson, Mary, 238, 240, 243
Stewardess-Nurses (Sues)
　in accidents and derailments, 226–230. *See also* Accidents and derailments
　commentaries of. *See* Commentaries
　duties of, 223, 226
　end of service of, 231
　experience vignettes of, 231–238
　historical sources for, 319–320
　inauguration of, 223–227
　overviews of, 223
　photographs of, 223–224, 226, 242–244
　requirements of, 223–224
　roster of, 238–243
　service of, 223–231
　Sidetracked Sues, 231
　supervisors of, 223–225, 239
Stewart, Gladys, 177, 182, 226–230, 240
Strauss, John F., vii, 13, 319, 321
Streamliner, The, 15
Stumm, Emil, 181, 208
Stumpf, Bill, 322
Sues. *See* Stewardess-Nurses (Sues)
Sullivan, Todd, 319
Summers, Ernie, 220
Supervisors, Stewardess-Nurses (Sues), 223–225, 239
Switchers, Baldwin DRS 4-4-15, 81

T

Tacoma, 5–6, 17, 216
Tally, Sydney, 232–233, 235–237, 240, 243
Tarabokia, Joyce, 240
Taylor, James C., 244
Television advertisements, 6
Tell Tale, The, 172
Tellinghuisen, Mike, 178
Thompson, Donna Lee, 240, 243

Index

Thompson, Patricia, 224, 239
Thompson, Sharon, 239
Thorp, 254
Three Forks, 253, 270
Timetables and time folders, 3–4, 7, 29–30, 171, 320–321. *See also* Scheduling and train servicing
Titus, Hazen J., 97
"Tomorrow's Trains on Yesterday's Tracks" (Trains, September 1970), 319
Townsend, Dave, 179–180, 191–192
Track mileages, 29
Traffic handling crews, 190–194, 201
Train crews. *See also* Crews
  description of, 210–214
  districts, 205–213
Trains
  cars. *See* Cars
  consists. *See* Consists
  lines (cars). *See* Lines (cars)
  locomotives. *See* Locomotives
  modeling of, 297–312. *See also* Modeling information
  No. 1 (The Mainstreeter), 8, 10, 15, 17–18, 54, 84, 154, 158, 167, 171–173, 192–193, 206–208, 213–214, 220
  No. 2 (The Mainstreeter), 8, 10, 15, 17–18, 54, 84, 154, 158, 167, 171–173, 193, 206–207, 213–214, 220
  No. 3 (The Alaskan), 193, 206, 213
  No. 4 (The Alaskan), 54, 193, 206, 210
  No. 5, 54
  No. 6, 54
  No. 7, 210
  No. 25, 8–16, 26–35, 39–145, 171–200, 205–220, 250–251, 266, 269–270, 276–277, 280, 282, 287–289, 291, 319–321
  No. 26, 4–17, 26–28, 53–60, 70, 92–96, 124, 142–143, 171–219, 222, 254–257, 265–268, 283, 285–286, 289, 301, 304, 319–321
  No. 407, 54
  No. 408, 54
  train sets, 23
Trains, 319–321
"Trains of Note" (Passenger Train Journal, April/May 1976), 319
Traveller's Rest Buffet-Lounge cars (Pullman-Standard). *See* Diner cars (Pullman-Standard)
Trestles
  Marent Trestle, 287
  O'Keefe Trestle, 287
  Skones Trestle, 16
Tri-Cities, 260
Trip commentaries. *See* Commentaries
Troutwine, Kay, 241, 243
Tunnels
  Bozeman, 125, 268, 288
  Stampede
    No. 2, 152
    No. 3, 192, 259–260, 263, 277, 285
    No. 4, 153
Turah, 18, 278–279
Twentieth Century Limited, 26

U

Ulricksen, Shirely, 239
Ulyatt, E. S., 182
Umtantum, 216
Union Pacific railway. *See* UP (Union Pacific) railway
Union Station, Chicago, 40–42, 96, 142, 258, 263
Union Station, Tacoma, 216
UP (Union Pacific) railway, 160
U.S. Highway 10, 281

V

Valley City, 259
Vintage Rails, 319
Vista-Dome cars (Budd). *See* Dome cars (Budd)
Vista-Dome North Coast Limited era (1954-1970)
  accidents and derailments. *See* Accidents and derailments
  consists. *See also* Consists
    actual, 165–163
    evolution of, 149–154
    seasonal changes of, 149–154
  crews. *See also* Crews
    assignments of, 204–210
    brake system, 194–204
    dispatchers, 215–221
    engine, 190–194
    introduction to, 187–189
    people skills required of, 214–221
    Stewardess-Nurses (Sues), 223–244
    traffic handling, 190–194
    train, 210–214
  description of, 7–13, 293–295
  equipment and maintenance
    cars. *See* Cars
    Como Shops, 24–26, 84–94, 124, 189
    description of, 23–36
    lines (car). *See* Lines (car)
    locomotives. *See* Locomotives
    Pullman Company shops, 24–26
    running repairs, 24, 27
    trains. *See* Trains
  insider tour
    first class accommodations, 101–145
    locomotive to diner, 49–100
    overviews of, 39–47
    photograph gallery of, 265–292
    reference point (1959) of, 10–13
    scenic route highlights, 15–22, 247–263. *See also* Scenic route highlights
  modeling trains of, 297–312. *See also* Modeling information
  overviews of, vii, ix–xiii
  schedule and train servicing
    description of, 29–36
    servicing, 32–36
    timetables, 30
  timeline of, 8–9

W

Waco, 265
Wagner, Paul, 192
Wall calendar advertisements, 3
Walt, Karen, 188, 240, 243
Walters, Barbara, 241
Warren, McGee, 220
"Was this the Greatest Streamliner?" (Passenger Train Journal, November 1981), 319
Water-baggage cars (Pullman-Standard) 200-series, 300
  400 NP, 8, 12, 58–60, 165, 168–169, 299
  401 NP, 8, 58–60, 166, 168, 170
  402 NP, 8, 58–60, 168, 177, 181, 268
  403 NP, 168–170
  404 NP, 8, 58–60, 168–170
  405 CB&Q, 8, 58–60, 169, 174, 185–186, 299
  406 NP (conversion), 300
  407 NP (conversion), 300
  408 NP (conversion), 300
  409 NP (conversion), 300
  410 NP (conversion), 300
  411 NP (conversion), 300
  description of, 4, 10, 50, 55, 57–60, 162–163
  modeling of, 299–300
Waterstreet, Julie, 241, 243
Waukesha type air conditioning systems, 74
Weberling, Irma, 239, 243
Weights, cars, 50
Welch, 259, 275, 277
Welligrant, Jr., Don, 235, 322
Westbound commentaries, 247–257. *See also* Commentaries
Western Pacific railway. *See* WP (Western Pacific) railway
Westminster Hill, 252
Weyerhauser, 119
Whitehall, 249, 275
Whittendale, Nona K., 224, 239
Wildung, Gary, vii, 24, 31, 265–277, 280, 282, 284, 287, 291
Williams, Clyde, 69
Willis, Art, 192–193
Wilson, Jeff, 319
Windsor, 140
Wing, Warren, 55
World's Fair (1962), 160, 169, 186, 238, 249
WP (Western Pacific) railway, 8
Wright, Steven, 293
Wurdeman, Herb, 193

Y

Yakima and Yakima River, 254, 259, 283, 285
Yanta, Geraldine, 223, 239
Yellowstone National Park, 261
Yellowstone River, 18, 124, 249, 259
Yogi Bear (cartoon character), 94

Z

Zabel, Joelle, 236–237, 239
Zelinski, Jack, 322
Zepp, Barbara, 231, 241
Zimmerman, Karl, 319

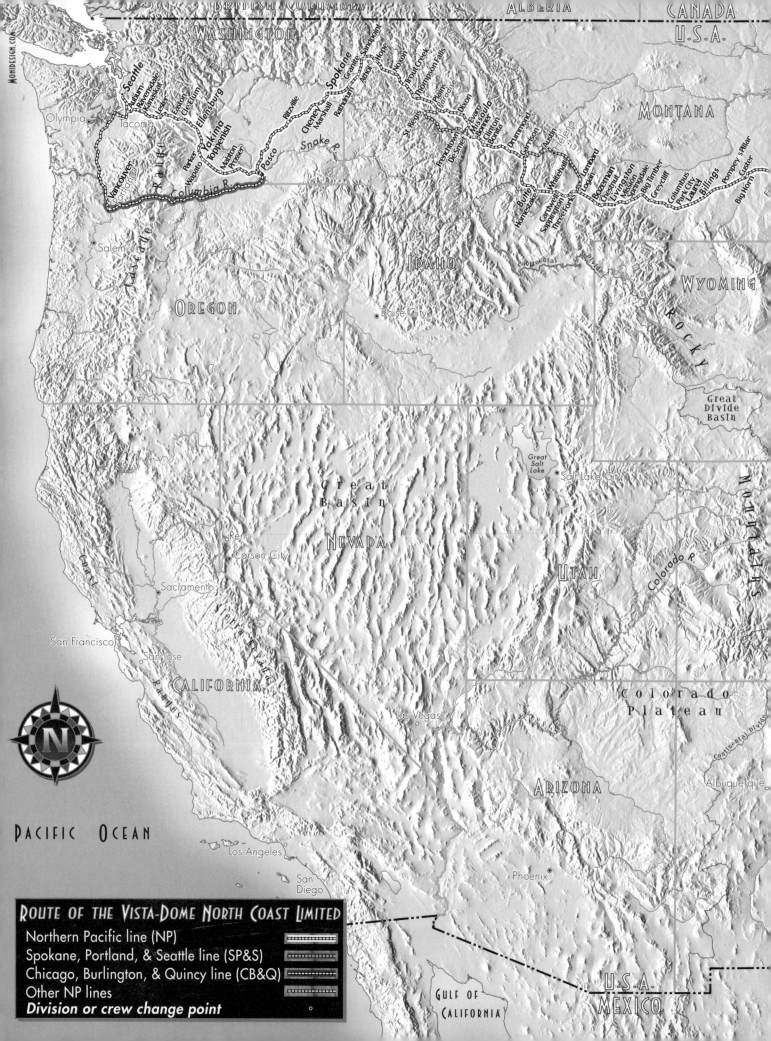